WITHDRAWN
SELLING
PLACES

...u on or before

STUDIES IN HISTORY, PLANNING AND THE ENVIRONMENT

Series editor   Professor Anthony Sutcliffe

SELLING PLACES

The Marketing and
Promotion of
Towns and Cities
1850–2000

STEPHEN V. WARD

First published 1998
by E & FN Spon, an imprint of Routledge
11 New Fetter Lane, London EC4P 4EE

Simultaneously published in the USA and Canada
by Routledge
29 West 35th Street, New York, NY 10001

Typeset in Times by Keystroke, Jacaranda Lodge, Wolverhampton
Printed and bound in Great Britain by Butler & Tanner Ltd, Frome and London

This book was commissioned and edited by Alexandrine Press, Oxford

British Library Cataloguing in Publication Data
A catalogue record for this book is available from the British Library

Library of Congress Cataloging in Publication Data
Ward, Stephen V. (Stephen Victor)
    Selling places : the marketing and promotion of towns and cities,
    1850–2000 / Stephen V. Ward.
        p. cm. — (Studies in history, planning, and the environment
    ; 23)
    Includes bibliographical references and index.
    ISBN 0–419–20610–8 (pb)
    1. Cities and towns—Marketing—History. 2. Public relations—Municipal
government—History. I. Title. II. Series.
HT325.W37 1998
307.76—dc21   98-4002
                                                            CIP

ISBN 0 419 206108 (hardback)
ISBN 0 419 242406 (paperback)

Contents

ACKNOWLEDGEMENTS

Few books can have given their authors more happy hours of innocent enjoyment than this one. Researching it has taken me to many obscure corners of libraries, museums and archive collections, reclaiming the ephemera of place advertising. I have wiled away winter afternoons musing over interwar holiday brochures and marvelling at the bountiful joys of nature in suburban advertisements. Deep moral lessons have been revealed to me from the pages of outwardly unpromising material such as trade directories and business magazines. And, since so much of the raw material of my study has been destroyed or survives only by chance, its discovery – in unexpected places – has never failed to bring pleasure. All-in-all, the collection of the material in this book has been a delight.

Quite why it ever seemed sensible to embark on such a quest remains a little obscure. The research certainly touches base with an issue of great topical interest but there is much more to it than mere relevance. If I am honest, its origins go back a long way, to the 1950s, in fact. When I was very young my maternal grandparents left the mining village where we lived to open what was then called a 'Yorkshire boarding house', in Blackpool. For many years this was to be the setting for our family holidays. I can clearly recall how, in anticipation of what was probably one of the first of these, my parents sent off for that year's Blackpool holiday brochure. Its pages conjured up in my mind's eye a world of unimagined wonders (many of which, I should add, were subsequently fulfilled in ample measure). At any rate, this early exposure to the mainstream of British place marketing has obviously had a lasting impact.

There is, of course, a big gap between these childhood impressions and what now follows, which is the product of roughly a decade and a half's work. Inevitably a study like this accumulates in a random fashion rather than moves in a straight line from beginning to end. Over the first few years, odd nuggets uncovered in other inquiries were collected in box files for possible future use. Eventually I had a critical mass of material and the recognition dawned that there was something worth pursuing more single-mindedly. I am especially grateful to the School of Planning at Oxford Brookes University for the financial assistance that has allowed me to indulge this growing interest. Since 1993 especially, the amounts have been quite significant, allowing me to explore the US dimension in a more comprehensive way. The Canadian government also helped in this widening with a Canadian Studies Research Award in 1990.

Appropriately, however, most of the acknowledgements relate more to the acquisition of the material and development of the ideas within this book. In Britain I have received much assistance from the relevant staff of the Public Record Office in Kew, the Greater London Record Office, the London Transport Museum, the John Johnson Collection of the Bodleian Library, Oxford, the National Railway Museum in York, the Thomas Cook Archives, the John Laing Archives and numerous other local libraries and record offices. In the United States I have been fortunate to enjoy the warm co-operation of staff of the Virginia State Library in Richmond, the Boston Public Library, the Society for the Preservation of the New England Antiquities, also in Boston, the Chicago Historical Society, the Newberry Library, also in Chicago, the Library of Congress in Washington, particularly its Rare Books, Map, Picture and Local Collections, the Atlanta Historical Society and the Atlanta Public Library Local Collection. I also gained a great deal of understanding of the contemporary US scene from the Metro Atlanta Chamber of Commerce and the Atlanta Convention and Visitors Bureau.

In Canada much of my work was based at the Ontario Provincial Archives in Toronto, together with the Oshawa and District Historical Society. In addition, I have made full use of university library facilities on both sides of the Atlantic. Oxford Brookes and the Bodleian Library, University of Oxford have been my main supports, but important for particular aspects have been the University libraries at Waterloo and Toronto in Canada, the design libraries at Harvard University and Massachusetts Institute of Technology in Cambridge and the Virginia Commonwealth University library at Richmond.

In these and other settings specific individuals have been of special help and deserve to be mentioned by name. In no particular order of priority they are: Gerald and Elizabeth Bloomfield, Emily Clark, John and Margaret Gold, Michael Ebner, Robert Brueggemann, John Nix, Bernie Frieden, Ed Robbins, Chris Silver, Richard Dennis, Peter Edwards, Roy Darke, Jo Ann Haden-Miller, Brian Goodey, the late Jacquie Porter, Rob Woodward, Roy Cooper, Michael Thomas, Alan Reeve, Beverley Cole and Alan Thorpe. Tony Sutcliffe and the late Gordon Cherry, supportive to the end, facilitated bringing the work to publication. And I have benefited, as always, by Ann Rudkin's encouragement, wise counsel and sensitive editing. I must also thank her and the editorial staff at Spon for their patience.

My greatest debts, though, are owed to those who are closest to me. My much-loved family – Maggie, Tom, Rosamund and Alice – have to bear the many stresses and strains produced by my absences or distraction. They experience few of the selfish joys of scholarship yet provide so uncomplainingly the practical and emotional sustenance that makes it possible. Dedicating the book to them is the least I can do.

Stephen V. Ward
Oxford, February 1998

COVER PICTURES

Front cover: Poster of America's biggest resort, 1932. Unlike the smaller New England resorts, Atlantic City did not aspire to offer a place to get away from it all. It was essentially promoted as a place for *nouveaux riches* middle class social display. The vast Traymore Hotel (with cupolas) fully captures the style of the resort. (See page 75.)

Back cover: The most famous and enduring example of British seaside promotional art, John Hassall's jolly fisherman first appeared in 1908 to promote the Great Northern Railway's excursion to Skegness. Hassall was apparently paid £12 for the image, which was not produced with Skegness in mind. The 'so bracing' slogan is thought to have been added by the Chief Passenger Agent of the GNR. The image has been continually reworked to promote the resort through to the present day. This interwar example has lost the clouds of the original and gained a pier (probably reflecting the desires of the Skegness Advancement Association). The fisherman is jumping out of the frame, symbolic of how he had transcended promotional art and caught the popular imagination. (By courtesy of the National Railway Museum.)

Picture Credits

To Maggie, Tom, Rosamund and Alice

1

INTRODUCTION

The last quarter of a century has seen a massive worldwide growth in the practice of place marketing and promotion. Every town, city, region and nation, it seems, is now frenetically selling itself with assertions of its competitive place advantage. All places, even those least endowed with attractions, vie to ensure that the tourist gaze falls, however fleetingly, upon them. Traditional resorts find themselves competing with older industrial towns and cities as their abandoned factories and docks are recycled into the marketable commodities of heritage and leisure experience. Today's manufacturing towns compete for the uncertain favours of Japanese car makers, Korean electronics giants and other multi-national firms. Major cities compete for international prestige (and the investment in business services that goes with it) by selling themselves as 'cultural capitals' in the new Europe or as 'world cities', staging major spectacles like the Olympic Games. The collapse of Communism (where it has not precipitated a descent into ethnic barbarism) has signalled the comprehensive entry of the cities and nations of eastern Europe into the place marketing 'game'.

A specifically promotional policy repertoire has also emerged. Its staples include place logos, slogans, advertising, public relations, subsidies, tax breaks of various kinds, 'flagship' development projects, flamboyant architectural and urban design statements, trade fairs, cultural and sporting spectacles, heritage, public art and much else besides. At the core of these manifold endeavours is a concern with making and propagating place images that are sufficiently attractive to persuade place users, principally understood as visitors and investors, to part with their money. The place is packaged and sold as a commodity. Its multiple social and cultural meanings are selectively appropriated and re-packaged to create a more attractive place image in which any problems are played down.

This kind of competitive ethos of selling places now permeates urban public affairs throughout the world, modifying or even supplanting other policy concerns. In Britain and other European countries the extent of place marketing's contemporary dominance is certainly unprecedented. Yet we must not make the mistake of believing that the approach itself is in any way a novel one, even though much of the existing literature reinforces such a view. The main focus of this book will be on British experience, where comparatively little has been written about the history of place selling. But an almost equally important secondary theme will be to consider experiences in other countries, especially in the United States. As we will show, this trans-Atlantic dimension forms a highly pertinent comparison, because it throws into sharp relief many of the underlying factors that have triggered and shaped place selling activities. We can begin to get some clues about this from what others have already written.

THE EXISTING LITERATURE

There has been a quite startling growth in publications on the subject over the last few years. In the wake of Logan and Molotch's *Urban Fortunes* (1987), Bailey's *Marketing Cities in the 1980s and Beyond* (1989) and Ashworth and Voogd's *Selling the City* (1990), we now have Kotler, Haider and Rein's *Marketing Places*, Kearns and Philo's edited collection *Selling Places* (both 1993), Smyth's *Marketing the City*, Gold and Ward's edited collection *Place Promotion* (both 1994) and Duffy's *Competitive Cities* (1995). There are also many more localized studies of place marketing, for example Neill *et al.*'s recent comparative study of Belfast and Detroit, *Reimaging the Pariah City* (1995), Gold and Gold's *Imagining Scotland* (1995) or Rutheiser's study of a classic booster city, *Imagineering Atlanta* (1996).

Even more striking has been the increased attention given to place marketing approaches across a very wide range of recent publications on urban regeneration. A major source of inspiration has been David Harvey. In books such as *The Urban Experience*, a collection of his earlier writings, (1989*a*) and *The Condition of Postmodernity* (1989*b*) he has highlighted the rise of 'urban entrepreneurialism' (on which see also Harvey (1989*c*). This refers to cities throughout the world deliberately adopting policies, amongst them explicit place marketing, intended primarily to enhance and demonstrate their attractiveness to mobile investment and consumption. Where Harvey has led, many, especially in Britain, have followed, adding empirical detail to his synoptic sketches. A few significant examples here would be Healey *et al.* (ed.) *Rebuilding the City* (1992), Imrie and Thomas (ed.) *British Urban Policy and the Urban Development Corporations*, Bianchini and Parkinson (ed.) *Cultural Policy and Urban Regeneration*, and Law *Urban Tourism* (all 1993). It would not be difficult to suggest other titles.

Little sense of an activity with rich historical precedents appears in this burgeoning literature, however. There are occasional allusions, in passing, to earlier episodes of place marketing, sometimes of slightly doubtful provenance. Harvey, for example, dates the selling of places back to the civic boosterism of the Hanseatic League and the Italian City States in Medieval Europe (1989*c*). Ashworth and Voogd claim even earlier examples of place marketing in Viking Leif Ericsson's search for settlers to populate his newly discovered 'green' land (1994, p. 39). Whatever the validity of such assertions, and little evidence is presented, these places were not promoted in ways that bear much resemblance to the practices of today. The most immediate and important precedents for contemporary practice lie in the more recent past. A few vignettes into the nineteenth and early twentieth centuries are offered in Logan and Molotch (1987), Kearns and Philo (1993), Gold and Ward (1994), Gold and Gold (1995) and Rutheiser (1996). Otherwise very little comes through in the mainstream place marketing literature.

Outside this mainstream, there is a small, relatively obscure and very fragmented literature on aspects of the history of selling particular kinds of places in specific parts of the world. The North American literature is much the richest with several fine accounts of the role of place marketing in the westward colonization of both the United States and Canada (e.g. Gates, 1934; Quiett, 1934; Dumke, 1944; Elias, 1983). Drawing mainly on this experience, Boorstin (1965) has given a typically vivid and suggestive account of the central role of the local promotional, boosterist ethos in the emergence of the American nation. The promotion of the southern United States for industrial development has also been well treated, most comprehensively by Cobb (1993). Industrial place promotion in Canada has similarly attracted significant historical attention, especially by Bloomfield (e.g. 1983*a*, 1983*b*, 1983*c*). Meanwhile, in another part of the forest, Warner, Stilgoe, Jackson and many other urban historians have cast much valuable light on American suburban promotion.

Still more dispersed and fragmentary is the work on British and other European experiences. Such as it is, most of the existing historical writing focuses on tourist resorts and residential suburbs (e.g. Walton, 1983*a*; Jackson, 1991). Much useful work on the selling of both these place types has been done by railway and local historians, especially Jackson (1986) and Yates (1988). Another very important group of historical studies are those of railway advertising art in both Europe and North America, much of which had a place promotional intent. Fine examples are Shackleton (1976), Camard and Zagrodski (1989), Cole and Durack (1990; 1992), Runte (1994) and Weill (1994). Yet, in all these studies, even this last group, place selling remains only a secondary or incidental theme. There have been only a few, partial, attempts Holcomb (1990) and Ward (1994*b*, 1995) to synthesize the various episodes of place selling into a coherent overview. One of the most straightforward aims of this book is therefore to mould a coherent and comprehensive story from the current, rather fragmentary view.

Understanding Place Selling

What is Place Selling?

As a first stage in this process, it is important to think about how to conceptualize the place selling phenomenon. As already noted, place selling is not simply a specific area of urban policy or action. It is rather a broad entrepreneurial ethos or ideology which, at specific times, has permeated the common affairs of particular places. We have already identified some of the most familiar and obvious ways in which this ethos has found expression, but manifestations of it may be found across the whole urban policy agenda. Every aspect of public policy from street cleansing to the provision of housing, from equal opportunities to public transport, from the award of public contracts to sewage outfalls can be made to bear the imprint of the place selling ethos. But the reverse is not true: the existence of these common urban concerns does not necessarily imply that they are motivated by any significant impulse of asserting competitive advantage over other places.

A more specific example will give more depth to this point. In the late twentieth century it is well known that many post-industrial cities are busily investing in 'high' culture as a deliberate promotional strategy, to draw in tourists and encourage business investment (e.g. Bianchini and Parkinson, 1993). Over a century ago, British cities were also spending large sums on much the same material things: libraries, concert halls, art galleries and museums. Yet the motives then were very different, concerned more with demonstrating the success of industrial civilization (e.g. Briggs, 1963). Britain's cities did not need, at that time, to give priority to boosting their economies. Culture was the 'icing on the cake'; today it has become part of the 'cake' itself.

Yet this was not universal, even then. There were some cities, especially in the American mid- and far-West during the late nineteenth and early twentieth centuries which did, quite deliberately, use high culture as an economic promotional device. As of one of Sinclair Lewis' characters told the Boosters Club of the imaginary mid-West city of Zenith:

Culture has become as necessary adornment and an advertisement for a city to-day as pavements or bank-clearances . . . it gives such class-advertising as a town can get in no other way; and the guy who is so short-sighted as to crab the orchestra proposition is passing up the chance to impress the glorious name of Zenith on some big New York millionaire that might – that might establish a branch factory here! (Lewis, 1922, pp. 252–253)

The broad point behind all this is that cities were (and are) capable of doing very similar things for quite different motives. In the past some cities were obliged to become more entrepreneurial in the running of their collective affairs. Others, as we have seen, did not need to be. There is actually only one area of public policy and action which may be equated directly with the wider ideology of place selling. The existence of place advertising remains perhaps the surest single test for the existence of the place selling impulse. We certainly do not overlook the many other dimensions of place selling but, as we have argued, their intent is rarely as clearcut and unambiguous as place advertising.

The place selling impulse would normally, then, involve fairly public assertions of competitive place advantage by means of, but not confined to, place advertising. In practice, this means that it has often to be identified, especially historically, on the rather pragmatic basis of 'knowing it when you see it'. Such an approach militates against easy reliance on quantitative measurement or comparison of activity. In practice, place selling action within particular national jurisdictions have often followed certain common patterns during specific periods. But the possibilities of precise international or historical comparisons are very limited.

Moreover, a reliance on place advertising as a key indicator also brings its own unique research problems. There will obviously be a tendency to exclude place selling episodes which predate the emergence of modern print advertising. More seriously, however, advertising and other publicity are essentially ephemeral items. Unlike minutes, correspondence, briefing papers etc (some of which are clearly valuable in understanding the promotional process), it is almost unknown for bodies to hold archive copies of their advertising.

Beyond these operational problems lie some altogether more fundamental questions. Much the most basic of these is what we actually think about place selling. Do we begin from a critical standpoint, bemoaning the appropriation of the multi-layered meaning of places into a one-dimensional marketable commodity? Or can we be more positive, appreciating that the making and propagation of marketable place images can be worthwhile – an extension rather than a narrowing of the cultural meanings of place, even a source of enjoyment?

Not too long ago, most academic commentators on the contemporary urban scene would have found it easy to answer these questions. To the first, yes; to the second, no. Now the new mood of 'realism' that pervades the post-Thatcherite, post-Reaganite and post-Communist world adds a tantalizing uncertainty. All, left and right, have begun to show a real awareness of the importance of projecting positive place images and the need to work within a market framework. This is mirrored in recent trends in research work on place marketing and promotion.

Cultural Interpretation of Place Selling

Within this shift in prevailing attitudes we can occasionally detect faint echoes of sympathy for earlier episodes of place selling. Anyone familiar with John Betjeman's poetic and televisual evocations of Metro-land will immediately have some sense of the power of promotional imagery to stir deeply sympathetic feelings. Around the Metropolitan Railway's inspired attempts to market the suburban areas along its tracks in north west London from 1915 to 1932 has been woven the best known British celebration of the cultural aspects of place selling. As we will show in more detail in chapters 5 and 6, the characteristic Metro-land combination of fine illustrations and a highly contrived prose style created a romantic fairytale vision of suburban living. Across the decades it nurtures a deep nostalgia for a supposedly simpler age whose innocence is signalled by the charms of the hand coloured photographs and the quaintness of the language. There is, and was in the past, a humorous dimension to the appreciation, but the humour is gentle and sympathetic.

Though none achieve the emotional power of Betjeman's interpretation of Metro-land, at least as far as an English audience are concerned, there is much other writing in similar vein about place selling, especially of the suburbs and sea-side resorts (Jackson, 1991; Yates, 1988). Heroic tales of railroad building and town promotion are more typical North American themes, particularly evident in the works of Quiett (1934), Dumke (1944) and Elias (1983), for example. In the promotional puff and the often outrageous actions of the railroads and town boosters, such writers find a powerful metaphor for the deeper story they want to tell: the making of a nation out of relentless optimism, boundless hyperbole and sheer guts. In this way the idea of place selling and boosterism has become, as novelists great, such as Sinclair Lewis (1922), and obscure, such as Mark Lee Luther (1924), have shown, an integral part of the American dream. It reflects the competitive freedom of individuals and communities to better themselves by their own efforts, untrammelled by big government or powerfully entrenched aristocrats.

Not all cultural comment has been so positive, however. During the 1980s, insights drawn from the critical cultural studies began to be applied to place selling efforts. The real pioneering work had been done in the 1970s by a few behavioural geographers, particularly Gold (1974) and Burgess (1982). But the main shift came within cultural geography, influenced by both the new directions coming from cultural studies and Harvey's more general encouragement to critical exploration (e.g. Kearns and Philo, 1993). Some related work of great importance has come from sociologists and social anthropologists, notably O'Barr (1994) and Lash and Urry (1994).

One of the principal concerns of this body of work has been with decoding the promotional message itself, particularly the place image that is being sold. Much of the style of this decoding derives fairly closely from several studies on advertising such as Williamson's *Decoding Advertisements* (1978). As we might expect, given the Marxian intellectual origins of the whole cultural studies approach (Williams, 1980), the critical fire is mainly directed at the way place marketing supposedly 'commodifies' places. It is this approach which has largely inspired the academic critiques of place selling as a mere packaging of place as marketable product rather than an honest acknowledgement of its cultural depth and complexity. It is, in essence, the same argument as that made by Williamson about advertising in general, that it obscures and avoids the real issues of society, substituting an imperative to sell for reality and real emotions.

A recent trend is to focus on the discourse of advertising (Cook, 1992). This involves exploring the whole process of communicating advertising messages, not merely viewing the image in isolation. An important distinction is often made between the primary and secondary discourses of advertisements (O'Barr, 1994, p. 3). The former are more immediately concerned with the selling process, while the latter reflect the wider social significance of the advertising messages. On the whole those adopting this broad approach have tended to focus more on the wider social meanings, the secondary discourse, of advertising. Place marketing images can thus be viewed simply as exemplars of, for example, broader economic and political changes, such as the rise of the enterprise culture or post-modernism (e.g. Harvey, 1989*b*). Or analysing the discourse of tourist advertising might be a vehicle for exploring cultural and racial stereotyping (O'Barr, 1994).

Public Policy and Place Selling

A rather different approach to understanding place selling has been to view it as an aspect of local public policy and seek to understand it accordingly. In this view, policies must be evaluated on public interest and welfare criteria – how much they benefit the population of the place being sold, and specifically those least able to help themselves. These kind of criteria sit somewhat uneasily within the market-based notion of pursuing competitive advantage which is integral to the place selling ethos.

There is a general presumption within most work on public policy analysis that market forces have, at best, only limited compatibility with public interest criteria. Such presumptions derive in the main from the various currents of critical neo-Weberian and neo-Marxist new urban theory that became fashionable in the 1970s and 1980s (e.g. Castells, 1977; Saunders, 1981; Cooke, 1983; Harvey, 1989*a*). Moreover, when market processes are themselves under stress, all public policy analysts recognize that this compatibility between market and public interest is further reduced. In other words, the very economic circumstances that are most likely to give rise to place marketing initiatives are also those which make it most difficult to reconcile these initiatives with public interest and welfare objectives.

This approach has thus been very effective in highlighting the contradictions with traditional welfare and public interest policy objectives when public agencies embrace the place selling ethos. On the other hand, public policy researchers have preferred to concentrate on topics closer to their traditional concerns, such as local economic policies (Totterdill, 1989; Collinge, 1992; Eisenschitz and Gough, 1993), where welfare concerns have remained more overt. In contrast there has, until recently, been little work on place advertising and those aspects of place selling where the language is most overtly that of the market. We can see some signs of change, at least in the growing willingness of public policy researchers to explore such topics (e.g. Ward, 1990; Wilkinson, 1992; Madsen, 1992; Paddison, 1993).

In doing this their concerns begin to merge with the last approach, which focuses most explicitly on place marketing itself, rather than its wider social, cultural or political significance (e.g. Ryans and Shanklin, 1986; Bartels and Timmer, 1987; Bailey, 1989; Kotler *et al.*, 1993). As an approach it is rather pragmatic in style,

untroubled by the conceptual and ideological crosses some of the other approaches have to bear. Thus the 'commodification of place' critique, seen by some as the intellectual *coup de grace* for place selling, is regarded by marketeers, somewhat disarmingly, as the starting point for their work.

The conceptual inspiration is essentially drawn from the growth of a more 'scientific' approach to business, management and marketing since the interwar years (Ashworth and Voogd, 1990; 1994). Marketing practices try to make places into commodities (or 'place products') (Ashworth and Voogd, 1990, pp. 65–76). Yet places are, as we have already noted, complex packages of goods, services and experiences that are consumed in many different ways. This is not a problem *per se*, as it is for the cultural critics. Rather, it raises operational difficulties because it means that marketing's usual clear goal of sales maximization can easily be obscured. With many place activities, the pattern of 'purchase' and consumption is much more problematic and capable only of indirect measurement.

These types of issue present considerable problems for place marketing, not least in how it is to be organized and funded. They have also prompted much research activity that has, amongst other things, begun to engage with issues of deep concern to other research approaches such as the need to secure public consent and approval (Bailey, 1989; Kotler *et al.*, 1993).

A Synthetic Approach

The reader will not perhaps be surprised to learn that this book will continue and develop the trend to achieve better understanding of the place selling phenomenon by drawing different explanatory approaches. The exact character of the synthesis will become clearer as it is elaborated throughout the text. Its essence may, though, be shortly summarized here.

From the Betjemanesque celebration of place selling we borrow the concern for detail, texture and sense of emotional depths that lie beneath the commonplace and the ephemeral the place selling process. On a more prosaic but equally important note, the marketing approach serves to remind us of the need to think about how (and how well) the place selling process actually worked on its own terms. From the cultural studies critics we derive a sense of the wider social meanings. Some of the methods pioneered within this tradition will also be used to explore the symbolism of the images deployed in the place selling process. Finally, from the public policy tradition, we borrow the concern for precision in probing institutions, agencies and the often complex politics of place selling.

THE STRUCTURE OF THE BOOK

To understand the structure of this book, it is useful to set it within the context of a very simple historical model. A literature survey suggests that we can identify three main stages in the life cycles of urban and regional systems when place selling efforts are evident. The first is agricultural colonization, when a relatively empty land is settled. Dependent very much on the timing and scale of this colonization, place selling has sometimes played a central role in promoting settlement. Two distinct activities were involved in this process, settling the land itself and promoting the first towns. Both are examined in chapter 2 which looks at the settling of the American West, one of the most important ever episodes of place selling. Government agencies, railroads, land companies and other agencies made full use of advertising and other promotional devices to draw both farmers and town dwellers to the frontier.

The next stage may be termed urban functional diversity, when greater differentiation of specific urban functions becomes apparent within increasingly mature urban systems. In some circumstances, place selling has played an important role in encouraging and underscoring these changes. Most widespread geographically was the selling of the tourist resort. In Part 2 of the book we explore how this dimension of place marketing developed, mainly focusing on Britain, but with sideways glances at France, Belgium, the United States and some other countries. The breakdown of chapters in this part of the book sets a pattern for the rest of the book. Thus chapter 3 examines the process of resort marketing, looking at its evolution, promotional agencies and methods. The following chapter explores particularly the nature of the promotional message.

This same two chapter pattern is adopted in Part 3, which focuses on another specialist place type, the residential suburb. Again place selling was very widespread and intensively pursued. In this case, though, the area focus is mainly on the United States and Britain, with fleeting glimpses of France and Canada.

Part 4, selling the industrial town, reveals a rather different pattern, however. Here the emphasis was not so much on place selling or marketing as on promotion, with many incentives to draw industrialists. Nor was the activity as universal as resort or suburban promotion. It was largely confined to more marginal parts of urban and regional systems, Canada and the US South in North America, and in Britain, to localities experiencing particular difficulties during depressions.

This hint of a more regenerative theme becomes very much stronger in Part 5, which examines the main contemporary place selling episode, concerned with the post-industrial city. Viewed as part of the urban system life cycle, the post-industrial city has moved beyond the stage of stable maturity, into decline. The policy priority has therefore shifted to urban regeneration, seeking new sources of wealth to replace those which have gone. City marketing and promotional action have become key parts of this attempt to move beyond industrialism at a time of greatly intensified place competition. Finally, the last chapter draws together the main findings of the whole book on the incidence and character of place selling.

2

SELLING THE FRONTIER

---

*Young Man Life is too short To Be Wasted on a rented or worn-out farm,
when you can by Making A Start for Nebraska, secure a good farm and
competence for old age.* (CBQRR, 1881)

Thus promised one panel of a folding pamphlet issued in 1881 by the Chicago, Burlington and Quincy Railroad. Other panels reinforced the message. On one appeared the image of a key. The surrounding text contained what must have been one of the first place selling puns: 'Found – A New Brass Key (pronounced) NEBRASKA (That will unlock Vaults of Wealth for the Farmer and the Stock Raiser)'. The pamphlet was issued to promote the lands opened up for settlement by the new Burlington and Missouri River Railroad, a subsidiary of the Chicago, Burlington and Quincy Railroad (CBQRR). Its form and general message of masculine opportunity were entirely characteristic of the later phases of the settlement of the mid and far West of North America, perhaps the greatest ever episode of place selling.

In this chapter, which forms a critically important prelude to the major concerns of the book, we explore how the frontier and the first towns were promoted and marketed. It tells of the beginnings of place selling in the modern sense, where places were marketed via the printed word and the new mass media – the handbill, the pamphlet, the poster and the newspaper. It is also the story of how land formerly held collectively by indigenous North Americans became a private commodity. Henceforth it could be bought and sold by individuals and be the object of specula-

tion. It was a transformation that was crucial to the formation of the North American, and especially the US tradition of place marketing or boosterism. As new 'upstart' cities appeared in the newly colonized agricultural lands, their priorities were to attract people and investment as rapidly as possible. In its early stages, it was a process driven primarily by land speculation though other concerns gradually became more important. It involved the boosters of these upstart places trumpeting their advantages, real and imagined, to any who would listen in the highly mobile economy of the West.

This was an episode with no equivalent in long settled Britain or Europe. Odd, marginal areas of the 'Old World' had been deliberately opened up for settlement, but in nothing like the systematic manner of the 'New World'. The difference was an important one. In large measure it fostered the much greater American propensity to place selling of all kinds over the succeeding years. In the United States particularly, boosterism became an almost inherent characteristic of all manner of places. In Britain, by contrast, it has been both less familiar and more circumscribed. The relative silence of nineteenth-century Britain in the matter of place selling is also therefore important, forming a secondary theme of this chapter.

Selling the Frontier Farmlands

Beginnings

From almost the first stages of the colonization of the North American continent, there were conscious measures taken to attract settlers. One of the earliest forms of publicity to this end was simply a government notification of lands available for settlement. In 1773, for example, the Governor of Georgia, issued a proclamation relating to land secured by treaty from the Indians [*sic*] (Georgia, 1773). Land was to be made available on favourable terms according to how many and what types of settlers came forward. Thus a head of household could command 100 acres with 50 acres for his wife, each of his children and each male slave or white servant. Each female white servant aged 15–40 warranted another 25 acres. Amongst other details, the proclamation spoke of the fertility of the lands, the ease with which products could be distributed, the abundance of water and the promise of security. These were familiar themes, to be repeated over and over again in the promotion of colonization.

As settlement proceeded the land itself became a commodity to be bought and sold. Significantly, perhaps, land sales were the most common objects of advertising in newspapers and posters by the time of the War of Independence (Goodrum and Dalrymple, 1990, p. 13). Some of this activity might be understood as implying a wider area or place marketing intent, though this is open to interpretation. What it certainly indicates is the emergence of a vigorous market in land that gradually became an integral part of the place marketing impulse. Over the first decades of the newly independent country the settlement process gradually quickened as more public lands formerly occupied by indigenous peoples were made available for private appropriation.

Yet the process remained a fairly gradual one until the 1840s. From the outset there had been tensions between those who favoured larger land holdings and ideas of a nation of smaller yeomen farmers. Such political rivalries had affected the pace and pattern of settlement in the eighteenth and early nineteenth centuries. This tension remained important, though much larger forces began to intrude in the 1840s, making more dramatic changes inevitable. The introduction of the first regular steamship communication between Europe and North America made this decade a turning point. Greatly improved accessibility radically transformed the attractiveness of North America for migration. The same decade brought also the beginnings of steam railroads linking the Atlantic ports with the interior of the country.

Up to this time migrational flows, though influenced by published materials, had been stimulated more by personal contacts, often based on kinship or religious affinity, than by any organized selling of settler destinations. Now that the scale of the potential movement was greatly enhanced there was a clear role for organized and systematic area marketing. Before considering this, however, we need to understand something of how the colonization process actually operated.

Governments and Railroads

The principal agency in the opening up of the United States was the federal government in Washington. Under their control lay a vast area of the sparsely populated interior territories, mainly acquired in the legal sense by purchase, negotiation or cession from other sovereign powers or individual states of the union. The established position of the indigenous American peoples was largely ignored in such deals and successive internal treaties were rarely observed. At their peak the federal lands amounted to 1838 million acres, roughly four-fifths of the current area of the United States (Clawson, 1983). (This compares with a little over 30 per cent by the 1980s, mainly comprising forest and natural reserves unsuitable for cultivation.)

The settlement process was synonymous with the disposal into private ownership of those parts of the federal domain that could be cultivated. Over time the federal government adopted ever more ambitious methods of achieving this end. Large amounts of land (328 million acres) were simply handed over to individual states, often as endowments when they were established. Some of these lands were certainly used to promote settlement and development. The most important federal initiatives were, however, the homesteading scheme (288 million acres), military bounty grants to veterans (61 million acres) and the land grants to railroad companies (94 million acres). These three had the biggest impact on promoting settlement, though there were many other measures, especially for marginal lands.

Individual states also played an important role in encouraging immigration, settlement and development. Many of the earlier railroads in the eastern states were heavily supported by state (and, as we will see, local) governments. As the flow of immigrants and would-be settlers began to increase in the 1840s, the interior states began themselves to become more active promoters. In 1845 Michigan, for example, appointed an immigration agent to be stationed in New York to direct would-be settlers to the state (Gates, 1934, pp. 169–170). Four years later it began a very active advertising campaign in the east and in Germany. Wisconsin took similar action from 1852 and most of the other mid-Western states followed over the next few years.

It was about this same time that the federal government determined to encourage railroad construction in the largely unpopulated interior by endowing the companies with large land grants. These went much further than was necessary simply for tracks and other railroad requirements. They were intended for disposal to settlers, to provide a source of income for the railroads and involve them more deeply in the process of colonization (Mercer, 1982). The first land grant railroad was the Illinois Central (ICRR), which received almost 2.6 million acres

of land in 1850–51 (ICRR [Dupuy], 1855, p. 3). We will say much more about the marketing activities of the ICRR below. For the present we should note how it set the pattern for all the Western railroads over the next three decades (and was also imitated in Canada). The basic spatial character of these grants was a chessboard pattern of alternate sections of land spanning a wide band of territory centred on the route of the tracks. The basic land unit, the section, derived from the rectangular survey method. A section was a square block of 640 acres, though the more typical unit of disposal was the quarter section, 160 acres.

While the alternate section principle was intended to avoid a monopoly, there is no doubting the railroads' powerful role. It is clear that railroad directors and officials often speculated in land on the sections not granted to the companies, strengthening still further the railroad 'interest' in the emergent land market of these areas (Cochran, 1953, pp. 118–121). Yet against this tendency to strengthen larger interests, there were countervailing forces favouring the smaller settlers. One strongly established tradition from the earliest days was squatting on public lands. The 1841 Pre-emption Act supposedly guaranteed squatters the right to legitimize their claims at the minimum price (though 'claim jumping', buying land from under squatters, was common). Military bounty grants, giving land rights to former soldiers, were also significant in encouraging small farming.

Homesteading

But the ideal of a nation of small family farmers received its biggest fillip with the passing of the 1862 Homestead Act (Fitte, 1966; Milner, 1994). Under this legislation (which was imitated in Canada ten years later) any citizen could file a claim for a quarter section (Brown, 1948, pp. 336, 416–420). This right was enhanced, effectively to a full section or even more under other legislation, notably the 1873 Timber Culture Act, the 1877 Desert Lands Act, the 1911 Enlarged

Homestead Act and the 1916 Stockraising Homestead Act. Some states also encouraged homesteading rights to be used with pre-emption rights, offering further ways of amassing larger areas. The only requirements were single owner-ship and an agreement to farm the land for five years. If such conditions were met the land itself was free, though transfer and registration costs were payable. Although the settlement of some states, such as Illinois, was much more under railroad control, homesteading had a dramatic effect on the settlement of states such as Nebraska, South and North Dakota, Montana, Wyoming, Kansas and, above all, Oklahoma (Wishart, 1987).

The timing of the Act, during the Civil War, was significant. The Southern plantation states had been major opponents of Western settle-ment, especially by smaller farmers who did not need slaves on their own farms. Yet the railroads, although they stood to gain by homesteading, also found that it could interfere with the profit-able disposal of their own grants. In the cities too, the alternative of cheap land for landless workers had the effect of guaranteeing high wages and was therefore opposed by indus-trialists. And, on the frontier itself, there were many tensions between different interests, especially the big landowners and homesteaders or squatters (Gates, 1973). On the whole though, homesteading promised economic growth on the frontier and was supported by a wide variety of interests, particularly those who supplied equipment to the new settlers.

Yet it is clear that many homesteaders, or indeed others who acquired free or cheap land, certainly did not conform with the Jeffersonian ideal of sturdy yeomen farmers. Despite federal intentions, there was a great deal of speculative acquisition of land. Some homesteaders clearly behaved more like small scale speculators than family farmers. More obviously, there were also many land companies which controlled sizeable areas. This was especially so in the vicinity of railroads, where the prospects of speculative gain were highest. There was also rather more

renting of property than was intended, often as farm creditors foreclosed on unpaid debts.

Colonization consisted, therefore, of a simple ideal and a complex, contested reality. The most tragic figures in the process were the indigenous Americans whose interests were routinely over-ridden, often in a very cruel fashion (Bogue, 1994, pp. 288–294). From our perspective, however, the important point is the wide variety of interests with some kind of stake in promoting colonization. Many of them, moreover, were to some extent competitive with each other. State (or, more often, territory) certainly competed with state. Yet the agricultural states also com-peted with employers in the growing cities of the north east. As landowners, railroads would compete both with each other and with areas opened for homesteading. Land companies and other commercial interests added further layers of complexity. Overall therefore, this created the ideal conditions for the emergence of place marketing.

The Garden State of the West

We have already noted a little of the beginnings of such large scale marketing. The organization which set the tone for much that followed was the ICRR. Its land grants were a huge asset which, theoretically, might have been released for settlement only slowly, to capitalize on rising values. Yet a strategy of protracted speculation that attempted to engineer a scarcity of land was obviously unwise. Adjoining states were already actively marketing themselves with promises of cheap land. Although Illinois could now offer better access, it would have been quite easy for the federal government to have undermined such a position by giving other railroads similar grants, as in fact soon happened. Quickly there-fore the ICRR decided that its main interests lay in rapid disposal on favourable terms, promoting settlement and profitable traffic in agricultural produce. Land sales might give short term profits, but the ICRR saw its long term role as a railroad rather than a land company.

Yet it was also clear that the existing pace of settlement needed to be speeded up if this objective was to be met (Gates, 1934, pp. 169–187). In 1854 the ICRR started extensive advertising in the eastern states and across the Atlantic. Higher land costs in the older settled states meant that there were many frustrated farmers renting land or on farms that were too small. To reach these frustrated or ambitious farmers a combination of selling methods was used. The ICRR Land Department produced 100,000 copies of a promotional circular to be distributed directly to farmers and posted more generally throughout the eastern and southern states. Advertisements were also inserted in eastern and Chicago newspapers and specialist journals read by farmers. The railroad itself received a great deal of editorial newspaper coverage, reflecting its pioneering role and massive advertising campaign, which further stimulated settler interest. From 1854 the Land Department also produced a promotional handbook that was distributed in both the United States and England (ICRR, 1854). Another then novel method was the use of advertising placards on the New York street cars (Gates, 1934, p. 180).

These and other forms of printed publicity were only part of the story, however. Particularly important were the ICRR agents who canvassed the longer settled farming regions or positioned themselves at strategic points, such as New York or Niagara Falls, where they could intercept potential settlers. Increasingly, too, there was overseas activity. From the outset the ICRR had recognized that many European countries had large rural populations with little or no land to whom they could appeal. The troubled conditions in Europe also meant that many of these same people would be anxious to avoid military service. The problem was not so much to stimulate emigration, however. It was to ensure that migrants came to Illinois.

Within a few years the ICRR had begun to market its lands in Sweden, Norway, Germany, Britain and Ireland (ICRR, 1859; Gates, 1934, pp. 188–224). Its agents were especially active in Scandinavia and Germany, though there was opposition from major landowners and farmers to the threat to their supply of farm labour. The Civil War slowed migration to the United States, but it soon resumed. By the later 1860s the flow of Swedish and German migrants had increased greatly, allowing a reduction of marketing effort. Yet foreign efforts continued to be important. Particularly controversial were the efforts of ICRR agents in Canada, where they sought to divert would be settlers southwards.

Overall, the promotional spending of the ICRR was quite unprecedented. In 1856, for example, almost $17,000 was spent on newspaper advertising, $11,800 for printing and circulars and $14,400 for agents' salaries (Gates, 1934, p. 181). Within a short time the shareholders, many of them London-based, began to question the necessity of such expensive programmes. The later 1850s saw a cutback, but by this time other land grant railroads had begun to be active. Neighbouring states such as Iowa were also showing some competitive advantage in the promotion of settlement. By the early 1860s the ICRR's internal US campaigns were resumed with even greater intensity, promising 'homes for the industrious in the garden state of the west' (Gates, 1934, facing p. 186).

By the 1870s the settlement frontier had shifted westward. The ICRR's message was changed to remind would-be settlers that much land remained in Illinois (ICRR, 1878). Even in the 1890s the company was still advertising its lands in southern Illinois and along the line of a subsidiary company in Mississippi (ICRR, 1896a; 1896b). And there were even later campaigns (e.g. ICRR, 1912, p. 5). These were very much residual efforts, however. Most of the ICRR lands had by this time gone, eventually producing gross receipts of nearly $2.6 million (ICRR, undated, 13). Roughly a tenth of this income had been spent in advertising and disposal costs, producing net receipts of $8.96 per acre.

THE ILLINOIS CENTRAL RAILROAD CO., HAVE FOR SALE

1,200,000 ACRES OF RICH FARMING LANDS,

In Tracts of Forty Acres and upward on Long Credit and at Low Prices.

THE attention of the enterprising and industrious portion of the community is directed to the following statements and liberal inducements offered them by the

ILLINOIS CENTRAL RAILROAD COMPANY.

which, as they will perceive, will enable them, by proper energy, perseverance and industry, to provide comfortable homes for themselves and families, with, comparatively speaking, very little capital.

LANDS OF ILLINOIS.

No State in the Valley of the Mississippi offers so great an inducement to the settler as the State of Illinois. There is no portion of the world where all the conditions of climate and soil so admirably combine to produce those two great staples, CORN and WHEAT, as the Prairies of Illinois.

EASTERN AND SOUTHERN MARKETS.

These lands are contiguous to a railroad 700 miles in length, which connects with other roads and navigable lakes and rivers, thus affording an unbroken communication with the Eastern and Southern markets.

RAILROAD SYSTEM OF ILLINOIS.

Over $100,000,000 of private capital have been expended on the railroad system of Illinois. Inasmuch as part of the income from several of these works, with a valuable public fund in lands, go to diminish the State expenses; the TAXES ARE LIGHT, and must consequently every day decrease.

THE STATE DEBT.

The State debt is only $10,106,308 14, and within the last three years has been reduced $2,969,746 80, and we may reasonably expect that in ten years it will become extinct.

PRESENT POPULATION.

The State is rapidly filling up with population; 868,025 persons having been added since 1850, making the present population 1,723,663, a ratio of 102 per cent. in ten years.

AGRICULTURAL PRODUCTS.

The Agricultural Products of Illinois are greater than those of any other State. The products sent out during the past year exceeded 1,500,000 tons. The wheat crop of 1860 approaches

35,000,000 bushels, while the corn crop yields not less than 140,000,000 bushels.

FERTILITY OF THE SOIL.

Nowhere can the industrious farmer secure such immediate results for his labor as upon these prairie soils, they being composed of a deep rich loam, the fertility of which is unsurpassed by any on the globe.

TO ACTUAL CULTIVATORS.

Since 1854 the Company have sold 1,300,000 acres. They sell only to actual cultivators, and every contract contains an agreement to cultivate. The road has been constructed through these lands at an expense of $30,000,000. In 1850 the population of forty-nine counties, through which it passes, was only 335,591 since which 479,293 have been added; making the whole population 814,891, a gain of 143 per cent.

EVIDENCES OF PROSPERITY.

As an evidence of the thrift of the people, it may be stated that 600,000 tons of freight, including 8,600,000 bushels of grain, and 250,000 barrels of flour were forwarded over the line last year.

PRICES AND TERMS OF PAYMENT.

The prices of these lands vary from $6 to $25 per acre, according to location, quality, &c. First class farming lands sell for about $10 to $12 per acre; and the relative expense of subduing prairie land as compared with wood land is in the ratio of 1 to 10 in favor of the former. The terms of sale for the bulk of these lands will be

ONE YEAR'S INTEREST IN ADVANCE,

at six per cent per annum, and six interest notes at six per cent., payable respectively in one, two, three, four, five and six years from date of sale; and four notes for principal payable in four, five, six and seven years from date of sale; the contract stipulating that one-tenth of the tract purchased shall be fenced and cultivated, each and every year, for five years from date of sale, so that at the end of five years one-half shall be fenced and under cultivation.

TWENTY PER CENT. WILL BE DEDUCTED

from the valuation for cash, except the same should be at six dollars per acre, when the cash price will be five dollars

Pamphlets descriptive of the lands, soil, climate, productions, prices, and terms of payment, can be had on application to

J. W. FOSTER, Land Commissioner,
CHICAGO, ILLINOIS

The Illinois Central Railroad was one of the principal pioneers of modern place marketing, using mass advertising and other promotional techniques to dispose of its federal land grant, principally for agricultural settlement. This advertisement appeared widely in the early 1860s. It shows how illustration was beginning to be used to reinforce the optimistic message.

Uncle Sam is Rich Enough to Give Us All a Farm

By the 1870s and 1880s the competitive selling of the frontier was at its height. There were now many more railroads with huge endowments of federal land, all trying simultaneously to attract settlers (Fitte, 1966, pp. 15–33). More areas were also being opened for homesteading and there were many encouragements to pre-emptive settlement, either in advance of or in conjunction with homesteading (Wishart, 1987). In 1871, for example, one typical handbill, produced by an organization which sold information to settlers, promised 320 acres for every citizen under a combination of homesteading and pre-emption in the Dakota Territory. Headed 'Uncle Sam is rich enough to give us all a farm', the bill further promised 'homes for the homeless' and 'land for the landless' (Yankton Press, 1871).

Other areas that ultimately became the main mid-West farming states were also being promoted vigorously over these years, often by territorial and state administrations. Less typical was the promotion, from the late 1870s, of what became Oklahoma. Acquired after the Civil War, supposedly for the resettlement of freed slaves and indigenous tribes displaced by white settlement, ever more covetous eyes were cast on this area by those interested in promoting homesteading. In 1879, for example, the Indian Territory Colonization Society was advertising for colonists (ITCS, 1879). Another broadside in the same year promised, rather improbably, that the 'Indians are rejoicing to have the whites settle upon this country' (Carpenter, 1879).

The railroads continued to play centrally important roles in selling the frontier. After the defeat of the South removed the main political obstacle to the opening of the West, federal lands were used to endow the building of the principal east-west railroads. All followed the lead of the ICRR in extensive advertising to promote settlement and traffic (e.g. Fitte, 1966, pp. 27–30). Most prominent amongst these was the first trans-continental railroad, the Union Pacific, with its vast 12 million acre land grant (Zube and Galante, 1994, pp. 218–219). By the 1870s it was spending an average $80,000 per annum on advertising. In 1874 alone the railroad took space in 2311 newspapers and magazines. Like the ICRR, its settlement work continued for many years. In 1892, for example, it was promoting the 'Golden Belt of Kansas' (Shackleton, 1976, p. 29). Meanwhile in colder latitudes, the Northern Pacific Railroad was energetically wooing northern European settlers, especially Scandinavians. In 1882 it distributed over 600,000 copies of its publications, in English, Swedish, Danish, Norwegian and Dutch (Fitte, 1966, p. 28).

Increasingly by the 1870s, all the land grant railroads were running frequent special excursion trains for would-be settlers. The excursions themselves were widely advertised by letterpress posters and handbills. Fares were cheap and if purchase of railroad land resulted, then the cost of the fare was reduced or even refunded. Yet the volume of available land, especially after homesteading began, meant that even without this railroads would offer extremely cheap fares to stimulate interest. In 1876, for example, the Atchison, Topeka and Sante Fe Railroad, advertising the Upper Arkansas valley as 'the best thing in the West', was appealing both to homesteaders and to potential purchasers of its own lands (ATSFRR, 1876). Only the latter would get a refund on their fares, however.

In some areas rivalry became extremely fierce. During the 1880s the Southern Pacific Railroad (SPRR) and the ATSFRR competed intensely to open up California. Reflecting this, it was possible, for a brief period in 1886, to travel the 1600 miles from Kansas City to Los Angeles for just $1 (Dumke, 1944, p. 9). Both companies took full advantage of all available promotional arts. In San Francisco, for example, the SPRR had a permanent land agent during the 1880s who authored place selling literature such as *California: Its Attractions for the Invalid, Tourist, Capitalist and Homeseeker*. The very title shows how the promotional message was shifting,

The federal land grant to the Illinois Central set the pattern for Western settlement. These two bills are typical of promotional advertising in the 1870s. By this stage many railroads and other agencies were competing and cheap land excursions to Iowa and Nebraska from cities such as Cincinnati and Chicago were daily events.

especially as the frontier shifted from the flat, fertile prairies to the scenic splendours of the mountains, desert areas and the Pacific coast. In particular tourism began to be promoted, often as a possible prelude to settlement.

The same message came through in other promotional literature. A common device was the hiring by the railroads of freelance writers who specialized in promotional and travel writing. For many years commercial writers and publishers had been able to make money out of for sale guides to the new lands. Railroad patronage was a natural development. Much the most notable was Charles Nordhoff, author of *California: for Health, Pleasure, and Residence* (1873), a book credited with having brought more people to California than anything else ever written (Dumke, 1944, p. 30). Like those of the ICRR and earlier land grant railroads, such publications were distributed in their thousands. During the following decades neighbouring Arizona experienced the same treatment (Zube and Kennedy, 1990). After the territorial administration had initially tried to promote arable farming, the SPRR and ATSFRR began from the late 1880s to promote settlement based more on grazing, minerals and tourism.

Piling It on Thick

This diversity had not originally been an important part of the marketing message. Traditionally the frontier was portrayed in much simpler terms. Fundamentally the frontier itself was a symbol of agrarian opportunity. The language of promotion was directed very much at the farmer, with much discussion of soil fertility, climate and crop yields. Invariably, as with virtually all subsequent place marketing efforts, the message was optimistic. Thus the *Chicago Tribune*, reflecting on the pioneering advertising efforts of the ICRR, commented in 1887:

If an Eastern or European immigrant could doubt that the Garden of Eden of Palestine was a myth, and that the real scene of Adam and Eve's interview with the apple lay anywhere else other than down about Kankakee, he must indeed have been wedded to his biblical gods. In the vernacular of today, Mr Dupuy [the head of ICRR's Land Department in the early 1850s] 'piled it on thick'. (Gates, 1934, p. 177)

The difficulties of settlement, such as breaking the soil, securing timber or drinking water, the poor drainage, the prevalence of epidemics etc were often not mentioned. There were also more conscious attempts to combat negative eastern reports of the prairies. From 1857 engravings were used in pamphlets, quite deliberately to reinforce a much more positive image. Another member of the ICRR's Land Department called for,

a fancy sketch of *an ideal prairie farm*, with a neat house, an adjacent grove, distant view of the *much dreaded prairie* covered with waving grain, some good looking stock in the foreground, a living stream of water, handsome Maclura hedges, etc. (Gates, 1934, p. 176)

Playing down the dangers or difficulties of settlement remained typical, even as the frontier itself shifted. In 1873, for example, Nordhoff, the great publicist for California, wrote:

There are no dangers to travelers on the beaten track in California; there are no inconveniences which a child or a tenderly reared woman would not laugh at . . . when you have spent half a dozen weeks in the State, you will perhaps return with a notion that New York is the true frontier land, and that you have nowhere in the United States seen so complete a civilization. (cited Dumke, 1944, p. 30)

Another Californian example, from 1886, dismissed another persistent worry of many would-be settlers:

The whole number of persons in the southern half of the State (where thousands sleep all summer on the open ground) injured by snakes and poisonous reptiles, animals etc., in the last ten years is not equal to the number killed by lightning alone in one year in one county in many Eastern States. (cited *ibid*, p. 30)

Fertility Unsurpassed by Any on the Globe

With such difficulties played down, the central part of the frontier message emphasized bounteous prosperity. In the early 1860s, for example, settlers in Illinois were promised:

Nowhere can the industrious farmer secure such immediate results for his labor as upon these prairie soils, they being composed of a deep rich loam, the fertility of which is unsurpassed by any on the globe. (Gates, 1934, facing p. 186)

It was a pattern followed in all the prairie farming states over the following decades. Advertisements for the especially rich farmlands of Iowa were always anticipating bumper crops. Yet territories which proved less attractive to settlers, such as Nebraska, were promoted with praise that was especially fulsome. In 1875, for example, the Lands Department of the Burlington and Missouri River Railroad promised corn yields set to exceed those of southern Iowa. They also quoted the opinion that 'a bird never flew over a finer country' (see page 16).

Other territories and states followed suit, basing their advertising on farm settlement even in the most unlikely circumstances. A particularly cruel myth was fostered by dubious scientific experiment that rain would follow the plough. As soil was broken and vegetation grew, rain clouds would miraculously increase (Wishart, 1987, p. 271). Although expression of this idea grew more cautious by the 1880s, promotional claims were still careless with the truth. This was even true of desert or marginal lands such as Arizona. In 1886, for example, a promotional publication by the Territorial Commission of Immigration went a little too far when it referred to:

The grassy hills and plains, once the home of the deer and the antelope, are being transformed into green fields and blossoming orchards; capital's magical wand has touched the barren mountains, and streams of precious metals are flowing therefrom.

. . . Popular opinion has long considered Arizona a waterless region, but the truth is that few countries of the West are so abundantly equipped. (cited in Zube and Kennedy, 1990, p. 191).

Many similar claims were made in adjoining South-Western territories, sometimes more successfully than others. A few years later, for example, the Pecos Land and Irrigation Company showed how the New Mexico desert could be made to bloom and prosper as a fruit growing area (PIIC, c1891). Much of this effort sought to emulate the earlier example of California. In that much promoted state, the orange quickly became the main early signifier of fertility, perpetual sunshine and prosperity. In 1907 the slogan 'Oranges for Health – California for Wealth' began to be used in intensive joint railroad and fruitgrowers' promotional campaigns throughout the mid-West states (Elias, 1983, pp. 38–39).

Eventually notes of caution began to be inserted in promotional publicity, especially after over ambitious cultivation or grazing by early settlers had succeeded only in extending the desert. By 1859, for example, the ICRR was warning against purchasing too much land (in part necessary because the ICRR had fixed the price relatively high) (ICRR, 1859, p. 37). In more arid areas, later revisions of the promotional message could sometimes be more fundamental. In Arizona, for example, later publicity laid more emphasis on minerals and only the most extensive forms of agriculture. Scenic attractions in these more arid or difficult areas also began to form a progressively greater part of the promotional message by the 1890s (Runte, 1991; 1992; 1994).

Miss Dakota

Another important theme in the frontier marketing message was gender. Invariably, as we have seen, the promotional invitation was to young men, to make a new life for themselves. The role of women, though obviously crucial to the building of self-sustaining communities, was rather neglected. The Illinois Central made some references to children, both as a source of labour for some crops and in relation to the state school system. But women were generally neglected in literature promoting frontier settlement. This did not entirely mirror reality. Pre-emption law, for

This pictorial poster was issued in 1890 by the immigration department of the new state of South Dakota. One of a series using the figure of 'Miss Dakota', she is here presented to an admiring male world by Uncle Sam. The representational meaning of Miss Dakota herself is discussed more fully in the text but notice also the explicit (and entirely typical) invitation to settle on lands ostensibly reserved for indigenous peoples. Also worthy of comment is the citation of public institutions such as a 'school for deaf mutes', 'hospital for the insane', state penitentiary and reform school. Along with (from today's viewpoint) more conventional prizes such as universities and colleges, these institutions were also fiercely competed over because they offered secure markets for local produce.

example, only sanctioned claims by widows or 'heads of families' (Boorstin, 1965, p. 77). This did not stop enterprising maidens acquiring land by temporarily 'adopting' a child from obliging neighbours. The Homestead Act was used more openly and extensively by women, for a variety of motives including speculation, the desire for a dowry, aiding husbands or male relatives as well as a genuine desire to become farmers (Myres, 1982, p. 238–270). So far as most promotional literature was concerned, though, it was a man's world.

There was a definite sense though in which the frontier was represented as a feminine construct. This was done in a precise fashion in the promotion of Dakota. About the time the territory was achieving statehood, the Commission for Immigration used several fine coloured pictorial posters of Miss Dakota. In 1887, for example, she is portrayed as a modest, barefoot maiden holding a scroll for Uncle Sam's kindly consideration. Meanwhile Dakota's name is just being added to the other 38 states. Three years later, she has become South Dakota, more elegantly attired, no longer barefoot and with hair neatly tied back. But she remains essentially modest. An ebullient Uncle Sam shows off his latest state before approving male representatives of other nations at the 1890 World's Fair. Again she holds a scroll showing some of the new state's attainments, this time in visual form. Her image is surrounded by other tokens of the new state's achievements and promise.

Several readings of this are possible. There were certainly a large number of women homesteaders in the Dakotas in the 1880s. One 1886 estimate was that a third of the land was held by women (Myres, 1982, p. 258). It is possible that this is being alluded to in the posters. Yet the images of Miss Dakota certainly do not show her as homesteader. The surrounding vignettes of economic activity show only men; her role is more decorative and symbolic. The main underlying message of the Miss Dakota figure seems rather one of virginity and promised of fertility. The clear analogy is with marriage and reproduction. Young men should embrace the virgin lands, plant seed and be fruitful. Yet this itself only partly captures the meaning of the image. Certain parallels with the story of Pygmalion are also apparent. Rather in the manner of Professor Henry Higgins, Uncle Sam presents his protégé, transformed from a simple girl, to an impressed, masculine world. And behind the national stereotypes are figures of archetypal male homesteaders. This reading of the promotional message points to a deeper relationship, between American civilization and a changing frontier.

Such a marketing proposition came later in the promotional process, as the frontier lands began to change from their uncolonized, unowned condition into profitable use. The last major rush of farm-based settlers onto uncolonized lands came in the wake of the 1887 General Allotment Act. Ostensibly intended to draw the indigenous peoples into the new farming system, it served rather as the means finally to deprive them of what traditionally held land they had remaining (Wishart, 1987, pp. 265–266; Milner, 1994: 174). In April 1889 the last large areas of reserved Indian lands in Oklahoma, long anticipated by promotional advertising (Goodrum and Dalrymple, 1990, p. 19), were finally released (Boorstin, 1965, pp. 81–82). As we have seen, however, much land remained for settlement well after this period. The agricultural colonization of land in the far West continued well into the twentieth century (Wishart, 1987, pp. 275–277). Nor was agricultural settlement ever the only promotional concern.

SELLING FRONTIER TOWNS AND CITIES

Town Site Promotion

Given the priority to bring their huge land areas into the capitalist system, it was natural that early place selling efforts by territorial administrations, state governments and railroads would be dominated by agricultural settlement. Yet in such large and relatively empty areas towns were also needed as trading and administrative points for these farming areas. A few such towns, serving wider functions of trade, administration, education and culture, grew into large cities. Meanwhile some smaller urban places also began to develop more highly specialized functions within an increasingly national urban system.

At one level it is quite possible to rationalize these developments in terms of the impersonal factors of economy and geography. Yet the whole process was typically accompanied by quite intense place selling activity, as the merits of different places were competitively asserted. Because they had such a decisive impact on the prospects for settlement, the railroads themselves were well placed to promote new town sites on their lands. In part such promotions were motivated by convenience for railroad operation. Yet profit from land development was usually at least as important. The railroads' extensive publicity machines were used to market such places in the same way as agricultural colonization.

Railroad construction itself brought into being many temporary towns devoted principally to drink, gambling and other excesses. The life of such desperate places was extended where they coincided with more permanent railroad depots, mineral deposits and mining camps or, most promisingly, richer farmlands. The ICRR had a string of Illinois towns to its name (Gates, 1934, pp. 121–148). Its original charter had forbidden such ventures, though four had already been promoted through an ICRR Associates Land Company before a revised charter legalized the practice. Amongst these early promotions was the southern terminus at Cairo, whose investors included the novelist, Charles Dickens, one of the many British involved in the ICRR and related projects (ICRR, 1853; Gates, 1973, pp. 69–70). Further west the sparser landscape reduced the prospects for successful long term town development. Cheyenne, in Wyoming, was a notably successful town promotion by the Union Pacific Railroad (UPRR) in the late 1860s (Quiett, 1934, pp. 83–84; McKelvey, 1963, p. 26). Other railroad towns included Reno, Nevada, on the Central Pacific, and Butte, Montana, on the Northern Pacific.

Though the railroads were the most powerful (and best documented) agencies promoting new towns, there were others. Most immediately prominent were independent land speculators who were particularly attracted by the difference between undeveloped and urban land values, offering much larger gains than were possible in purely farming districts. This led to many more towns being proposed than had any realistic chance of being fully settled. Many of the most successful speculators were railroad officials, directors or investors, usually with access to privileged information. Advance knowledge of or inspired guesswork about railroad routes could be used to great effect. If land acquired at low cost was then subsequently to be served by a railroad (or, more importantly, if a subsequent buyer could be persuaded that this was likely), immense speculative gains might follow.

It was far better for land speculators if buyers never set eyes on the new towns that were being promoted (Reps, 1965). Advertising in the eastern states or even in Europe was common. Another favourite device to attract buyers involved frenzied auctions of town lots in the nearest semi-civilized city. Typically such events would occur shortly before the tracks actually reached the place concerned. It was at this time that the maximum speculative gain was possible. Elaborate engraved plans and sketches of the town were displayed at the auctions to suggest an established place with fine public buildings.

These fine engravings normally fell rather short of being literal representations and were more in the nature of speculative hypotheses, their potency all the greater because they could not easily be tested against reality. If the venture failed entirely the initial low cost of the site meant that little had been lost.

This was the basic mode of operation of the ever growing group of speculators and promoters both in the United States and Canada, many of them moving westward with the railroads. The intensity of the California boom of the 1880s owed at least something to this ultimate concentration of professional speculators. Yet there were also examples of more secure town promotions, where land developers took a longer view. The foundation, in 1871, of the health and pleasure resort of Colorado Springs at the foot of Pike's Peak in the Rockies by the railroad promoter General William Jackson Palmer was one such instance (Quiett, 1934, pp. 98–104). Palmer followed the familiar tactic of extensive optimistic advertising in the newspapers of the eastern states and England. Yet such efforts were underpinned by a site of innate scenic quality, careful and sustained attention to the details of creating an attractive resort and formidable marketing skills that drew a stream of dignitaries to visit the growing resort.

The Best Advertised City in the World

As communities became more settled a wider range of more local interests became part of the boosterist ethos, selling their towns to potential settlers and investors (Boorstin, 1965, pp. 113–168). Prominent amongst such interests were the local newspaper editors who used their columns to proclaim and reinforce a spirit of progress and enterprise. Local businessmen of all kinds vigorously promoted their towns, increasingly through collective bodies such as local Boards of Trade, Chambers of Commerce and Town Councils. A typical example of this process was Wichita, in Kansas, which grew from just 50 inhabitants in 1870 to a claimed

40,000 eighteen years later. By 1887 the town had a virile Board of Trade which was promoting the city with a breathless stream of superlatives such as 'the new Chicago'; 'the peerless princess of the plains'; 'the Jerusalem of the west'; 'the best advertised city in the world'; and many others in similar vein (WBT, 1887). Its local newspapers similarly talked up the city in supplements as, for example,

Wichita: Metropolis of the South West. The Largest City in Kansas. A city of fine educational institutions, Magnificent Business Blocks, Elegant Residences and Extensive Manufactures, with more railroads, more Wholesale Trade, more manufacturing, more enterprise than any other city in the South West. (*Wichita Eagle*, 1888)

Much of this kind of activity developed, as here, after the railroad links had appeared. Yet where such settled communities existed in advance of the railroads, the promise of rail connections posed a severe test of local boosterist resolve. This was because the railroads habitually demanded subsidies from the existing settlements they served, with the threat that they would follow another route to by-pass the town. As a counter measure business men in the larger centres might themselves use local capital to promote new railroads to ensure they remained on the map.

Either way, such practices meant that individual communities had to pay to be part of the emergent rail system. In smaller or more marginal communities particularly such payments were likely to be financed from local taxation. These practices were commonplace throughout North America, even in the most settled regions. By 1875 some three hundred municipalities in New York state had paid such subsidies to railroads (McKelvey, 1963, p. 24). A few years earlier the thriving frontier mining settlement of Denver had faced losing its dominant trading position in the Rocky Mountain region to the new Union Pacific town of Cheyenne (McKelvey, 1963, p. 26). Its response was to organize a local Board of Trade and raise $280,000 to pay for a link to the main line, opened in 1870. And so it went on.

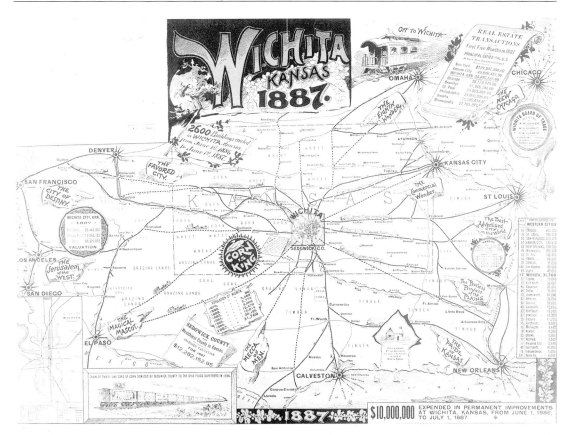

Booster impulses were strongly represented in emerging Western towns and cities. This 1887 promotional map for Wichita was produced for the local Board of Trade. The blank space in the top left would probably have been overprinted by local businesses. Great spatial distortions are apparent to emphasize Wichita's centrality and an entire family of promotional slogans are apparently being bestowed by admiring cities. Also visible is the trainload of local corn sent to relieve Ohio flood victims in 1884, its cars all evidently emblazoned with boosterist messages about the Wichita area.

General Palmer, building his Denver and Rio Grande Railroad southwards in the following decade deliberately fostered an air of uncertainty about the route (Quiett, 1934, pp. 105–107). The inhabitants of Pueblo and other towns were frightened enough to pay handsomely to ensure rail links. By 1879 there were loud complaints about similar behaviour by the Central Pacific Railroad in California (Quiett, 1934, p. 83).

In Canada too the same game was played and became even more institutionalized, following the 1852 Municipal Loans Act. By 1912 it was estimated that municipalities had raised 7 per cent of the total subsidies given to Canadian railway building, but the proportion had been much higher in the 1850–1880 period, especially in Ontario (Bloomfield, 1983*b*, pp. 59–61). Even by 1894 almost 10 per cent of the total municipal debt in Ontario was accounted for by cash payments, known as bonuses, to railways (Ontario, 1896). Toronto alone had a $1 million debt on such bonuses. The experience of other Canadian cities was similar. Thus Montreal, already a big city, and Winnipeg, not yet one, had similarly helped secure their future status by railway bonusing in the 1870s (Morris, 1989, pp. 55–56).

Already then, place selling was becoming a more complex process, involving more than just the securing of short term profits on land assets that had been the concern of most town site promoters. Settled communities took a broader and longer term view of the pursuit of economic prosperity. In selling themselves they recognized that to survive and develop, place marketing might need to recognize the principle of the loss leader. A place could not be sold on equal terms to all investors. Important investment, such as the railroads, with much greater bargaining power than individual towns and cities, might well need to be bought in order to enhance a place's attractiveness and lay the basis for more self-sustaining growth. What many North American towns experienced first with the railroads became more common with other attributes of growth in the later nineteenth and early twentieth centuries.

The Pecuniary Value of Cheek

Not all places were in similar positions, of course. A few cities such as Buffalo, Cleveland and Chicago and the big eastern ports were sufficiently well established for the railroads to come begging at their doors. Other, more upstart places benefited by playing railroads off against each other. Los Angeles, a city of just 7,000 people, had been obliged to pay heavily to secure the Southern Pacific, its first transcontinental rail link, in the 1870s. Yet it became the principal beneficiary of the cut throat competition between the Southern Pacific and the ATSFRR in the following decade (Elias, 1983, pp. 13–17). As we have seen, both railroads threw themselves into promoting California, especially the areas around Los Angeles, where the ATSFRR promoted many new town sites.

Meanwhile the remarkable concentration of land speculators in this rapidly growing area was reinforcing these efforts, changing national perceptions of the whole state (Dumke, 1944, p. 9). As the *San Jose Mercury* observed regretfully in April 1885:

Our brethren in the city and would-be state of the Angels understand how to advertise. The average eastern mind conceives of California as a small tract of country situated in and around Los Angeles. The mines, parks, vineyards, and redwood forests are all there or thereabouts . . . Circulars, posters, pamphlets, all singing the praises of Los Angeles were distributed by the millions; and all our ultramontane brethren whose lives have been spared through the recent awful winter are vowing that as soon as they can sell out they will emigrate to Los Angeles. The result shows the pecuniary value of cheek. Suburban lots at Los Angeles are worth a prince's ransom, and the appalling waste of alkali and sage brush in which the angels have built their city is almost as valuable to sell as our rich willow lands. (cited Quiett, 1934, p. 275)

But the 'pecuniary value of cheek' was at its zenith in southern California during the 1880s. Less favoured places had to work harder to secure a real basis for survival and growth. Railroads were necessary but not sufficient to ensure future prosperity.

One favoured tactic of new towns and cities was to make bids to state governments over the location of key state facilities (Boorstin, 1965, pp. 163–167). Places competed to be made state capital, or to become home to a state university, insane asylum or penitentiary. All of these brought more buildings, employment and business to local communities that might well be struggling after the initial railroad-fuelled boom had ended. Accordingly many thousands of dollars were offered to state governments in the pursuit of such prizes. There was, for example, a bitter four-way battle over the location of the University of Illinois (Gates, 1934, pp. 132–135). The eventual winner, Champaign-Urbana, had benefited from the strong support of the ICRR, which owned large amounts of land in the area. Further west, however, a university was not always so highly prized. When Canon City, Colorado, won the right to a state facility, it chose the penitentiary whose impact was more predictable (McKelvey, 1963, p. 30).

Another way to sell your town or city was to embellish it with handsome, large, buildings. We have seen how town site promoters regularly included images of non-existent fine public build-ings in their promotional engravings. As places became more established, the giving of reality to such buildings became a key indicator of the true worth of a place. Photographs, increas-ingly common in guidebooks and promotional brochures by the 1890s, were a way of vouch-safing the authenticity of such grandeur. The sense of stability and incipient greatness that the buildings created was crucially important in attracting persons of wealth and position, and the capital they controlled. Large hotels were typically the first large buildings to appear (Boorstin, 1965, pp. 135–147), though others such as banks, court houses, council chambers soon followed in places with some genuine growth potential.

During the 1890s a new North American design ideology took shape which was particularly well attuned to the boosterist ethic – the City Beautiful movement (Wilson, 1989). Stylis-tically, it combined classicism and landscape architecture, typically in the creation of new civic centres, parks and grand boulevards. Its grand scale, lack of challenge to the dominance of urban business elites and widespread legitimacy gave it great potency in competitive place selling. Thus City Beautiful planning became a way in which the cities of the mid-West and the West could assert themselves, both one against another and against the more established cities of the east. As Wilson shows, such sentiments were particularly developed in places like Kansas City and Denver, allowing them to distance themselves from their raw frontier legacy and market themselves as diverse and attractive cities.

THE UN-BRITISHNESS OF BOOSTERISM

A Long Settled Land

While the North American continent was undergoing this massive process of settlement promotion, Britain and its near neighbours in continental Europe were also changing drama-tically. Their industrial towns and cities were growing as never before or since. There were also huge changes in the countryside. Yet, for all this, there was practically no evidence of the competitive city advertising for migrants or investment that was typical across the Atlantic. With a few significant exceptions towards the end of the nineteenth century, the most striking point is how un-British American-style booster-ism actually was. While it is never easy to explain why things do not happen, the problem is fundamental to the chapters which follow. It is important therefore to think about its sources.

The most basic point is that the land of Britain, in common with most of Europe, had largely been settled for several centuries before 1800 (Darby, 1973). A relatively dense network of cities, towns and villages already existed. There were no longer any large and relatively empty areas into which agrarian settlers needed to be attracted. Moreover, the settlement of Britain had preceded any widespread acceptance of the concept of land as a commodity in a capitalist, market economy (Whitelock, 1972). Travellers' tales doubtless played a part in drawing migrants from the North German plain and Scandinavia. Yet such tales were not in the literal sense mar-keting Britain because there was no established commodity to market. As such they were pro-foundly different from the promotional advertis-ing of the US territorial and state commissioners, railroads and land companies, created with the clear objective of marketing land. The migra-tional patterns of Angles, Saxons, Jutes and Vikings into Britain were conditioned largely by bonds of family and tribal kinship. Capitalism and private land ownership came later.

But this fairly obvious feature can only be part of the explanation. Certainly it explains why there was no British equivalent of agricultural land disposal. Yet the question remains why the main arena of nineteenth-century change in

Britain, the towns and cities, was not the subject of competitive boosterism. The critical point here was that Britain also had much the most spontaneously flourishing economy in the world, at least until the later decades of the nineteenth century. Britain's industrialization occurred on the firm foundations of several centuries' worth of indigenous capitalism and successful accumulation. By international standards of newly industrializing countries, it enjoyed an abundance of capital, typically available locally within the industrializing regions (Payne, 1988). Its agriculture and trade were already very strong. Its rural areas were overflowing with people who were no longer needed for food production and could search for better prospects in nearby expanding towns.

Quite simply therefore the acute place competition for long distance migration and/or external investment that was critical to North American rural and urban settlement, especially in the West, the South and Canada, simply did not occur on any scale in Britain. In its absence, there was no need for active place selling on the pattern of American boosterism. The particularly favourable economic and demographic circumstances of Britain in the late eighteenth and early nineteenth centuries also had other consequences.

A Mature Urban System

The early industrialization that followed from these favourable circumstances and the urbanization that grew on an established settlement pattern combined to restrict the formative influence of the railways. These were, as we have begun to see, one of the most important agencies that fed place competition in North America. In Britain, by contrast, they were inserted into an already highly mature urban economic system. There was never any question of established towns or cities having to pay railways to serve them (Kellett, 1969). The railways themselves were invariably supplicants in their dealings with cities. Crucially, too, Britain's railways were, in

general, denied the powers to become the major players in the land market that they were in North America (Biddle, 1990, pp. 83–109).

The upshot was that, of the larger industrial towns and ports, only a handful were actually nineteenth century foundations. Middlesbrough, Barrow-in-Furness, Birkenhead and Ashton-under-Lyne were the most important of these. The railways themselves also created a few 'company towns' to serve their own industrial needs, the largest being Crewe. But the list of new nineteenth-century industrial town or port creations quickly tails off into the obscurity of places such as Aberaeron and Portmadoc. None of these British 'upstarts' ever seriously challenged the position of the much older established settlements, already prominent as regional centres by 1700, which grew to be the main cities of the industrial regions: Manchester, Liverpool, Birmingham, Leeds, Newcastle etc. (Chalklin, 1974, p.10). Still less was the dominant position of London as primate city ever under threat.

Historical geographers and urban historians have been undecided as to whether it is best to stress the relative stability or the dynamism of the British urban system during industrialization. There is no doubt important changes had taken place by 1800, as the main centres in prosperous agricultural regions such as Exeter or Norwich, and many county towns, lost ground to the new regional centres of the industrial areas noted above (Robson, 1973, pp. 37–41; Carter, 1978, pp. 371–378). These trends continued throughout the nineteenth century. Yet from this time there were strong tendencies to stability in size relations. By 1850 Britain had evolved an urban industrial system that in most key respects was to persist for rather more than a century (Carter and Lewis, 1990, pp. 42–66). Thus, as modern place marketing emerged in North America, Britain already had what was, by American standards, an extremely stable urban hierarchy.

There were, certainly, some upward movers which increased their relative importance after 1850, particularly the resorts and the suburbs. These were places which were actively marketed, as we will see in the next two parts of the book. Yet they were not important enough to destabilize the whole British urban system. Thus the basic size relativities of the main centres survived very large absolute population increases. Moreover the broad functional economic relationships within the urban and regional system also endured. Each region quickly found its own highly specialized economic niche, competing not so much with other regions as with other parts of the world. Cities such as Manchester, Birmingham, Newcastle or Glasgow remained throughout the largest cities and unchallenged command centres of their respective regions. Each was surrounded by a constellation of smaller production centres and other specialized towns.

This relative stability even in circumstances of growth was matched by the absence of precipitate decline even amongst places whose position in the urban hierarchy was declining. The main 'losers' of nineteenth century British urban growth, the historic county and market towns and the cathedral cities, clearly remained agreeable residential locations for the wealthy. Certainly at this time they showed no great propensity to challenge their relative decline with promotional strategies.

Competition between British Cities

The consequence was that the culture of competition between different cities was never as sharply focused in Britain during the nineteenth century as it became in North America. There was, certainly, a form of competition between the big British cities by the later decades of the century but it expressed itself more in the pursuit of a civilizing agenda (Briggs, 1963). It was about coping with the consequences of a spontaneously successful process of capital accumulation and population growth (Morris, 1989). There was no real scarcity of capital or people to fuel this growth and therefore no necessity to compete for such factors of production. Inter-urban competition in Britain was expressed in the grandeur of town halls and waterworks; the cultural riches of art galleries and public libraries; the efficiency of sewage farms and tramway systems.

North American cities began to show similar concerns, of course, but their motivations remained subtly different, especially so in the many upstart cities of the mid and far West. The growth imperative was never far from the surface, revealing an economic insecurity that British cities did not then have to face. In so far as the business men of British Victorian cities acted collectively to advance local economic activity, through chambers of commerce or similar bodies, their typical concerns were to remove the obstacles to the trade of the existing dominant industries. More typically the collective agenda of the urban political elites sought to enhance the social functioning of their cities rather than directly assisting in economic activity.

CONCLUSIONS

Overall then, the economic systems of the United States and Canada were characterized by instability and a strong sense of inter-place competition. The rapid settlement of the North American continent left a boosterist legacy that continued to pervade the urban agenda, in sharp contrast to the pattern we have identified in Britain. There was actually nothing that was inherently un-British about boosterism. As we have seen, British investors in American railroads or land companies were just as willing to become boosters as their US equivalents. It was simply that in Britain there was no imperative to settle so much land so quickly, nor to create an urban system to service this highly mobile economy. Relatively speaking, Britain's urban system was characterized by dynamic stability; North America's by dynamic instability, a situation where place competition was endemic. There were some British (and European) exceptions to these general principles, as we will see over the following chapters. But it has not been until much more recently, as the overall stability of Britain's urban system has been threatened, that we have seen the kind of all-pervasive boosterism that has been so characteristic of the United States.

We have then, set a broad agenda for the more detailed investigations in the next four parts of the book. The earliest forms of modern place marketing have begun to demonstrate much about marketing imperatives, agencies and messages. We will find ourselves returning to many of these themes in subsequent chapters.

3

HEALTH RESORTS AND WATERING PLACES

In the early 1990s the stagnating gentility of Eastbourne was assailed by a local publicity campaign meant to shock the town out of its complacent decline (EMG, 1994). Under the headline 'Eastbourne – the last resort?' the campaign highlighted closing down signs on the main multiple stores, a collapsed pier and rundown terraces bristling with For Sale signs. The tactic, intended as a first stage in breaking the town's 'elderly tourist' image and combating long term decline, was deliberate and successful. By 1992 the small group of businessmen and tourist operators who started the campaign had secured sufficient financial assistance, from local businesses, the local council and the English Tourist Board, to launch the Eastbourne Marketing Group. In turn the new Group set to work marketing and promoting the development and improvement of the town. It was an innovative and widely praised attempt to address deeply seated problems that had been affecting virtually all Britain's seaside resorts since the appearance of the foreign package holiday in the 1960s.

Yet in doing this Eastbourne was merely reverting to exactly the type of place selling tactics that had been critically important for the resorts in their heyday. Since the 1950s, in many ways since the interwar years, the resorts, with perhaps the singular exception of Blackpool, had simply forgotten the lessons of their own histories. In fact, the selling of the seaside was one of the few instances of genuine North American-style boosterism to be found in Britain's otherwise rather stable urban system.

In this and the next chapter we reclaim some of this largely unexplored history of resort marketing. The focus is, quite justifiably, mainly on Britain which was the original home of the mass holiday resort, particularly the seaside. Yet we will also consider some of the parallel efforts in other countries. In the next chapter we will move on to investigate the imagery of resort marketing in all these countries. Finally we will examine the more recent trends in resort marketing, considering both the new mass tourist destinations and the often struggling British seaside resorts which are attempting to regenerate themselves. Our narrative begins, however, at the other end of this historical process.

THE EMERGENCE OF THE RESORT

The Pre-History of Resorts

The two main social imperatives which underpinned the pre-history of the tourist resort were religion and health (Pimlott, 1976, pp. 21–48; Walvin, 1978, pp. 13–16). Since at least the late medieval period, certain places in Britain and much of the rest of Europe had begun to attract visitors. The places typically had some kind of religious association, often with saints or supposedly miraculous events. Water, with all its powerful associations with holiness, also held a special significance. Such religious overtones were not solely Christian. Where spring water effervesced or steamed from cracks in rocks or where it had an unusual taste from dissolved minerals or even where it was unusually cold, there had long been claims for its curative or magical properties. Despite some misgivings about such superstitions, dedications of such springs and wells to saints were common, so that they became religious sites of pilgrimage.

The religious role of the watering places declined markedly after the Reformation. Yet this was more than compensated for by the rise of scientific medical knowledge. A growing number of scientific treatises, the first in English published by Dr William Turner in 1562, attested to the value to health of bathing in the waters. It was the increasing flow of literature on these lines that laid the main basis for the emergence of the spa resort (Alderson, 1973; Hembry, 1990). The actual term spa came from a watering place with that name in what is now the Belgian Ardennes, which became known in Britain at about this time. As the spa resort emerged as a specific form in Britain over the sixteenth and seventeenth centuries, the religious partnership with health was pushed further into the background.

A new emphasis on pleasure replaced it. The spa typically offered facilities for bathing and drinking waters and a growing range of recreational and cultural diversions (Alderson, 1973; Denbigh, 1981). By the early eighteenth century the larger spas, such as Bath and Buxton, which had Roman origins, Tunbridge, Harrogate, Epsom and Scarborough (unique in being a spa by the sea) had become fashionable summer resorts for the upper classes, who would often spend the entire season there. Even health was now becoming a secondary theme. In the main resort, Bath, the attraction was increasingly the pursuit of pleasure within fashionable society

(Hembry, 1990, pp. 132–158; Wechsberg, 1979, pp. 9–27). Even Scarborough, a much smaller spa, could offer horse racing, gaming rooms, theatre, dancing and a circulating library, sufficient to hold the attentions of the northern gentry for the season (Walvin, 1978, p. 17).

Though the numbers of spa visitors were growing appreciably by the eighteenth century, as the expansion of trade and commerce brought new sources of wealth, the key feature of the spa remained its social exclusivity. Most people simply did not have the wealth to allow them to escape so completely from the normal routines of their lives. This point is significant in understanding how such places were marketed. Advertisements played only a very limited role, being used primarily to announce new spas that were trying to establish themselves. A very early (and utterly unsuccessful) promotional advertisement was that announcing 'London Spaw' (a renaming of the former Clerkenwell) in 1685 (Hembry, 1990, p. 100). Cheltenham Spa, founded in 1718, was also advertised in the Gloucester and London press over the few years immediately following. The spa ultimately proved very successful, but not because of this advertising.

The promotion of the spas was largely a matter of what today would be called public relations (Alderson, 1973; Wechsberg, 1979). It relied on associating these places with fashionable behaviour, creating a cumulative demand amongst the upper classes and aspirant members. Medical treatises, extolling the virtues of the waters of a particular place, were a necessary but not a significant part of this process. So too were guidebooks and descriptive accounts, which also proliferated. The promotional process was essentially conducted by word of mouth within the social networks of the upper classes. Patronage by prominent aristocrats or, for preference, royalty was essential in establishing that a particular place was fashionable. Thus it was the visit by Queen Anne in 1702 which confirmed and further enhanced Bath's position as the premier English spa. Even earlier Tunbridge had benefited by her attentions over many seasons. During the eighteenth century most of the main southern spas enjoyed royal visits, fuelling further their growth.

The Emergence of the Seaside Resorts

By this time the habit of resort-going was spreading to the seaside. Scarborough, although a spa, had begun to highlight the potential of the seaside itself (Walvin, 1978, p. 19). Some activities in the town's wide repertoire of sporting and recreational diversions made use of the beach. Certainly some of the town's visitors were bathing in the sea in the early eighteenth century. Meanwhile the wider establishment of the seaside resort as a distinctive form of place, different from the spa, was also beginning to occur. By the 1730s Brighton and Margate, along with Scarborough, had distinct seabathing seasons. Initially the pattern of the development of the seaside resorts followed closely that of the spas. The early seventeenth century brought medical assurances of the value of seabathing. Dr Richard Russell's study *A Dissertation concerning the Use of Sea-water in Diseases of the Glands*, published in 1752, was of crucial importance in providing the scientific basis for the development of seaside places as health resorts (Pimlott, 1976, p. 52–54). A little later, in the 1780s, the royal patronage, by the Prince Regent of Brighton and by his father, George III, of Weymouth supplied the other familiar element in the emergence of the high class resort.

Yet the story of the emergence of the seaside resort was not to be simply a re-run of the spa's development. The spa by its very nature offered exclusivity, focused around buildings and social institutions to which access could be carefully controlled (Denbigh, 1981). The central focus of the seaside resort was the beach and the sea itself which could not be privately owned. From the first the seaside resort had a more democratic dimension to it than the spas. Quite independently of the vagaries of upper class fashion and medical opinion, there were, certainly in

Lancashire and probably elsewhere, established social customs of seabathing amongst the common folk (Walton, 1983a, pp. 10–11). The growing upper class fashion for seabathing in the eighteenth century may have reinvigorated these customs, but did not create them.

Of course, the extent to which ordinary working people could enjoy the seaside was limited in time and place. Unlike the upper classes, they could not simply decamp in their carriages to the seaside, renting a house for the summer season. Their enjoyment of the seaside had to be brief and, in view of their very limited mobility in the pre-railway age, very localized. For the moment at least, the seaside resort remained the prerogative of an admittedly widening section of the upper and middle classes. The resorts were marketed largely by the combination of word of mouth, guidebook and medical treatise that still closely followed the practices of the spa towns. Though individuals offering property for summer rent at the seaside might publicize their services, overt advertising of a whole resort was still very rare.

The main single reason why this pattern began to change was improved mobility, based on the growing availability of cheaper mass transport. In the Thanet area of Kent, steamer services from the 1820s opened up the resorts of Margate and Gravesend to a much wider clientele than had ever been able to travel by carriage (Stafford and Yates, 1985, pp. 1–33). A few other resorts close to large centres of population were similarly affected, but for most resorts it was the railways which had the most decisive effect. Arriving at the seaside resorts from the 1830s the railways allowed a huge growth in the number of visitors. For example, in 1837 some 50,000 travellers had arrived in Brighton by stage coach. By 1850 the railway was managing to carry 73,000 in a single week (Walton, 1983a, p. 22).

Fundamental though they were to the subsequent emergence of mass holiday making, it is important not to exaggerate the effects of the railways (Walton, 1983a, pp. 22–32). Typically they brought big increases in absolute numbers of visitors, but most were simply day trippers. The innovation of the cheap day excursion train allowed mass working class access to the seaside, but it was not this alone which underpinned resort growth. Although they came in huge numbers, the amount working class trippers spent in the resorts was usually too small to provide a secure basis for growth. Excursion traffic was also rather uncertain, particularly vulnerable to economic swings and limited by sabbatarian disapproval in the early years, especially in the south (Walvin, 1978, pp. 40–43). This latter point highlights the continuing influence of religion and moral concerns on leisure activities. Paradoxically, however, employers, Sunday schools, philanthropic and temperance organizations in the North and Midlands used the day excursion as a supposed means of working class improvement. Such high ideals were not always realized. Nor did they prevent many of the more sedate resorts viewing the rowdy invasions of excursionists with some horror.

Much more important for resort prosperity in the middle decades of the nineteenth century was the less spectacular, though still very marked, growth in lower middle class holiday making. Just as the upper echelons of the middle class, dependent on trade and commerce, had begun to follow the leisured upper classes into the spas and early seaside resorts during the later eighteenth century, now the new lower middle classes of the Victorian cities were adopting the habit of staying at resorts. All resorts, even those, like Blackpool, which received the day tripper traffic with most enthusiasm, needed the greater security of longer stay visitors to provide the basis for growth. It was not until the later nineteenth century that these longer stay visitors began to include the working classes in any numbers. Blackpool was again a pioneer in this respect, partly reflecting the relative affluence of the Lancashire working class families that formed the core of its visitors (Walton, 1978). Even here though mass working class holiday making was a largely twentieth century phenomenon, when improvements in incomes and the increasing trend to paid holidays (evident particularly in the 1938 Holidays with Pay Act) removed the final barriers (Amulree Committee, 1938; Pimlott, 1976, pp. 211–237).

Resort Marketing in the Railway Era

Early Resort Selling Methods

Yet resort development was not simply a crude function of factors such as income, mobility and time. As the shift to mass holiday making occurred, so the role of place selling increased commensurately. As suggested in chapter 2, the resorts were an extremely unstable section of the whole urban system of nineteenth-century Britain. Although Brighton managed to hold on to its position as the biggest seaside resort throughout the century, Bournemouth moved from sixty-ninth largest resort in England and Wales, with a population of just 695 in 1851, to second largest in 1911 with a population of 78,674 (Walton, 1983a, pp. 53, 65; Soane, 1993). Over the same period Southend moved from

forty-fourth to third and Blackpool from forty-third to fifth. The intense place competition that lay behind these shifts continued into the twentieth century. By the late 1930s Blackpool, though not quite the largest resort town (Brighton and Southend were still larger), recorded much the largest number of visitors at about 7 million per annum. It became the ultimate mass resort in Britain. And it was certainly no coincidence that throughout most of this period Blackpool also had by far the biggest publicity budget.

When and how then did such active place selling practices originate? In the early railway age place advertising, though gradually becoming more common, remained fairly modest. At this stage place selling efforts were essentially individual or, if co-operative, not based on any permanent formal organization. Thus the catalogue of the Great Exhibition of 1851 contains advertisements for Great Yarmouth, Bath and Harrogate, apparently placed by hoteliers or proprietors of particular amenities in these towns (Official Catalogue, 1851, pp. 27–28, 33). This pattern of operation meant that sustained promotional campaigns were unlikely, because the intended benefits of resort advertising, increased visitor spending, would not be felt only by those individuals who had paid for the advertising. A more typical promotional device which overcame this problem was the guidebook, produced commercially for sale (e.g. Stafford and Yates, 1985, pp. 1–97). Often still focused heavily on medical matters, such books increasingly devoted more space to describing and illustrating scenic, historic, climatic, cultural and recreational amenities of the resorts. They were aimed very much at the upper end of the holiday market and probably did little to extend the social range.

The railway companies and the related efforts of publishers and excursion promoters began to point the way to change. Some of the first railway efforts in promotion were associated with day excursions which, by their nature, sought to widen the market for rail travel (Shackleton, 1976, pp. 9–30; Wilson, 1987). Rather crude compared to what came after, the publicity for these events usually took the form of newspaper notices, letterpress posters and handbills. Usually very little was said about the character of the destination as a place. They were still essentially promoting an activity rather than a particular place.

Yet, by associating specific places with the generally plebeian and boisterous experience of the excursion, the promotion of rail excursions often played a part in shaping or reinforcing particular resort images. Thus the early practices of the Lancashire and Yorkshire Railway, promoting 'Seabathing for the Working Classes' at Blackpool and Fleetwood by means of cheap Sunday excursions from the industrial towns were helping to establish the 'social tone' of the

area (Walvin, 1978, pp. 37–39, plate 6; Perkin, 1975). Some private excursion promoters, most notably Thomas Cook, adopted a more educative approach and often gave a little more description of the places to which they were promoting excursions (Brendon, 1991, pp. 28–73). In April 1873, for example, a Cook's excursion to Alton Towers referred to its 'Beautiful and Enchanting Gardens' (*Cook's Excursionist*, 1873, p. 23).

Another early promotional form associated with the railways was the descriptive guide book, published for sale as either an official publication of the railway company for sale, or by commercial printers. These guidebooks would give accounts of the various places served by a particular railway, with a rather low key place selling intent. The form of this kind of publication had become more refined by the 1870s, with guides that were more specific to holiday making. Yet these were still relatively muted in their marketing of particular places. And because they were normally for sale publications, they were essentially profiting from a widening tourist market rather than themselves widening it.

Blackpool's Pioneering Role

The selling of the seaside became ever more intensive in the last quarter of the century, reflecting a holiday market that was now widening to include the working classes. As the railway network was completed over these years, this widening population of holiday makers in the industrial areas found itself able to consider an ever greater number of potential holiday destinations. Meanwhile the resorts, at least the larger towns, were becoming more organized in the way they ran their affairs. As we will see, the railways from this time also began to play an ever increasing role in marketing the resorts. Yet many resorts were becoming resentful of the often arbitrary policies of the railway companies, which might alter services or increase fares or simply subordinate the interests of any particular resort to wider interests. The key shift came in the way that the resorts themselves sought to take a firm hold of their own destinies in the growing and highly competitive holiday market.

In all resorts, especially the large ones, local business networks and organizations appeared, acting as powerful voices for the holiday industry in local affairs. Increasingly active local governments were also coming into being. These municipal agencies addressed issues that were common throughout the Victorian urban system, such as public health, the provision of infrastructure and public utilities, the maintenance of order and, to an extent, social services. Yet the specialized character of the resorts always gave a very distinctive focus to such concerns. It also added other items, mundane and exotic, to their municipal agendas. Sea defences, promenades, deck chairs, ornamental gardens, municipal bands and other entertainments were typical concerns. So too was resort advertising.

It was Blackpool, where the local political hegemony of the holiday industry was almost complete, which led the way, as it did in so many other spheres of municipal action in the resorts. The critical decade was the 1870s. In 1872 came an abrupt change in the Lancashire and Yorkshire Railway's fare policy, threatening the growth in working class traffic which was so crucial to the town's prosperity. Yet the town's leaders were not inclined to accept meekly the consequences of such a change. A new Winter Gardens was opened in 1878, becoming the occasion of a massive exercise in public relations (Cross, 1990, p. 209). The Mayor of Blackpool invited the Lord Mayor of London, the Sheriff of Middlesex, together with the Mayors and Lord Mayors of fifty Northern and Midland towns and cities (and wives) to attend. The whole party were accommodated and entertained for a whole week at the luxurious Hotel Metropole, the expense being covered from public subscription.

The following year a more secure basis for marketing Blackpool was found. Within a local Act of 1879 the town gained powers that enabled it to levy a rate (local tax) of two (old) pence for its municipal band and 'maintaining at railway stations and in other public places advertisements

stating the attractions and amusements of the town'. In practice virtually all this special rate, the value of which increased hugely as the town itself grew, was devoted to advertising (Walton, 1978, p. 55). This special advertising power underpinned Blackpool's long standing domination of resort promotion. The new Advertising Committee began fairly traditionally with illustrated brochures, directed more at the middle class market, but from 1881 Blackpool's posters appeared ever more widely (Walton, 1983b, pp. 174–175). Their use reflected the growing influence of the local entertainments industry, eager to draw in day excursion traffic. These posters, supplemented with other forms of publicity, played a key role in publicizing Blackpool's burgeoning holiday attractions, most notably the Tower (1894) (e.g. Blackpool, nd c1896) and the Autumn Illuminations, introduced in 1912 to extend the holiday season.

French Resort Publicity

Despite Blackpool's early lead, it was France rather than Britain where the forms of advertising art that epitomized the selling of the seaside resort first appeared on a large scale. The key figure was an English railway executive, the chairman of France's Compagnie de l'Ouest, Edward Blount (Reid, 1902). The company was one of the major privately owned regional railway companies created by the French government out of many smaller networks. From the start Compagnie de l'Ouest, which linked Paris with the relatively undeveloped regions of Brittany and Normandy, struggled (Cobban, 1965, p. 67).

In an attempt to break out of what soon proved to be intractable unprofitability, Blount and his chief executive, Marin, began marketing specific tourist destinations on the Ouest's network. Initial efforts relied on the illustrated tourist brochure, an advertising form which the Ouest probably advanced rather than actually invented. The real innovation came in 1886, when the first lithographed pictorial colour posters to be used by railways were commissioned (Camard and

Zagrodski, 1989, p. 14). Over the next few years the Ouest and indeed the other railway companies in France and all other countries with well developed systems began to advertise pleasure destinations using this combination of media.

The French location of these innovations was not merely accidental but reflected dramatic increases in potential demand for tourism and, more importantly, artistic and technical developments within France. As in Britain, the building of France's railways, which occurred a little later than across the Channel, allowed pre-existing upper class fashions for seaside tourism to be more widely emulated. In contrast to Britain, however, French railways were inserted into a predominantly agricultural country which had experienced only partial industrialization. Perhaps reflecting this, the tourist traffic rapidly assumed a high priority in the development of railway business in France. From a very early stage international tourism became important, not least involving the British themselves (e.g. Pakenham, 1967).

Some Channel resorts, such as Boulogne, Dieppe or Trouville were already becoming well established but now saw their growth accelerate. Others, like Deauville (Ville d'Eau), were truly creations of the railway era, in this case 'invented' by the Duc de Morny, its railway station preceding the town itself (Kain, 1980; Camard and Zagrodski, 1989, pp. 11–14). Resort development on France's other coastlines was generally slower, reflecting their greater remoteness from the major centres of population and the strength of the summer sun in the south, not yet a tourist attraction (Haug, 1982; Soane, 1993). Nevertheless the Paris, Lyon and Mediterranean (PLM) and other railways pursued vigorous advertising campaigns, aimed at attracting *hivernants*, rich, usually foreign, winter tourists. There was also extensive publicity to promote inland spa, lake and mountain resorts.

This perceived need to build up tourist traffic coincided with important French developments in the artistic use of lithography (Hutchison, 1968; Shackleton, 1976, pp. 31–32). Litho-

graphic techniques had advanced significantly during the nineteenth century, replacing the original slabs of stone with zinc plates. It was, however, Jules Cheret's stretching of the technique's illustrative potential in the 1860s and 1870s which laid the basis for the new artistic and advertising medium of the pictorial poster that Blount and the other railway companies were then able to apply to railway advertising.

Land developers, casino and spa proprietors, hoteliers and, it would seem, municipal authorities in the individual resorts were also quick to adopt the new medium of the poster, usually in collaboration with each other and the appropriate railway companies (Camard and Zagrodski, 1989, p. 16). The *syndicat d'initiative*, which was to become an increasingly familiar agency within the French-speaking world, also became increasingly evident in tourist publicity from about 1900. Translating as 'syndicate for (tourist) enterprise' or, more freely, simply 'tourist bureau', the *syndicat* was used to harness private and public sector energies in localities or wider regions. The evidence of surviving posters sponsored by early syndicats, for example for Arcachon, Rochefort-sur-Mer, Finistere, Provence and the ski resort of Chamonix, suggests they were initially more active in the south and west (Camard and Zagrodski, 1989, pp. 39, 42, 53, 65; Conservatoire de L'Affiche en Bretagne, nd *c*1994, p. 39).

These French developments marked a new stage in resort selling methods. In their general features they were soon emulated in all other countries with well developed railway systems (Shackleton, 1976; Weill, 1994). Henceforth publicity expenditures devoted to promoting particular places were to be much greater. These costs were also now borne directly by increasingly sophisticated railway publicity departments and the resorts themselves rather than the tourist. In comparison to the cheapness of letterpress bills or the guidebooks sold to tourists, the new posters and brochures were expensive. It made sense therefore to use them for prolonged periods to promote places rather than squander them on one-off events such as excursions. In France the customary display life of railway pictorial posters was three years, though ambitious resorts such as Trouville commissioned a new poster each year (Carmard and Zagrodski, 1989, p. 16). Brochures would similarly be expected to have a lifespan of several years.

Resort Publicity in Britain 1890–1914

These French methods quickly became known in Britain, especially since the desire to attract British tourists soon brought the colourful new French posters to the railway stations of London. During the 1890s British railway companies themselves began to experiment with similar methods. By the early years of the twentieth century posters promoting holiday areas in a distinctively British manner were becoming well-established (Wilson, 1987; Cole and Durack, 1990). Supporting the posters was a growing volume of other types of area advertising material, such as pamphlets and brochures, increasingly free, giving details about particular areas. The London and North Western Railway, for example, was issuing thirty-seven free booklets by 1911, with titles like *The Spas of Central Wales*, *Scotland for the Holidays* and *The English Lakes* (LNWR, 1911, p. 76). This emphasis on quite wide areas mirrored a tendency that was apparent in many of the earliest posters which concentrated on areas such as Cornwall, Northumberland, Scotland or Wales, rather than specific places.

The relatively high costs of the new advertising media meant that the British railway companies approached them with greater caution than their French counterparts. Print runs of posters appear to have been lower than in France, where runs of 6,000 of each poster were usual (cf Camard and Zagrodski, 1989, p. 16; Wilson, 1987, p. 67). The railways were also reluctant to focus too closely on one place unless there was a likely direct increase in their traffic receipts. The Great Northern Railway, for example produced its own posters for selected individual resorts. Amongst

these was the hugely popular *Skegness is So Bracing* (1908), promoting its regular excursion services from London to the Lincolnshire resort (Shackleton, 1976, pp. 44–46). Yet the same company refused Woodhall Spa when it asked for railway advertising, unless the resort itself was prepared to contribute to costs (Hansard, 61 HC Deb 5s, 1914, c2052).

As we might expect, Blackpool had been quick to make use of the new colour lithographic techniques as part of its own unique advertising campaign. It also pioneered joint railway-resort advertising. Thus one of the earliest British colour pictorial resort posters surviving (from *c*1893) is of Blackpool, issued in conjunction with the Midland Railway. Yet Blackpool was always sufficiently well funded not to have to rely on such collaboration. In other cases where local authorities were less powerful, railways could sometimes play a central part in drawing them into resort marketing organizations. Thus Cambrian Railways played a central role in creating the Cambrian Resorts Association in 1909 (Wilson, 1987, p. 29).

Other privately organized local publicity associations were also formed. Yet such organizations were dogged by funding difficulties and rarely matched the vigour of their nearest French equivalents, the *syndicats d'initiative*. In Britain the resorts looked to their most powerful local organizations, the municipal authorities, already playing the central role in investing in resort development, to fill the marketing vacuum. But the problem remained that, with the exception of Blackpool, resort authorities still had no legal authority to spend money on advertising, whether alone or in conjunction with railways.

Exactly how Blackpool had managed to acquire its advertising powers so early remains a mystery. What is certain is that within a few years, other resorts had begun to press for similar powers, not least because they felt themselves directly threatened by Blackpool's publicity onslaught. In 1889, for example, Scarborough was complaining of the indignity of having Blackpool's attractions placarded all around their town (Walton, 1983a, p. 150). The Lancashire resort's clear intention was to use its advertising muscle to extend its catchment area throughout the industrial North and Midlands, even as far afield as London, the south coast and Wales (Walton, 1983b, p. 174). Yet when other resorts sought similar powers for themselves, the prim response of the Local Government Board was that invariably that the spending of municipal monies, especially those raised from local taxes, on competitive advertising was inappropriate (Hansard 61 HC Deb 5s, 1914, c2012). Blackpool's unique powers were explained as the result of parliamentary oversight (Hansard, 41 HL Deb 5s, 1920, c557). They were not to be regarded as a legal precedent for wider emulation.

If the Local Government Board ever thought that this ridiculous justification would satisfy other ambitious resorts, they were to be mistaken. More than in any other country the story of resort advertising in Britain was to be one of a struggle for municipal enabling powers (Ward, 1988b). Competitive fervour was further fuelled in 1894 when the Isle of Man, whose independent legal status gave it freedom from the strictures of Westminster and Whitehall, also embarked on an extensive publicity campaign (May, nd c1904, pp. 5; 10). Yet the absence of legal powers on the mainland was not always a complete barrier to promotional endeavours. Various subterfuges could be used to divert small amounts of municipal funds from sources other than the rates, such as various trading service accounts, into advertising (May, nd c1904). Most resorts at this time were reliant on local publicity associations, drawing on voluntary subscriptions that sometimes masked municipal contributions (Walton, 1983a, p. 151).

There were signs too of direct interest from the advertising industry itself. In 1895 a Health Resorts Association was founded by a London publicity consultant, G. W. May. The stated aim of the Association was to advance the interests of the resorts by 'systematic, judicious and economical advertising'. (May, c1904, p. 14). What the Association sought to encourage were illustrated resort guides, posters, and articles and notices in newspapers and other periodicals. Its members (and, May hoped, his clients) were mainly the local authorities and business organizations of the smaller resorts. Yet achievements never matched these intentions. The typical output was guides (which, even distributed free or at nominal cover prices, could increasingly be made self-funding by carrying accommodation and other advertising) and press and magazine notices.

Pressures for Municipal Advertising

Voluntary private or surreptitious municipal funding meant that most of the major British resorts and many smaller ones had some sort of publicity effort by the first years of the twentieth century. But the uncertainty of voluntaristic funding and the risk of challenge to unsanctioned municipal expenditures remained serious difficulties. Even with railway good will and assistance it was difficult for individual resorts to move into the new and more appealing territories of poster and brochure publicity. In 1906, for example, Bridlington's publicity expenditure was just £59 (Gee, 1949). Even Brighton, the biggest British resort and one of the few with a truly international reputation, had a derisory advertising budget. The income of the local Publicity Association had dwindled to only £217 in 1908 (Walton, 1983a, pp. 150–151). For comparison, it would have cost perhaps £125 to commission and print 3,000 copies of one coloured poster at this time (Wilson, 1987, p. 67). By contrast, Blackpool's potential advertising revenue had been about £2,500 in 1900, and grew rapidly to over £4,000 in 1914. The Isle of Man's advertising budget had been about £1750 in 1903 (May, nd c1904, p. 5).

Facing such uneven odds in the highly competitive resort selling game, many authorities continued to seek powers in local bills. Yet the litany of failures continued. Rateborne publicity powers were struck out of the Bills promoted for Cleethorpes (1902), Hunstanton (1903), Appleby

(1904), Ilfracombe, Llandrindod Wells and Whitby (all 1905), Hornsea (1911) and even mighty Brighton (1912) (Hansard, 41 HL Deb 5s, 1920, cc555–6). Signs of what was to become an acceptable formula for compromise were becoming apparent, however. Thus the local Acts actually passed for Buxton (1904), Margate (1908), Brighton (1912), Aberystwyth, Hove and Southport (all 1913) and St Annes and Weymouth (both 1914) all granted severely limited powers to advertise.

Although the exact details varied, the critical principle was that monies used could not be raised in local taxation. (The idea of a discretionary local hotel or tourist tax was so contrary to British fiscal tradition that it did not even appear as an option.) Income had therefore to be derived from the profits on various holiday services, such as deck chair hire, bandstand profits or admission charges. Reflecting a familiar divide of resort politics, such an approach to financing ensured that 'residential' interests, who looked on the resort mainly as a place to enjoy the fruits of investments or previous earnings, would not have to pay for a pet project of the 'holiday' interests, who actively sought the commercial exploitation of tourism (Walton, 1983b; Roberts, 1983). The value of the advertising budgets thus authorized was also restricted, usually to the equivalent of a ½d rate. Moreover, there were serious limitations too on the form of acceptable advertising, excluding posters and placards.

This creeping and rather half hearted legalization provided no permanent answer. The resorts, or strictly those interests within them who sought tourist development, remained profoundly dissatisfied. Pressure for change grew even stronger when a private member's Bill to give Irish resorts rateborne advertising powers was granted Parliamentary time in 1909 (Hansard, 11 HC Deb 5s, 1909, cc1977–80). The Health Resorts and Watering Places (Ireland) Act, as it became, did not pass unscathed. The original sanction for a Blackpool-style two (old) penny advertising rate was halved to win Local Government Board approval. It was also made clear that even this

was allowed because the Irish resorts were very underdeveloped, indeed unknown, compared to those in Britain.

Those scourges of public spending who had voiced fears during the debates on the 1909 legislation that it would soon provide a precedent for British action did not have long to wait. The resorts tried to secure comparable British powers in 1914 (Hansard, 61 HC Deb 5s, 1914, cc2007–62). Another private member's Bill was promoted. Its parliamentary sponsors reviewed the troubled history of resort advertising, but added an important new point that appealed to the fervid mood of patriotism that was building up during the spring of 1914. The vagaries of fashion which had originally drawn first the upper and later the middle classes to Britain's resorts in the eighteenth and nineteenth centuries were now changing markedly. Continental resorts in France, Belgium, Switzerland, Italy and elsewhere were growing in popularity amongst wealthier British tourists. Reflecting and reinforcing this trend, a large volume of extremely attractive poster and other advertising for these foreign resorts was appearing in Britain, especially in London.

The main opposition came from the government itself. In a speech that revealed much about prevailing British attitudes, the President of the Local Government Board, Sir Herbert Samuel, rehearsed all the familiar counter-arguments which his predecessors had been using since the 1880s (Hansard, 61 HC Deb 5s, 1914, cc2012–19). He voiced fears that Britain would be drawn into more general place competition comparable to that in the western United States, especially California. It would be wasteful and undignified; smaller resorts particularly would suffer. He also hinted that such competition could fuel dangerous sentiments when it had an international dimension, alluding to the competition over battleships between Britain and Germany. Little notice was taken of such arguments, however, and the Bill comfortably cleared its first Parliamentary hurdle. But it got no further. Ironically, in view of the way the Bill's sponsors had played the patriotic card, it was the outbreak of war which prevented further progress.

Pre-1914 Tourism Marketing in Belgium

Such pre-war fears about growing international competition to attract British tourists away from home resorts were well justified. We have already noted the important French role in the development of advertising practice. French resort posters continued to be those most commonly seen in Britain, through exchanges of advertising material between railway companies. By 1914 other countries had also entered the tourist market and were quickly selling their holiday areas, both to their own populations and internationally, in much more organized ways than was Britain.

Belgium provides a good example of the way a smaller European country was marketing its tourist areas at this time. Parts of its tourist industry were very long established, most notably the inland health resorts of the Ardennes, including the archetypal Spa. Tourist interest in historic towns such as Bruges was largely a phenomenon of the late nineteenth century, but obviously exploited a tourist resource that was long established. By contrast, seaside tourism was both recent, developing entirely after the creation of the Belgian state in 1830, and located in resorts that were also, with the exception of Ostend, entirely new creations. The demand side of the growth of seaside tourism relied on the familiar combination of royal patronage (of Ostend, by Belgium's newly established monarchy, especially Leopold II from 1865) and transport (Constandt, 1986, pp. 13–31, 49–51, 58–60). Railway building, beginning in the 1830s, regular ferry links with Britain, initiated during the following decade, and the coastal tramway system, dating from the 1880s, added the vital accessibility that enabled tourism to develop on a large scale.

Much less familiar was the active role of the Belgian government, seeking to emulate the essentially spontaneous development of Britain's resorts as conscious national policy. The state's ownership of the railway system, from the first considerable and almost total by the later nineteenth century, gave it major influence on coastal development (Girard, 1965, pp. 234–235, 263). The national government also ensured extensive funds for resort building, transferring a large portion of the gambling tax revenue derived from the licensed casinos at the well-established resort of Spa (Lombaerde, 1983). Such funds helped to build up the infrastructure and public amenities of the coastal resorts, especially Ostend and Blankenberge. These transfers occurred mainly during the 1860s and 1870s, though there were occasional later payments. Leopold II himself also directly provided funds for the development of Ostend. In turn of course such state expenditures made the resorts much more attractive for private developments.

This process of resort development had implications for the pattern of marketing. As everywhere, the publicity role of the railways was crucial. Yet the unified state ownership of Belgian railways brought considerable advantages. By 1909 the Belgian State Railways' spending on tourist publicity, running at 300,000BF annually, far exceeded that of any other agency (Constandt, 1986, p. 32). The existence of a national network facilitated the nation-wide marketing of all Belgium's tourist areas, unencumbered by the problems which arose from the very fragmented pattern of railway ownership such as existed in Britain. Such advantages were even more apparent in Belgium's early start in international marketing. Already, in the early twentieth century, the State Railways' Paris office was actively promoting French tourist interest in Belgium.

Yet it would be quite wrong to imply a purely state railways-led pattern of resort marketing. There were also many diverse local interests involved in tourist promotion. The rapid development of the coastline in the later nineteenth century had brought a great deal of place advertising associated with specific land development ventures. There was also strong interest by commercial advertising firms who were instrumental in the creation of the first French-style *syndicats d'initiative* on the coast (Constandt, 1986, p. 44). An early example was created in Coq sur Mer in or before 1898 (Weill, 1994, p. 20). It was not until after 1918 that such promotional agencies became firmly established in this area, however (Constandt, 1986, pp. 33–34). Meanwhile a variety of other local interests, particularly hoteliers and local authorities, were undertaking publicity, most notably Ostend and Blankenberge but also many of the smaller resorts. By 1910, for example, advertisements for *Ostend – The Queen of Watering Places*, were appearing regularly in international tourist journals (e.g. *Cook's Australasian Traveller's Gazette*, August 1910, p. 40). Already, since the 1890s, many attractive Belgian resort posters had been issued, as elsewhere prepared by varying combinations of local and railway initiative (e.g. Weill, 1994, pp. 20–21, 73).

The pattern of local action in Belgium's other tourist resorts was also varied. The older established inland resorts of Spa, Bouillon and Stavelot were evidently the first in Belgium to adopt the French-style *syndicat d'initiative* model (Constandt, 1986, pp. 33, 44–47). Bruges also followed the same pattern in 1909, developing in this case out of an earlier association called 'Bruges Forward: Society to Improve Tourism'. The latter had been established in 1900 and was only one of several competing local organizations wishing to promote tourism. The case of Bruges, which has been more closely researched than any of the others, confirms the general impression of great local variation in practice.

What is particularly noticeable in Belgium generally is that there was no automatic assumption at this time that the municipalities should be taking the lead on the British pattern. This does not seem to have been because of any particular discouragement from national government such as occurred in Britain. As we have seen, some councils were active. Others, for example in Bruges, were evidently content to take a minor role. The key point, perhaps, is that for all the Belgian desire to emulate British resort development, the municipalities had not been thrust into quite the same pivotal role that they occupied in Britain. The civic and business leaders of the British resorts saw them primarily as individual places that were competing with each other and served by private railways that were also competing with each other. In other words they were in a fiercely competitive market for holiday locations. This was quite different to the Belgian pattern where, in the context of a smaller and newer country with a tradition of much stronger national policies, the resorts identified their interests much more with those of the nation as a whole.

Thus it was that the major issue in Belgian tourism marketing at this time was to strengthen the international promotion of the country as a whole (Constandt, 1986, pp. 32–33). A further sign of this focus came in 1908 with the formation of the Ligue Belge de Propagande pour Attirer les Visiteurs Etrangers, a private, non-governmental initiative intended to bring together those interested in promoting Belgium as a tourist destination. In the run up to the Brussels World Fair of 1910, there was heightened interest in international tourism and the Ligue quickly attracted a membership of individual members, associations and local authorities. Ostend was a member by 1909 and Bruges the following year. Working closely with the Railways, the Ligue opened information centres in London, New York, Cologne and Paris, with representation also in Berlin, Stuttgart, Zurich, Budapest and Vienna. The Ligue's achievements were comparatively modest and further moves, more ambitious and more official, were to follow after 1918. Yet it is important because it demonstrated clear and early action on a subject which in Britain went no farther than a blustering reaction to foreign tourist publicity.

Marketing Tourist Resorts in the United States

Belgium's growing national involvement in international tourism marketing was certainly more typical than Britain's relative inaction. Many other countries were also promoting themselves for international tourism at this time. Railways normally carried the main burden of publicity for their respective countries, with embassies or high commissions also playing a role. Official government departments of tourism were also beginning to become important, especially in more remote or exotic locations. New Zealand was an example of a highly state-led approach, proceeding from state ownership not only of the railways and internal shipping services but also many of the hotels and the actual resorts themselves. A Government Department of Tourist and Health Resorts was supervising and marketing these tourist resources by the early twentieth century (NZGDTHR, nd c1906). Its advertising was apparently targeted particularly at imperial officials and other ex-patriate residents in the less temperate zones of the British Empire in Asia (*Cook's Oriental Traveller's Guide*, January 1910, p. 55).

Yet a highly statist, nationally-based approach was not essential for an international marketing presence. The premier United States' resort of Atlantic City, New Jersey also maintained its own European office, in London, by 1909. Atlantic City was, however, a resort which made even Blackpool seem coy. Its claimed numbers of visitors, 8 million in 1909, certainly exceeded Blackpool's (ACPB, 1909, p. 25). While scepticism about such advertising claims is always necessary, Atlantic City, before the emergence of Florida or Las Vegas or southern California as mass holiday locations, undoubtedly dominated American tourism.

As all this rather implies, Atlantic City was not altogether typical of US coastal resorts at this time (Funnell, 1975; Lewis, 1980). During the early nineteenth century the eastern seaboard had seen the development of a string of seaside settlements, offering summer diversion for the wealthy. Newport, Rhode Island, stood at the pinnacle of this pattern of elite tourism, though the former fishing communities of Nantucket and Martha's Vineyard in Massachusetts enjoyed some early importance, as did Cape May in New Jersey (Brown, 1995; Thomas and Doebly, 1976). The pattern involved escaping, by steamer and railroad, from the summer heat and humidity of Boston, New York, Philadelphia or the other cities. In the original manner of the British aristocracy, elite families would decamp for the summer season, staying in their own seaside homes, summer cottages or rather refined lodgings. Though some advertising materials were produced (e.g. Hussey and Robinson, 1865), word of mouth and the sense of a social exclusivity that would be demeaned by overt publicity was, as we might expect, critical for the selling of such seaside places.

Atlantic City sought to appeal to the snobbery of a very rapidly growing urban lower middle class by offering them something of the social cache of a Newport or a Cape May. But it actually signalled the beginnings of mass commercialized tourism in the United States. Though the analogy remains inexact, Atlantic City was in its promotional methods far closer to being a Blackpool than a Newport (or an 'American Brighton' which was a label first applied to it in 1880 (Funnell, 1975, p. 7). Its early growth followed the course of much US town development, with the familiar close combination of railroad and land development interests leading to the initial foundation in 1854.

From the start aggressive boosterism and publicity were hugely important. Railroad advertising played a critical part in early development but the growing resort benefited from railroad competition as other lines were built from the late 1870s. Except in the early years, therefore, its destiny did not lie exclusively in the hands of one railroad and, rather like Blackpool, the resort increasingly took greater responsibility for its own advertisement. Like Blackpool there was a tremendous flair for public relations that kept the resort continually in the news.

Unlike Blackpool, however, this boosterist spirit was expressed through co-operative private rather than municipal initiative. In 1900, for example, Atlantic City hoteliers raised $16,000 to advertise in sixty newspapers in twenty cities (Funnell, 1975, p. 18). Travel bureaux were established in New York, Chicago, St Louis, Toronto, Montreal and ultimately, as we have seen, London. The Atlantic City Publicity Bureau, founded in 1906, was a formalization of earlier business co-operation, a joint venture of Atlantic City's Board of Trade, Hotel Men's Association and Business League (BIP, 1906). It produced a regular flow of free illustrated brochures, packed full of Atlantic City superlatives.

Such highly organized co-operative local boosterism was more typical of the larger non-resort cities in the United States before 1914. Atlantic City, with a permanent population of almost 45,000 by 1909, a little smaller than Blackpool, was an unusually large resort by contemporary US standards. Even as tourism became more commercialized, it was the rail-roads which did most to publicize what were usually fairly undeveloped destinations (e.g. *Cook's American Traveler's Gazette*, July 1910, pp. 44–49, NYNHHRR, 1910). Individual hotel-iers, owners of springs or other attractions and the inevitable land speculators played their parts (e.g. Lawrence, 1873; Quiett, 1934, pp. 98–105). So too did other transport operators, especially steamboat and electric trolley lines (e.g. NBSC nd *c*1907; ASLR, 1909). But only the railroads, had the potential to promote smaller resorts to increasingly wider mass tourist markets. As we noted in passing in the last chapter, it was the Western railroads, particularly the Northern Pacific, Great Northern and Southern Pacific, which played the key roles in the promotion for tourism in the publicly-owned and still largely empty Western lands which were designated as National Parks from 1872 (Runte, 1991; 1992; 1994).

Overall, the United States before 1914 showed many similarities but also some important dif-ferences to the British pattern. Both exhibited predominantly place-competitive approaches to tourism marketing, with little development of nationally co-ordinated approaches. As elite gave way to mass tourism, the similarities between the eastern United States and Britain are relatively easy to see. Yet it is clear from the Atlantic City example that co-operative local boosterism was capable of being a much stronger place market-ing force in the United States than it was in Britain, where the municipality was expected to assume the key role. Further west the strong federal government role in railroad development and the direct control of some tourist areas in the National Parks produced quite different situations to any yet experienced in Britain. But if similar circumstances had generated nationally orchestrated approaches in New Zealand or Belgium, they certainly did nothing of the kind in the United States. Once again the emphasis was on competitive place marketing, dominated by the railroads. In Britain meanwhile, the railways and local authorities were beginning to move into closer partnership.

Railway-Resort Partnership in Britain after 1914

Apart from killing the resort advertising Bill, the Great War brought other important changes. The flow of British tourists to continental resorts was temporarily disrupted. As a result, some of the more refined inland resorts benefited. Llandrindod Wells was one such and viewed the return of peace with some trepidation as its wartime visitors returned to Wiesbaden and the other continental spas. On this basis the town in 1920 sought and got local advertising powers that went well beyond those secured in local legislation before 1914 (Hansard, 41, HL Deb 5s, 1920: c557). This small Welsh spa was now permitted to have an advertising budget equivalent to a two (old) penny rate, normally funded from holiday services, but allowing any deficits to be covered out of the rates. In effect parliament, without being asleep at the time, had put Llandrindod Wells on a par with Blackpool.

This new precedent gave further encouragement to those pressing for municipal publicity powers under general legislation. Also in 1920 the 1914 Bill was reintroduced. Despite some opposition, it passed the Commons unamended (Hansard, 130 HC Deb 5s, 1920, cc832–48). The Lords, however, baulked at the familiar hurdle of place advertising funded out of local taxes (Hansard, 41 HL Deb 5s, 1920, cc548–62). The Bill was thrown out, but with the understanding that if it were amended to a 'holiday services' funding formula they would drop their objections. The following year the Health Resorts and Watering Places Act was finally passed (Hansard, 45 HL Deb 5s, 1921 cc274–5; PRO HLG, 52/114). This gave resort municipalities, but not rural districts or county councils, the right to spend up to a one (old) penny rate equivalent on specified forms of advertising. Specifically, they could advertise in newspapers, other than those in the resorts themselves; they could prepare handbooks and leaflets and they could display placards at railway stations.

Despite continuing dissatisfaction, the 1921 Act laid the basis for resorts to make firm agreements with railway companies to undertake advertising. There was much variation in the arrangement of early resort advertising partnerships, some of which had begun on a more *ad hoc* basis before 1914 (PRO RAIL 1080/581, 15.2.21; PRO RAIL 645/89, 19.2.23; 5.3.23). Yet the early 1920s were also a period of upheaval in the railway industry. The 1921 Railways Act provided for the re-organization of the previous 120 railway companies into four major groups. Fears had been expressed when the Health Resorts Bill was going through Parliament that these new groupings would be less committed to resort promotion than their smaller predecessors. These fears generally proved groundless, however, and each of the new companies welcomed the new possibilities for advertising partnership on a more standardized basis.

By 1928 the London, Midland and Scottish Railway (LMS) had 101 such agreements (PRO RAIL 425/7). Seventy-one of these, including forty-two in Scotland, were simply joint schemes, funded on a 50–50 basis with individual resorts. The remainder, including one in the Irish Free State, were funded jointly with other railway companies. In these arrangements the resorts would still usually contribute half, with the companies sharing the rest equally. Spending on joint schemes was still fairly modest. In 1928 the LMS spent just over £11,000 on such schemes out of a total advertising budget of nearly £240,000. In the same year the London and North Eastern Railway (LNER) spent nearly £16,000 out of a total budget of nearly £265,000. Such figures obviously exclude the resorts' spending and probably underestimate actual railway spending on resort advertising. Certainly no rents were charged for resort posters on railway sites. It seems likely too that other costs of resort schemes were apportioned under other items.

Nevertheless spending on individual resorts clearly came pretty low on the Blackpool scale against which such things were invariably measured. In 1923 for example, the Southern Railway (SR) was contributing £150 to the Isle of Wight and £137.50 (matched by the Great Western Railway (GWR)) to Weymouth (PRO RAIL 645/89, 9.4.23). The main beneficiaries of the approach were undoubtedly the smaller resorts, which benefited from the expertise and the economies of scale of increasingly sophisticated railway publicity machines. This example given by the head of the SR's Public Relations and Advertising operations in 1926 gives something of the flavour of this interaction:

Seaford, in Sussex, approached the Southern Railway this year and said they were going ahead with their attractions and would like a poster. An artist was chosen by the Advertising Department and sent down to Seaford. There he conferred with the local authorities, made some sketches, and after these had been discussed at Waterloo, he completed a design which, displayed all over the system, has already had good results. (PRO ZPER 12/4, p. 259).

During the 1920s railway publicists began to think more strategically about the overall effectiveness of all their advertising. As at Seaford, posters and other advertising received particular encouragement when new attractions were on offer. Concentrated promotional campaigns, spanning several advertising media to promote particular holiday districts, became more common. Faced with the inherited tendency for an untidy clutter of advertising matter in stations, publicity departments encouraged neat and themed displays of groups of posters to enhance their impact. There was also a more sophisticated understanding of the varied nature of the holiday market and the character of different resorts. The SR, for example, recognized from the first the critical importance of fairly continual advertising of Brighton and adjoining resort areas because of the existence of a year-round 'impulse' visitor market (PRO RAIL 645/89, 8.1.23). Other resorts with a more established seasonal traffic were promoted accordingly.

The Problems of Partnership

Resort-railway relations were not quite the model of harmonious and rational marketing that all this implies. Railway companies could easily become irritated with the demands of individual resorts. The problem was well described by a GWR publicity consultant in 1925 (PRO ZPER 38/17, p.179). As he saw it, every resort wanted its own poster, even though few were distinctive enough as places to generate images that really stood out. Moreover, few had enough money to commission anything really eye-catching and continued to rely on the railways to subsidize them. He also called for county-wide publicity associations, relying less on localized posters (which he wanted banned), and more on the press and local guidebooks.

The joint advertising schemes did begin to adopt some of these ideas. The pictorial poster of an individual resort remained the most obvious fruit of collaboration, especially during the 1920s (Cole and Durack, 1992). But the use of the press increased greatly in importance from the late 1920s, taking advantage of the favourable rates

the railway companies were able to command (e.g. PRO RAIL, 425/7, Memorandum 5/29). Free locally produced resort handbooks also became more common, giving full details of climate, facilities, entertainments, accommodation etc. The resorts themselves, railway information services or travel agents would distribute these to enquirers.

Meanwhile the railways also continued to pursue their own publicity agendas, usually without resort financial involvement. By the later 1930s the peak pressure on rail capacity in the big resorts was near breaking point (Pimlott, 1976, p. 225). The companies were therefore anxious to spread the load, both in time and space. The latter reinforced their traditional interest in encouraging smaller resorts, sometimes in association with particular sports or recreational activities. It also gave further encouragement to the established trend of promoting wider areas, rather than particular resort destinations. The LNER for example issued successive series of posters to promote the East Coast in general (Cole and Durack, 1992, pp. 15–23; 146–147; Hewitt, 1995). And there was much material in this vein from all companies. Hugely popular were the annual for sale holiday guides. The first, the GWR's *Holiday Haunts*, had appeared in 1906 and it was quickly imitated (Wilson, 1987, pp. 104–121). Each of the post-1923 companies had their own. By 1939 each had over 900 pages and total sales ran to 367,000, with *Holiday Haunts* still the front runner with 170,000 (PRO RAIL 1080/590, 24.9.47). By this time, however, other important changes had begun to occur.

The Pressures for a Greater Municipal Role

For their part the resorts also recognized that joint advertising only served part of their marketing needs. The railways could still seem infuriatingly highhanded in their treatment of resorts. Local authorities often felt that quite legitimate requests for more literal representations of their towns on posters had been brushed aside (e.g. Cole and Durack, 1992, p. 21). The railways also took the opportunity of the early 1930s' Depression to seek a reduction in their proportionate financial stake in joint schemes (to three-eighths) (PRO RAIL 1080/ 586, 13.7.32; 14.9.32; 12.10.32). The LMS stood out in opposition, perhaps because of its established programmes to develop traffic to the smaller resorts, but the others all implemented reductions.

Such moves only encouraged resorts further along the road of seeking fuller responsibility for their own marketing. More of the resorts had in any case developed dimensions of their publicity functions that were quite independent of the railways. One important reason for this was simply that the numbers of visitors arriving by motor vehicles, especially coaches, was growing very dramatically during the 1930s. Blackpool received an estimated 5,300 motor coaches on the August Bank Holiday weekend of 1937 (Walton, in Cross, 1990, p. 229). It also received 425 special trains. Yet the railways, as we have seen, were struggling to cope with the traffic demands generated by the bigger resorts.

The major new growth was coming on the roads and most of the big resorts invested very heavily in this new transport medium (Ward, 1988a, p. 164). Coach companies, with their inherent reliance on a public road infrastructure, carried lower overhead costs than the railways and could operate on a smaller scale with great route flexibility. They were not, therefore, as financially committed to particular destinations. From the outset it was clear that they would never be likely to play as important a role as the railways in advertising the resorts. And what was true for the coach was to be even more so for the motor car, numbers of which were also growing rapidly by the 1930s, especially in more middle class resorts. Even Blackpool received not far short of an estimated 40,000 cars and motor cycles at its peak August 1937 weekend.

Also important was the sheer scale of enterprise and the phenomenal rate of growth that was represented by the bigger resorts at this time. Throughout the interwar years the resorts (with the residential suburbs) had exhibited much the fastest population growth of any class of settlement. Brighton, Southend, Bournemouth and Blackpool had populations of over 100,000 by 1931. The numbers of visitors were immense in this heyday of the resorts. By the late 1930s Blackpool reportedly received annually 7 million visitors and Southend 5.5 million. Nearly 3 million were claimed by Hastings, 2 million each by Bournemouth and Southport and 1 million by Ramsgate (Pimlott, 1976, pp. 239–240).

These and the many other striking indicators of growth which could be quoted had several important consequences for resort marketing. One important effect was that their rate bases were growing rapidly. This meant that their potential advertising budgets under the 1921 Act, though not directly drawn from the rates, were also increasing. Yet at the same time the growing self importance of the resorts made them more inclined to challenge the constraints of the Act. The holiday services formula produced great funding uncertainties. Yet surely, resort leaders argued, if they could undertake huge investment programmes in holiday facilities, they must be capable of being trusted to undertake much smaller advertising programmes to promote those facilities? Meanwhile the privileged position of Blackpool and the seemingly unrestricted ability of foreign resorts to advertise in Britain continued to rankle.

The pressures for change manifested themselves in various ways. Local authorities pressed further for advertising on the rates in their local legislation, resulting in almost all cases in disallowance or voluntary withdrawal (PRO HLG 52/117, 5.2.36). This was the fate of Thornton-le-Cleveleys (1922), Morecambe (1924), Dartmouth (1928) and Torquay (1934). Nor were the seaside resorts the only seekers after these powers. Perhaps looking to build itself another economic identity, the depressed shipbuilding town of Barrow-in-Furness sought and failed to get powers to advertise its amenities on the rates in 1925. Warwick (1928) and Oxford (1933) also tried their luck, indicative of the growth of tourism in historic towns.

Only one of the local authorities which applied for rateborne advertising powers met with any success. In 1931 Brighton gained powers that eased some of the problems of the 1921 Act by allowing it to use rate income to make good any shortfalls in holiday services income. Meanwhile, however, the Conference of Health and Pleasure Resorts, the increasingly active representative organization for the resorts, began pressing during the 1920s for a general extension to advertising and other marketing powers (PRO HLG 52/115). One particular interest was the development of information bureaux as resort marketing agencies. Beginning with Folkestone (1920) and Ramsgate (1922), nineteen resorts and historic towns had such powers by 1930, including Southend, Bournemouth, Hastings and Southport (PRO HLG 29/179). Blackpool had no specific powers but had, as usual, gone farthest with a London information bureau, 'of doubtful legality'.

The 'Come to Britain' Movement

A much bigger issue lay behind all this. Through their representative body, the resorts now wanted to develop joint information bureaux to market Britain's resorts internationally. Since before 1914 there had been some overseas marketing of British resorts, most notably through the exchange of publicity materials with French and other European railway companies. On the whole, however, this was a rather haphazard process in which British railway publicists had diminishing faith (e.g. PRO RAIL 1080/584, 12.3.30). With its high budget, Blackpool had also managed to make a specific impact on the continent. In 1918, for example, off-duty British soldiers visiting the battlefields at Waterloo in Belgium had been surprised to see 'GO TO BRIGHT BREEZY BLACKPOOL' posted on the gable end of a hotel there (Cross, 1990, p. 209). But despite such enterprise, by the 1920s there were far fewer foreign tourists coming to Britain than there were British tourists visiting other countries.

In line with pre-1914 experiences, tourist destinations in other countries were usually marketed for international tourism more effectively than were their British equivalents. The emergence of just four new railway companies in 1923 clearly promised a more co-ordinated approach. To some extent this was fulfilled in a joint initiative by the British railways in the United States. By 1926 they were spending annually over £30,000 there, though this was about £70,000 short of what was thought necessary to be really effective (PRO RAIL 1080/583, 5.1.26; 23.4.26).

By any standards, however, continental marketing of British tourist destinations by the railways remained weak. In 1928, for example, the LMS and LNER together spent under £10,000 on continental advertising, compared to almost £26,000 on American advertising (PRO RAIL 425/7). The SR was certainly more active, but probably not by much (Cole and Durack, 1992, p.12). Moreover the effects of some of this expenditure, because it often still involved exchanges of material with foreign railways or travel organizations, would be to market continental tourist destinations to British people. From the point of view of the British railways this was not a problem since it would also generate rail and ferry travel.

There were also fundamental weaknesses in the whole approach to marketing British resorts. Relatively little publicity material was produced in other European languages (though this improved during the 1930s). Moreover, the growing suspicions of the publicity exchange arrangements with continental railways led British railway publicists to rely increasingly on direct newspaper advertising on the continent (PRO RAIL 425/7; PRO RAIL 1080/584, 12.3.30). This obviously limited the continental penetration of the attractive and colourful promotional material that was available in Britain. There was also a deliberate reluctance on the part of the railways between the wars to undertake overseas publicity too well (PRO RAIL 1080/583, 5.1.26). Financially pressured from the outset, they were very reluctant to take on the role of a national tourist office by default.

It was the existence of much stronger national dimensions to tourism marketing that was most noticeable virtually everywhere else in Europe. After World War I Belgium, for example, replaced the privately-organized Ligue, referred to earlier, with the Press and Publicity Department of the national Ministry of Railway, Maritime, Mail and Telegraph Affairs (Constandt, 1986, pp. 33–34). In 1924 the Ministry took a further step and formed the Office National Belge du Tourisme. In 1926 this itself was replaced by the Conseil Superieur du Tourisme en Belgique.

No enduring national framework was found until after 1945. (In 1931 the Conseil Superieur was itself replaced by a semi-official agency OBLUT (Office Belgo-Luxembourgeois du Tourisme) which served the national tourism promotional interests of both Belgium and Luxembourg.) But the priority and national leadership provided by these interim agencies was still important. Posters and other publicity material were created for specific resorts, especially the smaller ones, and wider areas, such as the coast as a whole. The stronger national organizations were also able to encourage more formal local agencies to promote tourism within the national framework. In 1926, for example, the Conseil Superieur du Tourisme sponsored the formation of the Federation des Syndicats d'Initiatives et Groupements Touristiques de l'Ouest du Littoral Belgiques. Again it was the smaller resorts which gained most from such ventures.

Meanwhile, the position was also beginning to change in Britain. Although central government remained deeply suspicious of the attempts of resorts to spend ratepayers' money competing with each other, there was more sympathy for a co-ordinated attempt to sell Britain as a tourist destination. Such sentiments were encouraged further with the formation of a 'Come to Britain'

movement in 1926 (GLRO MET 10/559). At first this initiative had nothing to do with the resorts. Its main early backers were predominantly London-based interests associated with international travel and trade. They included the major hotel groups, shipping lines, travel agencies, the national press and central government in the guise of the Board of Trade. As fund raising began however, contributions were sought more widely so that the movement began to link up to more localized place marketing agencies. The railway companies were soon drawn in, though they remained profoundly suspicious, regarding it as a ploy to get them to fund an organization from which other interests would derive more direct benefits.

After almost two years of weak organization and negligible achievement, the movement began to be put on a firmer footing (Hansard, 80 HL Deb 5s, 1931, cc1181–2). Douglas Hacking, the Minister of Overseas Trade, forged a new organization, the Travel Association (TA) of Great Britain and Ireland. It was to be the first officially approved national organization to promote overseas travel to Britain. Central government involvement and the £5,000 annual grant that went with it helped win over the railways, who were persuaded to stump up £5,500 between them (GLRO MET 10/617; PRO BT 56/41/CIA 1800/123, 6.2.33). More funds came from other travel and tourist interests, though always less than the railways and the TA itself wanted. From the first, however, Hacking wanted to widen the TA's funding base. Conveniently enough the resorts and other local authorities were taking a keen interest in the new body that was emerging.

Advertising on the Rates

In November 1927 the Association of Municipal Corporations (AMC), the main local government body, gave its powerful support to these moves towards an approved national body to sell Britain as a tourist destination (PRO HLG 52/116). Moreover, it urged that local authorities be given powers to contribute from the rates to such a body, producing a draft Bill to this effect. The resorts rushed to press further this case, allowing Hacking in turn to press the Ministry of Health to permit advertising on the rates. After much deliberation during 1928–30 the AMC's proposals (which extended beyond mere tourist advertising, with important ramifications that we will explore more fully in chapter 7) were accepted. The essential principles were that advertising would involve co-operation not competition between places, that it would be channelled through an approved single organization, and that it would apply only to overseas publicity. It would also be very modest, limited to a ½d rate.

This compromise, introduced as a private member's Bill, became the 1931 Local Authorities (Publicity) Act (Hansard, 245 HC Deb 5s, 1930, cc836–57; 251 HC Deb 5s, 1931. cc1919–30; 80 HL Ded 5s, 1931, cc1180–4; PRO HLG 29/179). Like earlier legislation, it satisfied no-one very much. The newly renamed Travel and Industrial Development Association (TIDA), though its funding was now more secure, was still not sufficiently well endowed to be able to generate more than a small amount of its own materials. And the resorts took the view that if they were paying they also wanted to ensure their particular message was getting through. A cumbersome financial arrangement was devised whereby three-quarters of the money paid to TIDA was remitted back to the local authorities to generate publicity materials. Inevitably this money became rather tangled up with general resort publicity accounts, so that the overseas limitation on advertising was hard to enforce in practice.

By the mid-1930s, the Ministry of Health had virtually given up trying to enforce the strict letter of the law on the 1921 and 1931 Acts. They quietly told their auditors that, provided there were no scandals, 'we do not wish to be too alert in discovering possible malpractice' (PRO HLG 52/116, 1.3.35). There was also, finally, a recognition that competitive advertising of resorts might actually be a good thing, increasing the overall amount of tourist expenditure in the country (PRO HLG 52/117, Briefing Paper, 5.2.36). Given such attitudes, it is clear that the Association of Health Resorts and Pleasure Resorts (as it was now called) was knocking on an open door when, yet again, it asked for general powers for rateborne advertising.

The 1936 Health Resorts and Watering Places Act gave these powers, allowing a one and one-third penny advertising rate. The slight increase on the one penny rate equivalent of the 1921 Act was more apparent than real. The Association had wanted a 3d advertising rate, but this was summarily rejected. The new limit was no more than what had come to be the 'tolerance zone' under the old scheme. Other aspects of the Act gave more flexibility in how publicity could be undertaken. Information bureaux were finally made legal for all resorts and poster display powers were no longer directly linked to the railways, as they had been under the 1921 Act.

Thus, by 1936 all resorts had finally obtained reasonably flexible, if still modest, powers to sell themselves in the mass advertising media.

The Golden Age

The later 1930s were in many ways a golden age of competitive resort advertising. Everyone associated with selling resorts was acutely aware of the tremendous surge in potential demand for holidays that was occurring at just this time (Pimlott, 1976, pp. 214–222). In April 1937 about 4 million workpeople (earning less than £250 annually) were entitled to paid holidays. Partly reflecting the 1938 Holidays with Pay Act, the figure rose spectacularly to over 11 million by June 1939 and was set to expand further. There was a huge new market to compete for, with real prospects for smaller resorts especially to reposition themselves. Not all wanted to, of course. Sidmouth, for example, clung to exclusivity and resolutely refused to sell itself, sneering at resorts like Ilfracombe which took the opposite course (Fogarty, 1945, p. 381; 1947,

p. 257). But such complete abstinence was rare. Most resorts wanted to stake a claim, if not directly for the new holiday makers then at least for those likely to be deflected from the bigger resorts by the growing press of working class bodies.

The railways, as we have seen, were less active in selling specific places than in the 1920s, but their output remained very important. Meanwhile municipal publicity budgets were very buoyant compared to what they had been. Blackpool still had more funds than anywhere else, with over £20,000 in 1938–39. Brighton had just over £10,000, nearby Worthing had a little over £3,000 and Ramsgate £2,200, though this last was a net figure (Fogarty, 1947, p. 71).

What then did the resorts do with these budgets? The most elaborate publicity machine was, predictably, in Blackpool. By the late 1930s, it was despatching each year approximately 89 tons of advertising propaganda. Most prominent (in weight) was the free annual holiday guide, running to about 150 pages, of which about two-thirds were paid advertisements for accommodation (BCPC, 1939; Cross, 1990, p. 208). Though none were so lavish as Blackpool's, all other resorts had similar publications if they were serious competitors in the mass holiday market. Circulations were very large; medium-sized Bridlington, for example, had a print run of 40,000 for its brochure by 1939 (Gee, 1949). Although those for smaller resorts often changed little from year to year, guides for the bigger resorts were beginning to have clear annual themes (Yates, 1988, p. 26). Blackpool's 1938 guide had a door as the front cover with the instruction to 'Open the Door to Holiday Happiness' (BCPC, 1938). Ramsgate's 1939 guide took the form of a 'Holiday Recipe Book' (Stafford and Yates, 1985, pp. 109–110).

These and other holiday booklets were brought to public attention through a growing volume of newspaper and related forms of advertising (Fogarty, 1947, pp. 217–219). This was one of the fastest growing areas of publicity in the 1930s, paralleling railway practices. A more traditional advertising form, the poster, remained important, with all resorts now able to advertise themselves beyond the confines of railway stations. Joint railway schemes themselves were still significant, but were now a lesser proportion of resort advertising than in earlier years. Under a fifth of Brighton's 1938–39 budget went to all co-operative schemes.

More direct attempts to gain public attention were also being used. Bridlington, for example, had a publicity van with amplification equipment that toured industrial towns and cities in the North, Midlands and Scotland (Gee, 1949). To coincide, the resort also arranged for prominent window displays in the biggest department stores of these places, supported by 'Mr Bridlington' who would distribute literature and generate interest. Meanwhile all resorts were giving great of attention to public relations, with often inspired attempts to create media interest. The hosting of various newsworthy events such as entertainments or sports and the contriving of news stories were favoured devices. Blackpool played the game with consummate mastery. As a local newspaper columnist exulted in March 1938:

Publicity, Publicity, Publicity!
    Every day and in every way we get it in brimming measure.
    . . . it's so brilliantly managed that it takes in those men who think they're the smartest guys on earth – the news editors of the daily papers. And for every penny we spend in the advertisement pages we get a pound's worth in the news columns.
    The biggest marvel is how we keep it up, year after year, winter and summer alike.
    But we do! (cited Cross, 1990, p. 208).

Another important trend was the growing appreciation of the different tourist markets. As we have seen resorts had long recognized the distinction between the excursion and holiday-maker markets. During the twentieth century differentiation in the various seasonal markets was also being acknowledged. The south coast resorts for example soon realized that they could better hold on to their high class visitors out of the summer seasonal peak (e.g. Brighton, nd *c*1929). Some northern resorts, notably South-port, also tried the same tactic (Southport, 1931, pp. 21–22) The attraction of conferences was also another device used to bring off-season visitors to the resorts. Although much less developed than it later became, by the 1930s most of the larger and medium sized resorts were trying to target trades unions, professional bodies and the like. Meanwhile, at the other end of the market, a working class resort like Blackpool was recognizing the need to continue building up the holiday-making habit amongst the working classes who had hitherto only been able to afford day trips (Walton, 1978, p. 39; Cross, 1990, p. 210). From 1929 its agents had created a network of holiday saving clubs in Glasgow, Bristol, Bradford, Leeds, Birmingham and Nottingham.

These practices reflected a deepening or an intensification of a tourist market whose geographical limits remained firmly British. Despite their espoused interests in overseas publicity, the seaside resorts kept their eyes fixed almost exclusively on Britain. The spas showed greater awareness of the potential foreign market, though less to win foreign visitors than deflect British tourists from foreign spas (Pimlott, 1976, p. 256; Cook's UK Brochure, 1922, p. xxx). Apart from the former residents of British colonies in the tropics who retired in significant numbers to spas and the more sedate seaside resorts, especially on the south coast, precious few tourists who could ever be described as foreign came to Britain's holiday resorts. Despite interwar pressures towards the international-ization of leisure culture through architecture, the cinema and other influences, they remained deeply British places, veritable laboratories of Britain's social system and values (e.g. Walvin, 1978, pp. 156–165).

European Tourism Marketing in the 1930s

Even if the resort publicists had wanted to, the later 1930s were not the most auspicious time to attempt to change this. Currency devaluations and other financial controls made it difficult for many European nationals to travel to Britain (PRO RAIL 1080/589 11.1.39). Despite their own currency difficulties, Americans with money continued to visit Britain. Yet the resorts, except perhaps Brighton and Bath, figured barely at all on the typical American tourist itinerary which was structured more by a pursuit of history and the varied metropolitan attractions of London. As we have noted, the railways played a significant part in maintaining such interests with a regular flow of promotional images which fostered the American idea of Britain. TIDA and various local and regional bodies with which it operated also made their own contribution to the international promotion of tourism in Britain. Generally the quality of TIDA publicity material was much inferior to that of the railways but because the Association routinely produced its brochures in other European languages, it improved the presentation of Britain within Europe (e.g. GLRO MET 10/617).

The scale of European efforts to promote foreign tourism within their countries during the 1930s remained well in excess of British action. If anything, the gap may well have widened. Britain's railway publicists estimated in early 1939 that the governments of Germany and Italy were spending annually as much as £200,000 each on tourist promotion, while the Swiss government was spending about £100,000 (PRO RAIL 1080/589, 11.1.39). Certainly such estimates were consistent with the contemporary volume of English language tourist advertising and publicity material produced by national tourist agencies in these countries (e.g. *Cook's American Traveler*, 1938–39). For comparison TIDA, the nearest thing Britain had to a national tourist office, had an income of just £60,500, of which only a quarter came from central government (Fogarty, 1947, p. 71).

The geographical organization of tourist marketing within other European countries also improved within this national framework.

Following its initiatives of the 1920s, Belgian tourist marketing continued to become more organized, especially in the British tourist market. In West Flanders, the Belgians managed in 1935 to bring together local interests in a body that covered the whole coast (Constandt, 1986, pp. 36–38). The new agency, usually known as 'Westtourism', promoted the whole coastal region, a pattern of marketing that many railway publicists had hoped to see develop in Britain. The Southern Railway (of Britain) had in fact become closely involved with the precursors of Westtourism (one of which was known as the Committee for Anglo-Belgian Publicity) during the early 1930s (Constandt, 1986, pp. 34–35). SR had begun to treat this co-operation in similar fashion to a British joint resort publicity scheme, paying 50 per cent of the costs. Though intended as a two-way arrangement, the Belgians undoubtedly derived most of the benefit and, scarcely able to believe their luck, sought to widen the arrangement to the whole country in 1937.

Despite the clear evidence of the priority given to international tourism it would be wrong to leave the impression that domestic tourism was only important in Britain. Everywhere home tourism was increasing. Belgium, for example, went through exactly the same political and trades union debates over paid holidays as in Britain during the 1930s. Equivalent legislation to that passed in Britain in 1938 had been enacted in Belgium two years earlier (Constandt, 1986, p. 33). By the time war broke out arrangements were well in hand for a new national Belgian tourist authority, the General Commission for Tourism, intended principally to deal with the anticipated huge growth in domestic tourism. Clearly, however, the habit of co-operative working between different resorts which had been apparent from the beginnings of modern Belgian tourism, in large measure to strengthen international tourism marketing, would also pay dividends in the effective management of domestic tourism. Britain too was obliged to change its approach to the marketing of holiday destinations.

The War and After

In fact, the working class paid holiday-making surge that was expected in Britain during the late 1930s did not occur immediately (Pimlott, 1976, pp. 221–222). 1938 and 1939 were slacker years than 1937, reflecting a weakening of the economy and growing fears of war. Moreover the 1939–45 war itself greatly disrupted holiday making patterns and was particularly harsh for the resorts as holiday areas. Many, in vulnerable areas in the South and South East, had been virtually closed down. Some, like Margate, suffered serious war damage (Stafford and Yates, 1985, pp. 155–157). Other resorts had a relatively good war. Relocated civil servants, rich evacuees and the billeting of military trainees helped many north western resorts (Walvin, 1978, pp. 126–129).

Yet, although it boosted resort economies, such wartime activity was not an ideal preparation for the great surge in numbers of holiday makers when it finally came in the late 1940s and early 1950s. Numbers of people entitled to paid holidays continued to rise relentlessly. By 1945 it was estimated that 14 million working people, about four-fifths of the total, had such entitlements. A decade later virtually everyone was entitled. By the end of the war central government had begun to plan as never before for the huge potential demand for holidays that now existed. A new body, the British Tourist and Holidays Board, was established to oversee the problems of the industry (PRO HLG 52/1395). After an uneasy period of tension it was merged in 1950 with the Travel Association (as it had again become) to form the British Travel and Holidays Association, continuing the pre-war publicity links with local authorities.

In this atmosphere of austerity and government planning, attitudes to resort advertising were somewhat contradictory, however. Central government was eager to extend holiday making, recognizing the critical role it could play in social welfare. Central grants for tourist publicity were greatly increased (to £407,000 in 1949–50).

On the other hand general shortages and several years of resort under-investment meant that the principal concerns were, as never before, to spread the load in time and space. It was also recognized that many resorts faced an up-hill struggle from wartime disruption. In the circumstances the government granted a further expansion of advertising powers under the 1948 Local Government Act. Municipalities could now raise a 3d rate for advertising subject to the other limitations of the 1936 Act. Yet it was typical of the mood of the time that they were immediately asked to use this new spending power sparingly (PRO HLG 52/1395, 1.5.48). Paper shortages also restricted the range and quantity of publicity materials (e.g. Gee, 1949).

Superficially resort advertising resumed very much where it had left off in 1939, but the keen edge of direct place competition between the bigger resorts was never again quite so sharp. The overarching imperatives were now, even more, to spread the holiday season and to encourage smaller resorts and rural areas to take more of the load. The railways continued to play a significant part in resort advertising but their relative importance declined further compared to the towns themselves. On the eve of nationalization in 1947, new arrangements for joint resort advertising were agreed which retreated from the universal financial formula of the interwar years. The new pattern involved a much more careful calculation by the railways as to how much benefit they themselves would get from the promotion of particular resorts (PRO RAIL 1080/590, 8.10.46).

Yet the 1950s became something of an Indian summer for the joint resort publicity scheme. Its most typical manifestation, the poster, enjoyed a partial revival (Palin, 1987). But the shift to road was by now inexorable. The relative decline in the importance of rail for holiday traffic in the 1930s turned into absolute decline in the 1950s. In 1947 for example, two-thirds of visitors to Skegness had come by rail (Walvin, 1978, p. 136). By 1955 the proportion had halved. Nor were numbers of visitors to the big resorts expanding as they had done between the wars. The figures in the mid-1960s were very similar to those of the late 1930s: Blackpool 7 million; Brighton and Hove 4–5 million; Hastings 3 million; Bournemouth and Southport 2 million each; Scarborough and Eastbourne 1 million each. The real growth was coming in smaller holiday centres with fewer of the trappings of the big resorts.

Growth in overseas holidays was also beginning. Austerity and its aftermath had interrupted the pre-war growth of international European tourism. This was, as we have seen, something which British tourism marketing had never handled very well. The circumstances of the early post-war years allowed them to pretend that it did not matter very much. It did, of course. In 1964 over 0.7 million Britons took holidays in Spain; by 1973 the figure was nearly 2.8 million and growing. No other foreign destination matched this but the trend to overseas holidays was inexorable. Although a few managed to buck the trend, the stagnation of most of the main British resorts now began to turn into real decline.

CONCLUSIONS

The story of how resort marketing evolved is, then, a complex one. Between them, the resorts and the railways developed an impressive range of promotional means to sell the seaside. We have focused particularly on the cutting edge of this selling process: resort advertisement and other forms of publicity. We have explored its reality as an often contentious aspect of public policy, noting how, by international and especially European standards, central government remained aloof from the business of tourism marketing.

Instead it was the privately owned railways and the resort municipalities which bore the brunt of tourism marketing. While railway involvement was typical everywhere, Britain appears to have been unique in the degree to which local governments were obliged to give leadership in publicity matters. Although private or quasi-autonomous publicity associations existed they generally lacked the vigour of those in Europe or in some of the larger American resorts. The focus on local authorities brought many weaknesses, not least the grudging reluctance of central government to grant adequate publicity powers (a theme we will meet again in other chapters). There were also other limitations. At times the municipalities groped towards wider frameworks of action, but essentially they were limited by their own organizational natures and geographical extents. Yet the achievement was still an impressive one, particularly if we consider the huge municipal investment in the tourist attractions that accompanied the rise of resort promotion. There was something very tangible to sell. We must now examine how the promotional message was put together.

4

THE NATION'S TONIC

Few aspects of place selling have been quite so evocative of time, place and experience as that developed for seaside resorts. For generations who now have little or no direct knowledge of the traditional seaside holiday, resort posters and publicity conjure up vivid, if vicarious, experience. The images of strapping young women playing leapfrog in the latest, daringly abbreviated, swimming costumes of the 1930s, children in innocent seaside play or ancient pipe-smoking fishermen populate not so much a reality as an ideal. A key promotional word like bracing, absolutely central to the British concept of the seaside holiday, was expressive of far more than a climatic reality. It embodied a particularly British ideology of personal and social renewal through holiday-making. The growing interwar promotional emphasis on sunshine, originally a symbol of the enlightening effects of travel, heralded a shift in that ideology, faithfully reflected in the promotional message but not the reality of the British weather.

As we probe more deeply, we find messages about class, culture and race. Advertising and publicity were, as we have seen, a central part of the primary discourse of selling the resort. But they were also mirrored deeply held social values. In this chapter we explore both levels of discourse about resort publicity. We begin by examining exactly how the resort promotional message was constructed, identifying and analysing recurrent images. The main point is, perhaps, that resort marketing was much more than the literal representation of successive cycles of resort development. Certainly the resorts were developing their tourist resources, but selling the resort was never solely about what was there to sell. Like all place selling it involved the creation and projection of images that only occasionally needed to coincide with experienced reality.

More typically the marketing message was an idealized representation. It exaggerated or in other ways distorted place to articulate desired themes and engender pleasant feelings and associations. Moreover the actual process of image making was not merely a function of a rational marketing process. Although much resort advertising had to go through a screening process of municipal, railway or other committees, there remained an intuitive and creative element in both the production and the understanding of the final image. We focus initially on the basic building blocks from which the image was constructed.

THE RESORT IN MARKETING IMAGERY

Image-Making: The Slogan

One of the most important components of early resort advertising, especially in Britain and the United States, was the slogan. In the few words which preceded or followed the resort's name on posters, in press advertisements and in brochures, it was possible to suggest the essence of a place, its appeal and its main market. This practice was less common elsewhere. Thus slogans on many early French resort posters did little more than name the place, list the main attractions, such as beach, bathing, casino or theatre and the time taken from Paris. 'Summer in Dieppe: The Only Beach 3 hours from Paris' was fairly typical of this approach in the 1890s, though slogans were occasionally used, for example 'Luchon: Queen of the Pyrenees' (Camard and Zagrodski, 1989, pp. 31, 49). Later French examples often gave only the simplest details, placing much greater reliance on the image (and the contact address for further details) though occasional, more lyrical slogans can be found, such as 'Parame-Rotheneuf: The Pearl of the Emerald Coast' (Conservatoire de L'Affiche en Bretagne, nd c1994, p. 46). A few more subtle slogans also appeared, for example 'Winter in Monte Carlo – The Chic People Are' (Weill, 1994, p. 79)

In Britain and the United States however, slogans were much more commonly used on posters and in brochure titles. Predictably, American boosterism generated more unqualified superlatives in its resort slogans. By the early twentieth century Atlantic City was 'America's Greatest Resort'; by the interwar years it was 'The Playground of the World' (ACPB, 1909; NCPC, 1922). The more sedate resorts of New England were promoted with less extravagant individual claims, though the collective slogan 'The Vacation Land of America', used consistently by the railroads, hinted at a similar boldness (e.g. *Cook's American Traveler's Gazette*, July 1910, p. 49).

By comparison, British and other European practice appeared rather reticent. Blackpool occasionally gave prominence in its advertising to subsidiary slogans such as 'Outrivals all foreign resorts – Blackpool – The Nation's Tonic' (Cook's UK Brochure, 1922, p. xxxiv), but generally even it lacked something of American chutzpah. The others seem decidedly timid and, in some cases, unoriginal. Thus Scarborough claimed to be 'Queen of Watering

Places', competing directly with Ostend's simultaneous use of the same title, noted in the last chapter (*The Traveller's Gazette*, June 1914, p. 65). The same slogan was also used at times by Brighton (1929) and Douglas (IMPB, nd c1925, p. 26). Other resorts managed more distinctiveness. Southport's long time slogan 'The Seaside Garden City' suggested sedateness (Southport, 1931). 'Dr Brighton', enjoying a recurrent popularity, retained the traditional sense of a genteel health resort (Frames, 1927, back cover). Snappy alliteration along the lines of 'Bright Breezy Bracing Bridlington' (or the famous 'Skegness is So Bracing', where it was reinforced with sibilance) was often used to suggest somewhere more down to earth. As these also suggest, climatic allusions were also commonly used, a theme we will investigate more fully below.

In other cases there were more literal attempts to represent a resort's physical character, such as 'Hornsea – Lake-land By The Sea' (Cole and Durack, 1992, p. 7). Exotic foreign comparisons were also made, most famously in 'The Cornish Riviera' (Wilson, 1987, pp. 33, 53, 72) a theme echoed in 'Torquay: The English Riviera' (Torquay, nd c1925). The particular vulnerability of British spas to continental competition encouraged many slogans on this theme, such as 'Cheltenham: The Most Continental of British Spas' (Cook, 1922, p. xxxv). Other devices involved emphasizing a place's historic or literary associations, though this was an approach more commonly applied to historic towns (such as Stratford-upon-Avon or Oxford) than seaside resorts. The South Eastern and Chatham Railway was, however, advertising the Kent Coast as 'Caesar's Choice' by 1913 (Cole and Durack, 1990, p. 59).

Image-Making: The Visual Representation

A visual element usually accompanied these slogans, adding further layers of meaning to the overall projected image. Many resort posters, press advertisements and covers of promotional

The Vacation Land of America was a slogan used by several railroads serving New England c1910. Notice particularly the attempt to cater for people of different incomes but without losing the emphasis on refinement.

brochures used general views, attempting to show everything the resort had to offer. Another earlier variant was the 'series of vignettes' type of poster, whereby the advertising image was constructed from several views, highlighting key attractions. Many of the earliest French resort posters used this latter approach, often in somewhat awkward conjunction with a dominant female figure in a bathing costume (e.g.

Weill, 1994, p. 14; Camard and Zagrodski, 1989, pp. 17–71).

In Britain, however, the persistence of more literal representation was particularly associated with local publicity committees. Such bodies were often sceptical of more artistic, impressionistic attempts to suggest the spirit of their town. What they wanted was detail and plenty of it (Cole and Durack, 1992, p. 21; Hutchison,

Sunny SOUTHPORT
ENGLAND'S SEASIDE GARDEN CITY

Slogans were a very common feature of resort promotion. For many years, Southport used this slogan to stress its distinctive and genteel appeal.

1968, p. 121). It was an approach that Punch had satirized as early as 1912 with a spoof poster for the mythical resort of 'Mixingham-on-Sea' (*Punch*, 17.7.12, p. 54). And, as the artist Walter Shaw Sparrow complained in 1924, the ideal poster for such local interests would have been a lithographed photograph with a colour tint. A few actually took this form (e.g. Cole and Durack, 1990, p. 71), though railway publicists tried to raise artistic standards by moving away from general views (PRO ZPER 38/17, pp. 8–9).

Another basic type of visual representation involved the use of human figures, sometimes completely dominating the scene, in others more a supporting or incidental figure. The intention was to use these figures and any interplay between them, or between them and the setting, to evoke pleasant or other desirable feelings and associate them directly with resorts. In part the practice of using figures to dominate visual representations of resorts arose somewhat accidentally out of early poster advertising practice, initially in France and later in Britain and elsewhere. Stock images were first produced by artists and

only then selected for use in association with particular places and slogans. Backgrounds would be generalized seaside rather than resort-specific, though a few details of buildings or natural features could be added to appease local concerns.

The potency of the advertising message depended directly on the attractive, symbolic or empathetic qualities of the dominant figure, in association with the slogan which was added. Designs using dominant figures were deployed in a more considered fashion in the interwar years. Commissioning advertising managers or committees would give the artist a much clearer idea of their wishes before the image was created. Local publicists still wanted to show off their resort's facilities but these now became at most a backdrop rather than the principal subject. Several broad types of figures recur regularly, though there were important national differences in their incidence over time, for reasons we will explore more fully later.

The next stage is to explore and decode the main elements of this promotional repertoire. By this means it is possible to reveal how the promotional imagery worked in the marketing process. It will also involve exploring the wider social meaning of its imagery of tourist pro-motion. It is not difficult to begin probing the significance of the stock promotional figures or the particular qualities which are being stressed. Yet such meanings need to be located within a wider social and cultural history to understand fully what the selling of the resort actually entailed. In doing this we focus on five central themes in the development of resorts and con-sider how they were dealt with in promotional imagery.

. . . So Bracing

Health was, as we have seen, a critical element in the emergence and selling of the seaside resort as a distinctive settlement form. The initial focus on the therapeutic value of seawater drinking soon gave way to an emphasis on seabathing. During

This poster for Blackpool, c1893, shows the town before the famous Tower was built. An early example of railway/town co-operation the poster is very typical of this period, linking a general view and a series of vignettes. The promoted impression is rather more sedate than the plebeian reality on an excursion day.

the nineteenth century, however, another shift occurred, putting much greater stress on the health promoting qualities of the sea air. This was important because air was all pervasive, capable of being enjoyed by everyone without necessity for immersion in a sea that, in Britain, was only occasionally other than downright chilly. The new emphasis was summed up in a term which soon became absolutely central to the marketing imagery of the British seaside resort: bracing.

The term became very widespread during the second half of the nineteenth century. An early use was in the advertisement for Great Yarmouth, referring to healthy and bracing air, in the 1851 Great Exhibition Official Catalogue. By the end of the century it had become quite unthinkable that any seaside resort could be promoted with anything but very prominent use of the term. Many resorts, as we have seen, made it a central part of the marketing message. To take one, not untypical, example, Blackpool in a promotional pamphlet (nd c1896) gave un-rivalled pride of place to its bracing air. This was mentioned no less than eight times, far more than any other quality, in a short pamphlet of about 600 words. Every medical and other authority quoted in praise of the resort used the term with supporting adjectives such as 'tonic', 'invigorating' and 'healthy'. For comparison, several words referring to temperature could only muster six references in total. Sunshine was only mentioned three times and dryness twice. The sands warranted just one mention and the sea as a medium for bathing also appeared only once. As if to reinforce the central significance of bracing air, however, there were four references to sea breezes or sea air.

SHOWING THE BRAVE EFFORT OF A POSTER-ARTIST TO DO JUSTICE, IN THE LIMITED SPACE AT HIS DISPOSAL, TO THE VARIOUS ATTRACTIONS ADVERTISED BY THE MUNICIPALITY AND SPORTS COMMITTEE OF MIXINGHAM-ON-SEA.

The promotional construction of a general resort view showing everything was already becoming a rather hackneyed device by 1912 when *Punch* satirized the approach in this poster for a mythical resort.

Such references were at their peak in the years before 1914, though they remained very common throughout the interwar years and continued to feature strongly even into the 1950s, especially in the northern resorts. Blackpool, Lytham St Annes, Ramsgate, Scarborough and Weymouth still mentioned the term in the advertisements included in Thomas Cook's 1951 UK brochure (1951, pp. 32, 39, 41–42, 46). Scarborough, for example, stressed that 'The tonic air stimulates the visitor so that he soon feels braced up and keen to enjoy wholeheartedly the countless delights which this beautiful resort provides' (*ibid*, p. 42). 'Tonic air' was also mentioned by Brighton, Bridlington and Newquay while Portrush claimed 'the most invigorating air in the United Kingdom' (*ibid*, pp. 34, 41, 47).

What then lay behind the bracing quality that was held to have such potent touristic attraction? In part it was simply a straightforward extension of the health-promoting qualities of the sea itself, transferring themselves to winds that were 'iodine-impregnated' or 'ozone-laden' (Pimlott, 1947, p. 106). Much was also made of the movement of the air. As a group of eminent physicians reported in 1932:

... the bracing quality of the air leads to increasing cooling of the body, larger demands on digestion and tissue charges, increased activity of the excretory organs, and more nervous activity and exercise.'(PRO ZPER 12/10, p. 2)

Yet the concept drew also on beliefs that had been widely accepted within Victorian urban

This year – a
SCARBOROUGH
TONIC
HOLIDAY !

DEEP BLUE SEA
SAND WITHOUT SHINGLE
MODERN SWIMMING-POOL
YORKSHIRE MOORS & DALES
DANCING; CONCERT PARTIES
GOOD MUSIC
UNIQUE OPEN-AIR THEATRE
UP-TO-DATE MEDICAL BATHS
TENNIS, GOLF
CRICKET, BOWLS, FISHING
and 101 other distractions

Lots of sun. *Less* rain. And the most bracing air in Britain, to put new life into you, give you energy that lasts for months.

Do exciting things. Play every game. Meet charming people. Dance, swim, relax. Listen to good music ; watch gorgeous sea-scapes, ride in unique country.

A Scarborough holiday's the best tonic you can have ! Come this year. GET THE BOOK ★

★ *To* THE VISITORS' SERVICE BUREAU, Town Hall, Scarborough.
Send me " Scarborough—the Tonic Holiday "; packed with magnificent photographs, and full details (including accommodation).

Mr./Mrs./Miss_____

Address_____
                                                              C.H.10

A 1936 advertisement emphasizing the traditional British seaside virtues of bracing, tonic air while reflecting the new interest in the sun. All the bigger resorts were also stressing their entertainments and sporting attractions.

society. The notion that diseases were spread by miasmas, bad airs, though scientifically disproven by the 1880s, retained widespread currency (Frazer, 1950; Taylor, 1952, pp. 75–77; Sutcliffe, 1981, pp. 51–52). We can detect something of the same impetus that motivated the public health drive to ventilate urban slums in the search for pure sea breezes, uncontaminated by the fetid and smoke-laden airs of the industrial cities.

The desirability of the quality also carried within it echoes of the theory of climatic determinism which was widely accepted in the heyday of British imperial power. In this, British economic and imperial strength were rationalized in terms of an invigorating temperate climate which stimulated enterprise and spawned civilization. It was a theme which was elaborated most completely in the early twentieth century, especially in the writings of the American geographer Ellsworth Huntington (1915). Variants of the same approach can be identified in the various works of C.E.P. Brooks and other climatic theorists during the 1920s (East, 1965, pp. 42–43). Yet such expositions merely extended commonly held late nineteenth-century ideas about climate, civilization and race. In seeking understanding as to how a small country could become such a dominating force in the world, climate seemed to be an obvious part of the explanation. And since the sea itself was such an important arena of British imperial power, we may speculate that such notions would have had particular potency at the seaside.

As this line of argument implies, the heavily promoted desire to be 'braced up' at the seaside was a particularly British trait. There were certainly variations of emphasis between resorts – Scarborough, Margate and Southend were decidedly more bracing than Bournemouth or Torquay. Yet the value system remained a common British one. No equivalent emphasis was apparent in French, Belgian or even American resort advertising. The Americans, for example, though they occasionally used the term, tended to stress the relief that sea breezes brought from the summer heat and humidity of the eastern cities (e.g. ACPB 1909, p. 3; NYNHHRR, 1910). But that was as far as it went; the accompanying visual and literary images suggest a balmy and relaxed pleasantness on the beaches and boardwalks. An even stronger atmosphere of sensual languor pervades much French resort advertising (e.g. Weill, 1994, pp. 70–81). The nearest equivalent French words to the English 'bracing' – *'fortifiant'* and *'tonifiant'* – seem to have been completely unknown in resort poster advertising.

It was this contrast in style which underpins Weill's notion of the 'British folly' as an internationally distinctive type of tourism promotional image (Weill, 1994, pp. 82–91). The image type is characterized by groups of people, often families, in scenes of considerable animation, frequently jolly and often comic. Weill himself merely implies the connection, yet this representational genre actually rests squarely on the centrally important concept of bracing. The busy group or family activity that is so characteristic of this type has been stimulated by the bracing climate.

There are, of course, some real climatic differences. Perhaps the people on British beaches actually did have to move around vigorously to avoid feeling cold. The insistence on the positive effects of bracing air might simply be understood as making a virtue of necessity. Yet it went beyond this. Blackpool clearly does have a cooler summer climate than Atlantic City or Nice, but the distinctions between, for example, Dieppe and Brighton or Ostend and Ramsgate are much smaller. And while American resorts went to some lengths to play down their negative features, for example the problems of mosquitoes and other airborne insects which were the down side of their summer warmth (e.g. Funnell, 1975:, p.11), the chilly summer breezes on Britain's beaches were positively trumpeted. Thus, in an official Torquay brochure from the mid-1920s, we find this pained rejection of the slightest hint that it might be warmer than other places:

There are many who have formed the opinion that, because Torquay is on the extreme South coast, it must, of necessity, be correspondingly warmer in the hot months than other places further north.

Such an opinion, however, is a libel on the town . . . While England swelters, Torquay breathes ozone-laden breezes from the wide ocean. (Torquay, nd c1925, p. 6)

Nor was this some bizarre peculiarity of Torquay. Tenby made a particular point of showing how *its* summers were even cooler than Torquay's (Leach and Morrison, 1928, p. 10).

The pattern, in fact, was fairly general throughout Britain. The typical British promotional insistence on cool summers and bracing air was therefore making the most of what British resort promoters genuinely believed to be a virtue.

The Sun Shines Most . . .

At least, that is, until the 1920s. During that decade the supposed health-giving qualities of prolonged exposure to the sun, already practised by a few before 1914, began to be more widely recognized. In 1923 Auguste Rollier, 'the high priest of modern sun-worshippers' published his influential book *Heliotherapy* (Brendon, 1991, p. 260). The following year the National Sunlight League was founded in Britain. By 1932 the cult of sunbathing was evidently well established. Thus David Adams of the National Smoke Abatement Society commented: 'To-day . . . we are returning to that most ancient of faiths, the worship of the Sun, in ceremonial interblending of his vital rays with our receptive bodily framework' (cited Bourke, 1996, p. 25)

The 'solar revolution' laid the basis for the development of the South of France for summer tourism (Weightman, 1970; Pimlott, 1976, pp. 262–263). It also began to push British seaside resorts onto a more awkward advertising terrain where truth blurred into untruth. While continuing to emphasize bracing qualities, the resorts were obliged also to show how well suited they were for the new fashions of sun bathing, in increasingly abbreviated swimming costumes (Stafford and Yates, 1985, pp. 115–118). Many resorts tried to reconcile this contradiction by changing the product they were selling. Seaside councils began to create outdoor swimming pools with large pool-side areas, sheltered from the wind, which were designed with mass sun bathing in mind (e.g. Southport, 1931, pp. 14–15; BCPC, 1938).

Often such facilities were featured in resort advertising. More noticeable was a universal trend to introduce the sun and/or shadows into advertising visual imagery. The sun was not unknown in pre-1914 publicity. It was, for example, a popular motif in the early travel posters of Thomas Cook (Cook, 1993). But whereas the sun had then been deployed as a symbol of enlightenment, demonstrating the educative value of travel, it was now intended to signify a desired climatic reality. Even by 1914 advertisements for 'Sunny Weymouth: The English Naples' had begun to appear (*Traveller's Gazette*, June 1914, p. 64). The London and South Western Railway also used a sunshine logo (*Traveller's Gazette*, January 1914, p. 58) while the London, Brighton and South Coast railway dubbed itself 'The

Sunshine Line' and advertised the 'Sunny South Coast' (Cole and Durack, 1990, p.13; *Traveller's Gazette*, October 1914, p. 33). By the early 1920s it was jointly contributing to a Sunny South Advertising Committee with at least some of the resorts in its area (PRO RAIL 645/89, 5.3.23).

After 1923 the new Southern Railway which incorporated the earlier companies took over and further developed these concerns. 'The Sun Shines Most on the Southern Coast' became a regular slogan during the 1920s (PRO ZPER 12/5, p. 102) and in 1930 Milton, the SR's Superintendent of Advertising, introduced Sunny

As sun became more highly prized, it entered more fully into British promotional imagery. One of the best known examples was the Southern Railway's Sunny South Sam, introduced in 1930 to highlight how much more blessed was the south coast than other parts of Britain. The slogan was a few years older.

South Sam, a supposedly typical SR guard, who continued as a regular figure in SR advertising. The competitive trading of sunshine statistics became increasingly common during the 1930s, with Sunny South Sam himself one of the main carriers of the glad tidings. The resorts themselves had already begun this in the 1920s. In 1922, for example, Worthing claimed to top the list for hours of sunshine the previous year, despite being flatly contradicted by Weymouth on the opposite page of Cook's UK brochure (1922, pp. xl–xli).

As this suggests, the basis for many of these claims could be very dubious. Though it recognized that it could not possibly win in the sunshine race, the LNER, serving the east coast, retaliated with 'The Drier Side of Britain' (Hewitt, 1995; Cole and Durack, 1992, pp. 18–19, 22, 146). It neglected to mention, however, that this result was achieved in many resorts by low winter rainfall, outside the holiday season. Individual resorts tried many different ways to make their statistics appear more impressive. One favourite tactic was to argue that the rain fell mainly when everyone was asleep in bed (e.g. Torquay, *c*1925, p. 9; Southport, 1931, p. 7). Sunshine statistics were particularly prone to very partial presentation, such as giving the average only for the best months, concentrating only on good years, giving so many abstracted details in a prolonged discussion that the overall picture is obscured, and so on.

Downright deception was also not unknown. Resorts could claim to be the top of any list if the criteria were carefully enough selected. Thus, by surreptitiously moving Berwick into Scotland, it was possible to claim that it too had often topped the national list of health resorts for sunshine. The claimed effects of Berwick sunshine were especially miraculous:

One has only to look into the faces of the Glasgow and Border people . . . They go home bronzed and fit, ready to tackle their tasks anew, and go about with lightsome hearts. (Berwick, 1940, p.26)

Anecdotal evidence suggests even more dubious practice, with allegations, usually made by one neighbouring resort about another, that weather stations were deliberately positioned to reduce recorded rainfall and increase sunshine. The ultimate was tampering with sunlight recording equipment, a practice which one former City Engineer of a major British city reported witnessing in an unnamed Lincolnshire resort in the 1950s.

Even for resorts not plumbing such depths, British claims based on sunshine and, explicitly or implicitly, dryness were giving dangerous hostages to fortune. It was, of course, rather easier for many French resorts to present themselves as sun-drenched. Not surprisingly perhaps, few of them gave quite as much emphasis to the sun in their advertising as did British resorts by the 1930s (Camard and Zagrodski, 1989, pp. 82–134). The earlier view that the summer sun in the south was too harsh for comfort was not immediately supplanted. Certainly the upper classes continued to treat the Riviera as a winter resort, leaving its summer enjoyment to the middle classes.

In the United States, however, the sun was used as a major selling point in the interwar growth of new tourist areas. Here sunshine was presented literally as a vital life force, uninhibited by older preconceptions of its possible harmful effects in excess, still less puritanical British beliefs in the value of being 'braced up'. Thus 1920s advertisements for Florida spoke of it as 'a land of sun-bronzed men, beautiful women – eternally youthful – working, playing and actually living in the fullest sense of the word' (*Cook's American Traveler's Gazette*, March 1927, p. 58). Even more, California's many promoters managed to associate the state irrevocably with eternal sunshine, to the continued benefit of its tourist industry and much else besides. It was no accident that the Southern Pacific Railroad promotional magazine for the West, launched in 1898, was called *Sunset* (Elias, 1983, p. 18; Runte, 1991). (It is significant also that the huge national promotion of Californian oranges beginning in 1907 (see chapter 2) used the brand name *Sunkist* (Elias, 1983, pp. 34–38).) Similarly

See the Famous EAST COAST

A land of sun-bronzed men, beautiful women—beautiful women—eternally youthful—working, playing and actually living in the fullest sense of the word.

Visit St. Augustine, Ormond, Daytona Beach, Miami, the romantic Keys, and finally Key West, the Island City. Swim in the warm surf, golf on the rolling dunes, play tennis, ride, speed through the shining waters in motorboat or yacht, fish in either sea or inland waters and actually live for awhile on the East Coast—and all this at any season of the year.

Modern hotel accommodations to suit both your taste and your purse, also furnished apartments and cottages at reasonable rates. Through Pullman service to all East Coast Resorts—less than 36 hours from New York —12 hours from Havana via Key West and the Over-sea Railway. Write for rates and illustrated booklet.

FLORIDA EAST COAST RY.
FLAGLER SYSTEM
NEW YORK OFFICE   GENERAL OFFICES
2 West 45th Street   St. Augustine, Fla.

the development of the Hollywood film industry fostered still further this popular image of Californian sunshine. In such circumstances the deployment of the same imagery in formal tourist advertising was but a ritual reaffirmation of perceptions that were already deeply entrenched.

. . . The Most Moral Town in England

Perhaps the most common type of promotional figure used in British resort advertising in the pre-1914 period was the child, usually depicted in some activity on or near the beach (e.g. Cole and Durack, 1990). It was a type which continued to be popular even into the 1950s, but its heyday had been before 1914. Such images clearly capitalized on the sentimentalization of childhood by the late Victorian middle classes. An essential part of this sentimentalization was the notion of childhood innocence, so that by choosing to represent seaside resorts in this way, the advertisers were projecting them as essentially innocent places. The underlying implication was for the adult too to regain something of the enjoyment and innocence of childhood.

All this is rather different from the most typical figures used to promote French resorts during the pre-1914 period. Bathing belles, often straightforwardly seductive or saucy in pose, sometimes more elegantly depicted, were extensively used in French resort advertising before 1914 (Camard and Zagrodski, 1989, pp. 17–72). By contrast the pre-1914 British use of young women figures was both rarer and altogether more reticent, tending to treatments that were ethereal or ethnic (for example in traditional Cornish or Irish attire). The depiction of young women in the company of men was also under-

This 1927 advertisement for Florida is fully expressive of the growing sybaritic appreciation of the sun after the First World War. The new cult of sunbathing was a great impetus to holiday destinations such as California and the South of France as well as Florida.

The child was one of the favourite subjects of pre-1914 British resort publicity. Building on the Victorian tendency to sentimentalize childhood, such images were expressive of a very innocent idea of the seaside holiday. It was in marked contrast to the promise of adult pleasure that was common in French (and even some American) tourist publicity.

taken very cautiously in Britain, to avoid any sense of impropriety. Earlier French treatments of such encounters also tended to be more daring, sometimes showing overt male ogling or active pursuit of young women (who showed every sign of being available). Elsewhere treatments of male-female encounters varied though none went as far as the French. Yet American resorts, even in puritan New England, were sometimes portrayed with a surprisingly strong suggestion of romantic, even sexual, promise (NYNHHRR, 1910).

This 1896 Ouest poster for Cabourg was, like many French posters of this period, much more explicit about the sexual possibilities of resorts than British posters. Overt male ogling or pursuit of likely young women was commonly shown. The treatment here is unusually humorous, however, with the young woman clearly outpacing her pursuers.

This use of attractive young women in resort advertising was evidence of a place product appeal that was promoted on the basis of altogether more adult enjoyments than were openly admitted in Britain. There was the explicit recognition that sexual encounters were possible. Yet these young women were also a means of associating French resorts with a more general range of worldly pleasures including, for example, casinos, that were simply not available in the British resorts. All of this of course is consistent with long held and deeply cherished mutual perceptions of the British and the French. Yet it is important to recognize that these were not closed cultural value systems. Some of these French posters were intended for display in Britain and were

quite deliberately building on the less puritanical French image to appeal to the British. A particularly interesting example was an early twentieth century Boulogne/Compagnie du Nord poster. Using the slogan 'The Beach of the Entente Cordiale', it showed England's white-haired John Bull exuding a decidedly raffish air, with the shapely young female figure of Republican France on his arm (Shackleton, 1976:, p. 41).

Weill continues to find important evidence of British unease with such themes in the inter-war years. In his view the British showed an internationally unique predilection for portraying wholesome and often rather jolly family groups of adults and children. Again, such figures were signifiers of a more morally conservative idea of

Although New England was traditionally thought straitlaced, a tone of greater permissiveness began to creep into resort advertising by about 1910, anticipating the greater freedoms of the 1920s. The cover of this promotional brochure for a Rhode Island resort conveys an unmistakable air of romantic, even sexual, promise, further encouraged by the main text. In Britain such an approach at this time would have been deemed far too suggestive.

the seaside holiday, untouched by random sexual possibilities (Weill, 1994, pp. 83–84). It is, however, undeniable that the British bathing belle made her appearance during these years, clad in costumes that became progressively more abbreviated. Yet British bathing belles were usually treated in a way that was more graceful, elegant and artistic, more modest and less overtly seductive, than earlier French examples (Weill, 1994, pp. 76–77).

Interwar French practice had, however, moved in the same direction. There was also a clear Gallic reaction to what had become a rather indiscriminate use of bathing belles on resort posters before 1914, in favour of approaches which gave a more specific representation of the resort. Where young women were featured, however, there remained a hint of sensuality which still contrasted with the essential modesty of much Anglo-Saxon treatment, especially in railway publicity. Another important theme, apparent everywhere but particularly so in British and American resort advertising, was the active woman, playing tennis or beach sports, swimming, golfing or horse riding. Clearly such emphases were reflecting the new freedoms of

This poster promoting Boulogne refers to the Anglo-French Entente Cordiale, agreed in 1904. The rather raffish depiction of England's John Bull, on the arm of the shapely figure of Republican France, mirrors much of the promoted appeal of French resorts for the straitlaced English upper middle classes. (La Vie du Rail)

1920s Belgian resort publicity. Reflecting the pattern of tourism development on the Belgian coast and the state ownership of the railways, its resorts were typically promoted collectively from an early stage. The promotional message, though sometimes using some French style bathing belles, generally projected similar values to those of Britain.

women between the wars and would certainly have had an appeal for women themselves, more so than the more male-oriented bathing belle.

For British resorts the image of the active woman offered a way of reconciling the traditional concept of the bracing holiday with the newer fashion for bodily exposure to the sun (Cole and Durack, 1992, pp. 110–111). It also allowed an acceptable degree of sexual suggestion to creep into resort publicity, without breaking faith with traditional puritanism. In

resort brochures such images could sit comfortably alongside the pictures of young children and families playing crazy golf or admiring floral clocks (e.g. BCPC, 1938). As might be expected, the incidence of these 'active bathing beauties' was markedly higher in the brochures of the more popular, down market, resorts. The late 1930s brochures of Blackpool and Ramsgate, for example, contained many more glamorous pictures of bathing belles (and with a bigger proportion wearing the latest, briefer costumes)

The greater social and moral freedoms of the 1920s were reflected in Britain in a more adventurous approach to the use of women in promotional advertising. Still some way from earlier French practice, this early 1920s poster was nonetheless frank in its use of female attraction. The tower provides a convenient phallic symbol to reinforce the message.

than resorts such as Brighton or Bournemouth (Cross, 1990:, pp. 181, 209; Stafford and Yates, 1985, p. 172).

Yet if promotional imagery suggested, however cautiously, greater sexual possibilities in the mass resorts, these were magnified greatly by a popular culture of postcards, freak sideshows, comedian's patter, comic songs and prodigious consumption of beer. Mass Observation, studying Blackpool in 1939, found it a place whose appeal was built disproportionately on sexual expectation. When, however, they attempted to measure the reality, using field research techniques that would have astonished (if not always convinced) Kinsey, they pronounced Blackpool 'the most moral town in England' (Cross, 1990, p. 190).

Although this claim was palpably less reliable even than those based on sunshine statistics, it was nonetheless a serious piece of black propaganda, prompting audible disappointment in the town's publicity department.

. . . No Appeal to the Cheap Tripper

The imagery of promotional advertising was also a way of signalling an ideal of a resort's social tone and character. From the outset, Britain's resorts had, quite openly, appealed to snobbish instincts. Even when word of mouth was more important than the impersonal assertions of advertising, promotion had rested very much on the notion of joining an exclusive group. Thus the

The active woman provided a promotional image that could appeal both to men and women. This posed bathing belle alludes vaguely to the active woman approach but is clearly intended to attract male interest. The outdoor bathing pool, providing more shelter than the beach, was very typical of interwar resort investment, especially as sunbathing became more popular.

growth of the spas had rested very much on the notion of the aristocracy emulating a royal pattern of behaviour, in turn being emulated by the upper middle classes (Wechsberg, 1979). Despite the more essentially democratic nature of the seaside, these snobbish notions persisted as the coastal resorts began to develop and as advertising proper became more common. Nor was it a peculiarly British phenomenon. The promotional propagation of the idea of admittance to select circles by visiting a resort, gaining at least a symbolic social mobility, also became very familiar internationally. Partly no doubt this was because the British were initially so important in wider European tourism. But east coast American resorts were also fully immersed in this same tradition (Funnell, 1975).

There was, of course, a glaring contradiction in trying to persuade very large numbers of people to adopt simultaneously a practice which was being portrayed as joining a socially superior and rather exclusive referent group. Ambitious resorts had to appeal to a widening market without entirely suggesting that just *anyone* could go there. Exactly what balance individual places struck would depend on the market they were aiming for, but it was a dilemma that all faced, even the most proletarian resorts.

How then was this achieved in promotional literature? In some cases the snobbery (and the contradictions within it) were explicit:

Torquay is roughly 200 miles from London, but that is not a disadvantage. It ensures that the town cannot be over-run with trippers of a class whose room is preferable to their company. Torquay makes no appeal to the 'cheap' tripper. But tourist tickets and excursion fares bring this wonderful beauty spot and health resort within reach of people with refined taste but moderate income. (Torquay, nd *c*1925, pp. 48–49)

In other cases visual imagery could be more subtly deployed. The general views or the compilations of several views that were commonly used on posters and for brochure covers could be very suggestive of social tone. Thus the 1893 Midland Railway poster for Blackpool, focuses on the smarter northern end of the seafront. The subsidiary views, though they include the rather notorious Raikes Hall, manage to give an extraordinary impression of a sedate, church going, county town, quite at odds with the realities of the mass resort and the 'golden mile' of proletarian amusements that was just emerging.

100% ENJOYMENT
FOR 99% OF PEOPLE

What kind of holiday do you like best—quiet walks through glorious downland or seacoast scenery—plenty of exercise, including golf (on 9 courses), tennis, swimming and rowing—long, lazy days passed sitting in the sun—dancing, theatres, cinemas and all such excitements?

Well, BRIGHTON has them all—and with them that special brand of sparkling air which makes a man eat like a horse and sleep like a log.

Whatever kind of holiday you enjoy

YOU CAN'T DO BETTER THAN

BRIGHTON

Send for FREE copy of the Book of Brighton by K. R. G. Browne, beautifully illustrated, to C. H. S. Browne, Corporation Publicity Department, BRIGHTON.

Brighton (1936) emphasized the way its size allowed it to offer a diverse range of activities for all tastes. Again though the promise of sunshine is central, with some continuing emphasis on the quality of seaside air.

Clearly the poster was aimed particularly at the more middle class holiday maker, reflecting a shifting balance of opinion within the town about its principal market (Walton, 1983*b*, p. 174). All references to cheap excursion trains that brought most working class visitors were omitted.

Even where cheap day tickets were mentioned, the visual imagery could still convey a dominant impression of gentility, for example in the 1913 North Eastern Railway poster for Bridlington

(page 76). Though apparently a general view of the resort, the scene actually shows the Royal Princes Parade, a section of promenade where a 4d pedestrian toll was charged for the enjoyment of its refined diversions (Walton, 1983*a*, p. 203). The more proletarian amusements of the harbour area, where most trippers headed, are not visible.

As these two examples suggest, the appearance, activities and general demeanour of the figures shown in promotional visuals, even at some distance, could be important in reinforcing the tone of social refinement. As we have already shown, the 1930s' resorts which used many close views of bathing belles were automatically positioning themselves down market. Yet the overall impression of the figures shown in resort brochures was important. Invariably everyone shown distinctly was smartly dressed, even in the general, unposed pictures. Men wearing ordinary flat caps rarely received much attention. But even for resorts like Blackpool which, by the later 1930s, liked to portray a more glamorous, even sexier, side to appeal to the young adult visitor, the market was too diverse to rely solely on such approaches. There might be allusions to the new arbiters of fashion, film stars rather than aristocrats, but the traditional signifiers of resort promotion remained prominent (e.g. Lidster, 1983, p. 14). Children and family groups continued to be commonly used, leavening the posed film star glamour of the bathing belles with solid respectability.

As all this rather implies, resort advertisements might suppress real activities or social categories if they did not fit the desired image. As well as flat caps, and despite its being one of the essential lubricants of working class culture in the late 1930s, beer drinking was almost entirely absent from posters and the editorial pages of resort brochures. This was rather at odds with the realities of the seaside summer season. Mass resorts such as Blackpool were very far from being oases of abstinence (Cross, 1990, pp. 162–167). Publicists may, reasonably, have been reflecting the concerns of their residential populations, that public drunkenness was already

a problem which needed no encouragement. It was, however, another triumph for the social values of middle class respectability.

But at least when they were dressed in their best clothes on the promenade the massed ranks of the British working classes could safely be included in the official brochures, if only at a distance. Black visitors to Atlantic City remained quite invisible in its publicity. The reality was that, even before 1900, a significant black excursion traffic from Philadelphia had been established (Funnell, 1975, pp. 29–31). Yet the familiar need to attract middle class vacationers, invariably white at that time, to occupy the hotels meant that excursions were played down in publicity, black excursions particularly. Generally the only blacks to appear in US tourism advertising, from about the 1920s, were shown in roles which serviced white tourists, typically as railroad porters or sleeping car attendants (O'Barr, 1994, pp. 131–134).

. . . The Unhurried Life of Our Great-Grandfathers

Black or white, it was rare to portray in promotional advertising those whose menial labour actually serviced the resorts and their visitors. The Blackpool landlady was a favourite of comic postcards but not the publicity department's official brochures or posters. Still less was there any hint at the appalling drudgery that was the lot of many who laboured in the boarding houses, hotels and other parts of the tourist industry (Brunner, 1945). When locals were shown, it was to lend the upstart seaside resort a sense of that older relationship with the sea based on fishing and coastal trade (Hewitt, 1995, pp. 303–304). The chosen signifiers were not so much typical members of the resort labour force as romanticizations of traditional notions of the seaside.

The usual promotional stereotype figure was the old fisherman, whitehaired and bewhiskered, with cap or souwester, gansey, breeches, boots and, usually, pipe. This broad type appears in the promotional imagery of all countries, with some ethnic variations in dress (e.g. Weill, 1994, p. 21; Camard and Zagrodski, 1989, p. 67; Conservatoire de l'Affiche en Bretagne, nd c1994). Typical poses involved exerting skilful control of a rowing boat, moving lobster pots or simply looking on, lending reassurance to the seaside scene (e.g. Palin, 1987. pp. 36–37). The LNER's famous *East Coast Types* poster series, designed by Frank Newbould in the early 1930s, uses the stereotype in several guises, including as a deck chair attendant (Shackleton, 1976, p. 120). Such direct linkage of traditional maritime and newer resort economies was very rarely portrayed. The approach adopted by John Hassall in his famous 1908 Skegness poster was, however, quite unique. Depicting a very jolly fisherman frolicking on the beach, Hassall managed to add a brilliantly comic touch of the surreal to a stock character.

Something of this same exploitation of the past was also apparent in the period figures sometimes used to promote historic towns and seaside resorts with historic associations. Brighton and Hastings for example used Regency and Norman characters to emphasize their traditions and distinctiveness. Closely related were the traditionally dressed figures deployed to advertise particular countries or especially distinctive regions. Many of the smaller European countries, such as Belgium, Holland and Switzerland, and some of the larger ones, for example Germany, used this approach to some extent (Weill, 1994, p. 20; Reinders and Oosterwijk, 1989, pp. 12–3; *Cook's American Traveler*, 1938–39). Within France and Britain the approach was used to promote distinctive regions such as Brittany, Provence, Alsace-Lorraine, Scotland or Cornwall (e.g. Conservatoire de l'Affiche en Bretagne, nd c1994;

This charming 1925 poster for Nantucket by John Held Jnr reworks the traditional approach of the general view with vignette to evoke the atmosphere of a traditional fishing and whaling community appropriated by the wealthy as a relaxed and unostentatious summer address.

Cover of promotional brochure of America's biggest resort. Unlike the smaller New England resorts, Atlantic City did not aspire to offer a place to get away from it all. It was essentially promoted as a place for *nouveaux riches* middle class social display. Its advertising almost invariably shows crowds of people, usually dressed to impress. The more working class excursionists, especially if they were black, were omitted.

Camard and Zagrodski, 1989, pp. 83–84; Cole and Durack, 1990, pp. 51, 63). The latter particularly occasioned a huge volume of interwar promotional literature which harped endlessly on its historic, timeless qualities (e.g. GWR, 1935). Looe, for example, promised the 'cheerful, serene, unhurried life of our great-grandfathers' (GWR/Looe, 1931).

We can, perhaps, argue that some of these figures, Hassall's fisherman in particular, have become willing converts to the cause of seaside fun. Where such figures appear in actual photographs, however, the received impression is not always so favourable. A 1931 Southern Railway

pamphlet for Weymouth, for instance, features a scowling local boatman surrounded by three artfully-posed bathing belles, grinning idiotically (SR, 1931). More generally, this use of images that evoke traditional meanings of place in order to promote tourism, something that was potentially destructive of that tradition, raises important questions. It alludes to a sometimes painful process of transition from small traditional settlement to commercialized resort.

Pre-existing fishing communities in what became resorts did in some cases find themselves literally dispossessed (Walton, 1983a, pp. 207–208). Shorelines formerly used by fishing boats

The same basic message of ostentatious display is even more apparent in this 1932 poster. The vast Traymore Hotel (with cupolas) fully captures the style of the resort. Amongst vacationers, the style is a little more informal than in 1909 but being seen is still clearly very important.

A North Eastern Railway poster promoting Bridlington c1913. Like the poster on page 58 it attempts to show a wide range of the resort's attractions in a general view, in this case closer and without supporting vignettes. It too greatly exaggerates the 'social tone' of the resort by showing only the Princes Parade, the most select part of the promenade.

were sacrificed for new promenades, as in Hastings. At Newquay, the real Cornish fishermen who were so romanticized in promotional art actually rioted when a hotel was built on their net drying area. In other cases the transition was certainly less harsh. Yet everywhere the rough and ready nature of fishing communities was marginalized as holiday making became established. It is therefore appropriate, perhaps, that all the fishermen are old; the authentic way of life of which they were part had passed, except to support and give a diversity of appeal to the new resort economy.

Typical example of late 1930s high profile national tourism advertising by European countries in the United States. This appeared in the issue of *Cook's American Traveler* current when war was declared, and belied much of a promotional message which would, in any event, invite rather different interpretations today. Notice, however, the strong emphasis on supposedly traditional life, very typical of how national tourism was often promoted.

A GLORIOUS VACATION IN

Gay Germany

Music and joy . . . smiling faces and happiness . . . you'll find Germany gay and carefree. The great seaports of Bremen and Hamburg open their hospitable portals. A swift streamliner speeds you to Berlin—that dynamic metropolis full of life. Leipzig, Dresden, Nuremberg, Bayreuth . . . cities of romantic history, great art treasures and fascinating festivals. Then Munich, city of art and fine living . . . Salzburg of festival fame . . . gay Vienna and the Blue Danube. The German Alps with sky high peaks, emerald lakes and picture book towns. The virgin charm of the Black Forest. A glorious Rhine trip on white steamers, past ancient castles and famed vineyards, to Mainz and Frankfurt, Cologne and Duesseldorf —each city alone worth the trip. Or, for rejuvenation, a pleasant stay at one of Germany's famous health resorts. A trip to Germany is the realization of your dream of a real happy and sensible vacation.

It is inexpensive and simple, too. We help you in your planning. A swift ocean liner carries you across—and big money-saving advantages are yours:

60% reductions in railroad fares
"Travel Marks" save about 40%

These reductions to foreign visitors bring the cost of travel in Germany within the means of everyone and add to the enjoyment of a pleasant trip.

SEND FOR BEAUTIFUL BOOKLETS!

Interesting illustrated booklets give you reliable information about Germany today Write us your preferences and we will send booklets covering your requirements. Address Dept. 94.

For further information consult your travel agent, or

GERMAN RAILROADS INFORMATION OFFICE
11 WEST 57th STREET, NEW YORK, N. Y.

MARKETING AND THE PROBLEMS OF THE CONTEMPORARY RESORT

The Crisis of the Resort

By the 1990s that very resort economy that had appeared in Britain during the nineteenth and early twentieth centuries, supplanting the older economy of the sea, was itself showing signs of chronic strain. The kinds of contradictions we have identified in resort promotional imageries were no longer manageable. The rather over-optimistic promises of sunshine and claims of dryness were simply unsustainable. For far too many visitors the rain did not fall at night, the sun did not shine and it was cold. Moreover the sense of the resort as an exclusive experience was completely lost as everyone, literally, did go there by the early 1950s. The traditional seaside resorts had become a commonplace experience, offering rapidly diminishing quantities of that faint aura of aristocratic good taste or film star glamour that had still been present in the 1930s.

By comparison the newer resorts of Spain and other parts of southern Europe offered mass holiday experiences that were increasingly attractive. Hot sunshine was virtually assured and 'abroad' replaced something of the lost fashion-ability of going to the British resorts. Low labour costs and favourable currency exchange rates combined with all-in package holiday deals to keep costs very low. As a whole, the British resorts became ever more reliant on visitors who were older and/or poorer than the national average.

For the majority of the population, holiday and social expectations were rising steadily through the 1950s and 1960s, yet Britain's resorts gained only a diminishing slice of this growing cake. By the 1970s and 1980s real decline set in. The English resorts have lost over 50 per cent of their 'long holiday' business since 1970, with a 30 per cent decline over the 1980s alone (ETB, 1991, 1992). Actual numbers declined from 135 million holiday nights taken at the seaside in 1978 to 102 million in 1990. Day trippers, increasingly travelling by car, became a much bigger part of resort business, with all the attendant problems of congestion and unsightly central car parking.

The decline in numbers came against a background of the biggest ever growth in world tourist numbers. Astonishingly, however, in the face of this, the quantity and quality of investment in Britain's resorts, already stagnating, declined markedly from the 1960s. A vicious circle of underinvestment was established (ETB, 1991, pp. 7–8). It was difficult to promote viable investments in the face of declining numbers of tourists who were also poorer. Moreover, the 16–20 week holiday season, something which smaller resorts never managed to break out of, compounded the difficulties. Recognizing these problems, resort councils were often forced into poor decisions, permitting crassly inappropriate development that degraded the quality of the resort environment. Key issues of environmental quality, in buildings, beaches and sea water were scandalously neglected. Maintenance of the existing fabric also languished, so that the very structures and environments that epitomized the British seaside – the promenades, the piers, the theatres and pavilions, the ornamental gardens, the seafront shelters and railings – frequently became degraded and tawdry.

While all bore some resemblance to this stereotypical pattern, the fates of individual resorts varied (Mills, 1994). Some of the bigger towns like Blackpool, Brighton, Bournemouth, Torquay and Scarborough have built up strong conference businesses, normally on the back of major municipal investments (Hutchings, 1995). Linked with this, others managed to diversify out of tourism with new sources of employment. Brighton, Bournemouth and Morecambe benefited by major higher education institutions in or near their areas. Office employment, sometimes the result of deliberate government policies, also developed significantly in resorts such as Bournemouth, Southend, Southport, and

Lytham St Annes (e.g. Soane, 1993). By their very nature, however, many resorts were in peripheral locations, literally on the edge of the land, making it difficult for them to diversify their local economies.

Some of the changes which affected resorts were unrelated to local employment. Most resorts within commutable distance of big cities, especially those on the electrified rail networks of southern England, developed further their identities as commuter settlements. Even bigger resorts such as Brighton or Southend (or Southport as a suburb for Merseyside) were greatly affected by such trends, already well established by 1939. The resort identities of places like Herne Bay in north Kent or Whitley Bay on Tyneside were all but eclipsed by these suburban identities. Seaside retirement settlement was also increasingly popular, especially in the more genteel resorts of the south. Waggishly dubbed the 'Costa Geriatrica', it was a trend which re-inforced the notion of resorts as old people's places (Karn, 1977). It also placed particular burdens on the social services of local authorities in the areas which were particularly affected. A more recent trend has been the use of cheaper resort boarding houses and smaller hotels as homeless bed and breakfast accommodation, even more damaging to the touristic image of the resorts.

Virtually alone, Blackpool managed to maintain itself as a mass resort on the pattern of the boom years. There were several basic reasons for this success. Perhaps the most fundamental was that Blackpool's appeal had never, at least since 1914, been based on premises that were demonstrably false. At a fairly early stage (and it was certainly well established between the wars) Blackpool's publicists had decided it was better to guarantee fun and good value rather than appear to promise good weather.

Yet in maintaining its ability to guarantee fun and good value, it was also necessary to ensure reinvestment in the resort to re-equip it for the second half of the century. Here Blackpool benefited by its much longer season; the town could offer real prospects of investments paying for themselves. While all resorts were obliged to take measures to cater for motor traffic, no other resort (indeed precious few other larger cities) secured the direct motorway accessibility that Blackpool had in the M55. The range of its entertainments and facilities remained wide and well chosen. Spectacular new amusements were added at regular intervals, ensuring it never slipped from the forefront of places in Britain that could literally excite the money out of people's pockets. In effect it became an entertainment centre by the sea, attracting huge numbers of visits, 17 million at the last count, mainly by day trippers. Even here, however, major investments, particularly in sewerage treatment and new conference facilities, are long overdue (*Guardian*, 24.6.95, p. 9; Hutchings, 1995).

Yet Blackpool has always, so far at least, been able to close the marketing gap between promoted and real product. Other resorts, faced with diminishing tourist numbers and perhaps reflecting the dilution of their very identities as resorts, allowed their marketing budgets to dwindle (e.g. Stafford and Yates, 1985, pp. 169–170; Yates, 1988, pp. 26–27). Yet Blackpool continued to publicize itself with great vigour and imagination. The mastery of the news media was almost as dazzling as ever. Thus when the Berlin Wall came down in 1989, the resort's publicists managed to find an East German couple who proposed to use their new found freedom to visit Blackpool, an item which duly found its way onto ITN's major national TV news broadcast. Potentially damaging news reports, especially about poor water quality, were skilfully managed away.

At the other extreme were those many resorts peering into the abyss. The worst affected were typically freestanding small or medium-sized resorts, not well served by transport networks and with few possibilities for economic diversification (ETB, 1991, 1993). Since local government reorganization in 1974 many had become parts of larger and more diverse districts, marginalizing the resort 'interest' in local politics. Ilfracombe was a particularly acute example of all these trends, though larger resorts like Weymouth, Bridlington and Skegness faced many of the same issues. Even ostensibly better located resorts such as Eastbourne or Weston-super-Mare were also struggling, however.

New Strategies

For many years, the worst affected resorts did not know even how to address, let alone solve, their problems. Fatalism and loss of confidence were widespread. The lessons of Blackpool were often crudely misinterpreted, so that resorts with radically different traditions embarked on hopeless quests to imitate what they mistakenly saw simply as a 'cheap and cheerful' formula. Rather than developing credible strategies that would enhance their distinctiveness as places, which was the real lesson of Blackpool, the resorts increasingly merged together in public (and tourist industry) perceptions. Even investments in climate controlled fun pools, which enjoyed a great vogue from the late 1970s and which were useful additions to resort facilities, partly missed the point.

Resorts were very slow to recognize the tremendous potential of their historic built environments. Blackpool always wore its unromantic attitude to the past with great pride. It was, for example, the last local authority in the country to designate conservation areas. As one witty commentator observed: 'At Blackpool, everything is new, no matter how old it is' (cited in Urry, 1987, p. 30). While such an approach might have worked in Blackpool, there is no doubt that the Blackpool 'formula' served many other resorts very badly indeed. One advantage of underinvestment was that there were few pressures to replace older buildings. Against this, dereliction and ill-considered conversions, for example of hotels to residential homes or flatlets, often eroded the quality of fine older buildings.

By the late 1980s, some genuine signs of change were becoming apparent. The English Tourist Board, set up under the 1969 Development of Tourism Act, with a network of regional boards beneath it, began to look very seriously at the resorts and their problems. The traditional autonomy of the resorts in their own tourist development and marketing, combined with the ETB's remit to build up and market new tourist opportunities, meant that for many years the main creative energies of the Board had been directed elsewhere. By the start of the 1990s, however, the ETB was anxious to give a lead. In 1990 it commissioned a detailed review of the problems of four resorts – Weymouth, Bognor Regis, Skegness and Morecambe. The results, published in summary form as *The Future for England's Smaller Seaside Resorts*, were a frank recognition of the problems facing all but the very largest resorts (ETB, 1991). There was a clear recognition that the resorts could not improve their positions without assistance.

Many of the key deficiencies were identified in marketing. As a first step the ETB launched its 'Discover the English Seaside' publicity campaign, in late 1991, in conjunction with the regional boards, thirty-five individual resorts and some private interests (ETB, 1992, pp. 2–3, 8). Worth about £1 million in the first year, the campaign has been credited with useful early results. Weston-super-Mare, for example, has claimed a 30 per cent increase in the circulation of its holiday brochure. The ETB also began to highlight and give further encouragement to the good practice of individual resorts in marketing and product development. The approach was pioneered in the late 1980s in Torbay, Bridlington and the Isle of Wight. By the early 1990s six projects, covering Eastbourne, Weston-super-Mare, Weymouth, Brighton, and the Lancashire and Lincolnshire coasts had been given Local Area Initiative status, assisted by the ETB to the tune of £300,000. More has been promised for further initiatives.

Meanwhile individual resorts have begun to respond to this lead. A growing number, including Brighton, Margate, Eastbourne and Weston-super-Mare, now have clearly articulated strategies for tourism development (ETB, 1992;

ETB, 1993; Mills, 1994, p. 3). Several are seeking to reinvent their images; Eastbourne for example has sought to counter its elderly image by promoting a new image based on sports and fitness. One of the key buzzwords of 1980s' urban regeneration, partnership, has also now found its way into the language of resort promotion as local councils seek closer links with private sector interests in marketing and development opportunities. Again Eastbourne and Weston stand out in this respect. Yet, despite such attempts to harness private sector funds, funding remains a serious problem. The 1993 review of regional assistance gave many authorities assisted area status, which is likely also to enhance access to European financial assistance. The British Department of the Environment's evidently greater awareness of the particular problems of resorts may also bring greater flexibility in regeneration funding.

Yet for all this, local authorities are still often strapped for cash to maintain or enhance the quality of the resorts and to upgrade marketing operations that remain remarkably primitive. Little, for example, has been done to create UK resort-based holiday packages that can be marketed by travel agents in the same way as foreign destinations. Travel agents, key gatekeepers in the industry, have been shown often to be woefully ignorant of Britain's resorts. As the ETB's 1991 report indicated: 'Travel agency staff know where Benidorm is, but have difficulty locating Bridlington' (ETB, 1991, p. 18). Moreover Britain's resorts have, as yet, taken little advantage of computerized marketing information, enabling targeted mailing of, for example, particular holiday products, such as short breaks.

Although the biggest resorts may be able to continue to act independently, co-operative marketing offers perhaps the only way smaller resorts can achieve the £500,000 bare minimum needed to make any significant impact. Even then the prospects for success are not huge. But increasing boredom with packaged European holidays offers some scope for a UK resort-based holiday product that is more carefully refined. (Benidorm, interestingly, felt it necessary by the 1980s to employ a British-based public relations consultant simply to counter negative media stories about the resort, hinting at a certain defensiveness.) Increased fears about sun-induced skin cancer and interests in sustainable tourism may also work in favour of Britain's traditional resorts. It is, however, unlikely that they can ever recapture much of the primary holiday market. The exceptionally fine summer of 1995 gave Britain's resorts their best season for many years but this was more the result of serendipity rather than strategy. A more sustained growth in second holidays is certainly not inconceivable, however, especially in places that can offer quality and genuine distinctiveness.

The extent and number of Britain's coastal resorts and their pioneering place in the international development of large scale tourism brings particular problems. Yet the resorts of other countries face problems that differ only in degree. Recognizing the international dimension to the problems they face, some resorts have begun to participate in pan-European initiatives. The COAST (Co-ordinated Action for Seaside Towns) network brings together several UK resort areas (Blackpool, Morecambe, East Sussex and Down in Northern Ireland) with similar areas in Corsica, Rugen in the former East Germany, Campania in Italy, the Balearic Islands in Spain and Loutraki-Perahora in Greece (Masters, 1994). In part the intention is to lobby the EU to devote more attention and funds to coastal resorts, but there has also been exchange of information and practice about resort economic development.

CONCLUSIONS

The recent past, then, has seen something of a renaissance of thinking about the promotion and development of holiday resorts. The complacent acceptance of decline, at least, is being challenged, even though its realities have yet to prove susceptible to reversal. Place marketing, which was so central to the original emergence of the resorts as major tourist destinations, has once again become a crucially important element in their regeneration and associated attempts to define more distinctive new identities. At one level this new marketing will need to involve much of the latest practice of targeted mail shots and computerized databases that is worlds away from the earlier practices. In another sense, however, past marketing regimes and imagery remain as abiding resources that can inform present endeavours.

Some resorts certainly draw directly on these resources. John Hassall's jolly fisherman continues to pervade Skegness' advertising and promotion. For many years a man has been employed to take the part of the fisherman during the summer season, disseminating a spirit of fun. In early 1995 an animated cartoon fisherman was also used in TV advertising for Skegness and the other Lincolnshire resorts. More generally, past endeavours have a crucial importance in defining the nature of the seaside holiday. Just as much as the buildings, they form a part of the heritage of the seaside, more ephemeral certainly,

but precious nonetheless. If today's resort marketeers wish increasingly to sell their towns as historic experiences, then it will be equally important to underscore this with interpretations of the images and experiences of past holiday making.

There are also more fundamental conclusions to draw, about the broader forces underpinning the place selling phenomenon in relation to resorts. A keen sense of place competition has been crucial to this story. We have shown how the peculiarly spontaneous and competitive pattern of resort development in Britain was especially conducive to the emergence of localized marketing. In countries where there was a stronger overall national hand guiding resort development, for example in Belgium, the marketing pattern was, almost from the first, more co-operative and nationally based. In many respects the British pattern embraced the worst of both worlds because its very localized initiatives were inhibited by the restrictions of central government. Yet they received no decisive lead from the centre until much later than any European competitor. It remains uncertain what would have happened if all British resorts had been able to promote themselves with budgets the size of Blackpool's. We can be certain, however, that the long term growth of the promotion of Britain as a destination for international tourism suffered greatly from this highly localized tradition.

5

MASS TRANSIT AND HEALTHY HOMES

If the mass marketing of the seaside resort was a story that could be told largely in British terms, this will certainly not be true of any other type of place we will examine. The residential suburb, arguably, was an English invention of the early nineteenth century. By the 1840s it was clearly visible not only in London but also in the emergent industrial cities, such as Manchester or Birmingham. Yet for many decades, the enjoyment of suburban living in Britain's growing cities remained the prerogative of social elites. In a way that closely paralleled the story of the resorts, suburban 'marketing', such as it was, was conducted through the informal processes of fashion, envy and emulation within the widening urban elite. The very possibility of suburban living for the masses remained remote until the end of the nineteenth century. The reality of mass suburbia only appeared between the two world wars. Organized, formal, procedures to sell these suburbs therefore only emerged over this same timescale.

Britain's experience of selling the suburb will thus be, a later, if very important, episode of this story. In searching for the origins of large scale suburban marketing, we must look, not to London or Manchester, but to the city that replaced Manchester as the epitome of modern urbanism in the last decades of the nineteenth century, Chicago. Historians have largely found the symbols of Chicago's new role in the vanguard of urban change in its skyscrapers, its elevated railway, and the World's Fair of 1893 (e.g. Briggs, 1967, pp. 381–384). But another important Chicago innovation of the late nineteenth century was the large scale packaging and marketing of suburbia. The main innovator was a quite extraordinary figure called Samuel Eberly Gross, 'the world's greatest real estate promoter' (Gross, 1891, cover). Operating and advertising on a scale that was huge even by Chicago standards, Gross had by 1896 subdivided and sold 44,000 lots and built 7,500 houses around the city.

Much American suburban development continued to be, in Sam Bass Warner's phrase a 'weave of small patterns' (1978, p. 67). Inevitably therefore marketing also remained on a small scale. Increasingly, however, the methods first popularized by Gross became more widely practised throughout North America. Gradually too, knowledge of such American innovations also spread to Britain. Although underlying social changes were also important, the main single reason for this shift lay in the marked improvements in British urban public transport which began to occur during the later 1890s. Many of these improvements drew very directly on American experiences, bringing in tow an awareness of suburban marketing techniques. In one very important instance there was a direct linkage to Gross himself. There were also significant developments elsewhere in Europe, especially around Paris, where the well established French techniques of pictorial poster advertising were put to early use in selling suburban *lotissements*.

In this and the next chapter we trace the origins and development of the selling of the suburb. Before doing so, however, we should note a more fundamental point. There was a basic difference between the nature of the sale that was being sought through the marketing of the suburb and that of the resort. Selling the resort essentially involved the sale of a non-exclusive and temporary right to enjoy a place in its totality. By contrast selling the suburb was literally that. Like the selling of the frontier, discussed in chapter 2, the ultimate intention was to produce multiple transfers of property ownership. Those buying the suburb were getting exclusive and permanent rights to a small part of the whole suburb together with non-exclusive rights to enjoy the place in its totality.

Doubtless this distinction contributed something to the vigour and inventiveness of suburban advertising by individual developers. In Britain at least, we have seen that hoteliers preferred to rely on collective promotional agencies to advertise the resort as a whole. In practice, though, we will find these differences were less fundamental than they sound here. One of the key reasons for this convergence was because of the important place selling roles, in both cases, of transport operators. Although they accepted the fundamental distinctions, their own particular concerns were to maximize their traffic receipts, whether of commuters or holiday makers. As in the resorts, however, we can better understand these individual marketing agencies if we review the period before they became active and the circumstances which prompted their operations.

SELLING THE AMERICAN SUBURB

The Roots of American Suburbia

In the late twentieth century, the United States has perhaps the most suburbanized culture in the world (Ebner, 1993). Its concentrated cities remain key points of geographical and cultural identity and still clearly represent important centres of business activity. But since 1930 the proportion of the US population living within them has been static, at around 30–32 per cent. Meanwhile the suburbs have grown from under 14 per cent in 1930 to a little over 46 per cent in 1990. Increasingly too business activities, especially retailing and manufacturing, have shifted into suburban locations.

It is not surprising, therefore, that America's urban historians have shown persistent interest in the sources of this remarkable shift. As Jackson (1985), Fishman (1987) and others have demonstrated, the origins of the American suburb lay, unequivocally, in England. The process by which the environmental values were transmitted was not a simple once and for all act of transference. There is no unanimity as to exactly how it occurred, but the essentials are reasonably clear. As early as the seventeenth century, something of the English elite's antipathy to urban living was apparent around many early American cities as the rich began to acquire landed estates beyond the city. A key element of the cultural value system that underpinned suburbia had thus begun to be established in the New World even before true suburbs had appeared. By the nineteenth century, however, it was a more direct awareness of English elite suburbs that was influencing the aesthetic and social conceptions of the suburb in the United States.

The development of railroads from the 1830s allowed greater scope for a way of life to develop that was at once linked to but also separate from the urban core. The railway was, of course, a British innovation but its potential for moving commuters was recognized much earlier in the United States than in Britain. Between 1839 and 1845, for example, there was a substantial re-orientation in the policies of railroad companies around Boston. As Binford (1985, p. 91) has noted, they

. . . rebuilt their facilities to encourage suburban travelers, introduced specially designed and scheduled commuter trains, developed an array of commutation tickets, and plunged heavily into advertising and selling house lots.

In part this probably reflected other factors in the United States that were particularly favourable to suburban development. Thus, in contrast to the rather complex and varied patterns of land tenure that existed in Britain, the United States had developed a very straight-forward pattern. This facilitated transfers in the ownership of land and thus its promotion for building. It is also probable that a larger proportion of the US urban population had incomes sufficient to aspire to a suburban way of life earlier than in Britain. Yet specific marketing measures were also important even at this early stage (e.g. Binford, 1985, pp, 127–128). By mid-century, all the same devices that were being simultaneously applied to sell the frontier were being deployed, on a smaller scale, to sell the suburb. Railroad and developer advertising extolled the virtues of suburban living. Special trains carried prospective suburban settlers to view likely places to live.

The Impact of the Street Car

When British railway promoters began to show the first real awareness of the potential of sub-urban railways in the 1850s, commuter rail traffic was already well established around Boston. Similar patterns were also evident around New York, Philadelphia and other older US cities (Jackson, 1985, pp. 35–39; 87–102). They soon appeared around Chicago after the first railroads came in the late 1840s (Keating, A.D., 1988, pp. 14–20). Evident too was the gradual emergence of a more ordered suburban environment, allowing a greater degree of privacy and separateness for the individual home. Yet both the numbers of suburbanites and the distance of suburbs from the urban cores were still quite small in both Britain and the United States. The real gap between the two countries opened up with the development of the street car, especially the electric street car, and related forms of urban

electric transit, the elevated railway and the subway. The greatest of these was, however, the street car. Almost all the key innovations in its development were American, including the grooved rail (1852), the cable car (1867) and the electric street car (1887) (Jackson, 1985, pp. 33; 103–109).

Britain was noticeably slower and more half-hearted in adopting these innovations. The electric street car had a particularly dramatic effect on US cities. By 1897, 88 per cent of American street car mileage was electrically operated, compared to just 9 per cent in Britain (Byatt, 1979, p. 32). American lines were also longer and soon extended well beyond the built limits into open country. In 1895 Chicago had more route miles of street car and boasted longer average journeys than any other city in the world (Jackson, 1985, p. 110). Many city-based lines terminated at amusement parks (often called trolley parks), specially developed by the street car companies to encourage travel (e.g. Gold-sack, 1993). Extensive interurban trolley car routes, largely through open country, were also being created by the early twentieth century (Stilgoe, 1983). By 1914, for example, it was possible to travel by this means between Boston and New York on a journey that took 18 hours and cost just $3.75 (BSSR, 1914, p. 10).

Coinciding with a period of hugely increased immigration into the United States and the grow-ing prosperity of the cities, such rapid investment obviously had huge potential for encouraging suburban development. Almost invariably street car operators worked on the principle of expan-sion, maximizing receipts by increasing the numbers of passengers carried. There was also little interest in the differential fares, graduated by distance, that were typical of British practice. For urban street cars the flat fare, typically five cents, was universal, regardless of distance travelled (Warner, 1978, p. 26; Jackson, 1985, p. 119). Costs to the operator were seemingly a secondary consideration. The main reason why this apparently reckless strategy worked, at least for a time, was that many operators had other identities as land developers or speculators (Jackson, 1985, pp. 120–124; Keating, A. D., 1988, p. 69).

One of the best documented examples is that of Henry Whitney, operator of Boston's West End Street Railway and the driving force behind the West End Land Company (Warner, 1978, pp. 21–29, 125; Edel, Sclar and Luria, 1984, pp. 205–214; Karr, 1984). By 1886 Whitney owned, or controlled with others, a large area of north Brookline, a still largely undeveloped part of a growing Boston suburb. Whitney now launched an ambitious scheme for a high class residential area, serviced by his company's street cars. When competing lines began to show an interest in the area he bought them. By 1887 the West End Street Car Company had become the largest system in the world.

The way Whitney marketed his new suburb reflected both its intended elite character and his general mode of operation. Promotional advertising played no very significant part in his development. The high class credentials of the scheme were established by Whitney's use of the well known landscape architect, Frederick Law Olmsted, to prepare a plan for the main boulevard linking the area with Boston. The West End Company's tracks, operated by electric cars from 1889, were tastefully incorporated on a central reservation. Land was also made subject to important restrictions on the way it could be developed. Covenants ensured a predominantly residential character, specified high minimum values of building, generous building lines and restricted any trades offensive to residential use.

Thus the social character of the development was signalled by processes altogether more subtle than vulgar advertising. The existing upper middle and upper class residents understood it as a consolidation of elite Brookline. Both they and aspirant new residents recognized it would be a social and ethnic rampart, secure against invasion by Boston's poor Irish immigrants. Yet there was also another reason why more impersonal marketing methods were not yet used. Although the scale of Whitney's development was very ambitious, he himself had no involvement in building or marketing the actual houses. He simply sold on land very quickly, often to other developers, at values now hugely enhanced by his actions. Ultimately the lots would filter down to those who actually built the houses, typically operating on a very small scale. And such individuals would themselves rarely need to undertake elaborate advertising to dispose of their houses; in many cases they would have been built to order.

The Suburb spreads down the Social Scale

In North Brookline, then, the potent new force of the electric street car was incorporated into an otherwise traditional pattern of elitist suburban development. By the 1880s, however, especially in the most buoyant cities such as Chicago, the preconditions were being established for a massive widening of social access to suburban living. On the demand side, the US population grew by 193 per cent in the half century from 1860. Remarkable though this was, the urban population grew over the same period by an astonishing 575 per cent. And cities of over 100,000, the very places most likely to spawn suburbs, increased by 669 per cent (Pred, 1965).

Increasingly by the last decade of the century foreign immigrants were more likely to move to Eastern or Mid-Western ports and industrial cities, rather than become frontier farmers. What drew them to the cities was the real prospect of high wages. As we have seen in chapter 2, the continued availability of rural land for agricultural settlement offered migrants a much more attractive choice than was available in Europe. It meant that if urban employers wanted workers to come to the cities, they had to offer wages that were rather higher than those across the Atlantic.

These general elements of demand were reinforced by more specific factors. The cheap, flat fares of the street cars made them increasingly available to the lower middle and working classes. Electric traction allowed the flat fare to apply to greatly extended routes, no longer restricted by the need to rest or change horses. Accordingly ever larger areas of cheap peripheral urban land became ripe for building. Meanwhile important developments in building technology were cheapening the costs of house production. The important changes came with the mass availability of sawn timber to standard dimensions and the development of cheap machine-made nails. The more specific invention of 'balloon frame' construction in Chicago in the 1830s has also been reckoned by many commentators (e.g. Jackson, 1985, pp. 124–128; Boorstin, 1965, pp. 148–152) to have been crucial. Although more recent work is evidently casting doubt on the notion of a single revolutionary innovation, the shift away from heavy jointed construction to light frames, nailed together to give strength, certainly brought dramatic reductions in building costs.

It was, therefore, the modest Boston street car suburbs of Roxbury, West Roxbury and Dorchester that were much more typical than elite Brookline of what was happening in the suburbs of American cities in the 1880s and 1890s (Warner, 1978). Instead of elegant brick built houses and apartment blocks, there were modest wooden single family detached cottages, along with two and three family houses. Instead of Olmsted's elegant centrepiece boulevard, there was a myriad pattern of small developments offering lots and residences of varying sizes, graded by price. Roughly 22,500 dwellings were built in these three suburbs between 1870 and 1900, yet no one developer was responsible for more than 3 per cent of them. There was no equivalent of Henry Whitney, though some of his methods were used on a more modest scale. As in Brookline, restrictive covenants were an important regulatory element, but reflecting here the infinite gradations of social position and disposable income amongst the lower echelons of the middle class.

Nor was suburbia any longer a purely middle class phenomenon. The inner districts of Roxbury were soon housing large numbers of working class families, including many Irish and other immigrants. The districts, and to a large extent the houses, were those progressively abandoned by the lower middle class for more distant locations, as street car services improved. Yet there were also growing signs, certainly in the newer cities such as Chicago, of the creation of suburbs built specifically for working class residents (Keating, A. D. 1988, pp. 20–22). One important reason for this was the growth of suburban industry.

During the late 1880s, for example, a developer called Turlington Harvey began to buy land south of Chicago's city limits in a rather slow growing factory district begun in 1870 called South Lawn (Keating, A. D. 1988, p. 27). Within a few years he had renamed it Harvey and converted it into a mixed industrial and working class suburb, run on strict temperance lines. Restrictive covenants were imposed on the residential lots, prohibiting the sale of alcohol. Marketing played a significant part in Harvey's development. Advertisements for settlers appeared in local newspapers in North Dakota, Missouri, southern Illinois, Michigan and Ohio. The promise of an alcohol-free place to live and work was attractive to the respectable rural families who Harvey wanted to buy his lots. Industrialists were also promised a reliable and steady work force, free from the temptations of liquor. By 1892 Harvey had 5000 inhabitants and ten factories. The early decades of the twentieth century brought further rapid growth.

In several respects, not least its moral dimension and its very close integration of housing provision with employment, Harvey was rather unusual. But its more general characteristics were not. The growth of suburban industry and consequent development of nearby working class housing were becoming increasingly common by the late nineteenth century (Harris, 1994). In many Eastern and some Mid-Western cities, co-operative building and loan associations played a key role in facilitating this growth (Board of Trade, 1911, pp. xxvii, 82, 266; Daunton, 1990). Yet there were also a growing number of purely speculative developers who were beginning to target the lower middle/working class housing market. This was especially so in boom cities like Chicago, where building and loan associations were unknown (Board of Trade, 1911, p. 144). In turn, such changes created a growing role for more formal marketing techniques.

As we have seen, advertising had not been unknown even in selling early, elite suburbs developed in a speculative manner. Yet the strength of informal marketing processes within urban elites had restricted the need for impersonal forms of publicity. Similarly, where co-operative approaches to the financing of working class housing were prevalent, we may surmise that it was also less necessary to undertake large scale advertising. As speculative provision for the mass market became more common, however, large scale advertising was essential to bring forward purchasers. Other marketing techniques also developed, designed to make it easier for the new, more marginal, suburbanites to take this new step. There was no greater master of advertising and the other marketing arts used in the selling of the suburb under the speculative 'Chicago system' than Samuel Eberly Gross (1843–1913).

Samuel Eberly Gross

Just after the Civil War, Gross, then a young man in his twenties, had moved to the rapidly growing Mid-West capital of Chicago and begun work as a real estate promoter (Clark and Ashley, 1992; Berger, 1992, pp. 113–120). Little is known of the detail of this early work in the late 1860s, though he was clearly involved in various real estate ventures. Chicago's Great Fire of 1871 destroyed a large area of the city. It provided further encouragement to urban change and land development in what was already the fastest growing city in the world at that time. Gross, who had had the presence of mind during the Fire to row all his business papers out to a tugboat moored in the Chicago River, was well placed to seize the initiative. Like others though, he was slowed down by the nationwide depression after 1873. For a while his real estate

activities became a sideline as he established a legal practice.

It was not until the early 1880s that he began operating on the very large scale that set him apart from all other suburban promoters of the time. In late 1880 he founded his real estate business, with a main downtown office and sales offices on each of his subdivisions. The 1880s were an extraordinarily active period for his business. In 1889 alone he reported sales of over $2.5 million and was providing employment for 15 departmental superintendents, 35 clerks, 185 salesmen and 20 distributors of advertising material, 'besides an ARMY of contractors, carpenters, masons, laborers etc' (*Chicago Tribune*, 1.1.1890). By 1891 he had sold over 30,000 lots and more than 7000 houses in sixteen different suburban districts around Chicago (Gross, 1891, p. 2). Many were originally beyond Chicago's boundaries, though extensions in 1889 brought most of them within the city limits.

Gross's basic mode of operation was to buy land where accessibility was good and/or improving. Following the common pattern of the time, he himself had direct involvements in public transit lines (which, as elsewhere, were improving dramatically in the last two decades of the century). Gross was a director and shareholder of the Calumet Electric Railroad serving his subdivisions at Dauphin Park and Calumet Heights in the industrial areas on the south side (Clark and Ashley, 1992, p. 9). He also reached agreements with other transit operators. In 1887, for example, Gross entered into an understanding with Charles Tyson Yerkes, the notorious dominating figure in Chicago's public transit during this period (Clark, 1995, p. 187). The intention was that Gross would extend one of his subdivisions in an area served by a Yerkes' street car line. The agreement was not a success, however, ending in litigation and mutual recriminations in 1899.

Other relations with transit operators were happier, particularly those with the Chicago, Burlington and Quincy Railroad (CBQRR). It was this railroad which played the key role in the success of Gross' most ambitious (and distant) subdivision, 'Magnetic' Grossdale, later renamed Brookfield (BHBC, 1994, pp. 18–47). Gross provided Grossdale's railroad station, modestly claimed as 'the handsomest suburban depot on the entire line' (Gross, 1891, p. 6). Meanwhile the CBQRR co-operated in the running of promotional excursions and regular services from downtown Chicago.

In addition to ensuring improved access, Gross also made important improvements to the infrastructure and amenities of his subdivisions. The intention was to make them more attractive to purchasers and the extent of these improvements varied with the hoped for final value of the houses and the remoteness of the subdivision (Keating, A. D. 1988, p. 76). His first development, Gross Park, catered for factory workers. Improvements there were limited to the grading of the streets and planting of trees. Remoter Grossdale, aimed at more middle class residents, provided sewers, gas, water, parks, trees, paved streets and the S. E. Gross School. The last was funded partly by levies of $2 per lot, though Gross himself contributed $1300 (BHBC, 1994, pp. 39–40).

As we have seen, most of Gross' customers bought individual lots. Some were simply speculating but most seem to have bought with housebuilding in mind. Of these, some made their own building arrangements. Although the City of Chicago had stringent fire regulations after 1871, Gross encouraged cheaper timber frame houses, more easily self-built, on his developments beyond the city limits (e.g. Gross, 1883). Loans were available from him to assist housebuilding. He also offered his purchasers the option of having a house, available from a standard range of brick or frame designs, built by him on the lot. This total approach was still relatively uncommon at this time. The scale of his housebuilding activity, modest though it was by later standards, was unique at the time. For both lots and houses, Gross offered the option of flexible instalment payments. For lots this would usually involve a 10 per cent deposit, as low as $25 on his cheaper subdivisions, with the balance paid off in

one or two years. Where he was also building a house, his usual practice was a deposit of perhaps $100 with repayments then calculated at typical rental levels, perhaps as low as $10 a month.

Some contemporary comment credited Gross as the originator of the instalment plan. Certainly he was using it earlier than W. E. Harmon of Cincinnati, thought by some to have introduced it in 1887 (McMichael, 1949, p. 10). But Gross may well have merely picked it up from other Chicago subdividers. Some of these were certainly offering primitive instalment plans as early as the 1860s (Daunton, 1990, p. 272). No-one, however, had previously used the approach to the extent or in the flexible manner that Gross did. It was an approach that left him (or his backers) carrying heavy debts for long periods. Yet it provided an important mechanism for promoting owner occupation to people of modest means, an alternative to the co-operative building and land associations of many other US cities. At any rate, the approach undoubtedly encouraged many working class people to take the first steps into suburban home ownership. By 1890 owner occupation in the city stood at about 30 per cent, broadly in line with the US urban average (Harris and Hamnett, 1987; Dennis, 1995).

Gross's Marketing Methods

As for no other developer before or at the time, advertising and marketing were completely integral parts of Gross's operations. The speculative mode of his operations meant that he had to reach his potential market quickly. He had to persuade ordinary workers to move from the familiar concept of house renting to embrace the notion of home ownership. In retrospect it is possible to argue that such a concept was an integral part of the 'American Dream' (Harris and Hamnett, 1987; Harris, 1990). To both rural migrants to the city and new foreign-born immigrants home ownership offered a sense of stability and integration within rapidly changing cities. Yet marketing clearly played an important part in articulating such aspirations. Gross was a master at this. In the manner of all really effective place marketeers, Gross was a genuine showman. He knew how to capture and retain popular and press attention. His picture appeared regularly in his advertising and, as we have seen, in the names of his subdivisions.

One of the most bizarrely self-promoting episodes of his extraordinary life was his 1902 law suit. In this, he accused Edward Rostand, author of the world-famous play *Cyrano de Bergerac*, of plagiarism. Gross claimed Rostand had pirated the plot from his own play, *The Merchant Prince of Cornville*, a work which he had apparently written during the 1870s. Gross's work had been performed only once, in 1896, a year before Rostand's play was first staged in the United States. In his efforts to get the play produced, however, Gross had circulated copies of the play, leaving one in Paris during a visit to the 1889 exhibition there. Gross won the action, was awarded all the profits from Rostand's much better known work, and secured a ban on its performance in the United States. More than satisfied with the international publicity the action had brought him, Gross ostentatiously waived his rights to Rostand's royalties, accepting only a token dollar.

More significant evidence of Gross's literary skills lay in the huge volume of advertising material which flowed from his firm in the 1880s and 1890s. Although the exact authorship of advertising material is very difficult to establish, it appears that Gross himself wrote this material. A great deal survives, sufficient certainly to tell us much about his activities, though it is clear that a lot has also been lost. At the peak of his operations, in the decade and a half after 1880, Gross advertised fairly continuously in the Chicago and suburban newspapers. In addition he produced an annual catalogue, running to 74 pages in 1891, including details of all his subdivisions. Other publications included various engaging homilies about the virtuousness of home ownership, such as *The House That Lucy Built* (Gross, 1886) and *The Home Primer*

(Gross, 1888*a*). Gross also published collections of standard house designs across the price range. The inquirer at his offices could expect to leave with an armful of attractively produced free publicity.

In marketing individual schemes, Gross also made much use of free excursions, chartering special street cars or trains to bring the public to the subdivision. Nowhere was this method used more extensively than to promote Grossdale. By the early 1890s, the CBQRR was running regular excursion trains, 'the longest passenger trains ever leaving the Union Depot' (Gross, 1891, p. 15). The trains would be met in Grossdale by a band and the excursionists led by Gross himself to a large marquee set up in the park outside the station. There he extolled the town's virtues while they enjoyed sausage sandwiches and lemonade or beer (Clark and Ashley, 1992, p. 10; BHBC, 1994, pp. 22–23). The excursions were a popular summertime event, thousands claiming the free tickets on excursion days at the peak of his promotional campaign.

Gross also showed an acute awareness of the need to target his place marketing efforts. Chicago was a city containing large numbers of non-English speaking immigrants, especially Germans, Swedes, Italians, Poles and Jews (Park, Burgess and McKenzie, 1925). Many suburban developers, reflecting widespread social opinion, were reluctant to cater for such groups. Exclusionary restrictive covenants were beginning to be used in North American cities by the early twentieth century (Chase, 1995). (They soon became a dimension of the marketing message, one that we will explore in the next chapter.) Typical exclusions were non-Caucasians, in effect black people, Jews and Chinese, but this was occasionally extended to Southern and Eastern Europeans.

The great black migration to Chicago came after Gross had left the scene. Yet, in his attitudes to late nineteenth-century immigrants, he appears to have been rather more liberal than was usual. A large volume of his advertising appeared in German and Swedish, some also in Italian (e.g.

Gross, 1888*b*; BHBC, 1994, pp. 23; 33). He also advertised in Jewish newspapers. Special German and Swedish excursions were organized and the letters of satisfaction he published in his catalogues included examples in these two languages. He also employed salesmen who could speak with immigrants in their own languages.

Little work has been done to probe his marketing policies. A much later note of indirect criticism came in the 1920s when Theodore Dreiser's novel, *Jennie Gerhardt*, was published (Clark, 1995, pp. 189–192). Dreiser himself had been involved briefly in the Chicago real estate business during Gross's heyday. His fictional character, Samuel E. Ross, was transparently based on Gross. In the novel, Dreiser accused Ross, and by extension Gross, of only catering for immigrants and factory workers when his ideal clientele, the English speaking middle classes, had failed to respond.

Against this, however, there is much to suggest something more than mercenary motives. In 1889, for example, he was held in sufficiently high regard by the Chicago labour movement to be invited to be Labor candidate for Mayor (Berger, 1992, pp. 113–114). Immigrant communities also seem to have seen him as more than just a simple exploiter. His marketing to German immigrants seems to have been particularly well developed. Gross was not himself German but his name would certainly have appeared familiar to German speakers. He also seems to have deliberately named one of his subdivisions, Under The Linden, after the *Unter den Linden*, the famous tree-lined avenue in the German capital (Gross, 1891, pp. 52–55). Certainly this version was used in his German literature, again suggesting a sensitivity to the German market.

Gross's later career became even more colourful than his heyday. Yet his main development activities were over by the time he won his legal action. During the later 1890s his promotional efforts were largely devoted to selling unsold lots on subdivisions begun in earlier years (Berger, 1992, pp. 118–119). In 1900 he began building operations again, now concentrating more on the middle class market, where profit margins were higher. In these final years, he seems to have taken on responsibility for the whole development process, including the actual housebuilding. This presaged a pattern that was to become more common in the twentieth century.

In 1903, he embarked on his last building developments, in Chicago and Milwaukee. Severe weather delayed building, however, and he was unable to meet the demands of creditors. Faced with bankruptcy, Gross declared himself ill and, after a period of travel, took up residence in 1906 at Dr Kellogg's rather unorthodox but fashionable health resort in Battle Creek, Michigan (BHBC, 1994, pp. 28–29). (Michigan's more favourable bankruptcy laws may also have been a factor.) After eventually declaring himself bankrupt in 1908, he was divorced the following year by his first wife on grounds of desertion. Ten days later, however, he had remarried, to an eighteen year old would be singer with 'a rarely rich contralto voice' (Clark and Ashley, 1992, p. 19). Gross was sixty five and the marriage won him still more publicity. Returning to Chicago in 1911, he died in 1913. Obituaries appeared across the country, recognizing his role as a developer catering for the ordinary man.

Other Sellers of the Suburbs

Although the scale of Gross's activities distanced him from his contemporaries, he still exerted a great influence. Other developers, in Chicago and elsewhere, began to adopt and adapt his marketing tactics. All his advertising brochures were prominently copyrighted, suggesting a fear that it was not just French playwrights who might be prone to plagiarism. The use of newspaper advertising and pamphlets became increasingly common amongst other real estate promoters. In Chicago some even managed to find approaches that Gross had not used. Thus the developers of Lawndale and adjoining Shedd's Park, on the western fringes of Chicago itself, published a regular free promotional newsheet from the mid-1880s. Called the *Lawndale Hustler and*

Shedd's Park Cyclone, it was written in a more racy style than Gross's material and by 1888 claimed a circulation of 10,000 (LHSPC, Vol 3, no 36, 1888).

Despite their great impact on actual development and close links with developers, the street car lines as such seem to have taken little part in actually advertising suburban living. It is difficult to be certain quite why this was so. They were certainly not opposed to direct place marketing. As we saw in chapter 3, leisure and tourist destinations, including the trolley parks they had developed, were commonly being promoted by the early twentieth century (Goldsack, 1993). Yet this was a more marginal part of their traffic, where they perhaps felt it necessary to make special efforts. In contrast, their suburban commuter traffic was more secure core business, growing very rapidly with the rush to develop the suburbs. They may have been content to leave publicity to the individual developers, particularly since leading street car interests were, as we have seen, often very closely involved in land development. Certainly there would have been little sense of insecurity, so often the trigger for active place selling campaigns. In this respect, the inactivity of the street car lines was in sharp contrast to railroad practice.

As we saw in chapter 3 mainline railroads took full advantage of the growing sophistication of advertising media in the 1880s and 1890s. As well as promoting tourist destinations, passenger departments also began to issue attractive free illustrated promotional booklets designed to boost suburban living and hence traffic. Sometimes railroads were directly involved in suburban land development, as with the Illinois Central Railroad's subdivision at Flossmoor on the far south side of Chicago, developed from about 1900 (ICRR, nd *c*1900). Yet the most typical motivation for railroad suburban marketing was their increased fear of the impact of street cars on their short haul traffic, especially as electrification spread. Electric traction was inherently cheaper and more efficient than steam power. The

steam railroads found it difficult to compete with street cars on fares, especially on shorter haul journeys, so railroads tended to stress their comfort, speed (because of less frequent stops), freedom from congestion, and the more attractive areas it was possible to reach within a short time.

Around Chicago the CBQRR, serving the western suburbs, was the most energetic of the railroads promoting suburban development. As well as aiding Gross's efforts, the company issued regular promotional publications, tastefully and poetically extolling the virtues of the suburban areas along its tracks. Meanwhile its timetables and fare structures were closely tailored to the particular priorities of commuting businessmen. The desires of their wives and families to travel into downtown Chicago for shopping, theatres and even church attendance were also reflected in services and ticketing arrangements. The company also promised 'none but polite and courteous employes [*sic*]' (CBQRR, nd *c*1883) to assist ladies who ventured from their suburban homes into the rough city. Street cars meanwhile were roundly condemned as thoroughly uncivilized, where the hapless commuter was 'jostled, crushed, choked with dust or bedraggled with rain or mud. If the journey be homeward bound he arrives at home (?) too miserable and disgusted to eat his dinner' (CBQRR, nd. *c*1900).

If the CBQRR's suburban marketing approach was developed to an unusual extent, it was certainly not unique. Boston's Old Colony Railroad was producing similar, if rather more prosaic, publications by the later 1880s (OCRR, 1889). And over the succeeding decades railroad advertising was used to an unprecedented extent to promote even the most exclusive suburban areas. Thus Chicago's elite North Shore (Ebner, 1988) was promoted in a series of elegant brochures issued by the Chicago and North Western Railway [*sic*] with titles such as *The Beautiful Country Near Chicago* (CNWR, 1900) and *Beautiful Suburban Towns* (CNWR, nd *c*1909). Publicizing country clubs, one of the central elements of social consolidation in the elite American suburb, offered another way by which some railroads, such as the Illinois Central (ICRR, nd *c*1912), sought to encourage suburban living along their routes.

By the early twentieth century, therefore, the selling of suburban places in the United States was becoming very highly developed. The particular features of American urbanization had encouraged early and very extensive development of residential suburbs, catering largely for owner occupation. Advertising and other forms of marketing played an important role in organizing this market for the suburbs. The practices which had appeared first and developed most completely in Chicago rapidly established themselves throughout the United States, even in more 'backward' regions such as the South (e.g. Bishir and Earley, 1985).

In many cases the organization of suburban publicity was being incorporated into wider boosterist concerns, orchestrated by Chambers of Commerce or more *ad hoc* groupings of speculators and developers, often with the active involvement of transit operators and municipalities. One of the most impressive publicity efforts was that of the New York Borough of Queens, whose Chamber of Commerce was annually producing a large promotional book by the time the United States entered the First World War (e.g. QBCC, 1920). The pattern was broadly similar in neighbouring Canada, which had many features in common with the American suburban development process (Paterson, 1989). By the early twentieth century developers around big cities such as Toronto were undertaking extensive newspaper and other advertising of suburban subdivisions.

Between the Wars

In Britain, as we will see shortly, the interwar years brought major changes in the selling of the suburbs. Yet the pattern and practices of North American suburban marketing were already firmly established by this time. The main

changes came in the scale of activity, especially the inexorable shift towards a fully packaged approach to development and marketing. In contrast to the selling of lots which had formed the major part of Gross's business, the trend was ever more firmly towards the selling of completed homes (Keating, A. D., 1988, p. 77). Developers, especially on middle class subdivisions, still often offered the simple and traditional options of buying a lot, or buying a lot and having the developer build a house to meet the customer's specific requirements. This, for example, was the pattern being followed at Highland Park, Revere, a Boston suburb, in the mid-1920s (PLC, nd *c*1926).

More typically, however, cheaper suburban housing was by the 1920s being produced speculatively and in ever more standardized ways. We have seen how earlier developers, including Gross himself, had already developed some subdivisions in this way. Now it was beginning to become more usual, supplanting the 'weave of small patterns'. In one of the fastest growing suburbs of the 1920s, the New York borough of Queens on Long Island, large tracts of districts such as Elmhurst were covered with identical speculatively developed dwellings, such as W. R. Gibson's 'Perfect Low Priced American Homes' (QBCC, 1920, p. 209). They were sold to occupiers who bought them 'off the peg', as completed, standard products. Yet this important transition in the nature of producing suburbia brought no equivalent transformation in the selling process. Marketing practices remained very much those pioneered by Gross almost half a century earlier.

The truth was, of course, that very few had even yet managed to emulate the huge scale of Gross's activities. Moreover the North American housebuilding industry was acutely affected by the interwar depression. From about the mid 1920s suburban development slowed and was at a very low level for much of the 1930s (Dennis, 1995; Harris and Hamnett, 1987). Owner occupation declined noticeably. It was only with Federal support that recovery began to occur in the later 1930s (Harris, 1994). This in turn paved the way for American developers to operate on a much larger scale than had been common in earlier days. The main dimensions of that change only came about after World War II, however, bringing some further innovations in suburban marketing. We will discuss the significance of these in the next chapter. For the moment it is more important to examine the way in which the ideas and practices of selling the suburbs began to develop elsewhere, as American ideas spread to Britain.

Selling the English Suburb

American Influences in London

During the same 1889 European tour in which he left the subsequently plagiarized copy of *The Merchant Prince of Cornville* in Paris, Gross also visited other European cities, including London. While there, he claimed to have been approached by a group of English capitalists who wanted him to duplicate his 'Chicago system' of speculative housing development in London or any other great city (*Chicago Tribune*, 19.1.1890). Quite how much substance there was to this approach is impossible to say without corroborating evidence. We cannot discount the possibility that Gross may simply have invented or inflated the story to keep himself in the public eye in his home city. At any rate, nothing came of it. Yet it perhaps suggests some British awareness of Gross's activities and their role in the spectacular growth of Chicago.

It was, however, the application of electric traction to street tramways and underground railways in the 1890s that brought wider British awareness of American development practices. In 1893 a leading tramway authority spelled out to his fellow engineers the essential dynamics of electric street traction in the USA:

Probably few engineers on this side of the Atlantic are aware of the fact that electric traction in the United States is encouraged primarily by estate agents and speculators. The earlier tramways and railways are suburban lines, and they are constructed before there are roads and houses, for the principal purpose of developing urban estates . . . the profit derived by the speculation has in many instances more than paid for the electrical street railway. (cited Barker and Robbins, 1974, p. 17).

Within a few years, the dramatic appearance of American capital, technical expertise, managers and engineers on the British urban transport scene had reinforced this lesson. Nowhere was this more so than in London, where tramway electrification was slow, even by British standards (Barker and Robbins, 1963; 1974; Byatt, 1979, p. 41). Here, in the world's largest city, the prospective financial pickings for both electrical transport and suburban development must have seemed irresistible.

Though he was not the first American on the scene, it was Charles Tyson Yerkes, Gross's erstwhile Chicago partner, who definitively marked the arrival of American ideas about transit-led suburban development in the British capital (Barker and Robbins, 1974, pp. 61–84). A completely amoral and profoundly corrupt figure, Yerkes made Gross seem tame and colourless in comparison. Gross might have been accorded a cameo role in a Dreiser novel, but Yerkes, thinly fictionalized as Frank Cowperwood, was the central character of a trilogy of novels. The last, *The Stoic* (1947), which Dreiser died before completing, tells the (true) story of Cowperwood/ Yerkes's departure from Chicago, following a huge bribery scandal. It then charts, with great accuracy, his activities in London. Within a short period the real Yerkes succeeded in gaining the dominant position in London's emergent but stalled underground railway system.

During 1901–2 he secured control of the District Railway and most of what was to become the tube system of inner London. In 1902 he and his American backers formed Underground Electric Railways of London (UERL) to raise the finance to complete, operate and extend the lines. His concern from the outset was to extend the tracks into open country. In general the already approved routes had not followed this American practice, sticking to the existing built-up area. However Yerkes was soon able to secure parliamentary approval for an extension of the Hampstead tube to Golders Green, with a surface line ultimately to follow to Edgware (Jackson, 1991, pp. 43–44). Feeder tramways focused on Golders Green were also sought to enlarge further the area thus made ripe for building. These last proposals were rejected. Nevertheless Yerkes and his American associates still benefited by a land syndicate they had formed in Golders Green, controlling a section of what, when the new route was announced, immediately became a valuable piece of real estate.

Place Selling and Yerkes's Strategy

Yerkes died in late 1905 before any of his tube schemes came to fruition. Yet he gave an important and powerful impetus to the way in which suburban development was to be promoted in London. However, the American approach never entirely worked in Britain. Traffic grew much more slowly than Yerkes had anticipated, partly because of competition with other forms of transport, such as the new motor bus (Byatt, 1979, pp. 52–58). American-style flat fares, dependent as they were on high passenger numbers, were soon abandoned. The lack of confidence was such that, despite brisk development at Golders Green, private finance was not forthcoming for the surface extension to Edgware. The experiences of the electric tramway operators were not dissimilar for, despite early promise, extensions into open country were proving 'financially hopeless' by 1910 (Byatt, 1979, p. 42).

The truth was that, more generally, British conditions, even in London, were not yet quite ripe for a Chicago-style surge in mass suburban development. Compared to the possibilities of cheap timber frame construction in North America, London's brick-built suburban housing was relatively expensive to build (Jackson, 1985, pp. 124–128; Harris, 1994). In addition, real income levels in Britain were tending to stagnate by the early twentieth century, further weakening demand (e.g. Pollard, 1962, pp. 23–28). Another key factor was the comparative underdevelopment in British cities of the ideology of home ownership, so central to the promotional efforts of Gross and his emulators in American cities (Harris and Hamnett, 1987; Dennis, 1995). The overall trend was therefore that while local transport improvements might sometimes stimulate local housebuilding booms, financial returns to operators were disappointing (Byatt, 1979, pp. 52–58). The more general decline in housebuilding in the last years of peace did not improve confidence (Daunton, 1987, p. 25).

It is, then, against this background of a hoped-for but elusive transport-led suburban boom that we need to view the early efforts to market suburban places. As the new tube lines built by Yerkes began operating in 1906–7, publicity also began to promote the areas they opened up for suburban living. The first such efforts were initiated by Walter Gott, UERL's passenger agent, whose primary concern was naturally to publicize the services themselves (Green, 1990, pp. 8–9). Some incidental marketing of places followed from this of course, though there were also more explicit efforts. Most directly focused on the possibilities of suburban living was an attractive booklet, *Healthy Homes: Illustrated Guide to London's Choicest Suburbs Made Easy of Access by the New Tube Railways* (LUER, 1907). Appearing first in 1907, it sold for a penny. The first edition was 80 pages long with a format similar to contemporary resort brochures. Boosterist descriptions of the different districts took up roughly 40 per cent of the publication. The advertising section, featuring individual housing developers or agents, accounted for the remainder. Later editions followed, at least until about 1915, using the same main title.

As it became clear that initial traffic was well below estimates, publicity efforts were stepped up as part of a general improvement in management.

After Yerkes's death, UERL brought in new people to run the company. The American connection was reinforced in 1907 with the appointment as General Manager of Albert Stanley, the English-born but US-raised manager of the leading New Jersey street car operator (Barker and Robbins, 1974, pp. 141–142). Yet links with the most effective British railway practice had also been made the previous year when Sir George Gibb from the North Eastern Railway (NER) was brought in as Managing Director. With Gibb from York came his assistant, an extremely able young man called Frank Pick, who played a central part in the making of London Transport over the next thirty years. One of the first fields in which this important figure made his mark was that of publicity.

In 1908 Pick took charge of UERL's publicity, giving it a clear corporate identity (Barman, 1979, pp. 25–34). He also drew on his NER experience to extend UERL's advertising repertoire. The most important shift involved the introduction of pictorial posters, used in the manner so successfully adopted by the mainline railways. It was at this time that the high quality posters for which London Transport became justifiably famous began to appear. Pick himself seems to have brought from NER no more than a very general understanding of the potential of the poster in transport advertising. His early efforts therefore betray something of a learning process as he experimented with different approaches. From the first, however, the poster promoting particular places on the system, especially newly opened sections, became a common type.

Off peak leisure destinations were perhaps the most common place poster subject, consistent with the priorities of an organization that was struggling to increase revenue. Yet, in keeping with the Yerkes strategy, the longer term encouragement of suburban living was also a strong early theme of the posters. Golders Green, where the American approach of extending into open country had been tried most comprehensively, was promoted most strongly with several fine posters appearing in quick succession. Other

suburban residential districts marketed in this way included Osterley and Hounslow. There were also some posters that gave general encouragements to suburban living. Another early type was half pictorial poster, boosting the broader idea of suburban or country living, with the remainder left blank for overprinting with the details of specific districts.

The Origins of Metro-Land

UERL provided much the most direct example of the way American thinking was influencing British ideas about actively promoting suburban development. Yet other railways around London and other cities had also been moving in the same general direction in the last few years before 1914. One of the most prominent examples was the Metropolitan Railway (Jackson, 1986). This had originated London's steam underground railway system in 1863 yet remained still an independent business entity, quite separate from UERL. The core of its traffic had traditionally focused on inner and central London, venturing only gradually into the inner suburbs. By the last decades of the nineteenth century, however, there was a mounting awareness of a wider potential traffic. New construction and absorptions of other lines had taken its tracks far out into the country-side north-west of London by the end of the 1890s.

This was not the homegrown English version of American transit strategy that in retrospect it might appear to be. There was certainly some desire to build up suburban traffic, but this was not yet the dominating theme. If it had been, early electrification might have been expected, yet steam operation persisted, even on the inner underground sections, until 1905 (Jackson, 1986, pp. 157–193). The essential *raison d'être* of the Metropolitan's country lines lay in the ambitions of its founding genius, Sir Edward Watkin, to make the 'Met' into a mainline railway. Watkin wanted to link London with other major English cities and even, at one time, Paris, through a proposed Channel Tunnel (Barker and Robbins,

1963, p. 211). His many directorships allowed him to exert extensive influence over the policies of many British railway companies, so that these ambitions were not totally fanciful. In fact, Watkin had been the prime mover in bringing the last major main line railway, the Great Central, to London in 1899, achieved in very close association with the Metropolitan.

By the twentieth century the former grand visions of the Metropolitan's destiny were much diminished. The development of suburban traffic began to assume the central place in company strategy. One key reason was the growing competitive threats to the inner London core business posed by the new tube railways, electric trams and, increasingly, motor buses. Dividends fell steeply and stood at only half a per cent in 1907 and 1908 (GLRO MET 4/13, 31.12.10). The development of suburban traffic seemed to offer the only feasible way of reversing the slide in operating profits. A unique feature of the Metropolitan's powers also promised other sources of profit from the strategy. This was because, alone of all Britain's railways, it had extensive powers to hold and develop surplus lands (Jackson, 1986, pp. 134–140).

Under the terms of the 1845 Land Clauses Consolidation Act, British railways were not normally permitted to retain or develop land surplus to railway requirements (Biddle, 1990, pp. 107–108). In London, however, opponents of the building of the Metropolitan Railway had burdened it with unusually heavy land acquisition requirements. In turn these had allowed the company to plead for greater flexibility in its powers in relation to land. From 1879 the Metropolitan explored the potential of these special powers, developing first a building estate at Willesden Green in north west London (Jackson, 1986, pp. 140–142). An ambitious attempt to boost traffic had also come in 1889 with the development of Wembley Park as a sports ground and pleasure park (Barker and Robbins, 1963, pp. 205–206). The original scheme, pushed by the ever visionary Watkin, was to build a 1000 foot tower modelled on the recently erected Eiffel Tower in Paris, though only the lowest section was ever built. The Tower was a failure and eventually went into liquidation, but the park was initially successful.

By the early twentieth century then, the Metropolitan Railway, eccentrically English organization though it was, was becoming well placed to follow the classic American-style suburban development strategy. The crucial change came in 1905 when extensive electrification of the Metropolitan's routes finally brought greatly improved services. At about the same time the surplus lands policy began to be pursued more actively. A new attempt to develop Wembley Park, for building this time, began in 1906, with a specific company formed for the purpose (Jackson, 1991, pp. 15–17). Another new building estate was also created by the Surplus Lands Committee at Cecil Park in Pinner. By the end of 1912 many more sites were under active consideration, along with the proposal that a special estate development company should be formed (GLRO MET 10/322, 31.12.12).

Meanwhile there appeared the first serious attempts to publicize places along the country route, initially for leisure purposes. Penny brochures advertising country walks from outer stations appeared from about 1905 (Jackson, 1986, p. 239). Within a few years publications were beginning to show a more direct concern for the promotion of residential areas. Most, such as *The Homestead*, issued from 1911, were published jointly with the Great Central Railway, which shared part of the Metropolitan's route (Jackson, 1991, p. 159). Others, such as *Country Homes* (MR, 1909), were produced by commercial publishers on behalf of the Metropolitan Railway. Such publications broadly followed the form of the earlier UERL booklet, described above (and the numerous mainline railway suburban brochures that were also beginning to appear at about this time).

From 1908 the new General Manager, R. H. Selbie, brought more coherence to the evolving suburban strategy. The railway began, for example, to enter into closer relationships with estate agents, better to organize the marketing and development of suburban areas. In line with general railway practice at the time a specific publicity department was opened in 1911 (Jackson, 1986, pp. 210–212; 238–239). A promotional film was even being contemplated in the same year. By the time war broke out in 1914 the future direction of policy was, in retrospect, reasonably clear. Yet it is clear that Selbie had to rehearse the argument for suburban development fairly regularly for the benefit of his directors in these years, suggesting that it was still not a foregone conclusion. It was, in fact, explicitly endorsed as Company policy in 1915 (GLRO MET 1/27, 29.4.15).

Meanwhile the publicity department maintained a good deal of its advertising efforts through the war years. It was noticeable, however, that the emphasis was now more on enjoying the countryside than on the marketing of residential areas, reflecting the wartime decline in suburban housebuilding. Much the most important piece of wartime place marketing appeared in May 1915. This was the first edition of the famous *Metro-Land* booklet (PRO ZPER 39/36, p. 499). Attractively produced, with richly coloured illustrations, the main concern at the outset was with places to visit in the countryside. Yet it also marked the beginning of a powerful place marketing concept that was later deployed with great success in promoting suburban living, as we will see, below.

The origins of the term Metro-land are variously reported. One version attributes it to a ditty composed by George R. Sims, a journalist with some associations with the Metropolitan Railway:

I know a land where the wild flowers grow
Near, near at hand if by train you go
Metro-land, Metro-land
Meadows sweet have a golden glow
Hills are green as the vales below
In Metro-land, Metroland . . .

(Jackson, 1986, p. 350).

Another, more colourful account attributes its origins to the fevered imagination of James Garland, a copy-writer in the Met's publicity department. While ill in bed with influenza in 1915 the word suddenly popped into his brain, whereupon he leaped out of bed dancing with excitement at his breakthrough (*ibid*, p. 239). Either version reminds us that, influenced as it might have been by ideas and practices drawn from American cities, the Metropolitan Railway also remained firmly English.

Suburban Marketing by Mainline Railways

As in the United States, the great improvements in urban public transport of the late nineteenth and early twentieth centuries had a marked effect on the policies of the mainline railways. During the later nineteenth century there had been a growing awareness on the part of at least some companies of the great potential of suburban traffic, notably the Great Eastern in London, the Lancashire and Yorkshire around Manchester and Liverpool and the North Eastern on Tyneside (Byatt, 1979, pp. 58–61). The Great Eastern particularly had developed a strategy based on very low fares which had encouraged a marked outward spread in those parts of London where its services operated (Barker and Robbins, 1963, pp. 214–219; Jackson, 1991, pp. 1–2). But such a considered strategy was unusual. In most cases, suburban traffic was an afterthought, fitted rather uneasily into a railway system that was designed for longer distance services. Track and terminal congestion were often serious problems. Despite such problems, however, the later nineteenth century brought substantial growth in the amount of suburban traffic carried by the railways in London and the other great cities of Britain.

The appearance of electric tramways and other transport innovations began seriously to erode the railways' suburban traffic. Because electric traction allowed rapid acceleration, much more frequent stops were possible than with steam power. In the six years to 1909 five railways saw their annual London suburban passenger numbers fall by 54 million, not far short of a third of the 1903 total (Byatt, 1979, p. 65). And the problems were similar elsewhere. The responses of the railway companies varied. Some, such as the North Eastern Railway and the Lancashire and Yorkshire, responded promptly with electrification, offering reduced operating costs and faster services. A few of the London railways also pursued this option, if more slowly. The main pioneers were those serving southern suburban districts, led by the London, Brighton and South Coast Railway (LBSCR).

Yet most railways were unwilling or unable to invest in electrification. Even the Great Eastern, which had come nearest to pursuing a genuine suburban development strategy in the late nineteenth century, had to allow the opportunity to pass. (It did, however, experiment unproductively with the 'Decapod', a mammoth steam locomotive intended to speed up suburban services but largely unusable because of the damage it inflicted on track and bridges (Barker and Robbins, 1974, p. 161).) Most of the other mainline railways were obliged, at best, to defer electrification. Instead they made relatively minor improvements to track, stations and services. A few also added new routes. What they also did, however, was to begin the systematic marketing of their suburban districts, particularly those farther out which were less vulnerable to tram, bus or tube competition.

The most typical publicity for these marketing drives was the promotional booklet, similar to UERL's *Healthy Homes* and the Metropolitan's *Country Homes*. Earliest in the field was the Great Northern Railway (GNR, 1906), with a 1906 92-page brochure, *Where to Live: Illustrated Guide to Some of London's Choicest Suburbs*, promoting the 'Northern Heights'. Paralleling this an inquiry bureau was opened to give advice about homefinding on the GNR. The Great Central's more general *Guide to Holiday Resorts and London's Rural Retreats* was published as a free publication in 1908 while the Great Eastern's *By Forest and Countryside* was in its second edition by 1911. In the few years before 1914 similar publications were issued by the London and North Western Railway (*North Western Country Homes*), the LBSCR (*By Surrey Lanes to Sussex Shores*), and the London and South Western Railway (*Homes in the South Western Suburbs*) (Jackson, 1991, p. 159).

Other publicity methods were also used. When its new line to Cuffley was opened in 1910 the GNR co-operated with the owners of the Cuffley Garden Estate in a poster campaign (Barker and Robbins, 1974, p. 158; Levet and Montry, 1992, p. 174). The Great Eastern co-operated similarly with the development of Harlow Garden Village. The Great Central, the least established of the mainline London railways, worked hardest to build up its traffic with a campaign that involved posters and the regular magazine, *The Homestead*, issued jointly with the Metropolitan (Cole and Durack, 1990, pp. 19–20). This last approach was also followed by the Great Western Railway (GWR) which otherwise was probably least interested in the development of suburban traffic. From 1912–4 it issued a free quarterly publication *Homes for All: London's Western Borderlands* from 1912–14 (PRO RAIL 268/206; Wilson, 1987, p. 151).

London represented much the largest suburban market, for which there was greatest competition. It was natural therefore that most efforts were concentrated there. Some railways also issued comparable publications for the main provincial cities they served, however. The GWR, for example, began a short-lived Birmingham edition of *Homes for All* in 1913, sold for a penny and subtitled *Birmingham's Beautiful Borderlands* (Wilson, 1987, pp. 126, 151–152; Cherry, 1994, p. 117). Promotional brochures were more typical however, such as the LNWR's *Manchester and Where to Live on the London and North Western Railway* (PRO RAIL 410/1998). Generally though such efforts were on a much smaller scale than around the capital.

Early Advertising by Developers

Reviewing the pre-1914 efforts to sell English suburbs, it is striking how much more than in the

United States these were dominated by the efforts of insecure railway companies. Individual developers and house agents did advertise their houses, of course, but on a much smaller scale than in American cities. Before the interwar years there were no London developers who even began to approach the size of Gross's business, so that the absence of comparable developer place advertising is not surprising. And when most suburbanites were still renting, perhaps for only a comparatively short period, it was simply not worth incurring the expense of brochures. Already, by the 1890s, some of the larger and more ambitious building societies (such as the Halifax), were beginning to advertise owner occupation as a concept (Hobson, 1953, pp. 138–143). Such efforts had no direct links to specific developments, but already some of the generic characteristics of suburban living were being endorsed and linked with home ownership. Their main impact was to come later, however, in the more favourable circumstances of the interwar years.

Promotional brochures for individual estates, especially those featuring more expensive houses, were certainly becoming more common by the early twentieth century (e.g. CPE, 1908; SE, nd c1912). These gave a better sense of the new suburbs as places. But such efforts, handed out to prospective purchasers, were still far from being usual, especially for cheaper properties. Most individual developers placed their promotional advertising as whole or part page panels in railway brochures of the kind we have been describing or, increasingly, in newspapers. Local newspapers in developing districts often included extensive descriptions of new building estates, knowing that such attention would attract advertising from the developers. Several of the main London evening newspapers had also begun to adopt similar tactics by about 1910.

From about 1900 specialist commercial publications also began to appear, with titles like *The Househunter's ABC* (nd c1910), *The Housefinder* (1905) or *The Standard Househunter's Guide to London* (1908). Usually short-lived,

these and many others like them provided a showcase for (and were financed by) suburban home advertisements. In some cases these specialist publishers, such as the Homeland Association or Acme Engraving, put together brochures for the railways. By about 1910 an organization called the Residential Centres Bureau had also identified a market niche for a series of residential handbooks for particular towns, largely outside London. These brochures, produced by the well known Cheltenham firm of guide publishers, E. J. Burrows, included descriptive sections about amenities, schools, local services etc. To judge by a surviving example for Cardiff, the handbooks were financed by local tradesmen advertising and the sponsorship of a local estate agent, who would distribute them free to clients (RCB, nd c1910).

On the whole though, the efforts of developers and house agents to market the suburbs remained rather limited in scope. Even when developers did produce publicity material, the emphasis was normally very narrowly on the house rather than the place as a wider entity. With the partial exception of some of the commercial publishers, their efforts usually showed little aesthetic distinction. We may make a contrast here not only with the coloured pictorial posters of the London Underground and some of the railways but also with those widely used by Parisian suburban promoters by the early twentieth century (Levet and Montry, 1992). The typical French poster featured general views of the land to be sold, usually near a suburban railway station, with an inset plan showing the individual *lotissements*. The detail suggests they were normally commissioned by property agents from commercial printers specializing in pictorial posters. Given the prominence of the railways in many such efforts, it seems likely they would have been displayed on railway premises, probably at favourable rates.

This distinctive feature of Parisian suburban advertising should certainly not be taken to signify a more advanced property development industry than in London or Chicago. Clearly many of the same things were occurring in all three areas as suburban railways were opening up peripheral land. Yet the Parisian marketing emphasis remained exclusively on the sale of building lots. The concept of developers speculatively building entire estates of houses, increasingly apparent in both the United States and Britain by the early twentieth century, seems to have been absent from Paris. It seems more likely that this stylish Parisian way of selling suburbia reflected the highly developed state of French poster art, with many specialist commercial publishers. Accordingly, the poster was never as widely used by developers in Britain or the United States. In the interwar years there was obviously some greater use of it (Howkins, 1938, p. 248), yet developers never became major patrons and few examples have survived.

The Heyday of Metro-Land

Mass suburbanization finally arrived in Britain in the interwar years (Jackson, 1991; Richardson and Aldcroft, 1968). As never before, or since, the green fields around London and the other cities were converted into suburban homes. In the way that Yerkes and the Americans had always predicted, transport proved to be a key part of the equation. Yet other changes proved at least as significant. Low interest rates, low land and materials costs combined with high real incomes and a widening social desire for owner occupation to create a huge private building boom (Swenarton and Taylor, 1985). Government also played a key role by providing the loans to extend or electrify suburban rail systems around London. (Private capital remained justifiably worried about the profitability of such investments.)

In addition government also primed the pump, especially in the provincial cities, with extensive housing subsidies. This meant that over 30 per cent of the houses built between the wars were built outside the market system, by local councils (who often 'marketed' them as heroic municipal

achievements in commemorative civic booklets) (e.g. LCC, 1937; Liverpool, 1937; Manzoni, 1939). Yet this action also created great confidence in the building industry and accustomed many housebuilders to operate on a large scale. Some began to use this experience in developing large areas of speculative housing. They also created much more sophisticated marketing machines, so that by the 1930s it was they, rather than the railways, who were dominating the selling of the suburbs.

The only railway which managed also to be a suburban developer was, of course, the Metropolitan. After war ended the Company moved quickly to revive the suburban strategy it had been evolving in the last years before 1914. The wartime advertising of Metro-Land had helped establish the attractiveness of the country districts to the north-west of London. Now, with an obvious pent-up demand for new houses after the war, the Company was anxious to convert this into an active house development programme, taking advantage of its special powers in respect of surplus lands. Even before 1914 new sites were being prepared with this in mind.

There was, though, a niggling doubt that if the company made too free in using these unique powers there might be political objections. It was therefore finally decided in late 1918 to create a special organization, broadly along the lines that Selbie, the General Manager, had suggested in 1912–13 (GLRO MET 1/34: 21.11.18; 27.3.19). Although it was originally hoped that the new agency might be no more than a dependent adjunct of the railway company, legal advice was against this (GLRO MET 10/756, 1.6.19). Instead the development organization was to be made more independent of the railway company but with some directors and technical staff in common. It would therefore benefit by advance knowledge of the Metropolitan's intentions (and the reverse would also be true). There would also be sharing of the Railway's publicity and other expertise and by favourable treatment in the placing of its advertising. Most important of all, its close association with the railway was deliberately made clear in the very name adopted, Metropolitan Railway Country Estates Ltd (MRCE). This assured immediate public and business confidence in the new company.

MRCE was actually formed in June 1919 though a temporary syndicate had already been buying land on its behalf over the preceding months (GLRO MET 10/152, 15.6.20; 17.6.20). It began life with three estates at Neasden, Chalk Hill and Rickmansworth Park, totalling over 600 acres. More sites were acquired over the next few years in Hillingdon, Ruislip, Eastcote, Harrow and Amersham. Meanwhile the older Surplus Lands Committee of the Metropolitan Railway and the Wembley Park Company, in which the Committee held shares, also continued their operations (MR, 1923, pp. 58–60). Overall, it gave the Metropolitan Railway an important and direct involvement in the actual building of the suburban areas along its country lines.

The principal role of MRCE and the other development ventures of the Metropolitan Railway was to prepare estates for building, planning layouts and subdividing the land into individual building plots. MRCE would also build houses itself either at the request of individuals buying plots or where there would otherwise be little interest. This was the case in Neasden, rather unpromisingly located in a very industrial district. Here MRCE felt it necessary in 1921 to prime the pump by building a substantial batch of houses, initiating what became Kingsbury Garden Village (GLRO MET 10/327). Elsewhere, where the estates were aimed much farther upmarket, such expedients were often unnecessary. Building houses for individuals and the need to build shops meant, though, that by the end of 1928, MRCE had itself built over 800 houses and shops (GLRO MET 1/115, 20.12.28). Increasingly however, the pattern was that builders would take over sizeable sections of these estates especially those, like Harrow Garden Village, which were aimed at the middle of the market (e.g. MR, 1932, pp. 100–101, 118–123).

Marketing Metro-Land

Though demand proved to be brisk what was, by British standards, a huge marketing campaign accompanied these efforts. The concept of Metro-Land was relaunched in 1920 with a new version of the *Metro-Land* booklet, geared now much more to the concerns of home seekers (MR, 1920). A special song, 'My Little Metro-Land Home', was also commissioned (Jackson, 1986, p. 243). Free train tickets were offered to home buyers. The following year, the Metropolitan Railway arranged a special press tour of Metro-Land with a commemorative booklet that carefully argued the social and economic case for railways having such special powers (MR, 1921). Publicity and advertising for the new venture was intensive. The Railway estimated that by the late 1920s it was contributing annually about a £1000 worth of free press advertising to MRCE (GLRO MET 1/116: 24.7.30). It was also given free access to advertising sites on the Railway. And there were few examples of Metropolitan publicity that did not, in some way, also advertise MRCE. Route maps typically included panels about the country estates. At times even the Company's mail was sent out in envelopes that bore an advertising message for house hunters (GLRO MET 4/13: 70).

The showpiece of all this publicity was the annual publication *Metro-Land*, which assumed its more familiar role as a marketing tool for suburban homes in 1920. As such, it was a promotional publication of uniquely high quality, well written (albeit in a highly romanticized style) and with fine illustrations, several in colour. Sold for a token charge, it gave general descriptions of the areas served, the estates being developed by MRCE, the Surplus Lands Committee and other developers. It also included a large advertising section. It was supplemented by other slighter publications that gave more specific details of actual houses and individual estates.

There were also specific marketing drives to promote particular estates. The Kingsbury Garden Village proved especially worrying in the early years, prompting the railway to bring in special advertising at the nearest station (GLRO MET 10/327, 19.8.21). Wembley Park, something of a millstone around the Metropolitan's neck, finally took off when it was chosen as the site for the British Empire Exhibition in 1924. It is unclear how the site came to be chosen, though it provided a huge marketing opportunity (Jackson, 1986, pp. 244–245; GLRO MET 1/38, 25.6.25). The Exhibition was the dominating theme of that year's issue of *Metro-Land* (MR, 1924). There were, however, some limits to the Metropolitan's willingness to assist MRCE. In 1930, for example, it refused to offer special fare discounts on one, rather distant, estate (GLRO MET 1/30: 24.7.30).

Nor were its concerns limited solely to its own development agencies. The Railway continued to treat with other developers in their various requests for new stations, better services etc (e.g. GLRO MET 10/89; GLRO MET 10/339). Its unique experience in the suburban development business allowed it sometimes to be rather more acute in such dealings than perhaps would otherwise have been the case. But it maintained extremely detailed information on the development process in its areas. And, of course, all the developments in the Metropolitan area derived some benefit from its marketing efforts. For its part the Metropolitan regarded the strategy as successful, showing huge increases in its traffic receipts as population grew (GLRO MET 10/712). Dividends also increased during the 1920s, averaging about 4 per cent during the mid and later 1920s. MRCE dividends averaged about 6 per cent over the same period and rose even higher at the start of the 1930s (Jackson, 1986, pp. 248, 250).

But the conscious Metro-Land strategy did not last much longer. In 1933 the Metropolitan Railway finally joined most of the other parts of the capital's public transport in the new publicly-owned London Passenger Transport Board (LPTB). MRCE continued, but its direct link with the transport operator was severed. The publication of *Metro-Land* ceased after 1932 and

with it ended one of the most famous ever place selling campaigns.

The Underground and the Southern Railway

It was the Underground group, already the dominant player in London's transport, which shaped LPTB's policy under the joint leadership of Lord Ashfield (the ennobled Albert Stanley) and Frank Pick. Yet the end of *Metro-Land* proved to be more than just a loss of the Metropolitan's specific identity. Overt suburban marketing generally seemed to be slipping back from the high level of the 1920s and early 1930s. During these years the Underground had been very active in marketing the suburban areas along its routes, even without the benefit of the Metropolitan's special arrangements. Major extensions, on a much larger scale than anything the Metropolitan achieved, were opened during this period. The Yerkes strategy lived on, most notably in one of the earliest interwar extensions into the green fields of Edgware. This, it will be recalled, had been Yerkes's ultimate objective when he secured the Golders Green extension. But the proposal, though approved, had stalled for lack of funds. It was only government financial assistance which allowed it to proceed in the early 1920s.

The Underground was anxious to ensure the new extension, its boldest such venture to date, succeeded. Heavy advertising, urging people to move to Edgware, began appearing as the line opened in 1924 (Jackson, 1991, pp. 204–214). Yet history repeated itself and early traffic receipts were disappointing. The marketing of Edgware and other places along the line had to be intensified over the succeeding years. More posters and newspaper advertisements were apparently produced by the Underground group for Edgware than for any other suburban residential area between the wars. Their efforts were soon joined by local builders and estate agents who, in 1927, formed an Edgware Publicity Association. Morden, terminus of the second major extension, opened in 1926, warranted a few posters and other advertisements. Traffic there soon exceeded expectations, however, allowing marketing efforts to be diminished. Hendon, Sudbury, Osterley, Hounslow, Stanmore and other areas were also promoted to some extent. But the volume of surviving material for Edgware is far greater than any of these. During 1924–29, by which time traffic was looking a great deal healthier, the travelling and newspaper reading public of London would have found it difficult to avoid the Underground's urgings in regard to this new suburb.

Many of the newly consolidated mainline railway companies showed somewhat less interest in London suburban traffic than their pre-decessors had done before 1914. In effect, they realized that, without major investment, it was a competitive struggle with other transport media that they could not win. The London, Midland and Scottish was a partial exception to this, able to undertake a modest scheme of suburban electrification. After a long gap it issued a new residential handbook in 1929, the first since before reorganization, to promote the areas on its suburban routes (PRO RAIL 429/17).

But the only real exception was the Southern Railway which positively threw itself into the development of its suburban traffic. Building on the early work of its predecessors, especially the London and South Western Railway, whose management (and publicity machine) dominated the new company, it embarked on an intensive programme of electrification (PRO ZPER 12/16A, pp. 205, 322). The first phases of the SR's new schemes were opened in 1925 (Jackson, 1991, pp. 184–190). By 1939 the electrified routes extended well beyond the area conventionally understood as Greater London, including much of Kent, Sussex, Surrey and Hampshire. Many of these lines were electrified because of their evident promise for commuter traffic. Brighton, for example, already had 2,700 daily season ticket holders travellers in 1929, when the deci-sion to electrify was announced (PRO ZPER 12/7, p. 410). Yet the new investment allowed much greater growth in such traffic.

Marketing and publicity played a key role in developing this new suburban business. The way in which this was done showed that British railway managers still valued American thinking (Cole and Durack, 1992, p. 10). Thus it was Lord Ashfield, Chairman of the Underground group, who advised the SR about how to improve its publicity effort. More specifically, it was Ashfield's recommendation that led to the appointment of John Elliot, a journalist who had worked in New York, to head the SR's publicity drive in 1925. (In passing, we may note this friendly gesture as a symptom of the informal non-competition pact that evolved between the Underground and the SR after 1923. The direct competition represented by the Underground's Morden extension was not repeated.) Much of Elliot's work involved building up the image of the SR as a great modern undertaking extending rapid transit through southern England, very much on the pattern of the Underground. As well as the public and press relations activity in which Elliot excelled, he also energized the SR's advertising work.

A major campaign to promote suburban development along the Southern's routes was launched in 1926 (PRO ZPER 12/5, pp. 101–102). Posters appeared urging the public to 'Live in Surrey, Free from Worry' and 'Live in Kent and Be Content' while advertising in London and local newspapers repeated and reinforced these slogans. Meanwhile, following the best public relations practice, Elliot ensured that the same newspapers included regular news items and comment about the improved services and their impact. The advertising slogans themselves became the subject of humorous press comment and variants for other counties were suggested, all of which served to embed the message still further in public consciousness. The detailed end of the campaign was sustained by a new residential handbook, *The Country at London's Door*. The SR was soon congratulating itself with the success of the campaign. 'There is not the slightest doubt' it commented in April 1927 'that through this advertising scheme many new residents have been, and are being, attracted to Southern territory' (PRO ZPER 12/5, p. 102).

These successes and the continued investment in suburban services ensured a continuing role for such marketing efforts. The residential handbook was regularly re-issued, under a variety of titles, including *Country Homes at London's Door* (PRO RAIL 652/29). During the 1930s it became known simply as *Southern Homes* (PRO RAIL 652/32). Though it lacked much of the visual and literary charms of *Metro-Land*, the SR's residential handbook was the clear market leader and, at over 350 pages, always much larger than any rival publication.

Other promotional initiatives followed in the 1930s. The extension of electrification to Brighton and Hove, for example, saw a special drive to encourage new residents. A booklet, *Live in Brighton or Hove*, was issued jointly with the local councils and chamber of commerce (Mais, nd *c*1933). It was written by the well known travel writer S. P. B. Mais. (As well as tourist material for the GWR, he also authored *Southern Schools*, another regular SR tract aimed at the suburban middle classes (PRO RAIL 652/33).) A little later, in December 1934, the SR decided to create a new home finding service in its public relations office (PRO 645/26, 20.12.34, Minute 577). Intended to encourage new housing developments, the new section gave out information about housing, local rates, train services, fares etc, though stopped short of actually making itself an estate agency.

Overall, the suburban development strategy paid much bigger dividends for the SR than for any other British railway. The comparative absence of freight traffic on the SR and the strength of off peak demand made electrification (by a comparatively cheap system) a very attractive option indeed. The pay back on the investment (16 per cent by 1938) was sizeable, especially by contemporary railway standards. Even without direct appropriation of land development profits, the Yerkes strategy seemed to be paying real dividends.

The Growing Marketing Role of Developers

Meanwhile, as we have mentioned, there was a noticeable slackening in suburban residential marketing by Yerkes's natural heirs at the LPTB from 1933. The tube extension to Cockfosters, opened in 1933, was accompanied by little of the explicit residential exhortations that had been apparent at Edgware. Newspaper campaigns by the LPTB overtly encouraging the public to live in suburban areas continued for a while in 1933 (apparently in space long booked by the Metropolitan Railway) but soon lost momentum. In part this probably reflects the growing circumspection of what had now become a major publicly owned body. By this time there were growing arguments (for example, by the Greater London Regional Planning Committee) against indiscriminate suburban sprawl (Miller, 1992, pp. 189–209).

Pick himself, a resident of Hampstead Garden Suburb, was somewhat dismayed at the mediocre quality of much suburban development (Barman, 1979, pp. 244–250). More generally, the LPTB was doubtless anxious to avoid being too closely identified with what might easily be seen as a failed solution. These changes reflected a growing appreciation within LPTB of some of the most serious limitations of the Yerkes strategy, not least the almost inherent tendency to require heavy investment to cope with peak commuter flows between home and work. Situations like that of the SR, with its comparatively even loads were unusual.

But neither should we overemphasize these shifts. Advertising might be becoming more muted on the matter of encouraging suburban development. Yet the momentum of policy was such that a new and ambitious programme of suburban tube extensions was approved in 1935 (Barker and Robbins, 1974). Moreover, it was quite possible for the LPTB to have its cake and eat it because by the 1930s housebuilding boom the developers themselves were now assuming the main role in the selling of suburbia. The exact marketing equivalents of S.E. Gross had finally appeared in London.

The main source of the change was simply that housebuilders were now operating on a larger scale. The roles of housebuilder and developer, already converging, had become increasingly united by the interwar years. Hitherto the usual practice had been that builders would take over a few plots of an estate being promoted by a developer or would build individual houses to order. By the 1930s, however, a growing number of larger housebuilders were undertaking the whole development and building process themselves. Large estates were now being developed and built speculatively in this way,

Such moves towards mass production of houses made essential a parallel marketing operation that would bring forward occupiers. Moreover these houses, with few exceptions, were being built for sale, to a new and rapidly widening class of owner occupiers. The tenure shift to owner occupation put a further premium on marketing effort. It meant that the immediate value of the transaction between the provider of the house and the new resident was much greater than under renting, a major spur to active marketing approaches. Moreover, the sale market for houses was growing so much that advertising and other publicity were important simply to give product information to the new owner occupiers.

Marketing Methods

The earlier marketing efforts by building societies to establish the concept of mortgaged-owner occupation were also intensified during the 1930s (Gold and Gold, 1990, 1994). Posters, newspaper advertising and booklets were widely deployed by the larger and more ambitious societies. Much more than ever before, the tenure form of owner occupation and the environmental form of the new low density interwar suburb were now being equated in building society advertising. (We will say more about this message in the next chapter.)

None of this advertising referred explicitly to specific suburban places. But the very close alliances with individual building societies that developers were typically forming in the 1930s (notably the 'builder's pool' system) meant that such generic marketing of suburbia also had a more specific impact on particular places (Jackson, 1991, pp. 156–158).

It was, though, the bigger builder-developers, especially those operating on the largest scale like New Ideal Homesteads, Laings, Taylor Woodrow, Costain, Wates, Wimpey, and Davis, who were increasingly taking the lead roles in selling suburbia by the 1930s (*ibid*, pp. 64–73). The same methods which had been applied before 1914 were again deployed as business picked up in the 1920s. Yet the intensity of this promotional effort increased dramatically. All except the smallest developers, building only a few houses, now tended to control their own marketing and sales efforts, rather than relying on estate agents, as had been more common before 1914.

Brochures, confined largely to the smarter developments in pre-war days, now became practically universal for schemes of any size or where developers were building on more than one site. Familiar and basic promotional methods like the site noticeboard were typically enlarged and embellished (Howkins, 1938, p. 248). Wates, for example, created great advertising archways at the entrances to some of their schemes (Weightman and Humphries, 1984, p. 113) Newspaper advertising was also used ever more intensively. The number of commercial publications designed as showcases for developers' advertising proliferated. The early 1930s, for example, saw the appearance of *MAP Magazine* (Mainly about Property) and the derivatively titled *Houseland Gazette*.

The ephemeral nature of advertising and the comparatively short lives of many building firms mean that it is extremely difficult to build up a clear picture of how advertising and marketing efforts were organized. The larger developers at least were increasingly retaining specialist consultants to prepare their advertising and publicity material in a consistent and effective way. In the early 1930s, for example, John Laing began housebuilding on a large scale in the London suburbs. His earliest schemes, at Colindale and Golders Green, were marketed under the 'Little Palaces' slogan (Laing, nd c1930a; c1930b). At this stage it was Laing himself and his sales manager, Edwin Penney, who devised these slogans and put together the company's publicity (Coad, 1979, pp. 103–104). Later, however, Penney established his own advertising agency, specializing in creating advertising material for building estates. Whether he worked for other firms is not known, but his agency continued to play an important role in Laing's publicity, apparently originating most, perhaps all, of later advertising.

Spending by developers on advertising and publicity was often heavy. Jackson records one case of a bankrupt builder who spent £20,000 promoting an estate of 320 houses, equivalent to over £60 each for houses selling for less than £500 (Jackson, 1991, pp. 163–166). Howkins, author of the standard interwar handbook on estate development, felt that even half that figure was much too high, recommending only £5 per £1000 dwelling (Howkins, 1938, pp. 227, 248). It is difficult to believe that many developers followed this cautionary advice. The sheer volume and intensity of their newspaper advertising alone would have been extremely costly for large developers. John Laing routinely advertised in national newspapers such as the *Daily Express*, *Daily Telegraph*, *Daily Mail* and the *News Chronicle*, as well many London and suburban newspapers in the areas where they were building.

Promotional brochures were another large expense, particularly as production standards and the search for novelty increased. In a few cases, for example that for Goodwin's Hounslow West Estate (Goodwin, nd c1932), the cost was offset by advertising contributions from local tradesmen. Yet the bigger developers tended to be more restrained in drawing on such contributions.

They were more concerned to foster positive impressions of their estates with careful design and, increasingly, colour. Novelty publicity was used by some developers. One rather grandiosely titled example was the 'Davis Mystic Oracle', promising to solve the homeseeker's problems (Davis Estates, nd c1936). It was actually a card folder fitted with a movable dial that identified questions. When the folder was closed, magnetism ensured the oracle identified the correct answer by means of a metal arrow on the cover. The answer always, of course, involved a Davis home. S.E. Gross would doubtless have loved it. Thematic publicity, sometimes reminiscent of some of Gross's pioneering material, was also used. Laing (nd c1937a), for example, had one pamphlet produced *From a Woman's Point of View*.

There was much else to the selling of the suburbs besides printed advertising material (Jackson, 1991, pp. 162–165). As well as site sales offices (and prominent sign boards) several of the main builders set up premises at strategic points, usually either at or near major railway terminals. Laing built a show house adjoining Kings Cross; Davis Estates one adjoining Charing Cross. New Ideal Homesteads had a kiosk in Waterloo. Show houses on major West End streets or in actual stores were also common. Most developers gave out free travel vouchers to view houses, occasionally even free season tickets for the initial period of occupancy. Cars were also often used to take prospective purchasers to an estate.

Very much in the manner of Gross himself, some developers organized free excursions to their estates, usually with some form of refreshment provided. The value of free publicity was also well understood, as when a government minister visited an estate or opened a new sales office (e.g. Laing Press Cuttings, 11/36, 5/37). A particularly common promotional device was the organization of bonfires and firework displays open to the public. These allowed the disposal of pre-existing trees and bushes on the site before building started and were usually worth a story in the local newspaper. In one case Laing drew large crowds when they actually burned down an old building as part of one display.

The encouragements to buy continued right up to the point of sale. Financial incentives and gifts were very common. Developers at the lower end of the market, like New Ideal Homesteads, used the builders pool system to cut back the required deposit almost to nothing. The same developers also offered an automatic insurance scheme that would avoid mortgage payment defaults and loss of the house if the mortgagee became unemployed (Barrett and Phillips, 1988, p. 21). Morrells promised free removals. Free gifts of domestic equipment were also common. Davis were even offering free telephone connection by 1936. Laing, who aimed higher up the market and stressed the higher quality of their houses, avoided such devices (Parfitt, 1979). The firm also insisted on a relatively large deposit, at least £50, though they offered financial rewards to existing occupants who introduced new purchasers (Laing, 1935a).

All the larger developers and many smaller ones were then working hard to foster a comprehensive marketing approach. Publicity materials, incentives and the personal interaction with the potential purchaser were dovetailed as part of a total strategy. Exhibitions, particularly the *Daily Mail* Ideal Home Exhibition held annually at the Earl's Court Olympia, provided the opportunity for intensive sales campaign (e.g. Laing, 1935b). Yet even on a more day to day basis, developers in the London suburbs in these peak years of the 1930s private housing boom were running residential marketing and sales operations that were far more systematically organized than any previously seen in Britain. As the building boom spread throughout the country during the middle and later years of the decade, so spread many of these same marketing ideas. As yet though, few of the biggest builders built private estates very far from London, so that the typical scale of building and marketing activity, even in a major city like Birmingham, remained significantly smaller than around the capital (Cherry, 1994, pp. 117–118).

CONCLUSIONS

The outbreak of war in 1939 brought this golden age of British suburban development to an abrupt end. Eventually, after fifteen years of war and austerity, private housebuilding re-emerged as a significant force, but it was never again as freely undertaken as it had been before 1939. The 1930s remain the all time peak for private house completions, a reflection of a uniquely favourable conjunction of circumstances on both the supply and demand sides. Marketing, whether undertaken by the development industry or the public transport operators, played an important part in awakening and informing the widening potential demand for suburban living.

This, of course, was exactly what the pioneer of suburban place marketing, Samuel Eberly Gross, had done with such innovation and panache

half a century earlier. He managed to persuade people of quite modest means, including many recent immigrants, that they really could afford a suburban home of their own and travel to their work on street cars or railroads. In Britain, as we have seen, the market for suburban owner occupation was altogether less well developed at this time. The practices of Gross and his imitators spread to Britain in the wake of the technology of electric traction. Not surprisingly, therefore, the initial efforts to market the suburbs in Britain were dominated by the providers of public transport. Faced with disappointing traffic receipts arising from an overprovision of facilities for urban-suburban movement, a marketing campaign to stimulate building development was entirely to be expected. Eventually, when Britain's mass suburban revolution finally began to happen, the developers themselves began to dominate suburban marketing, more in the manner of Gross himself. We must now look at the nature of what was being sold by these marketing efforts.

6

REALM OF ROMANCE

More than any other form of place marketing, the selling of the suburb touched the very soul of popular aspiration. Although the intent was almost completely mercenary, to achieve a sale, the suburban promotional message spoke of much more than a material or functional notion of house or neighbourhood. Woven into the mundane detail of prices, number of bedrooms and train services was an altogether more poetic vision of how a widening section of the population thought they wanted to live. At best, the words of the copywriter or the images of the advertising artist or designer expressed that vision with a far greater clarity than that which existed in the minds of the recipients. They charged the material dimension of selling houses with deep and powerful meanings that reached beyond the usual rational calculations of cost, convenience and value for money.

What came through was the idea of home as an emotional construct, imbued with idealized notions of family life and of relationships both to nature and a wider community. Father, mother and children each had their allotted roles in this scheme of things. Together they were shielded from the dark threats and uncertainties of city and wider world by an evocation of nature and the security conferred by ownership. Poverty, disease, squalor and, not least, all the unfortunate people whose lives were blighted by these evils, could be safely forgotten. There were many comforting allusions to a romantic, pre-industrial notion of the home, framed by trees and gilded by nature.

In this chapter, we explore the promotional imagery of the suburb as it became a mass phenomenon in the late nineteenth and early twentieth centuries. As in chapter 4, the first concern is to provide a general review of the language and visual devices used to construct the promotional imagery. The second stage then involves exploring key aspects of the marketing message. Finally, we add a more contemporary dimension to the discussion, considering how the practice of suburban marketing has fared in more recent times.

THE PROMOTED IMAGE OF THE SUBURB

Constructing the Advertising Message

Advertising, as we have seen, was an integral component of the selling of suburbia. As with other forms of promotional publicity, the essence of the message usually derived from a combination of slogans, key words and visual images.

Quite how the message was constructed depended substantially on who was actually doing the advertising and what exactly they were selling. There were, for instance, likely to be inherent differences in the kind of publicity produced by a developer who was simply trying to sell house sites and the (increasingly common) builder-developer selling actual houses. The commuter rail operator, concerned with the promotion of a whole district, was inherently freer in the creation of an advertising message compared to either kind of developer. Even freer was the building society, concerned only to market a generic concept of the suburb, an idealized setting for its own specific aim of promoting owner occupation.

The most straightforward advertising device was the subdivision or estate map, used mainly when individual house sites were being sold. It was capable of very cheap and crude production in newspapers or on handbills, yet more sophisticated effects were possible with various kinds of embellishment or decoration. Gross, for example, added decorative detail to many of his Chicago subdivision plan advertisements. Thus his two Under the Linden subdivisions were, respectively, framed with trees and highlighted with a target roundel and arrow which has found its mark. Oak Park was similarly emphasized by having its plan framed within a star (Gross, 1891, pp. 52, 54, 58).

In other cases the plan might take the form of an aerial perspective view, allowing something of the wider setting to be shown. This approach was commonly used in plans for Parisian suburban *lotissements* from about 1900 (Levet and de Montry, 1992). Occasionally such plans might be combined with a pictorial illustration or a series of vignettes. These could be rather reminiscent of resort posters of the time, not least in their cluttered layout. Harlow Garden Village in Essex, for example, was promoted this way in a poster displayed on the Great Eastern Railway *c*1910, combining a location map and estate plan with scenes of various rural pursuits.

Pictorial images, used either alone or in conjunction with other representational methods, were another major way in which the promotional message could be disseminated. Builder-developers naturally wished to draw the main attention to their houses. Early examples in Edwardian Britain often took the form of simple record photographs of recently completed houses, the raw lines of their newness as yet unsoftened

by human occupance and horticultural efforts (e.g. Acme, 1910, pp. 28, 55, 60). The accompanying words often stressed solidity, value for money and other practical details.

For the small local builder, such a straightforward and unpretentious approach had its merits. For more ambitious developers who did a lot of advertising it was severely limited and could soon become tedious. In Chicago, S. E. Gross, in the 1880s, had recognized the need to develop an advertising repertoire wider than mere subdivision plans. Thus his booklets *The House that Lucy Built* (Gross, 1886) and *The Home Primer* (Gross, 1888a) promoted the wider concept of working class home ownership and self improvement. Something of the same realization of the need to sell suburbia with more sophisticated messages came to all but the smallest developers in Britain during the 1930s boom (e.g. MR, 1932, pp. 118–143). By then, their houses were more often shown as artist's representations, achieving a more sympathetic effect with softer lines, better sky tones, more vegetation and, sometimes, people. The photographs in brochures tended to be more flattering general views, of well established sections.

The most artistic advertising efforts were often those of the larger building societies and, more especially, the rail operators (Gold and Gold, 1990, 1994; Green, 1990). Both were, as we have noted, free of the very specific marketing role of individual developers. Instead they could promote more of the intrinsic virtues of suburban living with less pressure for literal representation. There was, for example, no necessity even to depict new housing. It was easier therefore to suggest more directly the abstract social concepts, such as domestic bliss or the rural idyll, the 'realm of romance' (MR, 1923, p. 9), that lay at the heart of the suburban dream. It was not so much that developers neglected these, rather that they had in their advertisements to tailor them so specifically to their own particular product that deeper meanings were sometimes partially obscured.

Yet a careful reading shows that all sellers of

Around Paris, *lotissements* were commonly advertised by posters from the late nineteenth century, typically with a site plan and general view. This example, *c*1900, also shows how, as in England, suburban development was taking its place within an agricultural terrain of villages and orchards.

suburbia consistently upheld the same core ideals and signified them in very consistent ways. This seems to have held true in the North American and English heartlands of suburban living and more traditionally urban European cultures. Throughout, however, a common promotional language and visual imagery can be decoded. In the sections that follow we explore the principal themes of this advertising language.

A Good Parcel of English Soil, Inhabited from of Old

The most deeply embedded of all the components of suburban promotional imagery was the countryside. Rustic references were pervasive in the architecture of typical suburban dwellings. As has been well shown by many other writers, the basic design conception of twentieth-century

Harlow Garden Village promoted by the Great Eastern Railway in conjunction with the developer, probably c1910. Notice the incorporation of the estate plan, the emphasis on health and the representations of rural diversions.

suburbia derived broadly from the garden city tradition, if rather freely adapted (e.g. Edwards, 1981; Oliver, Davis and Bentley, 1981). Half-timbering, leaded casement windows and other, rather eclectic, borrowings from traditional styles provided popular embellishments. The naming of developments or streets (and, as we will see, increasingly actual house types) further strength-ened such allusions. As Howkins advised (1938, p. 249):

Names which convey a pleasant suggestion either as to aspect, such as *Sunnyside*, or to sylvan beauty, as *Elms Avenue*, or to height, such as *Hill Rise* are to be preferred to others.

is for Gross, of whom Andrew reads
That, for those wishing homes he can fill all their needs,
He will build them a home on the installment plan,
For a moderate sum down, then per month what they can.

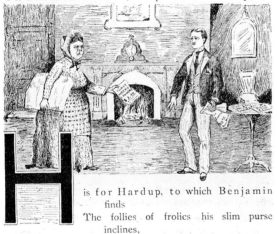

is for Hardup, to which Benjamin finds
The follies of frolics his slim purse inclines,
He's in debt to the livery, owes board-bill and laundry,
No wonder the poor fellow's in a great quandary.

The Home Primer (1888) was a charming example of the inventiveness of Gross's advertising. The contrast is between the spendthrift Benjamin, who is condemned to a miserable life of renting while the virtuous and wise Andrew resolves to save and become an owner occupier.

His list was suggestive rather than exhaustive. Key elements such as 'village', 'grove', 'park' can immediately be added to the list of names used to reinforce the sense of rurality. Yet this was not mere invention. The physical reality of the suburban product always gave at least

something that could be worked into an arcadian marketing message. Thus the very form of the garden suburb allowed great emphasis on nature and the distinctly un-urban activity of cultivation.

Whatever the arboreal realities of the residential areas into which the new suburbanite moved, the advertising images almost always showed the suburban house in a frame of leafy trees. Sometimes trees might also be depicted in blossom or bearing fruit. Gardens had typically reached a mature state, reflecting several years of occupance. Flowers were usually in full bloom. The general approach is that displayed particularly clearly in the well known 1908 Underground poster of Golders Green, showing the new Hampstead Garden Suburb. Yet, if they were rarely combined as charmingly as in this poster, the same basic elements were almost universal in suburban advertising. It was rare indeed to find a developer advertisement in interwar Britain by 1930, earlier in the United States, that did not betray at least something of such imagery.

The rural illusion was not sustained solely by botanical allusions, however. Many advertisements used birds, a particularly potent signifier of nature (and, through nesting, the concept of settling down and raising a family, to which we will return below). The Great Western Railway, for example, in a 1914 issue of *Homes for All* recommended 'the songs of the goldfinches, bullfinches and pipits' which congregated in the old pollard willows along the River Brent in Ealing, part of 'Rural London' (PRO RAIL 268/206, p. 11).

Animals and humans were also used in other ways to signify the 'natural' order of rural and, by extension, suburban life. For example, one 1910 Underground poster, used with overprinting to promote several districts, reworked the story of the town mouse and the country mouse. Now that the Underground allowed the town's pleasures to be reached easily, the life of the country mouse in the fields could be recommended. About the same time, the great English poster artist, John Hassall, juxtaposed comic characters to make the same point (Levet and de Montry, 1992, p. 174). A stout and ruddy faced farm labourer, white haired but still a picture of health, was contrasted with an anaemic and skinny office worker. The specific intention was to extol the virtues of Cuffley Garden Estate, reached by the Great Northern Railway.

Some advertisers went even further, equating suburban living with a more completely agricultural existence. Halden Estates, for example, quite seriously recommended beekeeping and poultry on their development in 1923 (GLRO MET 10/442). In other cases the references were fanciful and more symbolic, as in the enchanting Edgware 'sampler' poster designed by Helen Bryce for the Underground in 1924. Here, after planting fruit trees in their garden, the family of her story purchase poultry, ducks, a cow and a horse and 'prosper beyond all expectation'. Building society advertisers also occasionally spoke to suburban housebuyers in the visual imagery of agricultural life, as in the Halifax Building Society's well known 'Misery' leaflet of 1897 (Hobson, 1953, p. 142). It was though rare for most suburban dwellers to be allowed to indulge even the most modest of such agrarian fantasies. The keeping of poultry, for example, was often forbidden by restrictive covenant.

For some advertisers it was the historic associations of the countryside that were more significant. This was certainly the pattern of *Metro-land*, which in editorial content gave noticeably less illustrative prominence to new housing schemes than to the traditional rural scene. Historic cottage gardens, woodland or village scenes formed its staple images. The copywriters made much of the waves of colonization and settlement which had swept over the area over the centuries. In part such emphases reflected the original purposes of *Metro-land* as a recreational guide, but they were also deliberately used to shape the suburban promotional message. In 1927 (and later editions) for example, we find an explicit link:

This is a good parcel of English soil in which to build home and strike roof, inhabited from of old, as witness the lines of camps on the hill tops and the confused mounds among the woods, the great dyke which crossed it east and west, the British trackways, the Roman road aslant the eastern border, the pack-horse tracks worn deep in steep hill sides, the innumerable field-paths which mark the labourer's daily route from hamlet to farm.

The new settlement of Metro-land proceeds apace; the new colonists thrive amain. (MR, 1927, p. 30)

No other advertiser seems to have been quite so explicit in representing suburbanization as the latest wave of colonization, part of the long term historical process of settlement. Most alluded to it less directly. In 1924, for example, commuters were urged to seek a home of their own 'in the new country' opened up by the Edgware extension (Jackson, 1991, p. 204). In fact the accompanying visuals made clear that this new country was certainly not devoid of previous occupance. Yet the hint of primary colonization in the slogan offered a slightly different interpretation of the rural ideal, one that was more typical across the Atlantic.

O, When I am Safe in My Silvan Home

The much faster process of settlement in North America meant that, unlike Britain, there was no traditional, settled, countryside that was sufficiently mature to form an equivalent reference point as mass suburbanization appeared in the late nineteenth century. The twentieth century emergence of the 'Cape Cod' and the 'Colonial' standard types of suburban houses reflects something of the way this tradition was becoming established (Jackson, 1985, p. 240). There were also liberal borrowings from the imagery of the English countryside. But in North American usage, as Bunce (1994, p. 35) has noted, the word countryside is charged with far less emotional meaning than in England. Although the simple agrarian way of life represents an American ideal, this has not influenced aesthetic values to anything like the same extent as it has in England. The agrarian landscape of North America has tended to be utilitarian rather than picturesque. In

UNDERGROUND

SANCTUARY.

"Tis pleasant, through the loopholes of retreat,
To peep at such a world; to see the stir
Of the great Babel, and not feel the crowd;
To hear the roar she sends through all her gates
At a safe distance, where the dying sound
Falls a soft murmur on th' uninjured ear."
William Cowper.

J.R. & CO. LTD.

THE SOONEST REACHED AT ANY TIME

GOLDERS GREEN
(HENDON AND FINCHLEY)
A PLACE OF DELIGHTFUL PROSPECTS

Perhaps the most delightful of the early Underground posters marketing the suburbs (c1908). The emphasis on manicured nature, a social order with 'proper' allocation of domestic roles and the sense of a sanctuary from the city fully evoke the English suburban ideal, in this case of Hampstead Garden Suburb.

turn this affected early promotional imagery. Instead of promising a place within a traditional and picturesque historic landscape of farms and villages, the earlier American equivalents of *Metro-land* spoke more of establishing a more direct relationship with nature.

We can detect this sentiment, for example, in the promotional publications of the Chicago, Burlington and Quincy Railroad about the turn of the century. These suburban promotional booklets give an unmistakable impression of new suburban towns outside Chicago taking

LIVE LIKE A HEALTHY BROWN MOUSE
IN FRESH AIR AND FREEDOM.

UNDERGROUND

TOWN MOUSE:
Dear me! so you have
taken to the fields.

COUNTRY MOUSE:
The city's dust and
din one always
shuns.

TOWN MOUSE:
And city's pleasures
too?

COUNTRY MOUSE:
No, there again,
The way is easy when
one knows the runs.

LIVE IN A
NEW NEIGHBOURHOOD

24 MINUTES FROM PICCADILLY CIRCUS
INCLUDING CHANGE AT BAKER STREET

6d. PER DAY FOR SEASON TICKET

DOLLIS HILL

Another early Underground poster (1910) discussing the virtues of being able to enjoy both country living and access to the city's pleasures. The bottom section could be overprinted for different districts.

their place on a largely empty terrain. Reference to pre-existing rural settlement was lacking. It is as if the suburbanites were themselves the first wave of settlers, homesteaders setting up their homes in a new land. Even Gross, most of whose subdivisions were much closer to the city, was apt to give the same impression, of colonizing a pure and virgin land, untainted by the city. In one of his longer pamphlets he wrote of a Gross home as 'a tiny Eden in which there was no serpent's trail' (Gross, 1886. p. 9).

English (and French) promotional literature in

LIVE AT EDGWARE
and LIVE !

1925 Underground Poster taking the form of a charming embroidered sampler promoting Edgware. The emphasis on the keeping of animals is a fanciful allusion to the agrarian myth which lay at the heart of suburbia, especially in England. The references to the unhealthiness of the city are even more universal themes.

effect offered suburban encounters with a long established, slower, simpler agrarian way of life. American suburbanites were more likely to be invited themselves to become the pioneer settlers of a new land, communing directly with untamed nature (albeit with direct access to the civilized amenities of urban life). The notion was built very directly on the cultural traditions laid down by the transcendentalist movement, led by Emerson and Thoreau (Nash, 1973, pp. 84–95). The CBQRR indeed directly quoted some appropriate lines from Emerson's poetry in its promotional publicity: 'O, when I am safe in my silvan home, I mock at the pride of Greece and Rome' (CBQRR, nd c1883).

Yet we must not exaggerate the differences.

METRO-LAND
PRICE ONE PENNY

Metro-Land was the most complete evocation of the English idea of the suburbanites taking their place within a long settled countryside. This shows the cover of the 1920 edition, the first which was strongly oriented towards the marketing of suburban housing.

While the CBQRR gave prominence to Emerson, it also quoted liberally from English interpretations of the rural idyll, with lines by Keats, Bryant, Cowper and Spenser. We can also find examples of American promotional material that used an imagery that was unmistakably English, and deliberately so. Thus the Chicago and North Western Railway (and note the deliberate preference for the English form over the usual American 'Railroad') promoted the elite North Shore as a very 'English' suburban area in a series of promotional booklets. Its 1909 brochure *Beautiful Suburban Towns* (CNWR, 1909), for example, evokes a very English aspect, which would not have looked out of place in Golders Green. Others went even further. Thus the Boston

This 1891 Gross advertisement shows many dimensions of suburban promotional imagery. Notice the typical American sense of suburbanization as settling an uninhabited frontier, evident in the use of words like 'virgin soil' and 'prospecting'. The vignette of the home interior is also very typical of Gross. The father shows his interest in worldly matters by reading his newspaper. The female role is firmly domestic, signified by her needlework and children at her feet.

suburb of Felsdale (nd c1920), 'a rural community planned for modern homes of artistic harmony on the eastern slopes of Winchester Massachusetts' depicted the happy residents fox hunting, with their homes in the background.

By the time of America's 1920s housing boom, however, the more transcendental approach to suburban marketing was in any case becoming less apparent, certainly in the crowded urban regions of the East. Such was the scale of suburbanization around cities like New York, Boston or Chicago that it was simply more difficult to sustain the illusion of communing with nature. Suburban districts like Queens (New York) or Revere (Boston) were promoted with only the most token nods in the direction of trancendentalism. Queens might issue an invitation '[t]o everyone who loves the soil and grass, or who

cherishes the trees . . . ' but the promise went no further than 'neat suburban homes and gardens' (QBCC, 1920, p. 113). Nature was now much more tamed in gardens that were almost as tightly ordered as those in English marketing imagery.

Overall then, the evocation of the countryside to sell the suburb was not a single, simple message. The forces of nature were always a pervasive element in the appeal of the countryside. But they could be deployed in subtly different ways. The dominant English imagery throughout laid more emphasis on striking a bargain with nature by ordering it in ways that directly and deliberately echoed an earlier, historic agricultural way of life. It was a time-honoured existence that promised a more harmonious relationship with nature than was possible in the 'unnatural' city. The flowers, blossom and fruits cultivated in the garden, the

BEAUTIFUL SUBURBAN TOWNS

Issued by the Passenger Department of ···THE CHICAGO *and* NORTH WESTERN RAILWAY, *Chicago.*

The railroad residential handbook had become a standard promotional form by the 1880s. This example promoting suburban living around Boston dates from 1889.

foliage of the trees, the circling or nesting birds became symbols of prosperity and well being. American imagery, by contrast, especially in the early years, was more overtly transcendentalist. It suggested a more direct encounter with nature, rather than one mediated through an existing agricultural life. Yet the promise was broadly similar, if laying more emphasis on simplicity and enduring values.

Sun and Tonic Air

For the city dweller, the rustic references in suburban advertising were also intended to

An example of a more 'English' approach to suburban marketing. This residential booklet by the Chicago and North Western Railway (c1909) promoted many of the higher status Chicago suburbs. The carefully manicured garden, Arts and Crafts architecture and distant church spire are very reminiscent of Hampstead Garden Suburb or Metro-Land.

underline another, more tangible advantage. Because of their palpable connections with the countryside, the suburbs were generally reckoned much healthier than the city. Public health reformers and later the garden city, housing

Mid-1920s advertisement for a development in Revere, a suburb of Boston. Notice particularly the emphasis on elevation, dry and healthy sites, very typical of suburban advertising.

reform and town planning movements had all pressed this message from the nineteenth century (e.g. Cadbury, 1915, pp. 122–138). The sellers of the suburbs also added their powerful voices to this cause, further increasing public awareness. As in the seaside resorts, many of the healthy qualities stressed in suburban advertising rested on essentially nineteenth-century notions about the spread of diseases. Great faith attached to the value of air, partly reflecting traditional beliefs in the spread of disease by airborne miasmas. Clearly though, the ubiquitous air pollution produced by coal smoke in the densely populated and industrial parts of cities added a more obvious visible element. As such, it was regularly featured in promotional imagery, as something to avoid.

Even Gross, catering as he did for more working class suburbanites, often living close to factories, took care to stress the importance of health. His most up-market subdivision, Grossdale, was portrayed as 'high, dry, healthful

and surrounded by a handsome park, groves, river and forest . . . ' (Gross, 1891, p. 5). But the basic message of healthiness ensured by altitude, good air and good drainage was widely applied. Gross Park was similarly 'high, dry and healthful' (*ibid.*, p. 41). At Humboldt Park he guaranteed 'pure air and good health' (*ibid.*, p. 47). On the south side, Dauphin Park was 'high and undulating' with 'the purest of air' (*ibid.*, p. 23). And, despite its close proximity to the major factory district of South Chicago, Gross promised of Calumet Heights that 'no inconvenience will ever be experienced from dust, smoke and the ceaseless noise of the industries' (*ibid.*, p. 35).

Other, more up-market, American promoters of suburban living sang the same happy tune. The CBQRR spoke of

. . . the delights and benefits of a *home in a suburb*, where *pure air and water, spacious grounds, delightful drives*, and *healthful and independent living* can be had at small expense, and where children can *play*, and *grow* and *live*, comparatively free from the contagious diseases and contaminating influences of a large city. (CBQRR, nd *c*1883)

In a later booklet it promised that 'doctor's bills are lighter, because the general health of the individual is better, and the enjoyment of living is proportionately greater' (CBQRR, nd *c*1900). The pattern was repeated in the promotional publications of other railroads (e.g. CNWR, *c*1909) and other publicity material. In 1920, for example, the Chamber of Commerce of the New York Borough of Queens was offering ' . . . the tonic of ocean air, the sweep of breezes over sunlit fields, air untainted by smoke and soot . . . ' (QBCC, 1920, p. 119).

Such sentiments were readily taken up by suburban promoters in England, where early industrialization, urban growth and high urban death rates had already nurtured the idea of the unhealthy city. We have already noted how suburban life began to be advertised on the Underground under the general slogan of healthy homes. Frank Pick and the publicity department elaborated the theme in various ways. Thus a 1911 poster bore the message: 'Into the clear air and sweet sunshine at GOLDER'S GREEN out of the dull and smoky city by UNDERGROUND' (LTM, 1911, Y/1155). The illustration showed a murky central London, overhung with smoke and contrasting sharply with the luminescent and elevated countryside beyond. The theme of elevation was stressed in a 1917 poster with the recommendation 'Live on the Hills – The higher up the fresher the air', advertising the Bakerloo line extension to Watford (LTM, 1917, Y/1138).

Other rail operators were already pushing the same basic message. The language was remarkably similar to that used in seaside promotion, as discussed in chapter 4. The familiar concept of bracing air was regularly pressed into promotional service as a token of good health, by railways such as the London and North Western and the Great Northern. The latter particularly emphasized the healthiness of suburbs on the Northern Heights, served by its routes, claiming

it as 'one of the healthiest around London' (GNR, 1906, p. 1). Developers, too, had begun to stress the same points. Croham Park Estate was recommended in 1908 because '[t]he land stands high, in the healthiest part of healthy Croydon' (CPE, 1908). The practice of quoting local mortality statistics, invariably impressively low, had also become common by 1914.

And so it continued into the interwar years. Health was always prominent in the publicity for the Underground suburbs. In 1926, for example, a new home in Edgware was recommended to newspaper readers as 'the best tonic' (LTM, Newspaper Advertisements, 1926). The following year Osterley was marketed on the promise of good health, showing a suburban gate that carried the slogan 'No Doctors' as well as the usual 'No Hawkers' (*ibid.*, 1927). *Metro-land* meanwhile regularly rehearsed the virtues of its constituent areas. All, needless to say, were on high ground with 'bracing, health-giving properties' (MR, 1920, p. 44). For its part, the Southern Railway stressed the opportunities provided by its extensive electrification to find the even purer air of true country districts, far from London (PRO RAIL 652/29, p. 9).

By the 1930s developers were also beginning to make much of the healthy attributes of their estates. As we have noted for the resorts, the language showed how sunshine had become increasingly important, complementing the traditional focus on tonic or bracing air. Morrell's 1935 brochure, for example, bore the message 'Live in the Sun and Tonic Air of a Morrell's Countryside Estate', a message which was repeated in press advertisements (Jackson, 1991, p. 139; Barrett and Phillips, 1987, p. 21). About the same time Berg advertised their modernist 'Sunspan' houses as 'homes of tomorrow with sunshine laid on' (Berg, nd *c*1935*a*). In the same year John Laing advised the readers of local newspapers in Kent and south east London to 'Live where Hill and Sea Air Meet' at Shooters Hill in south east London (Laing Press Cuttings, 1935–36). By next year, however, the message was 'Leave the smoke of the valley – for the

Early Underground poster (c1909) showing the rather clumsy vignette approach also found in early resort posters. Healthy Homes was the title of the residential handbook issued by the Underground to promote suburban living along its new routes.

sunshine of the hills'. There was much more in the same vein (Jackson, 1991, pp. 139–141).

Although it was often difficult to believe it from the language of the advertisements, not all suburban developments were actually located in elevated positions. By the time of the 1930s boom, many lower lying areas of London clay were being built upon. Almost invariably, where developers did **not** mention the subsoil, they were building on clay. This coyness partly reflected a

SPRING IS HERE

Time for a Tonic. And the best
Tonics are fresh air and a change
of surroundings.

You will get both at EDGWARE.

Edgware is in London's north-
west countryside—a healthy spot
—300 feet above sea-level. It is
now linked up with London by
the Underground, and in consequence is developing rapidly as a
new and pleasant garden suburb.
You will have brighter outlooks
and daily doses of fresh air if you

Live at
EDGWARE
on the

E3'39'26

Strong emphasis on health in this 1926 newspaper
advertisement for Edgware, part of a major
campaign to promote a line which was slow to fulfil
its promised traffic returns.

continuing unease that clay, especially lowlying
clay, was cold, damp and unhealthy, especially
conducive to miasmas (Jackson, 1991, p. 140).
The term 'slum', connoting the exact opposite of
what the suburbanite was seeking, was probably
related to the German word *schlamm*, meaning
mud or mire, associated with low lying, water-
logged areas (LCC, 1937, p. 13). Not surprisingly
therefore, the sellers of suburbia went to considerable lengths to prevent any such fears about
their own developments. Promotional artwork
tended to show houses higher than the immediate
surroundings, whatever the reality. Occasionally
even more inventive methods were used. Jackson
found one case of a developer who claimed astonishing health improvements on clay soil, but this
was very much the exception.

Smoke was not always viewed as quite so
repellent, however. One, admittedly rather singular, commercial promotional effort of 1910
managed, in promoting Belsize Park, Chalk Farm
and Camden Town, to contradict everything it
had said in praise of the breezy Northern Heights
(alias the 'Cockney Appennines'):

... all people do not care to be 'braced' by a too
strenuous atmosphere: they prefer milder airs, even if
more generously tinctured with smoke (smoke, it is well
known, conduces to vividly chromatic sunsets and other
artistic effects); and enjoy the shelter afforded by the
northern rampart . . . (Acme, 1910, p. 85)

More typical were publicity efforts where
the nearness to industry was being particularly
pressed. There is a tendency to overlook the
extent of industrial suburbanization as a factor
influencing housing development. Rather than
being repelled by industry, as was the case in the
classic residential suburb, housing developers
in 'mixed use' suburbs might see it as a magnet.
We have seen how Gross was very careful in
wording his advertising copy for such subdivisions. Certainly he went nothing like as far in
this respect as the promoters of the Silverthorn
Park Addition subdivision in Toronto in 1912
(Paterson, 1989, p. 129). Here the residential
area was entirely surrounded by factories with
chimneys belching black smoke. More typical of

Leave the smoke of the valley— for the sunshine of the hills

ON LAINGS

SHOOTERS HILL ESTATE

Adjoins Golf Course and Park.   Close to Schools.   Gravel Subsoil.

This delightful Estate is built at the top of Shooters Hill commanding beautiful views and receiving the sea breezes as they drift up the Thames Valley. Every house has 3 or 4 bedrooms, 2 large reception rooms, fitted labour saving kitchen, tiled bathroom, 4 large bay windows and ample garden space. Each house is soundly constructed and architect designed.   The Estate is laid out with tree-lined roads and delightful lawns and shrubberies—a truly desirable place to live in.

MANY ADVANCES THROUGH WOOLWICH BOROUGH COUNCIL

£780 TO £1155

FREEHOLD

From 21/2 Weekly Rates 6/1

Write for FREE Illustrated Booklet K.1.

LAINGS SHREWSBURY PARK ESTATE, SHREWSBURY LANE or PLUM LANE, SHOOTERS HILL, S.E.18
or Phone : WOOLWICH 1495

From Charing Cross to Woolwich Arsenal Station (Southern Electric).   Bus Nos. 53, 53a, 54, 153 and 289a to end of Plum Lane, or Trams 44 and 46 from Well Hall Station, or bus No. 21a to Shrewsbury Lane, Shooters Hill.

By the 1930s British developers were producing high quality advertising, especially in newspapers. This 1936 example by John Laing stresses especially the values of elevation, away from smoke.

British experience were the advertisements for the housing estates near the motor car works in Oxford's industrial suburb of Cowley. The Sunnyside estate was advertised as 'delightfully situated', one minute's walk from the main factory (Hudson, nd c1933). Nearby estates similarly stressed proximity to work.

Overall though, these were but minor variations. The main suburban promotional message remained that pure, bracing, country (or sea) air, high ground, free drainage, absence of smoke and sunshine equalled health. But this environmental equation was not quite as simple as almost everyone believed. Its limitations became clearer as housing authorities began, with government subsidies, to apply the same suburban solution to former slum dwellers. Worryingly, their health did not always improve (M'Gonigle and Kirby, 1936). The larger truth was that those who had moved into privately developed suburban areas were healthier primarily because they were also wealthier.

Dare to Own Your Own Nest

And, though tenure was not itself a determinant of health, the new inhabitants of private suburbia

were also, in the main, buying their homes. As we saw in the last chapter, the intensive marketing of suburbia coincided in both North America and Britain with the rise of owner occupation. It was not unknown for developers building for rent to advertise but far more promotional effort was devoted to the actual selling of houses. This recognition of the potential for mass owner occupation was the primary inspiration of Gross's pioneering efforts in Chicago. It also coincided with the great surge in suburban promotional advertising in 1930s Britain.

The marketeers of the suburbs were then, in large measure, also selling the notion of home ownership. The positive allusions to the countryside, to nature, pure air and sunshine were consistently equated with ownership. Gross, for example, invariably associated renting with older, meaner properties and neighbourhoods. In his *Home Primer* (1888a, pp. 9–10), the renting agents are 'Old, House and Company', while most of their advertised properties are described as flats, rooms or even sheds, stables or shanties. The unfortunate couple who rent ' . . . at last settle down in a mean little flat'. Similar themes come through in British advertising, especially by the building societies. During the 1930s boom,

Nestmaking was a common image, often referred to in promotional texts. Yet few were as explicit as this charming French example, from the 1920s. Noisy le Grand now forms part of the new town at Marne-la-Vallée.

for example, a poster by the Planet Building Society directly equated tenancy with the gloomy and monotonous terraces of the smoky city. Ownership, by contrast, was signified by the familiar suburban ideals of space, light, nature and fresh air (Gold and Gold, 1990). Even more explicitly, the National Building Society advised that '[s]unshine is brightest when it falls on your own home' (Gold and Gold, 1994, p. 83).

The promotion of home ownership often rested quite explicitly on the premise that it was a dream achievable through virtue. This was a central part of the message of Gross's more general publicity. *The House that Lucy Built* (1886), for example, showed how thrift and hard work (interestingly, on the part of the wife, a theme we will explore more fully later) brought fulsome rewards. The *Home Primer* follows a similar line (with a more typical emphasis on male thrift and hard work):

CROHAM PARK ESTATE, SOUTH CROYDON, SURREY.

The Estate faces Croham hurst and is close to the Addington and Shirley hills. The land stands high, in the healthiest part of healthy Croydon.

The subsoil is chalk.

The Estate is within 10 minutes walk of South Croydon and Selsdon Road Railway Stations. 18 minutes of East and New Croydon Stations. Coombe Lane Station adjoins the Estate.

An early example of more imaginative developer advertising, this 1908 example conveys a highly romanticized impression of a fairytale rural world, reminiscent of a scene from a William Morris poem. As in much English suburban advertising nature is highly ordered. The turret helps suggest home as castle, while the pair of birds act as a metaphor for the nesting instinct.

E is for Earnings, which Andrew lays by
For a rainy day, which may come bye and bye.
For 'tis not what he earns – he knows full well –
But what he can save in the future will tell.
(Gross, 1888a, p. 4)

Meanwhile the spendthrift Benjamin is 'enjoying today with no thought of the morrow' (*ibid*, p. 6). Finally, with Benjamin and his wife forced to live in their mean little flat, the wisdom of Andrew's thrift becomes clear:

O is for Ownership, and Andrew remarks,
'Dear Mollie we're free from house renting sharks.
For we're in our own home, and, I'd think every man
Who could would get one on this installment plan.'
(*ibid*, p. 9)

The same message was also being purveyed in Britain by the more ambitious building societies at the end of the nineteenth century. The Halifax's 'Misery' leaflet of 1897 compares the outcomes of thrift and want of thrift. The latter shows a rural scene of disorder and despair, a tumbledown cottage with broken fences. To complete the descent to ruin there is a public house nearby. Meanwhile thrift promises a neat sturdy cottage, well ordered garden and family happiness. A church replaces the public house. Should anyone miss the point of this heavy handed visual imagery, thrift promoting homilies flank these illustrations.

By the interwar years, there was less overt emphasis on such high moralizing. All the promoters of suburbia were now anxious to stress that home ownership in the suburbs was a dream that could be achieved on easy terms. The National Building Society, for example, portrayed an idyllic vision of a 1930s suburban family, content in their own sunny garden with the slogan '[t]heir happiness can be yours . . .' (Gold and Gold, 1994, p. 82). Developers, particularly those who catered for the lower end of the market, were especially keen to emphasize the ease with which ownership could be attained.

But the notion never entirely disappeared that home ownership needed the aspiration of self-betterment, underpinned by the solid virtues of steady labour and careful financial management. Thus H. Dare and Sons, one of Birmingham's larger developers and builders of 'Dare's Distinctive Houses', expressed the notion of rising to a challenge in their slogan: 'Don't imitate the cuckoo, Dare to own your own nest' (Dare, nd *c*1933, p. 13). Instead of the heavy handed moralizing of earlier days, the necessary precondition to the achievement of this aspiration, thrift, was now signified more subtly. The many promotional images which showed fathers leaving or, more usually, returning from their work underlined the need for a dependable source of regular income. The images of neat,

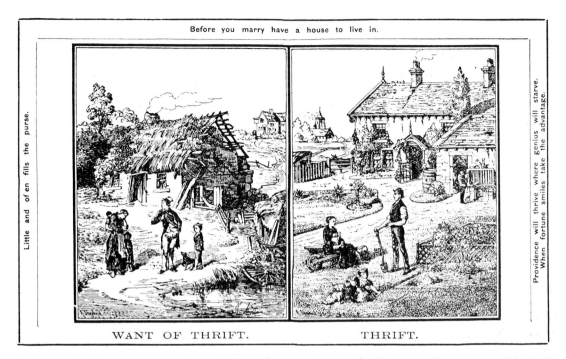

Before you marry have a house to live in.

Little and of en fills the purse.

Providence will thrive where genius will starve.
When fortune smiles take the advantage.

WANT OF THRIFT.   THRIFT.

Ambitious building societies such as the Halifax were beginning to advertise by the late nineteenth century. Heavy handed propaganda is used here to promote the ideal of thrift producing a more ordered way of living, significantly in a rural setting.

well cultivated gardens also stood as testament to the hard work of the inhabitants.

If ownership required aspiration on the part of the purchaser, the seller had to be able to suggest that commensurate benefits followed from this big step. Security was one of the main benefits, understood in both a financial and a deeper sense. No effort was spared by developers to show the physical and financial soundness of their properties, whether justified or not. The virtual certainty that values would rise was a continual theme of Gross's advertising. Understandable in the context of Chicago's speculative boom, such claims were not always so common, however. Many developers preferred to stress the structural soundness of their dwellings. By 1926, for example, Highland Park, in Revere, near Boston was being sold on the claim that each home was 'built to endure' (PLC, nd c1926).

Given the immense quantity of new housing built in interwar Britain, there was little chance of rising values, at least in the short term. Nonetheless the house owned by its occupier was often represented as a valuable and enduring asset (e.g. MR, 1923, p. 8). Much, of course, depended on the quality of construction. Laing made a great deal, with justification, of the high design and construction standards of their houses. In 1934, for example, they included in one advertisement a photograph of the first house built by the family firm, in 1848, showing it 'as good as new, and worth more to-day than when it was built' (Laing Press Cuttings, 1934). Yet many other such claims were more doubtful, especially at the height of the 1930s boom. Thus, despite their extravagant publicity claims to the contrary, Morrell's had the extremely poor quality of construction on one estate exposed in a famous legal action (the Borders' case) in 1939

Their happiness can be yours ..

BUY YOUR HOUSE THROUGH

The **NATIONAL**
BUILDING SOCIETY

FOUNDED 1849

Your Estate Agent will advise you

Building society advertising between the wars increasingly emphasized the accessibility of the suburban ideal, as in this 1930s' example. The scene evokes the full suburban stereotype of an ordered and bounteous nature, sunshine and health. Domestic bliss is much in evidence. Father has evidently just arrived home and relaxes with his pipe. His wife manages at once to be both stunning yet content with her domestic role (knitting needles can just be discerned). The faithful dog guards the untroubled scene.

(Jackson, 1991, pp. 157–158; Craig, 1986; McCulloch, 1990).

Symbolism also played its part in suggesting the benefits of security through ownership. The deeply rooted notion of home as castle was sometimes invoked, even in the most unlikely settings. Inevitably perhaps, it was even deployed on occasion by Gross (e.g. 1886, p. 13). Less surprisingly, it was often alluded to by building societies in Britain. The Woolwich Equitable, for example, adapted lines from Thomas Carlyle's poetry: 'This my house, my castle is / I have my own four walls' (Gold and Gold, 1994, pp. 84–86). Developers also occasionally made overt reference to home-as-castle. The Rectory Estate at Wylde Green in Birmingham was perhaps one of the most explicit, if in the process straying perilously close to the suggestion that it was merely building castles in the air (BCDP, 1978, p. 46).

A Sovereign in the Land of the Free?

The promoted merits of ownership included also the deeper notion of security in the sense of belonging. The firm foundations of the houses and the implication of well established roots for the mature trees which almost invariably framed them were a subtle way of suggesting that homeowners too could similarly belong and find emotional security. We have seen how the promise of becoming part of the true, rural, England featured heavily in suburban promotion. References to buying one's own piece of England were common, especially in building society publicity, and the meaning of home was sometimes patriotically extended to suggest country (e.g. Gold and Gold, 1994, p. 85).

Such sentiments, of course, became much more highly charged in the inherently insecure urban society of the United States in the later nineteenth and early twentieth centuries. Home ownership in the suburbs was often promoted as part of becoming an American. This was a recurrent theme in the advertising of S. E. Gross, directed, as so much of it was, at first generation urban Americans. Thus the *Home Primer* (1888*a*, p. 7) celebrates the signing of the deed of purchase with a celebration of America itself:

K is for King. Andrew's prouder than he
For he is a sovereign in the land of the free . . .

In both Britain and North America, however, sentiments which promoted an accessible dream of suburban home ownership in order to 'belong' sat rather uneasily with a powerful desire for social exclusivity. The fostered sense of escaping from the city was not merely a search for pure air and greenery. It involved an escape from all the perceived undesirability of urban society.

Promotional advertising had therefore to balance carefully claims of a socially accessible way of life with an unmistakable assurance that this could be combined with an exclusion of undesirable elements.

Rectory Estate, Wylde Green.

What all desire—

A

MODERN

LABOUR-SAVING HOUSE

The idea of home as castle often appeared in suburban imagery. This 1930s example from Birmingham was particularly explicit, although it seems to be suggesting castles in the air rather than reality.

Such exclusive messages were particularly strong in North America in the first half of the twentieth century. Restrictive covenants began to be used very extensively to limit movement to the suburbs by non-whites and non-Protestants. In 1914, for example, a promotional brochure for the elite suburb of Cameron Park, Raleigh, North Carolina promised that 'premises shall not be occupied by negroes or persons of negro blood', adding helpfully that 'this shall not be construed to prevent the living on the premises of any negro who is employed for domestic purposes by the occupants' (Brown, 1985, p. 31). Occasionally racial exclusion became a major theme of general advertising. At Loopway Park, Bradenton, Florida, the developer prominently promised in 1926 that the lots '[c]an never be deeded to anyone but the Caucasian race' (Johnson, 1926).

Normally, however, promoters were a little more circumspect in mentioning racial or ethnic exclusions in their general advertising, especially outside the South. Thus Oak Hill Village in Newton, Massachusetts was being marketed, also in 1926, as 'highly restricted to preserve old New England traditions', ensuring 'clean and wholesome neighbours – the kind you like to visit . . . ' (Oak Hill, 1926). The message was unmistakable, aimed here at deterring Boston's large Irish and Italian populations as much as at the usual targets of Jews and blacks. The truth was that, as Chase (1995) has recently shown for Wilmington, Delaware, restrictive covenants by the 1920s virtually always included racial or ethnic restrictions. It was only necessary, therefore, to adopt phrases such as 'The Ideal Restricted American Settlement for American People' or simply to mention that restrictions applied in order to get the message across. The practice was also common in Canada (Paterson, 1989).

Such overt approaches to the promotion of suburban social exclusion based on race and ethnicity have not been found in Britain. In part, of course, this reflected the fact that Britain was racially and ethnically a far more homogeneous

society than the United States. Yet sizeable Irish and Jewish populations existed within Britain, with much overt prejudice against them. There seems, however, to have been no evidence of their institutionalized exclusion from new suburban areas in Britain in the manner common in many American cities. One of the most heavily promoted London suburbs, Golders Green, soon acquired a strongly Jewish character. Laing were also keen to market their estates to Jewish buyers in the 1930s, building on the favourable reputation they had established in 1934 as contractors for the Edgware Synagogue (*World Jewry*, 7.9.34, p. 450). This did not mean that social exclusion formed no part of the suburban promotional message in Britain. Rather than being based on racism, however, it pandered to the more simple sentiment of snobbery.

Restrictive covenants or equivalent restrictions were certainly common from at least the late eighteenth century (Chalklin, 1974). Their role in social exclusion seems to have been to keep the working classes away from building estates which were intended as high class developments. This could be achieved by the relatively simple expedient of specifying minimum building values or plot size on land being sold for building (Thompson, 1982). Both the Metropolitan Railway Surplus Lands Committee and its associate Country Estates Company continued to practise and advertise this traditional approach in the interwar years (e.g. especially MR, 1926, p. 82). Yet, as the development process shifted to the more fully packaged provision of finished houses, restrictions were clearly of less consequence in the active shaping of suburban character.

English suburban advertisements often tried to suggest a degree of social exclusiveness, however. Laing, for example, referred to the 'good tone' of their estates (Laing, nd *c*1936, p. 3). In many other cases the character of the houses themselves became an unmistakable surrogate. Thus E. S. Reid promised 'you will not have a nasty cheap mass production house anywhere near you' on his development at Harrow Garden

HARROW GARDEN

TYPE "A." Compact semi-detached seven-room residence. Ideal for small family. A marked advance on that obtainable elsewhere. Weekly repayments 28s. 5d. Deposit £50.

PRICE £895 FREEHOLD

TYPE "B." Delightful detached self-contained seven-roomed house. Pleasing and practical elevation, well-proportioned and conveniently arranged rooms, good garden. Weekly repayments 33s. 7d. Deposit £50.

PRICE £1,050 FREEHOLD

TYPE "C." Specially large seven-room semi-detached residence. A very popular type of house. Good garden. A house of which you can be justly proud. Weekly repayments 34s. 4d. Deposit £50.

PRICE £1,075 FREEHOLD

TYPE "D." Tudor type seven-room semi-detached house complete with verandah and spacious porch. Without question the finest value obtainable. Weekly repayments 33s. 5d. Deposit £110.

PRICE £1,100 FREEHOLD

E. S. REID
STATION ESTATE OFFICE

SAY YOU SAW IT IN "METRO-LAND."

Page 118

VILLAGE ESTATE

TYPICAL REID HOUSE, HARROW GARDEN VILLAGE

A PERSONAL STATEMENT BY E. S. REID

ON the adjoining pages are shown some of the types of houses erected by E. S. Reid and in addition to these there are many other types also to choose from.

From the accompanying plan it will be seen that E. S. Reid's estate has the particular advantage of being **self-contained** and wherever you choose a house on this Estate you may rest assured that you will be surrounded by other of E. S. Reid's houses, and by this it is intended to convey that you may be sure that you will not have a nasty cheap mass production house anywhere near you to lower the value of your own property.

In developing this section (immediately adjoining Rayners Lane Station entrance) **great care has been exercised,** without regard of expense, to keep right away from the monotony of mass production houses which are so swiftly covering the suburbs of London. **It must appeal** to every-one in choosing their house

Continued on page 120.

HARROW GARDEN VILLAGE
RAYNERS LANE STATION, MIDDLESEX

SAY YOU SAW IT IN "METRO-LAND."

Page 119

Part of a developer's advertisement from the Metro-Land booklet, published in 1932. Note the promise that cheap and nasty houses and, implicitly, their inhabitants, are not a risk in Harrow Garden Village.

Village in Metro-land (MR, 1932, p. 119). Hints that buyers would belong at least to the lower echelons of some traditional rural elite were common. S. P. B. Mais, for example, promised buyers at Ottershaw Park in Surrey 'the pleasant feeling of being a small country squire' (nd *c*1930: 21). In true English fashion, much was made of any genuine upper class associations. Rumble and Silvester, for example, boasted that the late Empress Eugenie, exiled consort of Louis Napoleon, chose 'out of all Britain' to live at Farnborough Hill, where they were now building (*Houseland Gazette*, 1, 1931, p. 11).

If aristocratic connections did not exist, they could always be invented, of course. We have noted how the naming of estates was deliberately used as a marketing ploy. Appealing by this

means to the snobbish instincts of intending buyers was common, even in the United States. 'Park', for example, was an immensely popular North American suburban suffix, more so, seemingly, than it was even in England. While in some cases such a name simply referred to a nearby public park, in many others it was clearly no more than a high sounding aspiration. In England, the near universal use of the term 'estate' could also be made to suggest aristocratic associations that were usually entirely spurious. (Gradually, though, the term began to acquire a less favourable meaning, especially as council housing estates became widespread in the 1920s.)

The shift during the interwar years to a fully packaged approach provided yet another opportunity to add snob value through names. In the

1890 newspaper advertisement shows another Gross promotional analogy with the boxing champion's belt. Notice particularly the favouring of 'park' or other names with rural connections.

early years of the 1930s building boom, developers typically tended to refer to their houses only by designatory letters (Laing, nd c1933). By the end of the decade, however, almost all Laing house types, for example, had their own specific names. The firm's Queensbury estate offered the 'Berkeley', the 'Argyll', the 'Gainsborough', the 'Hereford', the 'Belvedere' and the 'Marlborough' (Laing, nd c1937b). About the same time, Costin Houses were offering the 'Waverley', the 'Langham', the 'Chatsworth', the 'Mayfair' and the 'Cavendish' (Costin, nd c1935). Again

the dominant impression was of the seats of aristocrats or, at very least, county gentry. There were certainly no names which might be closely associated with urban industrial society.

Every Inch a True Man

The idealized construction of the suburban family in promotional literature also rested on the romanticization of a supposedly traditional domestic order. In passing we have already noted something of the essentials of this order.

For example, the fondness for avian allusion in suburban advertising largely reflected the idea of home as nest. Central to this was the pair bonding of male and female; there was no place for singles in suburbia. As Costin advised, '[n]o man should plan his dream house without a woman, no woman without a man' (*ibid*). It was on this firm foundation that the next generation was to be successfully raised. Yet it was also an approach that involved a very rigid, if not quite absolute, stereotyping of family roles. Firmly in charge of it all was the father, genially indulgent with his adoring wife and children, but also steady and wise. His only admitted vice was his pipe, that commonly deployed signifier (in England, at least) of reflective wisdom, masculine contentment and unchallenged authority.

The promoters of suburbia worked on the general assumption that 'women choose houses; men buy them' (Howkins, 1938, pp. 248–249). The man was usually felt to have the final say. Many promotional efforts, particularly those produced by commuter rail operators, spoke directly and explicitly to men. In 1929, for example, the LMS railway referred to a 'comfortable carriage and a good seat where you can enjoy your pipe and newspaper' (PRO RAIL 429/17, p. 10) on their commuter trains, in contrast to other, third person references to 'the wife'. Even where the language was less direct, there was a general appeal to the man's ideal of himself. Suburban man was portrayed as a worthy provider and head of the family, making sensible decisions that would bring contentment for himself, his wife and children. Some advertisers went so far as to equate ownership directly with manliness, a final rite of passage to prove fitness for marriage. Of Andrew, the virtuous hero of Gross's *Home Primer*, we learn that

. . . to-day he is feeling every inch a true man
For he's bought a snug home on the installment plan.
(Gross, 1888a, p. 7)

Perhaps more attuned to possible double meanings in this kind of language, British advertising adopted a more brisk and breezy approach on this slightly embarrassing issue. Typical of interwar Britain was Halden Estates' 1923 admonition that 'there really is no excuse for keeping that girl waiting any longer' (MR, 1923, p. 72).

More usually the men are shown firmly settled in their homes. A very familiar scene was the husband's morning departure or, more commonly, his evening homecoming. Wife, and sometimes child(ren), offer farewell kisses or waves of greeting to the master of the family. Such portrayals were common in Underground advertising in the late 1920s and are found too in developer and building society promotion in the 1930s (e.g. Berg, nd c1935b; Gold and Gold, 1994). These episodes were important symbolically because they represented a union of the two sides of suburban life. One side was the masculine world of paid work in the city, which made possible the neat suburban home. The other was the safe and happy domestic world represented by the wife and children, making it all worthwhile.

Beyond the threshold that separated the world of work from his own home, suburban man, according to Costin, dreamed of 'a garden and a fireside chair' (Costin, nd c1935). Garden and fireside scenes were indeed common settings in promotional literature. In his garden the man was normally equipped for business with spade or other garden implement (and the inevitable pipe). Having left the artificial world of the office and the city, suburban man could now indulge his 'true' agrarian nature. Fireside scenes, with all their associated connotations of hearth and home were also common, especially in American promotional literature. It was an image which recurred regularly in Gross's advertising (e.g. Gross, 1888a). The usual pattern was of the man occupying pride of place, reading his newspaper, while wife and child(ren) completed the picture of domestic bliss.

From a Woman's Point of View

The portrayal of women in this suburban dream was also revealing. Almost without exception, their role was firmly circumscribed, limited

Why not live at Hounslow?

Freehold houses, large gardens, garages: those are the homes.
Frequent fast trains to town from three stations: that is the service.

42 minutes to Charing Cross. 47 minutes to Mansion House.

SEASONS		1 Month	3 Months
	Charing Cross . .	27/-	75/-
	Mansion House . .	31/-	85/-

UNDERGROUND

M1/85/29

1929 newspaper advertisement by the Underground to live in Hounslow. The scene shows a suburban ritual: the morning departure of male providers, kissing or waving to wives and walking to the station. Despite growing numbers of female office workers, only one woman traveller is apparent and evidently not a regular commuter. The suitcase suggests a longer journey; her worry over time an unfamiliarity with the efficient tube service.

exclusively to the domestic realm. They were housewives and mothers, with no paid employment outside the home. The interwar reality

of the many employed suburban women, themselves going off to catch buses, trams or trains, was almost wholly ignored. Admittedly such women were unlikely to be mothers but many new suburban dwellers clearly relied partly on the incomes of unmarried daughters (and sons) to pay the mortgage. Yet such adult or near adult children were quite invisible in promotional imagery. For the sellers of suburbia, children had to be young enough to enjoy their games in the garden and to greet their homecoming father with unaffected delight. They were there, in short, to signify innocence and a need for security and protection. This was provided by loving parents and especially the mother, serene in her new suburban home.

The more detailed treatment of suburban woman in promotional advertising varied considerably. In many efforts, clearly directed at men, the female dimension is apparent only in a few passing references. Certainly this was the typical pattern of many male-oriented commuter rail publications on both sides of the Atlantic. CBQRR publications of the late nineteenth century, for example, provide literary images of the suburban wife at home cooking for her hard-working husband, and being rewarded with the occasional shopping trip (CBQRR, nd c1883). Those of interwar Britain still portrayed much of the same message:

For shopping or theatres, the wife will be able to run up from the country home to the town with an LMS cheap ticket or weekly season. (PRO RAIL 429/17, p. 27)

Occasionally such publications gave a more central place to the wife, though without ever according her any great strength of character or capacity for clear thought. S. P. B. Mais, for example, portrayed his own wife, Ann, as remarkably vacuous and simpering in a 1933 publication intended to promote residential Brighton. Part of the brochure (not one of Mais's best efforts) takes the form of a lengthy interview with a local estate agent, a man evidently possessed of a rare gift for extended exposition.

A very short extract from his peroration captures much of its hilariously contrived flavour:

Our rates are amongst the lowest in the kingdom. Ours, with one exception, is the cheapest water-rate in the country, and the fact that it is good may be gauged by the fact that water from here is sent daily to the King; our lighting is also extraordinarily cheap. You need have no fear on that score.

As the agent paused for breath before plunging relentlessly onwards, Mais records a typical contribution from his wife:

Ann sighed happily. (Mais, nd c1933)

By the 1930s, however, there was a growing volume of suburban promotional literature, mainly produced by developers, that spoke directly to wives. Laing, for example, produced a pamphlet called *From a Woman's Point of View*. The approach was still very much to stereotype women as housewives. There was great emphasis on easy cleaning and maintenance of Laing houses, allowing greater devotion to the pleasures of motherhood:

There is not a lot of work to do in a Laing house, it almost keeps itself clean, but there must be a little. However, when it is finished and the housewife has a little time at her disposal, what is more inviting than a stroll round a Laing Estate, where there is a lovely green to let the children have their games, and the shade of the tree invites a deck chair, a book or some knitting – leisure hours spent pleasantly and profitably. (Laing, nd c1937a)

Yet such marketing efforts were at least add-ressing women directly, acknowledging, albeit imperfectly, their importance in setting up home.

Some developers even stressed the joint nature of decision making between the sensible house-wife and her steady husband. Costin produced a remarkable pamphlet which acknowledged and examined his and her dreams of home, concluding that:

Seen from both masculine and feminine points of view, there is a stereoscopic quality about a Costin house. A dream house, surely, but how admirably her ideals are complemented in the fulfilling of his wishes. For her the

practical, labour-saving devices that remove drudgery from housework – for him the economic advantages of a home well within an income that at all events does not stretch under the requirements of setting up home. (Costin, nd c1935)

There were a few, very rare, examples where women were accorded a more active role than their husbands, however. Gross's booklet, *The House that Lucy Built* was a uniquely full portrait of wife as key player. While her husband believes he is paying rent, Lucy secretly begins house purchase on Gross's instalment plan, meeting the shortfall by taking in washing with the assis-tance of her faithful servant, Maggie. Yet, for all her initiative, the story did not seriously challenge the conventional power balance of the late nineteenth-century American family. Thus when Lucy secures management of the family finances, it is through the exercise of guile disguised with girlish teasing and charm, rather than any open renegotiation. First, she

... rolled her lord's easy chair before the fire, and when he had comfortably seated himself therein coolly perched her wee, little self upon his knee ... (Gross, 1886, p. 4)

The *piece de resistance* in her campaign was a pianoforte and vocal rendition of 'Home Sweet Home', 'with such power and pathos as brought tears to her husband's eyes' (*ibid*, p. 5).

Later, when the home is owned outright, she reveals to husband Charley that they have now become owner occupiers thanks to her initiative, hard work and good management. Yet at the very moment of her triumph she returns to domes-ticity. She mortgages the house (owned in *her* name, of course) to allow him to set himself up in business, while her thriving laundry business is turned over to the loyal Maggie. The response is particularly revealing when Charley jokingly asks for payment for all the jobs he has done in what is now her house:

For answer, Lucy pointed to baby's crib, and Charley Graham kissed his wife almost reverently, as he for the hundredth time murmured 'God bless you, darling'. (*ibid*, p.13)

In other words the underlying message of this promotional tale is less exceptional than at first appears. Lucy sees her real role as housewife-mother with Charley as provider. Happily, especially so for someone so dimwitted as to be incapable of detecting an extensive laundry business conducted for several years from his own home, Charley proves a very successful businessman. Inevitably they live happily ever after. The real hero is of course the developer. As Lucy herself says:

... every hour of our lives we render mute thanks to that large minded, public-spirited man – S. E. Gross – who has rendered it possible for every man or *woman* to own his or her home. (*ibid*, p. 13)

This apparent encouragement to women to become homeowners in their own right was not to be mirrored on any scale in reality until the late twentieth century. Women workers, both within and outside the home, undoubtedly played a significant, if ultimately unquantifiable, part in achieving suburban home ownership. Yet, like Lucy, their role was submerged in the notion, purveyed in suburban marketing efforts, that the man was the provider. It is a social construct which, even now, remains deeply embedded in the suburban dream.

MARKETING THE SUBURB IN THE CONTEMPORARY WORLD

Suburbanization in the Contemporary World

That dream was fulfilled on an even greater scale after the Second World War. Suburban living achieved a new ascendancy throughout the West in the second half of the twentieth century though the pattern of its implementation varied greatly between Britain and North America. The war ended Britain's private building boom and the beginnings of the mass consumer society that it represented. Post-war controls and austerity ensured that neither began to resurface on any scale until the mid-1950s. Even after the revival, annual private housing completions never again reached the heights of the 1930s. Moreover post-war suburbs were less likely to take the form of a continuous spread around the big cities in the manner of the interwar years. The ideas of town and country planning achieved unprecedented political saliency after 1945, channelling British suburbanization into spatial forms significantly different from earlier manifestations (Ward, 1994*a*). Almost from the outset, post-war planning in Britain became obsessed with urban containment (Hall *et al.*, 1973). First around London and then, from the mid-1950s, provin-

cial cities, the planning intention was, through green belts, to prevent the repetition of interwar style continuous suburbanization.

The original intention of post-war planning was to divert suburban growth pressures into planned, largely self-contained new towns and expanded towns beyond the green belts, developed with a very high proportion of public housing. The practice, however, soon began to diverge from this ideal of planned metropolitan decentralization. Certainly the designated New and Expanded Towns soon appeared amongst the fastest growing places in post-war Britain. Initially their housing was largely public sector provided, but by the 1970s and 1980s the balance was shifting with large amounts of private building especially in southern examples such as Milton Keynes or Swindon. Yet, for all their impressive growth, they accounted for no more than a small proportion of the population moving out from the cities. The more typical new suburbs of post-war Britain were around the many villages and smaller towns beyond the green belts. Commuter rail systems and, increasingly, the motor car allowed longer journeys to work which, in conjunction with planning restrictions on housebuilding on the urban fringe, encouraged much more dispersed patterns of living (e.g. Coppock, 1964).

More than interwar suburbanites, the new post-war commuters found they could detach themselves much more completely from the big cities. They could pretend to a lifestyle that was far more rural than had been possible in the 1930s. The picturesque allusions to farm and village which had pervaded interwar promotional imagery had now become reality of sorts. A romanticized rural lifestyle of village cricket, horse riding and Morris dancing was now available to commuting accountants and systems analysts. Yet the reality behind the bucolic illusion was degraded by ever more pervasive motor vehicles and the rustic superstores, retail warehouses and futurist filling stations which were appearing around the edges of countless country towns by the 1980s.

Moreover, for that majority of the new suburbanites, those who could not afford the older cottages or grander houses in the conservation areas of country towns or village cores, the new housing estates offered each buyer a much smaller parcel of English soil than their interwar equivalents. While planning allowed this urbanization of the countryside, it did so only with the imposition of serious restrictions on the supply of development land. Plot sizes tended to be noticeably smaller than in the interwar years. They were made apparently more so by the growing need for double, even triple car garages. Even these, on average, smaller plots were more expensive. Thus the land component of the cost of a new house, rarely more than 10 per cent in suburban London during the 1930s, often nearer 5 per cent, was topping 40 per cent in the South-East by the late 1980s boom (Carr, 1982; DOE, 1992).

The North American experience differed in several important respects. These differences were underpinned, essentially, by greater American affluence, even greater reliance on the car and a planning system much less restrictive than Britain's. With scarcely any exceptions, American suburbanization has proceeded at an astonishing rate, quite untroubled by containing green belts on the British pattern (Jackson, 1985; *Built Environment*, 1991). There has been a huge 'white flight' from older core cities to ever more distant suburbs. The old racially restrictive covenants that were so much a feature of American suburbanization in the first half of the twentieth century are no longer legal. Yet social exclusion based on wealth (and therefore, in large measure, still on race) is more deeply entrenched than ever. It is now reinforced by the institutional fragmentation of local governments and the effects of land use zoning (Johnston, 1984). Combined with real estate development practices which have eroded the idea of truly public space, the modern American suburb has become an ever more private and exclusive domain, insulated from the city (Fishman, 1992). We can detect similar trends in Britain though as yet they are much more weakly developed.

Sheer distance from the city is itself an important exclusionary mechanism in the United States. Sprawl, a criticism often applied to British post-war residential development, is actually much more appropriate in North America. Thus suburban lot sizes, and homes, have been huge by British standards. Unlike Britain, the size of yards (gardens) has tended to increase markedly from what was typical in the interwar years. Moreover, immense investments in major highway construction since the 1950s and very cheap gasoline have allowed an absolute growth in car-based commuting on a far greater scale than in Europe. In turn this and the absence of planning restriction has encouraged suburban sprawl to assume the distinctive form of 'leap frogging' growth, so careless in its use of land that undeveloped tracts alternate with new residential areas. Notions of steering development into comprehensively planned growth centres, on the pattern of the British New and Expanded Towns, were virtually absent. A few private ventures and an ill-starred federal new towns programme in the early 1970s made little impact on the general course of suburban development.

One important shift that has taken place on both sides of the Atlantic has been towards mass produced suburbia. There had been important moves in this direction in Britain during the inter-war years where the lessons learned on major council housing contracts began to be applied to speculative housebuilding in the 1930s. Yet the beginnings of a totally mass produced suburbia are to be found in the United States. It was on Long Island in New York state in 1948 that the Levitt company began building Levittown, the largest ever single private housing development (Kelly, 1993; Jackson, 1985, 231–8). Ultimately consisting of over 17,000 dwellings built as standard types, Levittown catered for a guaranteed and federally-supported market of war veterans looking to set up home. and televisions included within the price as incentives to rapid purchaser decisions.

Things were never quite the same again after Levittown. There were two further Levitt developments on a similar scale in Pennsylvania, begun in the 1950s, and New Jersey in the 1960s. Yet Levitt was not as typical of American suburban developers as has commonly been supposed. Rather like Gross in an earlier era, Levitt was a pioneer, someone who showed it was possible to build on a very large scale, but whose efforts were never matched by his contemporaries. In some ways the underlying lessons of Levitt were actually more fully absorbed in Britain. In contrast to the United States, Britain's large amount of state-provided housing, with all the attendant opportunities for large contracts, encouraged the dominance of the bigger builders. Thus the British private housebuilding industry, already showing very marked signs of concentration into a few large companies by the 1930s, has moved even further in this direction since the 1950s. Most of the big British private house-builders are now arms of major multi-national firms. By contrast the United States continues to offer more scope in the building of its late twentieth-century suburbs to regionally-based builders.

Suburban Marketing in the Later Twentieth Century

There have been some important changes in suburban marketing practices in more recent years. One obvious shift everywhere has been the greatly diminished role of commuter rail operators as sellers of the suburb. In Britain, the post-railway nationalization successor to the Southern Railway, British Railways Southern Region, carried forward something of its 1930s' promotional momentum. Yet, as was already becoming apparent before 1939, the emphasis was no longer on the London suburbs. Instead the potential of living much further away from London in new housing developments in villages, small towns and, increasingly, seaside resorts was being exploited. The new post-war planning restrictions on peripheral metropolitan suburbanization also played an important role in this deflection. It meant that the full potential of the regional electrifications of the SR, though substantially completed by 1939, was only realized in the 1950s and beyond, as private housebuilding re-emerged. Linked with this, the Publicity Committees of many of the smaller holiday resorts served by the Southern Region electric system became increasingly interested in attracting new residents during the 1950s (e.g. WBC, 1959).

However, as the motor car became progressively more important for journeys to work in outer metropolitan areas from the 1960s, what remained of the residential promotional role of the railways was finally eclipsed. This followed the pattern which had appeared on a massive scale in the United States from the 1950s. The interests associated with the motor vehicle showed little desire to promote specific locations. Petrol and car advertisements might suggest a generalized freedom to live away from the congested big cities. But the companies whose products they promoted had no vested interest in the development of particular places to the same extent as railways, with their heavy investments in track, power supplies and signalling which could only be recovered by generating traffic. As we noted for the resorts, motor vehicles used a road infrastructure that was publicly funded. The use or non-use of any particular road route made no difference to the profits of car makers or petrol companies.

Thus it was that most of the direct promotion of suburban living has been undertaken by the development industry itself. Promotional practices and images have changed remarkably little since before 1939. It is still readily possible to trace the lineage back to S. E. Gross himself. True, there is a greater slickness and self consciousness about corporate image than in the past. Certain marketing practices which were just beginning in the 1930s, such as the inclusion of kitchen appliances, popularized in North America by Levitt, have now become routine. The highly cyclical nature of the property market has also seen developers offering during slack periods to purchase their buyers' existing homes. Operating in societies with already very high levels of owner occupation such as Britain or North America creates different marketing imperatives from those which animated developers in the past. In the past suburban home purchase was presented as a once and for all staking of a claim. Now selling suburbia involves purveying the notion that existing owner occupiers should 'trade up' as frequently as possible, or at the very least changing the homes they own to reflect the different phases of their lives.

Yet there were many important continuities. The same rural values continue to pervade promotional imagery. Estate subdivision names on both sides of the Atlantic show the same familiar trends. Thus Lower Earley near Reading, the largest recent development of private housing in Britain, is made up of neighbourhoods with names like 'Pipers Dell', 'Meadow Vale', 'Greenbanks', 'Badgers Walk' and 'Swallows Meadows' (Short, Fleming and Witt, 1986, pp. 78–80). House and estate designs, especially in Britain, draw on the same vernacular and picturesque references, unleavened even by the occasional modernist efforts that appeared in

the 1930s. The pattern is a little more varied in the United States, but does not differ fundamentally. In both countries the naming of developers' house types, now virtually universal, continues to refer in the main to a world of pre-industrial landed estates, historic cities, nobility and patronage.

Even where developers try to introduce a little variety in this direction, the image often fails to match reality. To take one very specific example, Tarmac Homes, a major British housebuilder, was in early 1996 advertising houses named after poets, composers and artists on its 'Brambley Hedges' development at Brackley, Northamptonshire (*Oxford Times*, 12.1.96). (Like much recent British suburbanization, Brackley is a genuinely historic market town rapidly being expanded with new dormitory estates for car-based commuters.) Names such as the 'Masefield', the 'Elgar' or the 'Keats' might be said to match or at least not jar with the English neo-vernacular realities of the houses. Yet the similarly inspired 'Picasso', devoid of any apparent references to the artist's modernism and radical ideology, seems incongruous, to say the least.

Traditional rural imagery has found a new outlet in the corporate logos of the major housebuilders, something which was entirely absent in the 1930s. Recent years have seen Tarmac using as its logo a twig in leaf, Barratt a broad leaf tree, Bovis a hovering bird and Laing wild flowers. Other examples, if not obviously rural, still send an essentially traditional message, such as Persimmon's classical arch or Bryant's bricks. Such logos betoken the promotion of corporate images that, in Britain at least, are much more than mere marketing to potential buyers. They are also intended to influence wider public perceptions of the firms concerned.

This concern for wider marketing is one of the most important shifts of recent years. In part this is a simple function of the fact that the typical housebuilders are very large firms, operating on a national or international basis. Some developer advertising has particularly stressed the sheer scale of operations. The biggest UK housebuilder, Barratt, for example, for several years during the 1980s made much promotional use of its corporate helicopter, zooming over the landscape, searching out new places to make into happy homes.

Yet corporate image-making also reflected something of the need to 'sell' their developments within the planning system, to councillors, local residents and professional planners. Britain's highly restrictive planning regime has made it essential that housebuilders wishing to gain approval for their schemes present an image of sensitivity to nature, to the historic environment and traditional values. Nowhere was this more so than in the many proposals for private new towns, villages or freestanding satellite suburbs that have become more common since the 1970s, often challenging established planning constraints. These reached a peak with the unsuccessful new country town proposals of Consortium Developments, formed from the leading British housebuilders during the middle and later 1980s (Ward, 1994a, pp. 250–254).

Another more pervasive shift on both sides of the Atlantic has been a gradual recognition of changing suburban lifestyles, as two incomes have become increasingly necessary to afford the suburban homes. As we have implied, the realities of this have been grasped only slowly. Both Britain's and the United States' consumer societies in the 1950s and 1960s were fuelled by advertising images of the homebound suburban

mother seeking more efficient ways of servicing family needs and acquitting herself with honour on the domestic front. Developer advertising was no exception. In particular consciousness of the working mother and the ever smaller families was slow to penetrate the promotional images. The increasingly common phenomena of divorce and unmarried cohabitation took even longer to acknowledge.

But shifts certainly did occur. Building society advertising was increasingly acknowledging the frailties of marriage in the 1970s and the growing income equality of women by the 1980s (e.g. Williamson, 1978, p. 34). Developers also began to recognize that houses would increasingly be bought by one or more unmarried adults, rather than the classic nuclear family. The development of retirement housing for the more affluent pensioners was another symptom of this differentiation of what had once been a very generalized market for family housing, segmented only by price. Yet there was still a certain coyness in the language used to market this mix of housing types. The smallest homes might, in reality, prove particularly popular with male divorcees but this was not reflected in a promotional language which spoke, more optimistically, of 'starter homes'. Even as the realities of late twentieth-century society were accepted by the sellers of suburbia, there remained always the romantic echoes of a happy world of family homes.

CONCLUSIONS

Like the selling of the tourist resort, the selling of suburbia came to be an integral part of Anglo-American urbanization. The availability of mass transit and the realistic prospect of mass home ownership were the two key factors underpinning the onset of mass marketing. These variables, as we have seen, came together somewhat earlier in North America than in Britain. In both geographical settings, however, suburban marketing practices have become endemic. We can see this as reflecting two fundamental characteristics of

the suburb. Firstly the suburb, even more perhaps than resorts, constituted a readily commodified product, represented in real estate or traffic receipts, that could be immediately exchanged for money. The returns to effort for the suburban marketeers were clear, direct and uncomplicated. One persistent practical problem of much place marketing, that it benefits many who do not contribute to its costs, was a relatively minor consideration in the suburbs.

The second point was that the suburbs, like

resorts, constituted a particularly competitive sub-group within the whole urban system. In North America but also, more importantly, even in a more mature and stable urban system such as Britain, the suburbs were unusually dynamic places. Involved in their development were builders, sub-dividers and providers of transit who were in competition with their equivalents in other suburbs. All of this fuelled further the sense of place competition, underlining therefore the arguments for active place marketing. While planning policies, in Britain at least, have blunted some of the keen edge of this competition since 1945, it remains an endemic feature of the business of suburban marketing.

More striking is the clear link between the promotional messages of today's suburban promoters and the pioneering work of Gross, the London Underground or the Metropolitan Railway. The suburb is still, in the words and illustrations favoured by its promoters, a realm of romance. There is still something of the same air of an imaginary happy land. Those who live there are promised emotional security through ownership, safety from the disturbing influences of the city and a closeness to the comforting world of nature and rustic tradition. It is a vision which many intellectual commentators continue to despise. The reality is criticized as environ-

mentally wasteful and socially soulless. Yet it is difficult not to admire the sheer artistry with which, at best, it has been purveyed to an eager public. The departure of those great patrons of suburban promotion, the railways, certainly diminished some of the former artistic and literary distinction of this particular type of marketing. Meanwhile much developer advertising remains what it always has been, starkly utilitarian.

Yet the old magic sometimes breaks through. One example is a recent television advertisement for the Halifax Building Society which bears comparison with the very best of the past. It uses as its soundtrack the Crosby, Stills, Nash and Young song 'Our House':

... is a very, very, very fine house
with two cats in the yard
Life used to be so hard
Now everything is easy, cos of you

The really original aspect, however, is to show the house being built with its walls and roof constructed of people standing on each others' shoulders. The result, a home built of people, is both charming and arresting, suggesting a human organization dedicated to the furtherance of domestic happiness. Samuel Eberly Gross would probably have loved it.

7

SELLING PLACES OR BUYING INDUSTRIES?

The dominant theme so far in this book has, quite literally, been the selling of places. Identifiable commodities such as real estate or tourist experience (or the means of reaching them) were marketed to a potentially large number of purchasers. In the next two chapters, however, the emphasis shifts decisively to the subsidized promotion of places. Even though we will find many parallels in the methods and language of advertising and publicity, there were important differences. In particular, the targets of promotion were not a mass popular market but a small number of potential industrial investors. Moreover, it was places anxious to grow, or to replace declining industries, which normally undertook such promotion. Even one successful new industrialist could bring growth or restore prosperity to such a place.

These facts inherently changed the terms of the relationship between seller and buyer of place, compared to the selling of the resort or the suburb. Places seeking industrial investment were often so keen that they routinely offered financial or other inducements on a scale not found in the case of resorts or suburbs. We saw some signs of such inducements in the selling of the frontier, but much of that story was about the disposal of land which, without settlement, had had no market value. By contrast much industrial promotion followed another frontier practice, that of local subsidies for railroads, paying them handsomely for the growth it was fondly hoped they would

bring. In many places, therefore, industrial promotion might better be described as buying industries rather than selling places.

Once again, the narrative covers both North America and Britain. Canada, however, features much more strongly than before. This reflects its highly marginal position in the industrialization of North America. Anxious to gain a manufacturing base to underpin its separate national identity, Canada's towns and cities embarked on an extraordinary and, at the time, quite unparalleled episode of industrial promotion in the half century from 1870. In the desperate scramble for factories, places advertised, publicized and, above all, subsidized, to the tune of millions of local tax dollars.

Despite Canada's very strong links to Britain, such widespread actions were entirely, in the words of one legislator, 'contrary to British precedent' (*Toronto Globe*, 3.3.1899). Oddly though, within months of this assertion came the first, albeit much more timid, British moves towards industrial promotion. Caution remained typical of British actions in the early twentieth century. Even as long established industrial towns and cities tried to promote themselves when their traditional industries faltered, they found only limited possibilities for decisive action. The same central mistrust of local advertising which we identified in Chapter 3 severely restricted industrial promotion.

From the 1920s the principal inheritor of the

Canadian tradition of aggressive, even desperate, local industrial promotion was the American South. This was another area on the edge. For decades, boosterist rhetoric had flowed out of the post-Civil War 'New South'. Now it began to be backed with hard cash and other dubious inducements. What was remarkable, however, was that, unlike Canada, the selling of the South never stopped. The growing inclination of Canadian provincial governments was to restrain local promotion. Yet the Southern states managed, following the lead of Mississippi in 1936, to combine regulation with encouragement, creating a tradition of localized industrial promotion that remains unbroken. We begin, however, with the earlier and extraordinary experiences in British North America.

CANADA'S BONUSING CRAZE

Broader Motivations

Canada's manufacturing economy emerged much later than in Britain or the north eastern United States. The country had grown as a resource economy based on furs, fishing, timber and agriculture, heavily reliant on British capital (Marr and Paterson, 1980). Manufacturing developed very slowly and was essentially locally based, small-scale, 'penny capitalism'. Yet the creation of modern Canada under the British North America Act of 1867 brought a stronger sense of economic nationalism and a desire to advance the new country's manufacturing base (Bliss, 1982). The most potent symbol of this intent was the tariff on manufactured goods introduced in 1878. This signalled Canada's aspiration to transcend the role of resource exporter, reliant on imports of manufactured goods from Britain and the United States. Effectively, the tariff committed the country to developing its own manufacturing base. It brought an intensification of indigenous manufacturing activity, albeit with foreign capital and technical assistance. It also encouraged the proliferation of American branch plants, jumping the new tariff walls.

The undoubted importance of tariff protection for the emergent manufacturing economy has encouraged a consistent theme in Canadian historiography. This is the notion that economic growth was dependent on state intervention (e.g. Aitken, 1967). It has recently become fashionable to play down this theme (e.g. Drummond *et al.*, 1987). Or commentators have acknowledged the extent of government action but questioned its value (Bliss, 1982). Yet it remains indisputable that Canadian industrialization was far less spontaneous than in the north eastern United States or in Britain (Drummond, Cain and Cohen, 1988). By international standards, Canada was unusually reliant on both state actions and foreign capital.

These larger themes are central to the emergence of local promotional activity. They meant that Canada's would-be industrial towns could not expect a spontaneous, problem-free process of growth (Morris, 1989). They had to compete with their neighbours for such investment as was around (Naylor, 1975, pp. 130–160). They also had to be prepared to prove their commitment by offering inducements to supplement the apparently slender funds of capitalists. For their part Canada's new industrialists soon recognized that, so far as industrial locations were concerned, it was very much a buyer's market. The bonus-hunting manufacturer quickly became a familiar part of the Canadian scene, playing off one town against another for the best deal. Relocations simply to secure bonuses were common, especially in the 1880s.

In Chapter 2, we noted the municipal bonuses to railways during the formative stages of Canadian urbanization. This was symptomatic of the sense of insecurity that affected even the larger settlements in this young and rather empty country. By 1895 municipal aid to railways in

Ontario amounted to $10.8 million. In Quebec it totalled $4.3 million (Rudin, 1982, p. 6). Such amounts were not huge compared to total railway investment, but they made up a very large part of municipal spending. In Ontario in 1894, railway bonuses formed almost a tenth of total municipal debt, more than for schools, sewers or gas and electricity (Ontario, 1896).

Having established such practices in relation to railways, their extension to manufacturing was perhaps a natural development. Yet similar US experiences, of railroads routinely requesting local subsidies en route, triggered a backlash. Until the South redefined legal precedent in the 1930s, the notion of US municipalities openly giving financial assistance to industrialists was usually rejected. (Even in Canada, local assistance to industrialists, though very large by international standards, never matched the earlier railway bonuses.)

The very fact that higher governments in the United States (and Britain) inhibited municipal assistance adds a governmental dimension to its existence in Canada. The reconstruction of Canadian government following the 1867 Act created new provincial and dominion institutions. Clearly it took time for these new higher agencies to assert in practice their theoretical constitutional dominance over existing local administrations. Obviously too, the inherent divisions of responsibility in a three-tier governmental framework implied a more decentralized power structure. The position of economic policy, theoretically a dominion role, was particularly confused, again giving more scope for local independence. Nor, finally, should we underestimate the simple role of sheer distance as a factor encouraging local autonomy.

The Bonusing System in Practice

The inducements themselves took several forms. Strictly speaking, true bonuses were straight cash payments but municipal loans on favourable terms, usually interest free, were also common. So too were local tax exemptions and fixed assessments, whereby the level of local taxes was guaranteed at a low level for a fixed period. Other assistance included gifts or subsidized provision of land, factory buildings, water, electric power and various other incentives, such as connections ('switches') to railways.

An 1899 Ontario survey, covering all types of municipal assistance to manufacturers since 1870, recorded their total value at $2.3 million (Ontario, 1900). Such was the extent of unquantified assistance and omissions, however, that the true figure must have topped $3 million (Bloomfield, 1985). The same survey also showed how widespread financial assistance actually was in the province. Almost all cities, most towns and many villages and townships admitted assisting manufacturers. Case studies in other provinces suggested similar patterns. By 1900, for example, Quebec's municipalities had evidently outdone their Ontarian equivalents (Rudin, 1982). There is also evidence of great activity in the western and maritime provinces.

Misgivings already voiced in the late nineteenth century began to grow after 1900. Yet incentives remained common in the first decades of the new century. Elizabeth Bloomfield, on whose meticulous work this account often draws, has identified assistance worth $4.6 million granted between 1901 and 1924 in southern Ontario (Bloomfield, 1985). By this last date, however, most incentives were becoming unlawful. The western provinces took the earliest effective steps. Saskatchewan, for example, legislated against municipal assistance in 1908 and Alberta in 1913. Quebec introduced severe restrictions in 1919 and Ontario in 1922 and 1924, though the practice lingered in the maritime provinces (Bloomfield, 1981; 1983b, pp. 62–63). In all areas, however, many local exceptions persisted into the 1930s and even beyond.

Everywhere the most active municipalities, proportionately, were ambitious places in the small to middle size range. Thus by 1900, the big city of Toronto, with roughly 200,000 inhabitants, had granted only modest industrial tax exemptions, amounting to $150,000 (Ontario,

1900; Beeby, 1984). In the smaller Ontarian cities of Guelph and St Catherines, similar exemptions were equivalent to roughly $4 per capita. And so, generally speaking, the trend continued. Much the most active were rapidly growing smaller towns such as Berlin, Oshawa and Fort William/Port Arthur (all still under 10,000 inhabitants in 1901) whose experiences give the authentic flavour of what Naylor (1975, p. 130) has termed the 'bonusing craze'. Thus by 1901 Berlin (renamed Kitchener in 1916) had, over thirty years, passed more than fifty bonusing bylaws, mainly granting tax exemptions (English and McLaughlin, 1983, pp. 236–239; Bloomfield, 1983*a*).

Meanwhile Oshawa, already generous with assistance, boldly voted a $50,000 interest free loan in 1900 to the McLaughlin Carriage Company to keep it in the town after its factory had burned down (Oshawa Bylaw 480, 1900). Equivalent to over $11 for each inhabitant at the time, Oshawa's generosity reflected the fact that sixteen other municipalities had already made competing offers (Hoig, 1933, p. 95; McLaughlin, 1954). In the event, though, Oshawa's support proved prescient. McLaughlin's subsequently became General Motors of Canada, one of the country's manufacturing giants.

More common, though, was the backing of losers. Nowhere was this carried to the heroic proportions revealed in the fiercely competitive twin towns on Lake Superior, Fort William and Port Arthur (later united as Thunder Bay) (Tronrud, 1990). Between them they had less than 7,000 inhabitants in 1901. Yet they managed to grant an astonishing $1.15 million in bonuses to industrialists by 1913. Big payments by any standards, these were almost certainly the greatest per capita manufacturing bonuses paid anywhere. Despite this municipal largesse, two-thirds of the principal recipients failed within the timescale of their assistance.

If Port Arthur and Fort William were the most extreme examples, there were many others, especially in central and eastern Canada, that came close in the desperate scramble to bribe industrialists to come to – or stay in – their towns.

With municipalities competing so fiercely and expensively, it was quite natural that they would also wish to tell the world, or at least the Americans, who soon became the principal source of manufacturing plants, what they had on offer.

Spreading the Message

Advertising, publicity and public relations were central aspects of local promotion, becoming more so as the more outlandish financial incentives began to be curtailed. Advertising, the widest and most impersonal form of promotional communication, was always a powerful tool in reaching those external investors as yet unknown to local leaders. Because investors were so scarce, however, it was necessary to combine general advertising with more targeted strategies.

Any inkling that a firm might be considering a move, or opening a branch factory, would bring offers. Factory fires, as we have seen, provided wonderful opportunities for places to try their luck (e.g. Naylor, 1975, pp. 146–147). Another favourite prospect were firms in Toronto and Montreal, targeted by places offering cheaper land and buildings, lower wage costs and, often, specific inducements (Beeby, 1984. pp. 204–207). Usually, initial approaches would allude to possible incentives. If a local brochure were available then this would also be sent. Personal meetings, presentations and visits played their part as negotiations proceeded.

As well as local council leaders, the leaders of local boards of trade or chambers of commerce (often, in practice, the same people) would play key roles (Bloomfield, 1983*c*). Boards or chambers (the latter title more typical of post-1920 foundations) were the formal collective organizations for local business, existing in all but the very smallest communities. In selling the place to possible newcomers, they would naturally stress soundness in the local business climate and prospects for growth. They were also very important in the generation of early advertising materials for their towns and cities.

Special supplements of local newspapers were a very early means of selling places to industrialists (e.g. *Ontario Reformer*, 1911). Funded by local business advertisements, they offered an inexpensive if crude form of publicity. By the 1890s more elaborate and lavish brochures began to appear, using glazed, high quality paper with fine photographs and line illustrations. Sometimes these were locally produced by boards of trade, often as annual handbooks (Tronrud, 1990, p. 1). Berlin's board, for example, was very active in this, as in other promotional endeavours (Bloomfield 1983*a*, 1983*c*). In other cases specialist publishers became involved. The Canadian Souvenir Publishing Company of Toronto, for example, concentrated on 'advertising progressive Canadian towns' (Oshawa, 1898, p. 6).

The expense of these productions meant that local subscriptions or, increasingly, municipal subventions were necessary to underwrite them. Municipalities had never shrunk from advertising their towns when they felt it necessary. Even in the 1870s advertisements for ambitious Canadian towns appeared in newspapers and business publications across North America, sometimes paid for by municipalities (e.g. Bloomfield, 1983*a*, p. 219). Yet more formal municipal involvement came later. In 1897 all Ontario municipalities secured modest powers to spend up to $500 annually on local advertising ($100 for places with less than 5,000 people) (Ontario, 1897, s17). This greater financial security coincided with the appearance of high quality promotional booklets, uncluttered with the advertisements of local firms. Boards of trade or specialist publishers still usually produced them, but publication could now be backed by municipal funds. The volume and quality of journal advertising, typically in business publications, also increased noticeably.

Another trend evident in Ontario from the turn of the century was the appointment of specific local officials, departments or committees charged with industrial promotion and publicity. The larger centres tended to take earliest action, reflecting perhaps their desire actually to sell themselves rather than merely buy factories.

Hamilton, for example, created an Industrial Committee in 1903 (Middleton and Walker, 1980, p. 35), expanding on the work of an earlier Reception Committee. After similar initiatives in the late 1890s, Toronto appointed a Department of Industries and Publicity headed by an Industrial Commissioner in 1906 ('questions cheerfully answered') (Beeby, 1984, p. 219).

Smaller places soon followed. By 1910 Brantford and Fort William also had industrial commissioners and Owen Sound boasted its own Industrial Committee (*Heaton's*, 1910, pp. 308, 319, 437). Also in 1910, general Ontario legislation permitted all cities to appoint Industrial Commissioners (Ontario, 1910, s7). Not everywhere could or did take advantage of these powers but by the 1920s there was a general trend towards professionalism. Business directories or advertisements now included many more references to industrial commissioners, industrial or publicity committees or similar.

Compared to western Canada, however, local advertising and related efforts in Ontario and Quebec were rather limited. Because the 'frontier' promotional needs to attract settlers and dispose of land continued to be very important (perhaps also because there were fewer financial inducements on offer), advertising budgets were far higher than further east. Winnipeg City Council allocated extensive funds for advertising in the 1870s and 1890s. When a Winnipeg Development and Industrial Bureau was established in 1906, specifically to attract industry, it was rewarded with $112,000 of council grants over six years (Artibise, 1970). Though more modest, Edmonton City Council's similar grants to its board of trade in 1905 and 1911, $18,500 in total, were still more generous than was typical further east (Bloomfield, 1983*b*, p. 64).

The Local Politics of Promotion

In general terms, as we have seen, local financial inducements and advertising grew out of the prevailing circumstances of late nineteenth- and early twentieth-century Canada. Yet the exact local mix of influences and outcomes always varied. The strength of the desire for growth and willingness to commit local funds were not uniform. Ever more insistent voices of scepticism could be heard in many communities and, even more, in provincial governments.

There were many possible objections to active industrial promotion. Existing local businesses were obviously unhappy to see local tax revenues spent on new firms whose products competed with their own. Significantly, one of Ontario's first legal curbs on bonusing, in 1888, specifically ruled out the aiding of competitors (Bloomfield, 1981). That the province legislated so early on this shows the strength of local business fears. The measure was not fully effective, but this sign of *intent* was revealing about local political concerns.

Even if direct product competition did not exist, established local businesses might also worry that new firms would pay higher wage rates, creaming off the best workers and pushing up labour costs. Such opinions were commonly voiced in Berlin by the early twentieth century (Bloomfield, 1983a, p. 233). Another objection was that subsidized firms were often bad risks. That so many failed or left within a few years of being assisted clearly affected local opinions.

For their part, ordinary people, particularly in larger centres, typically wanted municipal funds used to improve the community, not bribing yet more industrialists. Many of the very places that spent most on industrial promotion remained primitive overgrown villages with muddy, un-paved streets and few public services. Even in early twentieth-century Berlin, with an extremely high success rate amongst assisted firms, the population at large began to tire of paying for further inducements (English and McLaughlin, 1983, pp. 93–102; Bloomfield, 1983a, p. 233). Sometimes workers objected to assistance given to notorious employers. In 1893, for example, there was vocal working class opposition in Hamilton to a bonus for the American McCormick Harvester Company (Weaver, 1982, pp. 88–89).

Such business and popular misgivings about assistance to attract manufacturers were gradually acknowledged within Ontario's provincial legislation. Increasingly, incentives became conditional on votes of all ratepayers, not simply council approval. Progressively stricter rules about the size of majority and proportion of ratepayers voting were also introduced. Again 1900 was a turning point in this respect. The general effect was to ensure that local objections could be voiced and decisions not simply pushed through by an alliance of council and board of trade.

These shifts in provincial law help explain how the mounting local political tensions about assistance to industry were managed and incorporated into decision making. Yet they also make even more remarkable the continued high level of inducements during the first two decades of the twentieth century. What was it which generated local commitment to growth, sufficient to override the obvious objections and mounting legal obstacles?

The Basis for Local Consent

The simple answer is that the local political culture of communities which pursued active promotional policies was dominated by a belief in growth based on factories (Bloomfield, 1983b). Something of the authentic nature of such beliefs is captured in this breathless editorializing from one of Oshawa's newspapers, in December 1873:

. . . in a place in the situation of Oshawa, surrounded by a very limited agricultural county, whose benefits are keenly contested for by many rival towns . . . there is but one outlet to prosperity – but one means by which we can attain rank among the centres of industry of the country, and that is by fostering manufacturing enterprise. Upon its attendant train of advantages, substantial and real, of population, trade, circulation of money, and all the impulses of vitality which it gives the community, nearly all branches of trade and commerce which go to contribute to prosperity mainly depend and therefore every portion of the community [is] to a certain extent as deeply interested, indirectly, in the success of these institutions as the promoters of them are directly. (*Ontario Reformer*, 5.12.1873)

In cities with extensive existing industries, it was inherently more difficult to pursue very active promotion. Even though Toronto's industrial base came under threat in the 1880s, the city's sheer size and diversity made it difficult to secure local consent for big subsidies (Beeby, 1984, pp. 212–214). Yet for less developed places the logic of promoting new industries was simple and more compelling: subsidies would build the basis for growth, in turn drawing more population to strengthen the local tax base, progressively reducing the costs of subsidies to each citizen and allowing other improvements.

This growth ethos became all-pervasive in the actively bonusing community. As we have seen, local newspapers were one of the principal sustainers of growth-mindedness within the community. Extensive and approving reporting of the activities and views of the local board of trade was usual. In turn the local business interest would play a critical role in ensuring the local council reflected and followed their viewpoint. Board of trade approved lists of candidates for councils or major municipal offices were common.

In the increasingly important popular votes on bylaws authorizing assistance, boards of trade also did much canvassing to secure the right result (Bloomfield, 1983b, p. 84). Sometimes the power of this business/council nexus was used corruptly, in support of bonuses to firms in which leading councillors secretly held shares, as in Fort William and Port Arthur (Tronrud, 1990). In other cases, such as Berlin, tax exemptions were shared around the factories as a way of cosily committing all businessmen to the principle of inducements.

This simple picture of direct manipulation of the political process by local business does not explain everything, however. Oshawa's generous loan to McLaughlin in 1900 was certainly not hindered by the head of the firm having lately been mayor and there being several family members on the council (Farewell, 1973, p. 78; Hoig, 1933, p. 95). Yet popular endorsement of the authorizing bylaw for this, the town's biggest ever inducement, was overwhelming (Naylor, 1975, p. 147). Behind it lay a genuine popular desire to keep this respected and important local employer.

Other towns came to their promotional policies by different routes. Some places, for example Paris and Hanover in Ontario, were anxious to lay a proper social basis for their communities to grow. Seeing the presence of marriageable women as crucial to this objective, they took particular care to support industries that would employ women (Parr, 1990). Berlin's ethnicity, as a predominantly German community, also assisted wider agreement over its industrial policy. Significantly, some of the most serious objections to its promotional policies came from non-German businessmen (Bloomfield, 1983a, p. 231).

Overall, however, communities which actively sought new industries did so because their business leaders told them it was a good thing and, for a while at least, they saw no major reason to disbelieve them. The many places which, in this extraordinary episode, committed community funds in the pursuit of factories felt they had no real alternatives. They must, as they saw it, bonus or be left behind.

BRITAIN: CONSTRAINED PROMOTION

Broad Motivations and Constraints

In 1899 the Chamber of Commerce and Borough Council of Luton came together to form a New Industries Committee. Within a few months the Committee produced what was almost certainly the first British industrial promotional brochure, *Luton as an Industrial Centre* (1900). It also began actively wooing new industries, quickly winning several important successes, including Luton's future mainstay, Vauxhall cars. Within a few years Luton's lead was followed elsewhere.

The Derby Borough Development Committee appeared in 1906 (Bonsall, 1988). By 1910 broadly similar promotional programmes had appeared in Letchworth Garden City, Wolverhampton, Worcester, Wigan and West Ham. Many similar schemes were in varying stages of development by 1914 (Ward, 1990).

There was, however, an important difference between most of these programmes and those we have identified in Canada. In Britain the main concern was a potentially vulnerable or actively declining industrial base. Luton's straw hatmakers were worried about their town's overdependence on one industry that was subject to increasing foreign competition and, moreover, gave employment to women but offered little for men (Dyer and Dony, 1975, p. 143). In Derby the concern was an overdependence on a shrinking engineering industry. We have seen that this fear of decline might occasionally have been a factor in Canada, for example when Toronto was losing firms in the 1880s, but Canada's bonusing craze occurred within an emergent urban industrial system. It was most actively pursued by communities that were extremely small by British standards.

With over 36,000 population in 1901, Luton was one of the smallest of the first wave of British industrial promoters. Yet it was already about three and half times bigger than Berlin and over eight times bigger than Oshawa. In Britain industrial promotion emerged within an already very mature urban system that was experiencing mounting economic insecurity. Only in the rather special case of Letchworth (and later Welwyn) Garden City did British towns have to create entirely new industrial bases (Miller, 1989, pp. 112–124). In short, British industrial promotion, particularly as it expanded in extent and scope during the interwar years, was essentially concerned with regeneration, searching for replacement industries, rather than true boosterism.

This regenerative emphasis must be seen within the wider setting of a changing manufacturing economy. The older staple industries faced increasing problems from the end of the nineteenth century. Closures and significant unemployment affected many areas before 1914 (Southall, 1988), a trend which intensified greatly between the wars. Meanwhile new industries such as motor vehicles, electrical engineering and consumer goods were emerging, less tied to traditional manufacturing locations (Barlow Commission, 1940, pp. 36–48). There was also a growing potential for geographical mobility of manufacturing investment. In part this reflected the impacts of new production and distribution technologies, such as electric power and the motor vehicle, easing former locational constraints.

Other factors were also involved, however. The appearance of more multi-plant national and multi-national firms was very important (Jones, 1988). The branch plant had been integral to Canadian industrialization from the outset, but it marked a distinct change in Britain where local capital had been so characteristic of early industrialization. Such multi-locational firms were now less tied to particular towns and were able to shift locations within a wider spatial framework.

As in Canada, these economic changes were intensified by national policies. Increasing Edwardian fears of import tariffs and, more specifically, the 1907 Patent Act encouraged foreign interest in direct investment in Britain (Jones, 1988, pp. 435, 438–439). They also encouraged individual towns to seek foreign firms. Luton, for example, renewed its campaign in the wake of the 1907 Act and quickly attracted the Swedish ball-bearing manufacturer, Skefco (*Bedfordshire Advertiser*, 6.11.08). Such policy shifts were not yet as important for foreign investment as Canada's 1878 tariff, however. Equivalent British changes only came between the wars, culminating with the ending of free trade in 1931 (Law, 1981, pp. 176–177). The impetus to local industrial promotional efforts was correspondingly large.

In other, more specific, ways national policies were much more discouraging to local promotion. British local governments had far less freedom than their Canadian equivalents to advertise or offer inducements. We saw in Chapter 3 how much trouble British resorts had in securing even the most modest powers to advertise. Competitive municipal advertising to attract industry was seen as straying even further beyond the pale by the Local Government Board and its interwar successor, the Ministry of Health. The very idea of local subsidies triggered nothing short of complete revulsion.

Early Promotional Efforts

Lack of sympathy from central government left several options to those localities which felt impelled to seek new industries. They could give up their ambitions, which few did, though most had to tone them down. They could rely entirely on private initiatives, which some certainly tried. They could take municipal action to advertise their areas, perhaps even offer inducements, and hope that no-one who objected noticed. This was very common, though very risky if large amounts were involved. Finally, they could press for powers to implement the local policies they wanted, again a very common strategy.

From the very outset the dilemmas were painfully apparent. In Luton, for example, the New Industries Committee immediately asked for a contribution from the council. Total expenditure was a mere £50, paltry by comparison with Canadian spending. Yet the council soon discovered it could not legally contribute even this. Despite little risk of surcharge, caution reigned and they contributed only £20. Meanwhile the Chamber of Commerce, with no equivalent legal restrictions was even more cautious, leaving the initial campaign £20 short (*Luton News*, 6.12.1900).

With variations, this same story played itself out in many towns. The bigger local manufacturers were often unenthusiastic. This was especially so when their own businesses were under pressure. As we saw in Canada, new industries could easily disturb established employers' control of local economies. Yet the typical British scenario of promotion against a backcloth of stagnation or

decline in an established industrial town intensified such jealousies. Existing employers felt that they, not new industries, should get any assistance or encouragement. Certainly they would not usually pay to attract new industries.

Other private interests partly bridged the gap. Local landowners could sometimes be important allies in mounting a private programme, ensuring that suitable sites were available on attractive terms. The schemes of both Luton and Cardiff benefited by such co-operation from the big estates (LNIC, 1900, p. 9; 1905, p. 28; *Western Mail*, 15 and 16.9.08). Very occasionally land owners dominated the whole process, as at Trafford Park, where a pioneering industrial estate was developed adjoining Manchester Docks, promoted by a single estate company (TPE, 1923). Railway companies were also important in a few places, but were never the major players they were in marketing resorts or suburbs.

Almost invariably, the eyes of would-be industrial promoters turned to local councils. In some cases, such as West Ham (Martin, 1966, p. 21; Powell, 1973, p. 78) and Cardiff, councils themselves actually took the first steps. The funding of poor relief, still before 1914 the principal safety net for the unemployed, from the same local tax base as councils meant that local economic distress was something they could not ignore (Finer, 1950, pp. 155–160). This concern grew especially early in West Ham, where socialist sentiments were strong and respect for central restrictions limited. Local public works to relieve distress were becoming common by the early twentieth century. It was natural that councils would also consider ways of avoiding such problems.

A powerful incentive in the hands of many councils was electricity supply. By 1901 municipalities accounted for 54 per cent of electricity sales, increasing to 68 per cent by 1914 (Finer, 1941, p. 58). Since the new, mobile industries also used electricity, it was an obvious inducement. However, price discrimination in favour of new users was illegal. But an efficient, high capacity local public supply system with attractive industrial tariffs was a powerful selling point before 1914. Derby, for example, made much of its new electricity service in its marketing. Rolls Royce's move to the town from Manchester in 1908 owed much to this (Bloomfield, 1978, pp. 130–132; Bonsall, 1988). West Ham meanwhile advertised that it had the cheapest power in the south of England (Martin, 1966, p. 21). Both towns also offered cheap rentals of electric motors, offering further savings to industrialists.

Electricity and other municipal trading services also had less obvious promotional uses. Surplus lands acquired for utilities were often marketed for industrial development (though this mainly occurred between the wars). More subtly, profits from such utilities often also funded promotional advertising (Fogarty, 1947, p. 73). There was, indeed, a certain legality because new industries would mean extra business for the utilities. Yet the credibility of this argument was frequently stretched, as when Sheffield decided in 1918 to fund the work of its new Development Committee from surpluses on its tramways account (Hawson, 1968, pp. 152–153). Moreover, higher utility charges to pay for promotional advertising could easily become counterproductive. Such inventiveness certainly did not provide adequate funding to promote the industrial town.

Thus it was that industrial towns and cities regularly joined the resorts in dashing themselves on the rocks of central government disapproval of competitive place advertising. Local powers permitting such advertising were sought by Liverpool (1905), Pontefract (1906), Cardiff (1909), Bristol, St Helens (both 1911), Bristol (again) and Ellesmere Port (both 1914) (Hansard, 41 HL Deb 5s, c556; 61 HC Deb 5s cc2016–17). With the partial exception of Bristol, all were summarily rejected. Bristol secured limited powers to advertise its municipal docks, on the grounds that competing railway-owned docks could advertise without restriction. It subsequently marketed part of its dock estate for industry (PRO BT 56/40 CIA 1800/64).

There was little legally most councils could do. They still had responsibility for valuation of property for local tax purposes (LLEC, 1914, pp. 652–656). Yet Canadian-style fixed assessments, or indeed any other exemptions from local taxes, were strictly illegal. It almost certainly occurred, however. West Ham actually dropped hints in its publicity, but even guarded references were very rare. In similar vein, the borough also made much of its laxer building and fire regulations compared to the neighbouring London County area. None of these rather desperate expedients altered the threadbare nature of local promotion, however.

Developments in the Early Interwar Years

Yet the worsening economic circumstances of the interwar years tempted more places to try their luck. Despite growing central responsibilities for unemployment benefit, local poor relief costs soared during the 1920s, as older industries decayed. By the end of the decade the relief of poverty accounted for over half of local tax-based spending in the worst affected areas. Tighter central controls on local borrowing in depressed areas also prevented large scale public works to create employment (Ward, 1984; 1986). To areas affected or at risk of decline, new private investment seemed the only way to avoid the vicious circle of economic and fiscal decay.

As before 1914, there was a varying mix of private and public initiatives. Some, like Edinburgh's Society for the Promotion of Trade (1921) (Stephenson, 1921), the Liverpool Organisation (1924) (PRO BT 56/41/CIA 1800/121, NW 1271/1931: 4) or the Tees District Development Board (1930) (PRO BT 56/39/CIA 1800/27), were largely business-led ventures. In other cases councils acted through quasi-private initiatives such as the Bristol Development Board (1928) (PRO BT 56/41/CIA 1800/121, SW Division Report).

Many councils continued to seek powers for an openly promotional role, however. Again, such sentiments were strongest in boroughs which tried (and invariably failed) to secure local advertising powers. Sheffield, clearly ill at ease raiding its tramways fund, fell first in 1920. It was followed, in quick succession, by Wigan (1921), Hull (1924), Newport (1925), Accrington (1928), Birkenhead (1929), West Hartlepool and Southampton (both 1931) (PRO HLG 57/357; PRO HLG 52/1392). Excepting the last, it is striking how these would-be promoters mirror the new geography of interwar unemployment (Ward, 1988a, pp. 18–23).

Some broadening of promotional action also took place. There were, for example, a growing number of exhibitions and trade fairs in the 1920s. One which came to be seen as a model for local and regional self promotion was the North East Coast Exhibition, held in Newcastle in 1929, which attracted 4.5 million visitors (Baglee, 1979; PRO BT 56/38/CIA 1800/1 and 2, memo 10/29). The municipal information bureaux that appeared in the resorts in the early 1920s also spread to industrial cities (PRO HLG 29/179; PRO BT 56/38 CIA 1800/11). Local support for these new initiatives partly reflected their importance for existing industries.

Yet new industries remained the great prize. The 1920s saw municipalities also finding new incentives, as older tactics lost their sharpness. Electricity supply remained an important selling point, but no longer gave individual places a real competitive edge. Local tax valuation also became more tightly regulated under the Rating and Valuation Act of 1925 (Finer, 1950, pp. 413–418). Any hint of offered exemptions from local taxes was immediately stamped on by the Ministry of Health (Ministry of Health, 1926, p. 86). In 1926, however, came the first sign of a fruitful future area for municipal incentives: site provision. The Stoke-on-Trent Corporation Act gave local powers for a surplus land preparation scheme, notable because it helped draw the French Michelin Company to Stoke in 1927. Over the next few years local land acquisition, preparation and disposal powers became important, if only semi-lawful, parts of local industrial promotion.

Industrial Promotion and the 1931 Act

The most widespread priority remained the power to advertise, against which the Ministry of Health had so firmly set its face. In the late 1920s, however, municipal promoters found an ally in central government. He was Sir Horace Wilson, the Chief Industrial Adviser, a resolute opponent of interventionist national industrial policies (Lowe and Roberts, 1987). His particular fear was that Ramsay MacDonald's second Labour government, in power from 1929 to 1931, would want to take drastic action to assist the depressed areas in the North, Wales and Scotland. Instead he wanted modest local or 'bottom-up' regional initiatives. The first such effort was the Lancashire Industrial Development Council (1931) (PRO HLG 52/1393). Equivalent bodies soon followed, for Scotland (also 1931), South Wales and Monmouthshire (1932), the North East (1934) and Cumberland (1935) (PRO BT 104/1; Fogarty, 1947).

Before these bodies could properly be established, however, they needed a reliable source of funding. Wilson wanted local authorities to be able to contribute to his new regional development agencies. Meanwhile, as we saw in Chapter 3, the resorts were pressing for advertising powers to promote overseas tourism, a campaign backed in 1927 by the Association of Municipal Corporations. Yet the possible extension of such powers to industrial promotion was firmly blocked by the Federation of British Industries (FBI) (PRO HLG 29/179; PRO HLG 52/116). The Federation rejected outright any extra local tax burdens on existing industries. Its stance reflected the familiar opposition of established businesses to municipal expenditure to attract new industries.

It was only when the 1929 Local Government Act exempted manufacturers from 75 per cent of local taxes that FBI opposition faded away (Mair, 1986). At this point Wilson added his powerful support. The desired modest local advertising powers could breathe life into his new regional industrial promotion agencies. These, in turn, could achieve his major aim of avoiding any expensive central commitments on depressed areas. The imminent ending of free trade added further arguments in support of the measure. Faced with such a powerful alliance of interests, the Ministry of Health conceded.

The resultant 1931 Local Authorities (Publicity) Act, as we saw, gave extremely modest powers: only a half penny rate maximum expenditure; only exercised overseas and through a centrally approved agency, the Travel and Industrial Development Association. That, at least, was the theory. Even more than in the resorts, where other powers were available, industrial towns widely ignored the overseas restriction (Fogarty, 1947, p. 74). Overall, the volume of promotion increased with speed and intensity during the 1930s. By 1939, Fogarty found 85 per cent of county boroughs and 35 per cent of other urban authorities engaged in some sort of promotional activity (*ibid*, pp. 18–19). As well as the already familiar advertising and brochures, more sophisticated approaches were being used, especially by the larger regional bodies. Research, commissioned from local universities, became more common. So too did targeted marketing, in one case extending to Jewish businesses in countries vulnerable to Nazi takeover (*ibid*, p. 227).

Local Promotion and the Special Areas

The mid-1930s brought a significant shift in direct central policy towards the depressed regions, some of which were designated as Special Areas (Ward, 1988*a*, pp. 211–225). Introduced in 1934, they marked a modest beginning for 'top-down' regional initiatives, a modification of the non-interventionist approach urged by Wilson. From 1935 Special Areas policies began to become closely associated with promoting industrial development, including industrial estate development and modest financial assistance for new industries.

The relation of these centrally-orchestrated actions to more locally based promotion was initially encouraging. Extra funding was provided for regional development bodies and some local agencies were actually nursed into being by the Special Areas office (e.g. PRO BT 104/1). The problem (or virtue in Wilson's eyes) was restricted funding. Many depressed areas gained little. Lancashire was almost totally ineligible. Even in officially scheduled areas, such as the North-East, the concentration of projects to enhance their promotional impact meant that many localities gained little (e.g. Loebl, 1988, pp. 152–164).

In such circumstances their local governments renewed their efforts to develop their own inducements, the main emphasis being now on land, buildings and loans. During the 1930s there was a marked growth in local Acts permitting development and disposal of surplus lands (PRO HLG 54/574, 12/44). A few also gave powers to grant loans to private businesses. In fact only three local acts, for Liverpool (1936), and Jarrow and Tynemouth (both 1939) made specific reference to factory developments. But many other municipalities, for example Rotherham, Manchester (Barlow Commission, 1940, p. 282) and Burnley (*Burnley Express and News*, 28.11.36; 3.4.37; Hansard, 324 HC Deb 5s c1161; 326 c3333) 'stretched' their local powers to cover factories, a move of dubious legality. Yet there is little doubt that, as a Ministry of Health civil servant later reflected, most municipalities seeking such powers '. . . meant in fact to erect factories every time in the north and midlands anyway!' (PRO HLG 54/574, 6.5.45).

In fact, Liverpool's (entirely legal) scheme was the largest of the pre-1939 local initiatives. It formed part of a city-wide strategy of economic and spatial restructuring, involving factory developments and loans to industrialists at Speke, Aintree and Knowsley and elsewhere (PRO HLG 54/265). Most pre-1939 attention was focused on Speke, where the industrial estate was part of a municipal satellite town scheme (Barlow Commission, 1940, pp. 282–283). It was, however, the case of Jarrow on Tyneside which brought to a head the emergent tensions between 'top-down' and 'bottom-up' approaches to promoting industry.

The town was acutely depressed, with chronic unemployment (Wilkinson, 1939). Central government action had closed the shipyard which employed virtually all its workers and offered nothing in return. As well as initiating the famous 1936 Jarrow Crusade, the town council also launched a new industries policy (*Newcastle Evening Chronicle*, 25.9.36). Its 1939 local Act was a Liverpool-style programme but with compulsory land purchase and additional advertising powers (PRO BT 104/11). Although funding, at £100,000, fell well short of what the council had wanted, it was still the most ambitious legally sanctioned local industrial promotion programme in interwar Britain.

The problem was that it cut across the emerging idea, then being considered by the Royal Commission on the Distribution of the Industrial Population (Barlow Report, 1940), of centrally-directed regional policy. Jarrow's local programme would compete directly with Special Area industrial estates. There were growing worries whether any local authorities, 'even of the calibre of Liverpool', ought to be allowed to possess local powers (PRO BT 104/11, 1/39). By the late 1930s, therefore, support was widening for the Ministry of Health's traditional opposition to local promotion.

Jarrow had suffered so much and won such public sympathy that opposition to its local powers would have been very difficult (*Hansard*, 348 HC Deb 5s, cc500–17). Yet during 1937–39 factory development or similar local powers were being refused to Southampton (1937), Birkenhead, Nottingham and Stockton on Tees (1938) and Bootle (1939) (PRO HLG 54/574, 9/41). The trend away from local initiative accelerated in the war years, particularly as new centrally-directed regional industrial policies appeared under the 1945 Distribution of Industry Act (Parsons, 1986, pp. 60–86). Later changes, for example the nationalization of electricity in 1947, further diminished direct municipal involvements with economic development.

The flowering of local initiative in Britain was, then, very brief. The most striking thing is how limited, even threadbare, were local inducements in Britain compared to Canada. Overall we must conclude that, even at its most ambitious, local promotion in Britain was too limited to restore prosperity. At best, in places like Luton or Derby, or later Burnley or Liverpool, promotion added a little to what places could already offer. It certainly helped focus local attitudes and signal a desire to attract investment. Yet success followed only if other factors were also favourable. At worst, though, local promotion did little harm, a conclusion which has not been universally endorsed for Canada or our final example, the US South.

THE SELLING OF THE SOUTH

The 'New South' and Industrial Development

The Canadian and British examples encourage the notion that localized industrial promotion is something that countries ought properly to grow out of. From the interwar period both followed locational policies for industrial development that increasingly transcended the locality. If inducements were to be given, then this was the prerogative of higher governments. Canada's tradition of vigorous local action was increasingly harnessed to wider provincial and federal planning strategies over the post-1945 years (Rea, 1985, pp. 217–221). Britain's more constrained local tradition was more easily subordinated to 'top-down' regional policies and assistance. In both countries, at least until the rejection of higher level spatial planning in the 1980s, localized industrial promotion moved into the background.

Our last example, the US South, shows that an

approach to industrial promotion that retained a very strong local dimension could, in some circumstances, continue through the post-1945 years. Telling this story, we draw heavily on Cobb's work, especially his masterly study *The Selling of the South* (1993, originally 1982). In it, he shows that the marketing of the US South since the 1930s can, indeed, be regarded as the most astonishing of all twentieth-century episodes of local industrial promotion.

As in Canada, the 1860s were a defining decade for the US South (Cobb, 1984). But while Canada was able to confirm its distinctly separate identity within North America, the South failed utterly in its attempt to create an independent Confederate nation. The post-Civil War decades witnessed the emergent vision of a 'New South', taking this failed nation beyond Confederate notions of an agrarian utopia based on slavery and the plantation (Gaston, 1970). The new vision was based on industrialization, yet the shortage of indigenous capital in the South meant that investors and industrialists had to be attracted from the North.

From the 1880s this message was spread at countless business club luncheons, in boosterist brochures and newspaper editorials. It had no greater champion than a young journalist and orator called Henry W. Grady, editor of the *Atlanta Constitution* newspaper. Indeed, Atlanta soon came to think of itself as the capital of the 'New South' (Russell, 1988). By boosterist rhetoric it asserted its dominance over rivals such as the old Southern capital of Richmond and the emergent industrial city of Birmingham.

Yet it took more than mere words to make the 'New South' become reality. Unlike Canada, the South had no tariff barriers that might have stimulated industrial investment. Distance, easily conquered by the new railroads, was the only barrier to the distribution of the industrial products of the northern states. As Grady himself observed of a Georgia funeral, everything except corpse and hole were from the North (Cobb, 1984, p. 12). Moreover, many commentators have detected a continuing anti-industrialism on

the part of the Southern planters who feared industry would destroy their profits and their way of life (Cobb, 1988). Apart from slavery, many of the economic and social realities of the 'Old South' survived the rhetoric.

There were exceptions. The South was very far from being a homogeneous region. Cities such as Atlanta or Birmingham changed sufficiently in the later nineteenth century to give the 'New South' vision some credibility. A tradition of competitive local promotional advertising, by chambers of commerce or various other business organizations and city councils soon established itself. A spate of advertising brochures poured from Atlanta by the 1880s and many other towns and cities soon followed suit. Atlanta's hosting of trade conventions, pioneering in the South, further boosted its image as a progressive business city. By 1886 Atlanta was being described by a Massachussetts newspaper as 'one of the best advertised cities in the United States' (cited Russell, 1988, p. 240). In 1890 another newspaper in its old rival, Richmond, directly equated Atlanta's growth with 'its determination to leave no opportunity underutilized to advertise the advantages which it has to offer'.

Yet neither Atlanta nor most other places were offering any significant special inducements to draw industrial development. There were many exhortations to local capitalists to put their money into new or incoming ventures, particularly cotton mills (e.g. Lemmon, 1966, p. 166). Tax exemptions at state or occasionally local level were not unknown, especially for railroads. But the signals given to external investors could often be bewildering. At the most basic level, the constitutions of most states, rewritten in the decades after the Civil War, precluded the giving of aid to private businesses, though legal interpretations varied greatly.

Apparently contradictory actions were common, even within the same states. Thus Mississippi simultaneously in 1896 revoked its tax exemptions to the Illinois Central Railroad and granted an automatic ten year tax deferral to new industries (Cobb, 1988, p. 53). At the local level, patterns could also be very variable. In 1902, for example, the Virginia town of Manchester was offering liberal tax exemptions to new industries, but its big neighbour Richmond promised nothing in the many promotional booklets produced by its boosters (Engelhardt, 1902, p. 162). The broad point is that there was nothing approaching the scale of Canadian bonusing at this time. And although the growth of Southern industry was impressive when viewed in isolation, the differential between North and South had actually widened by the early twentieth century.

Forward Atlanta

Gradually in the twentieth century the notion of a more progressive municipality actively promoting industrial growth began to take hold. This sentiment expressed itself in many ways. There were growing pressures for improved public services and facilities as were typical throughout North America or Britain (Tindall, 1963; Brownell, 1972). Education, highways, health and public transit were important areas where many cities tackled Southern backwardness. (This progressivism did not, however, extend to one of its key dimensions, racism.) Increasingly, these improvements in the social and physical infrastructure of cities in the South were linked with more active marketing to draw in industry.

The main reason was the onset of terminal decline in the traditional rural industries of the 'Old South' (Cobb, 1984, pp. 32–35). The boll weevil savaged cotton farming in the 1920s, pushing several states into more decisive policies to promote industry. Thus Georgia introduced the option of five year local industrial tax exemptions from 1924 as a direct response to this threat to rural economy (*Georgia Laws*, Pt I, Title VI, No. 73, 1925). Even now though, the shift was not yet total. Conservative interests continued to oppose the idea of an urban industrial South even as the agrarian alternative was rapidly becoming untenable.

Building on its late nineteenth century lead, Atlanta definitively pointed the way. As one commentator wrote of the urban South in the 1920s 'There is no God but Advertising, and Atlanta is his prophet' (cited Tindall, 1963, p. 95). This was no exaggeration. Atlanta's Chamber of Commerce set entirely new standards for the volume and quality of city advertising and marketing during the 1920s. These influenced not just its Southern rivals but cities in other parts of North America and even Britain. As we will see in Chapter 9, they have continued to influence Atlanta boosterism in more recent years.

The first moves came in 1924 when the Chamber of Commerce established an Industrial Bureau (Garofalo, 1976, p. 190). The Bureau was intended to liaise with and persuade new industrial investors in the city. Despite its confident launch, however, the following year brought mounting local business fears that the city was losing ground to Florida, where extensive land promotion was drawing migrants and investors from other parts of the South. The Atlanta business community, led by the Chamber of Commerce, decided to challenge this Southern rival with a massive advertising campaign (FAC, nd *c*1930, pp. 8–10). They established much the most aggressive city marketing machine ever created up to that time, the Forward Atlanta Commission.

Yet this bold initiative was fully supported locally with a major fund-raising drive. The biggest subscribers were the city itself and Georgia Power, each with $48,000. Next came the city's clearing banks with $37,500 and adjoining Fulton County with $30,000. The biggest single business subscriber gave $23,000. Locally-based Coca-Cola gave $12,500. But there were also very many smaller subscribers, totalling over 10,000 by 1929. In 1920s prices the resultant budget, over $722,000, was immense. By the end of 1929, over $500,000 had been spent on advertising in a wide range of magazines and trade papers together with newspapers in New York, Chicago, Detroit, Cleveland, Boston, Miami and Greenville, South Carolina (FAC, nd *c*1930, pp. 50–51). The campaign began in 1926–27 with an advertising blitz, alone costing over $130,000, in the popular *Saturday Evening Post*. An impressive array of supporting literature, some general, some specialized for particular industries, was used to follow up the advertisements (*ibid*, pp. 58–59; 71). By 1929 over 160,000 pieces had been distributed.

Fully professional in its organization, using a local advertising agency, Forward Atlanta was something quite new. As we will see in the next chapter, its advertising was well conceived and designed. As no city had ever managed before, its efforts rested on a clear and consistent marketing strategy, to make the city into the industrial headquarters of the South. Although the campaign sent out national and international ripples, the regional influence was indeed huge, encouraging many other cities into pale imitation. Thus Atlanta'a historic rival, Richmond, launched its own Chamber of Commerce-sponsored 'Forward' movement shortly after Atlanta (RCC, 1933). As so often in place selling, however, the publicity advantage went to the first, and boldest, in the field.

Balance Agriculture with Industry

Yet Atlanta had something definite to sell. Its rail communications, its natural resources, its openness and generally favourable business climate were its attractions. Financial or other obvious inducements were still not deemed necessary. This was less true for much of the rest of the South over the next few years. The 1930s brought worsening problems as the world depression triggered a collapse in primary product prices. Federal farm improvement policies further reduced the demand for farm labour. Rural local governments, even state governments, faced the real prospect of bankruptcy as outmigration and poverty increased.

It was against this background that the most desperate actions were taken, often by small towns in the more rural states in the early 1930s. Industrial plants were literally bought with municipal bonds, especially in Tennessee (Cobb, 1993, pp. 6–8). Liberal exemptions from local and state taxes were widely granted, especially in Arkansas, Alabama and Louisiana. Free or heavily subsidized sites, water and power were often offered. In some cases (such as Manchester and Dickson in Tennessee) workers given employment were directly covenanted to repay from their wages loans raised to build new factories or the taxes foregone. There were other, even more dubious, examples. Lewisburg, Tennessee built a shoe factory with public money, claiming it to be a town hall. Ellisville, Mississippi misused federal education funds to build a 'training' hosiery factory, using child labour.

An attempt, in Mississippi in 1936, to introduce some sanity, laid the basis for an enduring promotional approach (*ibid*, 1993, pp. 8–34). This was the so-called Balance Agriculture with Industry (BAWI) Program launched by Governor White. As Mayor of Columbia, Mississippi, White had first hand experience of the problems of attracting new industries during the early 1930s. Elected State Governor in 1935, he developed a scheme that allowed local governments to finance factory building for new industries by issuing interest-bearing municipal bonds. Since these were public issues, however, their interest was tax exempt. The factories themselves were public property and also, therefore, tax free. The rents paid by the new industries were very low and certainly insufficient to redeem the bonds, which were repaid mainly by the local tax payers. There were some safeguards, however. Bonds could not be issued beyond ten per cent of local assessable tax value. A two-thirds majority in a local referendum was also necessary.

In all these respects, BAWI was certainly comparable to Canadian bonusing but with one very important difference. The whole Program was overseen by a state-wide Industrial Commission whose approval was required before a project could proceed. This body, comprising three very experienced businessmen, undertook industrial marketing, carefully targeting and screening likely prospects. It also investigated their business soundness. Finally it brought incoming firm and individual community together. A locality had to show that it had a labour surplus equivalent to one and a half times the projected employment of the incoming firm. The Commission also took on much of the detailed negotiation with new industries.

The initial BAWI Program was not outstandingly successful in the number of firms it attracted. By 1940 just seven were operational with another five in process. Many were fairly low wage employers of female labour, not that this was at all remarkable in this very low wage state. Nor was the size of initial workforces particularly impressive. By 1939 the public cost per job was $600. It had also proved extremely controversial, prompting many claims that it was unconstitutional, socialistic and wasteful (e.g. Adams and Pollard, 1936–37). In 1940 the Program lapsed and the enabling legislation was repealed.

BAWI after World War II

A few years later, however, the picture looked very different. By 1943 the BAWI plants had expanded and now accounted for 23 per cent of Mississippi's industrial payroll. The public cost per job had fallen to $90, a much more impressive figure. Clearly the wartime boom made an important difference, but Mississippi actually had rather a bad war, industrially speaking, and got precious few of the new wartime plants. The prospect of peace held little hope for improvements without some conscious policy. BAWI now began to look like a model that Mississippi ought to repeat. Certainly neighbouring states had become very interested in emulating the scheme.

Many states had continued with various desperate measures through the 1930s to stem the tide of economic decline, poverty and out-migration. Tennessee, for example had continued with its various, entirely illegal, schemes to subsidize new industries. Louisiana instituted its own industrial programme with state-wide tax exemptions for new industries (Cobb, 1993, pp. 46–48). But in the early post-war years

BAWI-type schemes were adopted in Tennessee, Alabama and Kentucky as well as Mississippi itself (*ibid*, p. 36). By 1962 nine Southern and twelve non-Southern states had adopted the concept of municipal bond financing of factories. By 1968 only North Carolina in the South lacked such powers. And by the early 1990s all US states had them, a rare instance of Mississippi, infamous for its poverty and backwardness, leading in the ways of statecraft (NASDA, 1993).

There were important differences between most of these schemes and the original BAWI Program, however. The more enduring formula involved municipal industrial revenue bonds which were redeemed by the rental payments of the industries rather than out of local taxation. Though this meant that factory rentals were higher, the loans were still at low interest and there were still inbuilt tax exemptions for both lender and industrialist. In the post-war boom years, however, the backing of issues with the full faith and credit of local governments was largely unnecessary. Small to medium sized industries, and even larger firms seeking to cut costs, found much to attract them in such packages, especially in the low wage South.

In some states, particularly Alabama, such bond schemes were constructed in ways that gave much greater discretion to the locality compared to the original scheme (Cobb, 1993, p. 36). State legislation of 1949 authorized the formation of municipal industrial development corporations with powers to issue bonds to finance, build and equip factories. A further Act in 1951 gave cities the power to enter directly into contracts with industrialists, without a state agency acting as intermediary.

A Balance Sheet

Across the South, therefore, there developed a post-war pattern of active industrial promotion, expensive in tax dollars foregone but hugely impressive in numbers of new industrial jobs. Always this promotion involved local government, even though the exact extent varied from state to state. In contrast to Britain or Canada, however, there was little sense of local and higher governments competing for authority. Instead there was a genuine sense of partnership. Localities actively competed with each other for incoming industries through their chambers of commerce or local development councils while state governments policed the framework of local subsidies, avoiding the glaring abuses of the depression years.

The states also played a key marketing role, with increasingly sophisticated industrial development agencies. State governors such as George Wallace of Alabama (or, in later years, Bill Clinton of Arkansas) became super salesmen for their states (ibid, pp. 75, 89). Their political support depended on securing industries throughout the state so they were always willing to front promotional delegations and identify themselves directly with incoming industries. Southern political leaders also sanctioned huge marketing and advertising budgets. By 1964 a survey of advertising budgets in thirty-one states showed the Southern average over 70 per cent greater than the general average (ibid, pp. 90–91). Southern states made up seven of the top ten spenders. State expenditure accounted for the major share of place advertising, certainly more than three-quarters by the 1960s. But local efforts, especially in bigger cities such as Atlanta, paid fulsome homage to the memory of Henry Grady. In the early 1960s, for example, a further 'Forward Atlanta' campaign was launched, raising an astonishing $1.6 million in private subscriptions, of which about half was spent on advertising. Cities with tourist as well as industrial potential advertised on an even more lavish scale.

There is much more that could be said about this remarkable tradition of Southern boosterism, which is described and analysed in great depth elsewhere. For our purposes we have said almost enough, however, demonstrating that a viable tradition of localized industrial promotion thrived even as elsewhere it fell victim to the ambitions of higher governments. In one sense it may be a model that holds some appeal for latter-day local economists. If this is so, it is necessary to sound a much more negative note. For all the laudable merits of locality and community values which these schemes harnessed, much of the selling of the South served merely to reproduce many of the region's traditional problems within the new factories. Wages were normally very low. Worker and environmental protection was very poor. Unions were largely forbidden under euphemistic 'right to work' laws and many communities would refuse plants which were unionized because of the knock-on effects on existing work forces.

Furthermore, the policies were often tainted with racist sentiment. As well as being Alabama's super-salesman, George Wallace, it should not be forgotten, was also a super-segregationist. There was a growing reluctance by incoming industries to relocate in segregated cities, particularly as civil rights protests increased from the late 1950s (ibid, pp. 122–150). Atlanta, rather more moderate than the rest of the South, typically turned the peaceful desegregation of its own schools into a piece of promotional theatre. Yet very few Southern boosters displayed any real commitment to desegregation. At best there was a token acceptance of the inevitable. At worst there was the pretence of a problem that only existed somewhere else and a behind the scenes pressuring of blacks into silence on the grounds that complaints would damage the prospects for new industries.

There was then a very distinctive sociopolitical construction to the selling of the South, limiting its value as a wider model of local economic initiative. The economic weaknesses of the Southern model of industrialization began to be recognized in the late 1950s when the first moves to break the low wage, low skill syndrome became apparent. The promotion of the Raleigh-Durham Research Triangle in North Carolina represented the first Southern shift towards the new informational economy (ibid, pp. 171–176). Yet these and similar moves elsewhere were insufficient to transform the dominant character of Southern industrialization. In general, the promoters of the South got exactly what they paid for.

CONCLUSIONS

The episodes of industrial promotion we have examined in this chapter provide yet more evidence that local marketing and promotion are nothing new. They also show very clearly how such practices were most highly developed in marginal industrializing regions. Indigenous capital was short. Options were few. Incentives, therefore, often went well beyond what was prudent and sometimes touched on sheer craziness. Ideologically there also had to be a strong enough commitment to industrialization to generate local political acceptance for the advertising and subsidies to lure new industries. This was inherently easier to achieve in smaller towns where the pre-existing industrial base was limited, though we have seen how wider visions of a New South and a strong and economically independent Canadian nation were also extremely important.

There was no equivalent wider growth ethos in long-industrialized Britain. The vested local interests of existing industries were deeply entrenched. In addition, there were also much stronger institutional constraints on local promotional actions, even simple advertising, in Britain. Canada, for a time, and the South, seemingly in perpetuity, displayed great provincial/state sympathy for local promoters. In Britain central sympathy for local action was much more limited. Local autonomy had been eroded much further than in North America. Yet even in Britain, as elsewhere, there were specifically local forces that emboldened some localities to sell, or mortgage, themselves more than others.

This mixture of wider with more specifically local determinants of the selling of the industrial town is mirrored in the way the promotional message itself was constructed. It is to the advertising imagery of the industrial town that we now turn.

8

AN HONEST TALE PLAINLY TOLD?

Selling the industrial town was intended to be a down-to-earth, matter-of-fact business. There was, certainly, a recognized need to attract attention. Yet there was also a pervasive belief that campaigns which were too flashy might be counterproductive. The view was that the prospective new employer would be more convinced by an accumulation of relevant and accurate facts than by the beguiling imagery that was the essence of the tourist poster or the suburban advertisement. This, certainly, was the opinion endorsed by two of the most sophisticated place promotional agencies of the late nineteenth century, Atlanta's City Council and Chamber of Commerce. On the title page of their *Hand Book of the City of Atlanta* (Atlanta, 1898), they made absolutely sure the reader did not miss the point by quoting from Shakespeare's Richard III: 'An honest tale speeds best being plainly told'.

We must not accept such self-explanation without question, however. Certainly the mountains of factual data contained in most industrial promotional brochures seem at first sight to preclude deeper meanings. They are not the most promising terrain for the would-be breaker of place marketing codes. To be frank, many of them are deadly dull. But in starting the decoding process, it is important to recognize that such facts were being deployed to construct a picture of place as the boosters and regenerators would

have liked it to have been. The code was more cryptic, with fewer clues than for the resorts or the suburbs. But eventually they add up to give a picture, typically, of a place of destiny. Local history was selectively plundered to demonstrate the inevitability of success. The record of all present economic activity served, in the manner of its presentation, to bolster the same point. Everywhere in the promoted place there was efficiency, modernity and progress. Similarly, local social relations were portrayed, or implied to be, indicative of a desire to co-operate and succeed.

In this chapter we explore the generic variants of promotional language and visual image, both through general discussion and a more specific exploration of key parts of the promotional message. At the same time we also show that there were some distinctive local variations in both message and medium. We conclude these two chapters on the selling of the industrial town by considering present day practices of industrial place marketing. The shift away from traditional manufacturing throughout advanced industrial countries has decreased the emphasis on 'smokestack chasing' promotional approaches. Yet such mobile industry as is around is pursued as vigorously as ever and in ways that do not differ dramatically from the old established methods we have identified. We begin, however, with such promotional imagery in its original incarnation.

The Promoted Image of the Industrial Town

Image-Making: Key Words and Slogans

One of the most basic ways in which deeper meanings could be signalled was in the key words or slogans used to front promotional campaigns. Even the most worthy recitations of factual information for businessmen needed some title, usually of a very descriptive kind. Increasingly, however, there was a more conscious use of slogans designed to attract or focus attention on the place being advertised and to associate it with desirable characteristics. From a fairly early stage several distinct types of slogan were being used in industrial promotion. The most basic linked the name of the place with industry, prosperity progress or other positive sentiment. Key reinforcing words, such as 'centre', 'hub', 'gateway' or 'heart' were sometimes used.

Britain's first industrial promotional brochure, *Luton as an Industrial Centre* (1900), was a simple example of this type of slogan. Surprisingly though, several other places, clearly impressed by Luton's innovation, simply substituted their own names. This practice was followed, for example, by Cardiff (*c*1908) (*Western Mail*, 15.9.08), Sheffield (1918) (Hawson, 1968, pp. 152–153) and Derby (DBDC, nd *c*1928), amongst others. Other British variants on the same broad pattern were *The Industrial Advantages of Worcester* (nd *c*1909), *West Ham: The Factory Centre of Southern England* (*c*1910) (Powell, 1973, p. 78) or *Industrial Edinburgh* (Stephenson, 1921). Rather more inventive, by British standards, were *Trafford Park: Britain's Workshop and Storehouse* (TPE, 1923), *Nottingham: The Queen City of the Midlands* (1927) (Nix, 1995), *Derby: Bounding with Vital Industries* (DCPC, nd *c*1933) or *Birmingham: The City of A Thousand Trades* (BIB, nd *c*1939).

This simple way of constructing slogans was also common in North America. *Atlanta: The Twentieth Century City* (ACC, 1903), 'Toronto: The Capital City of Ontario' (*Heaton's*, 1910, p.

438), 'Hamilton, Canada: The Home of Industry' or 'Quebec: The Gateway of Canada' (both 1920) rested on already established positions (*Heaton's*, 1920, pp. 517; 520–521). One problem with this type of slogan was the temptation to try and cram in too much, making for a ponderous, even pompous, construction. An extreme example of this tendency was 'London, Ontario: Commercial, Industrial, Financial and Educational Metropolis of the Western Ontario Peninsula' (1920) (*ibid*, p. 501). After 1926, however, most places followed Atlanta's lead in theming their publicity around simple slogans, consistently used. 'Atlanta: Industrial Headquarters of the South', with logo, became the tagline on all Forward Atlanta's advertisements (FAC, nd *c*1930).

Another basic type of slogan construction involved snappy alliteration of the type employed in resort advertising. This approach had the advantage of avoiding some of the risks of pomposity noted above. Brochures with titles such as *Busy Berlin* (1910) (Bloomfield, 1983*c*, p. 85) or *Toronto: Favored Field for Factories* (1907) (Beeby, 1984, p. 219) were becoming common in North America in the early twentieth century. Equivalent British examples do not seem to have appeared until the interwar years. Again Britain's industrial promoters showed a quite remarkable lack of imagination and recycled similar titles many times over. Thus the less than snappy alliterative device in *Halifax Commercially Considered* (1928) (Smithies, 1974, p. 90) was used by Glasgow (1929) (PRO BT 56/39 CIA 1800/29), Barrow-in-Furness (Barrow, 1931) and Wakefield (Wakefield, 1932). *Burnley Means Business* (BCDC, 1935) was more original, though has not been without later, and perhaps unconscious, imitators. *Do It At Dundee* (DCDC, 1931) was another original slogan. It is not difficult to appreciate why it has remained unimitated.

More aggressive slogan constructions sometimes took the form of a more direct appeal, even a command, to the investor. These included the imperative, for example, *Place Your Factory in*

TORONTO

The Capital City of Ontario

KING STREET, TORONTO

Toronto offers to manufacturers Low Taxation, Cheap Water, High-Class Labor and Niagara Power at low rates. Excellent factory sites are available on two railways. For special opportunities see the Boards of Trade Register, page 324.

AN ILLUSTRATED DESCRIPTIVE PAMPHLET
will be sent free on application to

Commissioner of Industries, Toronto

Correspondence Invited   Questions Cheerfully Answered
When answering advertisements, please mention Heaton's Annual.

Even Toronto, much the largest city in Ontario, felt vulnerable enough to promote itself in the late nineteenth/early twentieth centuries. The reliance on a photograph of the central business district to show the essential character of the place was very typical of Canadian practice. This example dates from 1910.

Edinburgh (EDC, 1932). A variant of this was the accusatory question, such as 'MR MANU-FACTURER Why Aren't YOU in Our Town?' (*Heaton's*, 1920, p. 499) used by St Thomas, Ontario. (For good measure the town also claimed to be 'The Hub of the Best Section of Ontario').

Other refinements of the slogan were also apparent, including occasional puns, for example 'Tees-Side Bridges The World', used on a 1938 poster by the Tees District Development Board (Fogarty, 1947, p. 232). As yet, however, such subtleties or conscious attempts at humour were rare. If promotional advertisements caused amusement, it was almost always unintended.

Oshawa had one of the most aggressive industrial promotion policies of any Ontario settlement in the late nineteenth/early twentieth century. This brochure, dating from 1898, reveals something of its pretensions to greatness, albeit within a colonial frame of reference.

Image-Making: Key Visual Elements

Another window on the mythic vision of the promoted place was in the visual equivalent of the key word. The use of visual imagery was more restricted in industrial advertising than in the other areas we have examined in detail. Advertisements that were entirely word-based were not unknown. Even promotional brochures did not always feature illustrations in prominent positions such as on covers. Despite this, a visual language of industrial promotion was soon developed.

One of the most important and recurrent visual elements, especially in North America, was the map. A fundamental concern in place advertisements which were trying to draw investment in from distant sources was simply to establish where the place actually was. Many places were small and had names which were not unique to them. Moreover many of the key words used in promotional slogans, such as 'centre', 'hub' and 'gateway', were effectively claiming locational advantage. It was logical therefore to include a map to support such claims. Even larger places were not immune. Thus Atlanta's pioneering

promotional logo and tag-line incorporated a locational map.

Invariably such maps were distortions of spatial realities. The most common distortion arose because the map would, almost invariably, put the place being promoted at or close to its centre. It would also signify the place with a more prominent circle and larger lettering than other places shown. The impact of this alone could be very significant for a small town trying to talk itself up in the world, a very common condition in central Canada. When other distortions were introduced, such as the very selective inclusion of other places in the surrounding area, claims of local or regional dominance could be made to appear more credible. The 1920 advertisement for St Thomas, quoted above, was one such example, incorporating a map that omitted many larger centres in the vicinity. But there were many others.

Other dominant visual images included various kinds of broadly realistic representations of the promoted place. These might be in the form of photographs or drawn or painted illustrations. Some of the same comments apply to these as to their equivalents in the resorts. They were usually carefully selected views, designed to give a particular impression of place. In some cases actual scenes of industry were used, though since places were usually seeking to diversify, undue emphasis on particular industries could sometimes give the wrong impression (and perhaps stimulate local jealousies). More common, especially in advertisements for Canadian towns and cities, was the main street. This provided the opportunity to give the sense of a thriving community with impressive buildings and other attributes of civilization. This was, for example, how London, Ontario, sought to justify its grandiose claims noted above.

In Britain, however, we find a growing emphasis on anti-metropolitan locations, stressing more of the rural aspect. One of the pioneers here was Letchworth Garden City (e.g. FGC 1908a; nd c1908; nd c1909). Even stronger in this regard was the Forest of Dean. In the very unusual

STRATFORD

The Hub of Rich and Fertile Western Ontario

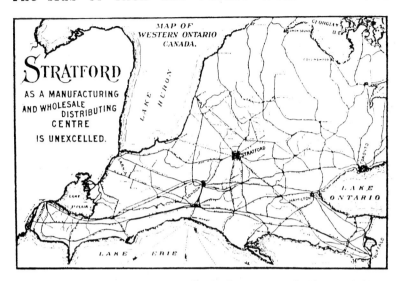

Stratford's Industrial Policy is Filling This Thriving City with Busy Factories

We offer excellent shipping facilities, Niagara power, a plentiful supply of skilled artisans, especially wood and iron workers, and generous civic assistance, including low fixed assessment.

We Shall be Pleased to Furnish Details

See description of Stratford on page 323

WRITE TO-DAY TO

The Secretary, Board of Trade

P. O. Box 353

STRATFORD, ONTARIO

When answering advertisements, please mention Heaton's Annual.

Typical early promotional advertising in Ontario. This example dates from 1910. The use of a map, centred on the promoted city, a slogan, based around a word – hub – that also asserts centrality and a promise of generous assistance are all very typical features.

circumstances of the early part of World War II, rural remoteness (for example from wartime bombing) was portrayed as a locational virtue (FDIDC, 1940).

Such emphases were, though, very uncommon. In larger cities, where the basic realities of civilization were less in doubt, the general views were sometimes deliberately presented as more impressionistic works of art. These were intended to associate the place with higher culture. Thus Atlanta, increasingly attuned to ways of asserting its metropolitan maturity, used an impressive

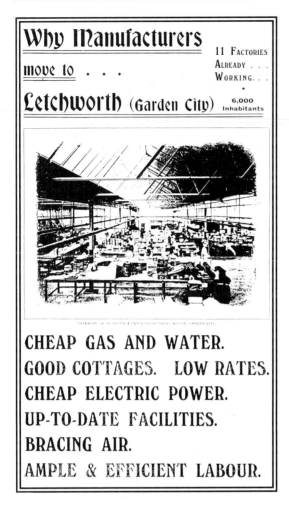

Why Manufacturers

move to . . .

Letchworth (Garden City)

11 Factories
Already . . .
Working. . .

6,000 Inhabitants

CHEAP GAS AND WATER.
GOOD COTTAGES.   LOW RATES.
CHEAP ELECTRIC POWER.
UP-TO-DATE FACILITIES.
BRACING AIR.
AMPLE & EFFICIENT LABOUR.

Letchworth (and later Welwyn) Garden City were amongst the most active British sellers of themselves in the early twentieth century. From 1908 industrial promotion became a priority, producing advertising of the kind shown here.

modern painting, *Atlanta by Night*, on the cover of its 1903 brochure mentioned above. The value of the painting as a realistic representation was decidedly limited, but it served to bolster Atlanta's big city credentials. One step further on was the Manchester Chamber of Commerce's artistic and beautifully produced 'slim volume' *Manchester: Heart of the Industrial North* (MCC, 1937), comprising a series of specially

commissioned watercolours that illustrated the city's life, with a foreword by the famous novelist and playwright J. B. Priestley. For a city that was known throughout the world as the first industrial city, this was a deliberate attempt to demonstrate that it had now achieved a higher plane of cultural development.

Landmark buildings or groups of buildings or engineering structures were sometimes used as a shorthand way of representing places. Richmond for example often included the Virginia state capitol as a central feature of its advertising (e.g. RCC, 1907; 1927). In Britain, Nottingham incorporated the castle and the Trent Bridge on the cover of its 1927 promotional brochure (Daniels and Rycroft, 1993). Bridges were especially popular devices in both British and North American publicity. This was perhaps because bridges combined visual interest with the suggestion of functional efficiency and a supremacy over nature that reinforced the theme of industrial progress.

It was, however, more difficult for the general run of industrial towns and cities to encapsulate their essence in one memorable building or structure. Quite simply, it was rare for them to possess anything which had sufficient visual potential to impress in this way. A common means of overcoming this problem and conveying the essence of place while avoiding the extremes of excessive realism or overly artistic treatments was to use a skyline, often in silhouette. This device did not need to be entirely realistic. Real buildings could be used, but often rearranged into a more exciting and dynamic juxtaposition. A very common variation was to produce two skylines (e.g. RCC, 1907; DCPC, nd *c*1933; BIB, nd *c*1939). One was industrial, comprising factories, chimneys (often smoking), and related structures. The other was civic, comprising churches, public buildings, universities and monuments. The intended effect was to show a place that had two facets, a workaday city of modern, busy industries, yet one that was also civilized. It was, though, important to show that these identities, though distinct, were not entirely separated.

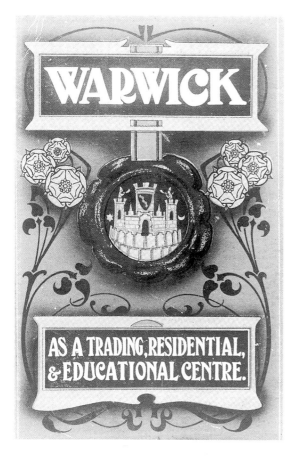

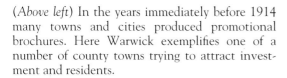

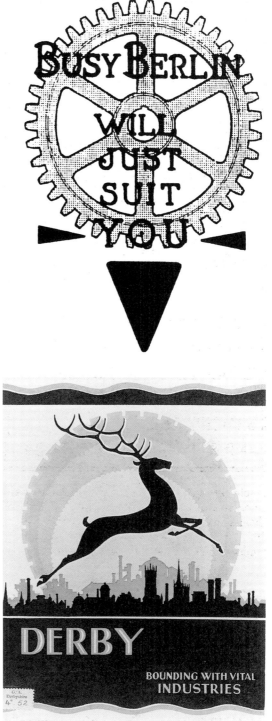

(*Above left*) In the years immediately before 1914 many towns and cities produced promotional brochures. Here Warwick exemplifies one of a number of county towns trying to attract investment and residents.

(*Above right*) Busy Berlin, one of the most active Canadian promoters, used advertising as well as tax exemptions to attract its largely German manufacturers. In this example from 1910 the cog wheel signifies manufacturing prosperity.

(*Right*)Early 1930s brochure from Derby. The conjunction of civic and industrial skylines and the cog wheel motifs were familiar promotional devices. The leaping stag and slogan were more original touches, however.

There were several possible ways of securing this effect, including superimposition and using railway trains to link the two scenes.

Another very common visual signifier in industrial promotional advertising was the cogwheel. In the era before electronics and high technology redrew manufacturing imagery, the cogwheel was one of the most powerful symbols of industrial well being. The turning wheel of industry gave the assurance of production, employment, prosperity and progress. It could also be used to signify that a place was at the centre of things industrially. Just as the cogwheel was integral to the proper functioning of the machine, so the place could be represented as an integral part of a wider industrial region. Accordingly we find cogwheel motifs used extensively within advertising compositions. Berlin, for example, used the cogwheel to reinforce visually the message of *Busy Berlin*. In Britain, Birmingham and Derby made prominent use of cogwheels in their 1930s' publicity. Birmingham – 'the city of change symbolised by the wheel' (BIB, nd *c*1939) embraced the full meanings of the cogwheel to reinforce its enduring 1930s slogan *Birmingham: The Hub of Industrial England* (BIB, nd *c*1932).

Other visual images were occasionally used in the construction of promotional advertising. In 1907, for example, Richmond adopted the device of the cornucopia, occasionally used in advertisements for western settlement but rare in industrial promotion publicity. From this horn, richly endowed with many advantages for business, came forth plenty, including a railroad locomotive, a cogwheel and miscellaneous boxes, barrels and other items. Compared to contemporary commercial advertising this was unremarkable in the extreme, but it represented a rare flight of fancy in the world of industrial publicity. Allusions to the same visual device are evident in the first Forward Atlanta advertisement, representing the nationally known firms which had moved to the city (FAC, nd *c*1930, pp. 86–87).

Overall though, the key textual and visual imageries of industrial promotion strayed only slightly from commonly perceived realities. Only rarely did they capture anything of the potency of the promotional ideology which underlay and motivated the advertising process. Still less were these concerns manifest beyond the covers, slogans and headlines of advertising materials. It is, nonetheless, important to give a sense of how promotional arguments were developed once the immediate impact had been achieved through slogans and visuals.

Use Facts, Not Generalities

Much of what was said in promotional brochures and advertisements was a direct description of facilities for supplying the main elements in production and distribution. Transport facilities, electricity, gas and water supply arrangements were invariably discussed in detail. Words such as 'modern', or 'efficient' were used liberally. Capacity was always abundant and costs were always attractive. Great attention was also lavished on existing industries, again emphasizing their modernity and efficiency. Photographs were normally used to reinforce the overall message and the reader was invited to admire gleaming power stations, gas works and production lines.

Similar treatment was meted out to the commercial and financial businesses of the city, underlining their importance for manufacturers. Further accumulations of impressive if arid factual information were typically included on other topics. One section that almost always appeared was that outlining the size and other favourable characteristics of the regional market within whatever radius of distance or travel time it was most impressive to employ. Educational facilities, public and social services, residential areas, cultural life and the opportunities for leisure also received the same relentless treatment.

In case the strict diet of statistical data became too indigestible, many brochures offered what were supposed to be tempting factual morsels at regular intervals throughout the text or, sometimes, handily collected together in one section.

Richmond, the traditional capital of the south tried hard to emulate Atlanta's impressive record of growth. This shows an early brochure produced in 1907 by the Richmond Chamber of Commerce. The jumble of images and text was very typical of much early place advertising.

By this means the distracted reader was able to marvel that, 'Within 80 miles of Manchester there is a population equal to the combined populations of Canada and South Africa' (LIDC, 1932, p. 8). Or that 'Richmond manufactures 500,000,000 regular-size cigars, 300,000,000 small cigars, and 40,000,000,000 cigarettes annually, in addition to vast quantities of smoking and chewing tobacco' (RCC, 1927, p. 17). The effects of such information on potential investors can only be imagined. Undoubtedly though the compilers of such brochures were placing an absolute premium on precision. In the last-quoted example, indeed, the reader was specifically urged 'when Speaking of RICHMOND Virginia Use Facts,

Not Generalities' (RCC, 1927, inside back cover).

In doing this, local promoters were, of course, trying to assure investors that such broader claims as they ventured were soundly based. Accurate, or at least detailed, information was everything. In 1898, for example, the compilers of the *Hand Book of the City of Atlanta* outlined their research methods in order to assure readers that their manufacturing data were based on a systematic local census, not wishful estimates (Atlanta, 1898, pp. 39–40). Other methods used to convince investors of their *bona fides* included the use of testimonial letters from established industrialists. Oshawa, for example, incorporated

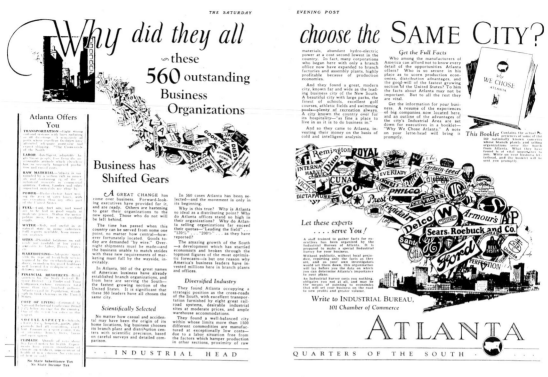

This was the first Forward Atlanta advertisement, in the high circulation *Saturday Evening Post* for 20 February 1926. All the main elements of the campaign are here. Note particularly, however, how existing successes, shown in a way that suggests a cornucopia, are central to the marketing proposition. Note also the offer of expert reports tailored exactly to individual business requirements, a practice at which Atlanta excelled.

facsimile letters of praise from the town's four main employers in its 1928 brochure (OCC, 1928: 56–59). Twenty years earlier Letchworth Garden City had produced an entire promotional brochure based on a complimentary speech by one of its earliest industrialists (FGC, 1908), supported with favourable press comments.

One section where brochures were often less than precise was in the matter of specific inducements and even, sometimes, available sites. Superficially this was rather surprising, but it actually reflected a rational approach. In part, places were anxious to avoid bonus-hunting industries coming solely to gain financial inducements. Their concerns also probably reflected a desire to avoid premature commitments when

the actual assistance finally granted would be a matter of negotiation on an individual basis. Similarly the inclusion of excessive detail about site availability might date the brochure too quickly. Practice did, however, vary on this. Some brochures included exhaustive details of sites as further testament of their commitment to precision.

A Spirit of Transcendent Energy

There are, however, parts of these promotional brochures which occasionally give greater insights on the mythic vision of place which underlay the factual overload. Amongst the most potent of these, at least in Britain and the US

South, was the potted history. Here, at least in the clearest form that promotional copywriters could manage, was the distillation of the supposed magic essence of place which would guarantee success. The tendency was present but much less well developed in Canada, perhaps because there was less history to recount. As we have already implied in the introduction, the US South, especially Atlanta, won hands down in giving grandiloquent expression to the underlying ingredient for success. These words, quoted from its 1903 Chamber of Commerce brochure, were already well honed from previous publications:

Atlanta is the result of a combination of advantages, on a commanding geographical location, turned to the best account by a spirit of transcendent energy, which surmounts all obstacles and builds even on disaster the fabric of success. The growth of this unconquerable spirit has been promoted by a unity of purpose which has prevented the domination of factions. Whatever local interests may clash, the good of Atlanta is always a rallying cry. (ACC, 1903, pp. 4–5)

Seeking northern investment, Atlanta's promoters were anxious to portray the city as the vigorous and progressive antithesis of 'Old South' torpor and backwardness. Rather like Britain's seaside resorts, the supposedly 'bracing' air of its elevated site was seen as crucial, albeit with even more extraordinary qualities:

Atlanta air is like Champagne; its people need no other stimulant. You can see it in their walk, and hear it in their talk. Few die and none resign their citizenship – those who go away come back when they can. There is no place like Atlanta, and no tonic like the 'Atlanta Spirit'. (ACC, 1909)

In a more modest way, we can find similar 'New South' sentiments informing the boosterist pamphlets of Richmond and other southern towns and cities (e.g. RCC, 1907).

In Britain it was not the experience of destruction in war, such a crucial test for the Atlanta Spirit, which provided proof of the will to succeed. That equivalent ingredient came from the country's experience as the first industrial nation, now invoked in a time of economic stress and decline. In 1932 the Lancashire Industrial

Development Council, for example, expressed the sentiments in terms that would not have shamed a Southern booster:

It is a strange but clearly traceable habit of nature to throw up constellations of talent that hang together at a given time in a given place . . . It happened that in Lancashire, less than 200 years go, there was thrown up a group of men as imbued with a passion for mechanics as a saint is with sanctity; and these men set going on the soil of Lancashire those forces and compulsions which were destined to turn the whole human race away from the method of living which till then it had employed.

It is not to be wondered at that Lancashire, the mother of industrial civilisation in this very real sense, has retained to this day powerful endowments from that fecundity which permitted her to people a world with new conceptions of living. (LIDC, 1932, p. 7)

Again the broad theme is not unique, even if aspects of the language, notably in relation to gender (to which we will return below), vary. The equivalent regional promotional body for South Wales and Monmouthshire made great play of its own history and traditions in its main publication, the magazine Land of My Fathers (*Hen Wlad Fy Nhadau*) published from 1935. The big British cities also displayed a particular fondness for celebrating past triumphs as evidence of their formula for success during the 1930s. As in Atlanta, the human basis of success was invariably stressed, capitalizing on the immanent advantages conferred by nature. 'This,' as J. B. Priestley wrote in one Manchester publication,

is good, but character is better. Perhaps the secret of the Manchester character is that it is nine-tenths hard north country grit, solid Lancashire bone and muscle and brain, plus a remaining tenth, acting as a leaven, of liberal minded and enterprising foreign influence, a contribution from Europe. (MCC, 1937, p. 5)

Character had also been invoked as the essence of Edinburgh's economic success in 1921, capable of transcending even the sinister new forces of socialism. Even, its brochure patronized, the 'local Labour M.P . . . is a fine type of the City characteristics – logical, persuasive and moderate' (Stephenson, 1921, p. 92). There were few cities indeed which did not try out such local spirit/character arguments at least to some extent, legitimizing them by local historical reference. Smaller places also recounted their histories and attempted to abstract some moral that pointed to a formula for success. The more lyrical flights of fancy were, however, associated with bigger cities and regional bodies.

Strikes Almost Unknown

Desirable local workforce characteristics were everywhere advertised with pride. Many brochures betrayed promoters' addiction to precision and detail on matters such as wage rates, skills and supply. Yet it is clear that copywriters, and those who briefed them, also wanted to promote an essentially romantic view of local labour relations. Typically this would draw heavily on the mythic vision of place and the 'spirit' or 'character' which had shaped it. In answering the question 'Why Industries Succeed in Sunderland?' (the very posing of which in 1931 in the face of a rapidly deepening depression was certainly indicative of a spirit of optimism), great emphasis was placed on the qualities of the workforce: 'Nurtured in industry, they are skilled, hardworking, thrifty, studious and healthy' (Sunderland, 1931, p. 17). With variations, these were very much the type of qualities which copywriters wanted to be able to stress.

It was, of course, very important to emphasize that local 'spirit' or 'character' was not expressed oppositionally, in labour organization or unrest. Where possible, places with strike-free records would use this in their advertising. In 1909, for example, Toronto advertised it had 'no strikes' (Beeby, 1984, p. 223). The following year Oshawa boasted, '[t]here are no union shops. Strikes almost unknown . . . ' (*Heaton's*, 1910, p. 317). By 1920 the increase in serious labour unrest had placed a premium on being able to make such claims. Hamilton advertised that it had a 'well supplied and contented labour market, which kept it free from strikes during the period of world unrest' (*Heaton's*, 1920, p. 517).

One city might also be able to score points off the notoriety of a neighbour or competitor. Issued at a time of acute national labour unrest Edinburgh's 1921 promotional brochure extolled, at unusual length, the virtues of local moderation:

What one might call the revolutionary element is almost absent, and class conflict, as compared with what is occasionally seen in other industrial areas – Clydeside for example – is conspicuous by its absence. (Stephenson 1921, p. 92)

Yet it was difficult to push this kind of argument very far. In its own 1921 booklet, Sunderland was forced to acknowledge that the times were abnormal amongst its workers but, it claimed, 'as a general rule they will be found industrious and thrifty, and the most cordial relationships exist between masters and men' (Sunderland, nd *c*1921, p. 6).

By the 1930s British brochures tended to say less about this topic. Some of the newer industrial districts, especially those which had known economic hardship, such as the Forest of Dean, could still make bold claims, however. As its 1940 brochure commented:

Disputes are almost unknown, and those minor ones which have occurred have been settled readily, by arbitration . . . The Forest inhabitants are steady, honest folk; those who have known the experience of having nothing to do are eager to recover the right sense of citizenship by proving their loyalty to their employers. (FDIDC, 1940, p. 26).

Yet, as so often, much of the most eloquent hokum on this topic came from the American South. In Richmond, for example,

Starting small and at a time when the closest co-operation between them was essential to the life of the infant industry, there was developed betwen [*sic*] employer and employee an understanding and appreciation, one for the other, which exists to this day. The influx of new blood has not been sufficient to break the bonds developed during those years and, in many cases, the sons preserve the relationships of their fathers.

As a result, Richmond has an established bond between employer and employee which makes labor disturbances practically unknown.' (RCC, nd *c*1923, p. 2)

Intelligent, Adaptable Anglo-Saxon People

Behind this lay a more specific Southern selling point, which Cobb has dubbed 'Anglo-Saxonism'(1993, p. 92), that became very common between the wars. We can trace the rise of these attitudes in the evolution of Atlanta's promotional publicity. In 1898 it was very much 'a cosmopolitan city': 'Almost every State in the North and West and every country in Europe is represented amongst its residents . . . ' (Atlanta, 1898, p. 85). Within a few years, however, the emphasis had changed, with 95 per cent of its people born in the South and the 'masterful spirit of the Anglo-Saxon' much in evidence (ACC, 1909). By 1926 this new theme had become a central part of the city's attractions: 'Intelligent, adaptable Anglo-Saxon people, free from the unreasonable attitude which elsewhere has so seriously hampered production and raised costs' (FAC, nd c1930, p. 86).

The underlying message was expressed even more clearly in a 1937 Louisville, Kentucky, advertisement, showing a worker, with the descriptive caption 'He speaks English!' (Cobb, 1993, p. 92). It went on to assure industrialists that 'Labor in Louisville doesn't require foremen who speak half a dozen different languages. Our workers are *American*. They talk and think American'. This was also the message that Richmond was purveying, with its boasts of '97% American Labor'. Behind these nativist sentiments lay a fear of trades unionism and socialism, closely associated in the American business mind with foreign immigrants in north-eastern cities.

Yet it was also part of a wider and more overt racist discourse. The prevalent and rather romantic picture of the dependable and loyal American-born Southern worker found echoes in specific portrayals of black workers. Again Richmond's boosters were the more explicit of the two main Southern cities in revealing prevailing attitudes:

Easily managed by those who understand him, tracable of temper, the negro practically has a monopoly in the manufacture of plug tobacco, in the heavier work of mills and some factories, and in other occupations best suited to him. (RCC, 1923, p. 2)

Though the increasing institutional formalities of racial segregation were not mentioned, the coded messages were clear enough. Brochures tended to emphasize that black workers lived in their own communities and were homeloving. In other words, they knew their place. Invariably there were bland assurances of an absence of racial tension. In its relentless desire to present all the facts Atlanta even went so far as to promise that lynchings and 'bloody scenes' had never occurred in the city (Atlanta, 1898, p. 87). Though seen as a selling point, it must actually have been rather alarming to be told this. Boosterist literature was not expected to conjure up such fearful images, even in the denial. It was in any case a promise that soon proved false. In 1906 Atlanta suffered some extremely bloody and widely publicized race riots. In 1915 an innocent Jewish man was removed from jail by an Atlanta mob and lynched. On such incidents the promotional literature was invariably silent.

Happy and Contented Employees

In explaining exactly what it was that made their workers so wonderfully loyal and compliant, promoters offered diverse reasons. In Britain, especially, many of the municipalities that had commissioned or paid for the brochures claimed at least some of the credit for themselves, on account of their social and welfare services. Yet, in doing this, municipalities were obliged to strike a careful balance. They had to show that their services were effectively operated and relevant to industry, but not so expensive as to create a serious tax burden. Local tax exemptions (or the general derating of industry in Britain after 1929) would in many cases have reduced the realities of this burden. But it always remained an important indicator of local political sensitivities to business.

Education, however, was a relatively easy area to justify expenditure. Technical education

The Competition
at your Gate

You may have the only product of its kind in the world — yet he in competition with a dozen other concerns, your neighbors.

If you are located in one of the old, congested American producing centers your costs are without question higher than they need to be. Your very location forces them up. There is just so much space, so much labor, no more. You compete with the factory across the street and around the corner for help. Your ground-rent is constantly climbing.

Come South and contrast your situation with conditions in the Atlanta Industrial Area. Here you will find factories whose locations cost very little, whose buildings were built for 20% to 35% less than is possible in other sections.

Their labor is willing, efficient, interested in the work—97% Anglo-Saxon. Their taxes are low. Raw materials come to them from close by at low prices. Power turns their wheels at rates among the lowest in America. Even climate is in their favor—equable, without the extremes of heat or cold which hamper smooth, uninterrupted operation in so many industries.

Dig into the actual dollars and cents figures here, and compare them with your own costs—and chalk up the savings against the cost of erecting a branch

plant here. Learn in how few years an Atlanta branch will pay for itself.

Then consider the marketing advantages. You know that you cannot get full volume from any section at a distance from your stock of goods under modern merchandising conditions. You know that trade demands overnight fill-in, that your competitors with nearby branches are getting some of the business to which you are entitled.

You know that the purchasing power of the Southern people has trebled in the last decade, that the South is America's fastest growing market. And your Southern salesmen will tell you that Atlanta is Distribution City to the South because of swift transportation by road, by rail—and now by 6000 miles of Air Mail service that radiates from this city.

Thus Atlanta presents a three-fold advantage as a branch location for your business. And those advantages translate themselves into better profits, bigger dividends for those who operate branches in this city and factories in the Atlanta Industrial Area.

The Atlanta Industrial Bureau is prepared to present a complete and unbiased survey of the region from the standpoint of your business, upon your request. This valuable work is done without charge or obligation, and in the strictest confidence.

Write INDUSTRIAL BUREAU, CHAMBER OF COMMERCE
Chamber of Commerce Building

Send for this Booklet
It contains the fundamental facts about Atlanta as a location for your Southern branch.

ATLANTA
Industrial Headquarters of the South

Another example of Forward Atlanta advertising, targeted directly at executives of factories in the North-East and Mid-West. The cheapness of southern locations is particularly stressed. Notice especially the claimed (and rather dubious) preponderance of Anglo-Saxon labour, very typical of southern industrial marketing. Black workers, already a sizeable proportion of Atlanta's workforce, are not mentioned.

in particular would enable the worker 'to rise high in his trade, benefiting his master and himself alike' (Sunderland, nd c1921, p. 6). Many promoters followed Derby in stating, quite categorically, that its educational facilities were 'meeting industry's needs' (Derby, 1928, p. 41). In fact most promotional brochures in all three countries, particularly those for larger centres, gave much attention to all aspects of education

(e.g. Atlanta, 1898, pp. 71–84; ACC, 1903, pp. 32–34).

Potentially more difficult was the heavy inter-war municipal expenditure on housing in Britain. This was given particular attention in most promotional brochures. That of Wakefield, which was proportionately the most active city housing authority in England and Wales, commands particular interest. In *Wakefield Commercially*

Considered, its 1932 industrial brochure, came the unapologetic comment that its policies had 'contributed largely to the solution of a social service problem that is of paramount importance to industry, realising that well-housed workers make happy and contented employees' (Wakefield, 1932, p. 7). Most other authorities took the same line, though these comments could sometimes conceal local tensions, especially in the more depressed towns.

The problems of working class housing did not arise or dominate the political agendas in the same way in Canada or the United States, so that it was not a heavy burden on local tax bases at this time. Discussions of housing conditions for working people were, however, very common. Where appropriate, promotional advertising emphasized the virtues of working class owner occupation. As the promoters of St Thomas explained in 1920, it had 'thousands of workmen who own their own homes, which tends to keep them here, thus stabilizing the labor supply' (*Heaton's*, 1920, p. 499). Oshawa's 1928 brochure specified more clearly what this stability meant: '80% of the workers own their own homes. The workers are conservative, productive and permanent' (OCC, 1928, p. 17). Similar sentiments occur in some American literature. Richmond, for example, emphasized the importance of home ownership as a producer of labour contentment, for both its white and black populations (RCC, nd *c*1923, p. 2). Although few British towns were yet in position to make much of the extent of working class owner occupation, those that were, like Burnley (BCDC, 1935, p. 48), did.

Other, wider, circumstances were also implicated in the shaping of local patterns of social relations conducive to profitable production. In the US South, much was made of the importance of churchgoing:

The religious and social atmosphere of Atlanta is wholesome and invigorating. It is a city of churches and the home of church-going people, and the community is honey-combed with fraternal organizations. (ACC, 1903, p. 9)

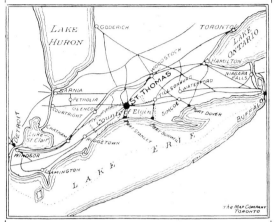

1920 advertisement for St Thomas, based around the familiar device of centralizing map. By now the references to direct municipal assistance were more muted, reflecting the tighter legal position. Note, however, the references to working class owner occupation and the offer of free rail interswitching, the latter a common Canadian incentive.

Outside the South this was, at most, a very minor theme in promotional texts. Some promotional brochures stressed the more secular diversions of parks, playing fields and other leisure facilities. The adage that 'all work and no play makes Jack a dull boy' was cited in several British brochures, with the appropriate moral being drawn (e.g. LNIC, 1900, p. 11; Sunderland, nd *c*1921, p. 6).

The Factory Mother . . .

A few promoters ventured into the homes of the workers, seeing the family as crucial in matters of productivity and labour relations. Although much publicity did not focus on this, that which did is important because of the insights is gives as to how industrial promotional images were constructed in relation to gender. In passing, we have already noted how rather general allusions to idealized notions of masculine and feminine traits appeared at the very heart of industrial promotional imagery, sometimes contributing directly to the creation of a mythic vision of place. In this section we subject the whole question of gender in industrial promotional imagery to closer examination.

At the more specific end of promotional image-making, we can identify several different attitudes in relation to women as factory workers. One approach rested on the notion that the typical worker was male, serviced by a supportive wife. Edinburgh's 1921 brochure, unusually revealing on all matters related to the workforce, expressed this viewpoint with particular clarity. While noting the presence of unmarried women in the workforce, it went on:

It is pleasant to be able to add that the 'married woman' class in Edinburgh industry is conspicuous by its absence, and what this means to the home and social life of the worker and of the community only those can appreciate who have lived and worked in centres where the factory mother is a regular feature' (Stephenson, 1921, pp. 92–93)

In Luton, the issue was handled rather differently. One of the underlying motivations of its pioneering new industries programme was to alter its late nineteenth century reputation as 'a place where the men were kept by the women' (Dyer and Dony, 1975, p. 128). There was a good deal of local unease at the way the highly seasonal work of hat making deflected mothers from their domestic duties for long periods, including at night. The new industries programme was essentially about providing better jobs for men, with the definite implication that mothers particularly

could thereby spend more time servicing their families. Yet the promotional arguments were subtly deployed and made much of the importance of unmarried women's work, by reducing their father's demands for higher wages:

. . . the head of a family in Luton can often afford to labour at 18s to 20s when he has three daughters each earning 15s to 20s. (LNIC, 1900, p. 11)

It is significant that the wage earning potential of the mother, which could often be at least as good as her daughters, was not mentioned.

Different again was Nottingham where the strong female representation in the workforce of both old established and newer industries was very fully reflected in the imagery of 1920s' promotional material (Daniels and Rycroft, 1993, p. 468; Nix, 1995). It was rare though to find British publicity moving quite so far in such detailed representation. Certainly by the 1930s, most places were pragmatic enough to acknowledge that many of the newer light industries which were creating most of the new jobs were looking for women workers. However, there was an underlying sense, which informed but was by no means specific to promotional literature, that these jobs were of only secondary significance compared to real, men's work. Even the promoters of a depressed Lancashire textile town like Burnley, where women were a hugely important traditional part of the workforce, showed a disproportionate interest in getting new work for men (*Burnley Express and News*, 28.8.37). Male work was felt to be the key to stemming outmigration.

In Canada in the early twentieth century, many towns had still not shed their raw and restless frontier image. Many towns' advertisements countered such impressions by stressing stable populations, living in their own homes etc. As we noted in the last chapter, the promoters of some places felt that women were a crucial stabilizing force (Parr, 1990). If women could be attracted or retained then families and a more settled community would surely follow. They therefore courted industries which employed women and girls at least as avidly as those which employed men. And if jobs could be provided for all family members this would offset the effects of lower wages and assist the accumulation of wealth and community development. Thus Paris, advertising itself in 1920 in overtly 'feminine' terms ('What a Pretty Town'), promised employment 'for every member of every family' (*Heaton's*, 1920, p. 418).

... Or Mother of Industrial Civilization?

Some places were, then, explicitly recognizing the importance of women as industrial workers. Yet this detail did not always accord with the deeper symbolism of promotional imagery. Although by no means universal, there was a recurrent underlying tendency in industrial place marketing to equate manufacturing strength with virility. Meanwhile the promoted place had to *attract* this masculine industry and facilitate its *reproduction*, both of which lent themselves to representation by female analogy. Such imagery appears in an exact form in the long extract from the Lancashire Industrial Development Council quoted earlier. In this, industrial innovation is repeatedly referred to as the work of men. Meanwhile Lancashire is clearly female, the 'mother of industrial civilisation', with words such as 'fecundity' and 'conceptions' added to strengthen the image.

Such representation of places in feminine imagery was not, of course, by any means unique to industrial towns. We have seen how images of virgin territory were used to sell the frontier, bathing belles to sell the seaside and female domesticity to sell the suburb. Indeed female imagery was more seriously strained in the context of the industrial town, since the traditional concept of industry as hard and dirty challenged contemporary notions of the feminine ideal. Yet

the interwar years were an important period of transition, from smoking chimneys to cleaner and brighter factories powered by electricity. This allowed a stronger association of industry with female imagery, something which was clearly apparent in, for example, Nottingham's promotional material. This used a regal female figure to represent its slogan *The Queen City of the Midlands* and to 'promote Nottingham as relatively pure and healthy, free from the grime and drabness usually associated with coalfield areas' (Daniels and Rycroft, 1993, p. 468).

A more traditional broad approach was that of Birmingham in the late 1930s (BIB, nd *c*1939). Industry is represented here by a giant blacksmith, suffused with the red glow of the furnace, wielding his hammer. He is framed by a cog wheel and towers over a city skyline contrived from key local buildings. Most prominent of these is the Council House clocktower which takes on an unmistakable phallic symbolism on account of its positioning in relation to the giant blacksmith. The imagery thereby becomes more overtly sexual. The subliminal message is therefore not so much city as mother of industry as guarantor of industrial virility and economic tumescence. The essential message reappeared in progressively cruder form in more permissive post-war years, perhaps reaching its nadir in the 1970s when nude female pin ups were used to attract industrialists to Aycliffe and Peterlee New Towns (Aldridge, 1996, p. 34).

Such approaches represent a few instances where the gender-based imagery is unusually highly developed in an industrial promotional context. They show that, despite its essentially prosaic character and frequent crudeness, the selling of the industrial town did not entirely lack symbolic depth. Sometimes at least, the promotional tale was less plainly told than appeared at first sight.

This is a particularly fine example of promotional art from Birmingham in the later 1930s. The familiar industrial and civic skylines and cogwheel are apparent, here with a god like male metal worker representing the city's industrial prowess. The positioning of the city council's clocktower makes it into a phallic symbol, as if guaranteeing industrial virility.

MARKETING THE INDUSTRIAL TOWN IN THE CONTEMPORARY WORLD

The End of Smokestack Chasing?

Much writing on contemporary place marketing in the 1980s and 1990s indicates that what is misleadingly termed 'smokestack chasing', is being eclipsed. (We know from earlier discussion that the process was, even by the 1930s, essentially about the attraction of relatively clean factories powered by publicly supplied electricity. Yet promotional imagery was, as we have seen, rather slow to reflect realities.) Now, however, place competition for factories, whether smokey or smoke-free, is diminishing. Heritage, tourism, tertiary and quaternary sector employment are heralded as the keys to a post-industrial future. In so far as manufacturing appears on the place

FOREST of DEAN
INDUSTRIAL
ESTATES

GLOUCESTERSHIRE

This 1940 promotional brochure produced for the Forest of Dean represents a rather different imagery to that which hitherto had been typical. The emphasis on environment in industrial promotion, partly here an attempt to stress remoteness from wartime bombing, presages a theme which became more important in the later twentieth century.

marketing agenda, there is now supposed to be less concern about attracting mobile industries, more with the fostering of indigenous enterprise. Industrial promotion is now about growing new small firms and encouraging established businesses. The indiscriminate throwing of advertising matter and subsidies at potential inward industrial investors is now, supposedly, *passe*.

Oddly though, despite this new conventional wisdom of the world of local economic development, the volume of investment-related promotional advertising is greater than ever. Nor are financial or other inducements unknown.

Certainly the objects of desire are no longer just manufacturers, as we will see in the next two chapters. But the prospect of a major new car or electronics plant is still sufficient to trigger an instant 'beauty contest' (more female imagery) between places. A few places might genuinely see themselves as beyond such competition, but many evidently do not.

As we noted in the last chapter, localized place competition was a continuous tradition in the US South. Unlike Britain or Canada, the hand of higher governments never overturned local initiative. The pattern in Britain moved farthest away from local promotion as central government developed its own distribution of industry policies from 1945, supported by incentives and advertising. Local promotion existed only within the framework of these policies. Powers to advertise and to create industrial sites came mainly through the time-honoured drip feed of local powers. As before 1939, these were often refused or granted only grudgingly. Where general powers existed they were typically conceded by central government as private members' legislation, such as the Local Authorities (Land) Act 1963 (*Hansard*, 672 HC Deb 5s, cc841–57). As before 1939, local authorities often used such powers with great ingenuity but the scope for truly independent action was very limited.

The Canadian pattern was broadly similar, although elements of local initiative survived longer (Rea, 1985, pp. 217–238). In both Britain and Canada, therefore, the recent growth of localized industrial promotion has marked the rediscovery of a virtually forgotten tradition. Meanwhile, even in the US South, the established promotional tradition was re-invigorated in the 1980s. There were two broad dimensions of these changes, one economic and the other political. Since the mid-1970s there have been major structural changes in the world economy, arising primarily from new technologies and a very marked global shift in manufacturing to low wage economies. Associated with this, more of the world's manufacturing has been undertaken by (or for) firms operating in more than one country. In addition, the cyclical fluctuations of economic activity have been much more severe in the last quarter of the twentieth century than in the long post-war boom. In the more advanced economies these changes have accelerated the decline of older established industries and intensified competition for the reduced amount of mobile industry that exists.

Such changes have been intensified by a dramatic shift in political cultures throughout most of the West, in favour of more market-oriented policies. Instead of national governments mitigating the effects of structural change and cyclical fluctuation, they have retreated from the notion that government can or should modify market processes. Since the late 1970s, this kind of attitude has brought a substantial dismantling of the spatial economic development policies which were so important in post-war Britain and Canada. Even in the more free enterprise-oriented United States, federal government has retreated from the stronger policies for regional development that were beginning to appear in the 1960s and 1970s. Everywhere, therefore, economic necessity and political design have played their part in heightening place competition. Faced with declining older industries and shrinking national government assistance, places have been forced to enter the fray.

Selling the Industrial Town in the Contemporary World

Examining contemporary promotional material or looking through the pages of specialist US relocation magazines such as *Expansion Management*, *Area Development* or *Business Facilities*, many differences with past experience are evident. Some of the promotional media have changed, now embracing videos, faxes, floppy disks and the internet. Some of the imagery has changed. The factory chimneys have finally gone; the cog wheels very nearly so. A new manufacturing imagery based on the computer and the electronic circuit has taken their place. More people now appear as the principal subjects of promotional material. Women and races other than whites feature regularly, and in a variety of guises. There are many more punning slogans. The graphics are more impressive and colour is more extensively used. Brochures are better designed and more professionally presented. The photographs are more artful. The quality of paper is much better, with high gloss or satin finishes. Meanwhile new promotional media allow the use of sound, allowing mood creation to influence attitudes.

Yet remarkable continuities with the past are also apparent. Many place advertisements are still constructed around the same basic devices. Maps remain very common. Alliterative slogans have reached epidemic proportions (and are often now combined with puns in a linguistic double whammy). 'Hub', 'gateway' and 'heart' remain familiar key words. There is the same underlying attempt to build a mythic vision of a happy and productive land. Infrastructure is invariably ideal. Contented, loyal, skilled and strike-free workers still people the places being promoted. Education is good, housing is good, recreation is good. The surrounding countryside is beautiful. Families are happy and harmonious. The list of businesses which have decided to locate in the town being sold is always impressive. Businessmen still provide authenticated testimonials about how successful they have been since they relocated. Sites and buildings and other incentives are attractive. Only the reader is jaundiced.

In other words, industrial place marketing remains almost as cliché-prone as ever, as may be judged from the accompanying illustrations. The conclusions of Burgess's seminal late 1970s study of British efforts (Burgess, 1982) have not altered dramatically, as Barke and Harrop (1994) have recently confirmed. This is not to say that some really impressive industrial marketing campaigns have not appeared. 'Make it in Livingston' was a very memorable campaign of the 1970s, advertising a Scottish New Town. Well funded, consistently pursued in all promotional publications, it benefited from an excellent

SET YOUR SITES on

Toronto

St. Thomas

New York

Detroit

ST. THOMAS CANADA

Accessibility

Centrally located in the Industrial Heartland with international market access.

Affordability

In our power: Electric and Natural Gas with Great Lakes water direct to your site.

Availability

A proud community of skilled and motivated employees.

Desirability

Business, Education, and Recreation provide the setting for happiness and growth.

ST. THOMAS GREAT "SITE" SEEING FOR BUSINESS AND PLEASURE

ST. THOMAS
Economic Development Corporation
Box 520, St. Thomas, Ontario N5P 3V7
Telephone: (519) 631-1680   Fax: (519) 633-9019

1994 advertisement for St Thomas. The use of puns is now more typical, but little else has changed. The map still asserts centrality (with the clear implication that investors still do not know where St Thomas is). Though less wordy, there is a similar attempt to articulate key themes of attraction.

punning slogan. While its literal meaning was about manufacturing, it also played cleverly on other social and personal meanings. Making it in Livingston meant a lot more than doing it at Dundee. We may doubt that more recent and entirely worthy campaigns such as 'Doncaster: England's Northern Jewel', 'Stoke-on-Trent: The City that Fires the Imagination' (Barke and Harrop, 1994, pp. 94; 101) or 'Wrexham: The Remarkable Development Area' (Expansion Management, 1994, p. 136) will manage to be quite so memorable.

Across the Atlantic the proportionate volume of place publicity effort is, as always, much greater, reflecting bigger budgets. Despite these, Holcomb (1994) concludes that US efforts are almost as cliché-ridden as in Britain. Bailey (1989) has, however, given qualified (and impressively quantified) approval of examples of good practice. Nothwithstanding the increasing problems of the older industrial cities of the north eastern 'rustbelt', Bailey shows how the tradition of Southern boosterism lived on in the 1980s. Surveying the general advertising expenditures of 135 city regions across the country between 1984 and 1987, he found the South made up half of the top twenty (Bailey, 1989, pp. 49–51). Ever true to their traditions, Atlanta ranked seventh and Richmond eighteenth.

At their best, these expenditures (which were usually paralleled in other dimensions of economic development policies) were used to stage more imaginative campaigns than were typical of Britain. What is particularly noticeable about high budget US advertising is the way in which individual print advertisements can be used in a more targeted way, making one clear point rather than attempting to say everything on one page. Richmond's Oreo advertisement of 1994 is a good example of this approach (*Expansion Management*, 1994, p. 125).

Old habits die hard, however, particularly if budgets allow only limited action. Beneath a superficial slickness, many North American advertisements today are remarkably similar to those of the early twentieth century. Newport

Richmond Helped Make It A Fortune Cookie.

Companies of all sizes have made their fortunes in Richmond, Virginia, from the hottest newcomers to the well-established Nabisco. In fact, 13 of the Fortune 500 call us home. For a prosperous future, make your corporate move to the Richmond area.

The Ninth Largest Home To Corporate America. **The Richmond Area**

The Counties of Chesterfield, Hanover and Henrico and the City of Richmond
Metropolitan Economic Development Council, 201 East Franklin Street, Richmond, Virginia 23219 • (804) 643-3227, ext. 220 or (800) 229-6332, ext. 220.

Punning 1994 advertisement for Richmond, showing the time-honoured technique of associating the place with a well known and successful product, in this case the Oreo biscuit. The simple presentation and message makes a striking contrast with the cluttered 1907 example for the same city, however (see page 171).

News, Virginia, for example, begins with a striking slogan and image, but then adds a text that says it all in the most predictable possible sense (*ibid*, p. 123). In other cases the links with past practices are palpable. In 1994 for example, St Thomas, Ontario, was advertising itself in a way that was eerily reminiscent of what it was doing 74 years earlier (*ibid*, p. 131).

CONCLUSIONS

There is still therefore much to depress (or amuse) in marketing efforts to sell the industrial town. This chapter has to a very large extent been a catalogue of clichés. As we have also seen, history is now, to a depressing extent, repeating itself in the promotional messages being transmitted today. In explaining this, we might conclude, as many critics (e.g. Massey, 1984) have done, that there is something inherently flawed in the whole system which forces places to compete for industries. When few can offer any really distinctive advantages, it may perhaps be thought inevitable that there will be a sameness in their marketing messages, imagery and tactics. The trouble with such a view is that other types of place, each offering broadly the same repertoire of attractions as their competitors, were advertised in ways that held more intrinsic

interest and drew on a richer and more varied imagery.

The puzzle remains why this should be so. Money provides some, but certainly not all, of the answer. Huge amounts of money were paid out, and often wasted, as subsidies. It would not have been difficult to divert more funds into publicity. Compared to the resorts or the suburbs, the under-representation in industrial promotion of 'enlightened' advertisers, such as railway companies, willing to commission skilled artists and illustrators, was also significant. Again, however, these were not the only place marketing agencies to produce attractive publicity for these other kinds of place, so this can only be part of the explanation.

Ultimately, most industrial promoters failed to infuse their publicity with any strong sense of

Ever Notice That The Good Stuff Is Always In The Middle?

Sometimes, getting what you really want means waiting to get to the *middle* of things. At last, the waiting is over. In the spring of 1992, one of the nation's largest and fastest growing metropolitan areas was changed forever. With the completion of Interstate - 664, the Hampton Roads area, situated on the world's greatest natural harbor, has become an even more unified, dynamic market. And in the *middle* is Newport News, Virginia.

Already the home of America's largest private shipyard, Newport News Shipbuilding, the City of Newport News has recently hosted the growth and location of such prestigious neighbors as Canon, Siemens, and the Continuous Electron Beam Accelerator Facility *(CEBAF)*. Like them, you can enjoy great access via air, land, and water, from a location that's in the *middle* of the Atlantic coast, the *middle* of America's history, and the *middle* of great recreational opportunities.

Not only that, Newport News puts you in the *middle* of a low-cost environment with a qualified, affordable workforce, and a truly satisfying quality of life. If you're ready to position your business for success, come get your share of the good stuff in Newport News, Virginia.

To find out more, call the
Newport News Department of Planning and Development:

1-800-A-SITE-4-U
1-800-274-8348

or write:
Paul F. Miller, Director of Planning and Development
2400 Washington Avenue • Newport News, VA • 23607

Newport News
In The Middle Of It All!

Another Virginia advertisement of the 1990s, this uses an arresting and original device in the lollipop with the chocolate centre, following the analogy through in the text. The advertisers have not, however, been able to resist itemizing all the familiar advantages which almost all industrial towns have always advertised, reducing the impact of the main devices.

underlying vision. Their primary inspiration came not from the distinctive qualities of the place they were promoting, but from what their competitors were doing. It was an approach that ensured that industrial publicity soon degenerated into self caricature, where it has largely remained. Now, in the late 1990s, the most imaginative place marketing work has moved beyond the industrial town. It is to this much more contemporary theme that we now turn.

9

MARKETING RE-INVENTED CITIES

'Chicago would like to remind you that the first four letters of its name are Chic' (cited Lawson, 1989, p. 68). Thus read one of a series of monochrome advertisements which began to appear in high quality glossy periodicals from mid-1989. They were soon joined by a series of TV commercials on the same theme. With an understatement that is rare in American television advertising, each of these commercials showed, also in black and white, a brief clip of electric blues, or ballet, or other cultural activities. They closed simply with a link to the name Chicago. There was, unusually, no insistent voice-over to punch home the sales message.

The campaign was by no means the first or the best known attempt by a city formed in the industrial age to redefine perceptions of itself. It was simply symptomatic of a shift in urban policies that had become noticeable from the later 1970s and had reached epidemic proportions by the early 1990s. Everywhere throughout the older industrial countries, cities were experiencing major structural changes as their older industries declined without obvious replacements. As it dawned on the leaders of these cities that they were indeed peering into an economic abyss, with all the associated demographic, social and political implications, they began to seek new sources of wealth and new ways of stating their importance as places.

City advertising campaigns were merely the most visible parts of a wider process of regeneration, normally to encourage growth in service activities. Common to all was the promotion of tourism, including the development or refurbishment of cultural attractions such as museums or art galleries, the boosting of business conventions and the hosting of major sporting or cultural events. Yet for larger cities, at least, such consumption-based initiatives were also intended to attract entrepreneurs and investors to live and conduct their businesses nearer the urban core areas. Particular prizes were the higher level business services that were felt to hold the key to future success. All this was, in turn, reflected in the physical renewal of derelict areas, typically creating up-market housing, speciality shopping and offices as well as cultural facilities. There was great emphasis on the quality of buildings and public spaces. Key developments were consciously promoted as 'flagships', intended to set the tone of what civic leaders hoped would follow.

In all this, of course, marketing and the image of the city were hugely important. Such regeneration policies flew directly in the face of deeply entrenched negative perceptions of the older industrial cities amongst would be tourists, entrepreneurs or investors. In many cases too, the inhabitants of these cities held exactly the same views, often more vehemently. To residents and non-residents alike the idea of tourists visiting Baltimore or Manchester or regarding Glasgow or Chicago as centres of culture beggared belief.

In this part of the book, we look at how the re-invention of older cities as post-industrial cities occurred. As in the earlier parts, the second chapter is largely concerned with exploring imagery and meaning in the marketing message. In this chapter we consider why and how this latest phase in place selling appeared and spread. As in several other areas of place selling activity, the story is largely one of North American innovations being adopted and adapted in Britain and Europe. Now, however, the game has become truly global as cities seek to achieve international prominence in the twenty-first century.

THE POST-INDUSTRIAL CITY

The End of the Industrial City

The decline of manufacturing has been a universal phenomenon in advanced capitalist countries for at least two decades. The United States lost about two million of its total factory jobs, roughly a tenth, between 1977 and 1993 (*Expansion Management*, 1994, p. 7). That was a very modest fall compared to Britain, where decline began in the late 1960s, becoming serious after 1974 (CSO, 1984; 1988; 1995). Two decades later, in 1994, there were 3.6 million fewer manufacturing jobs, a decline of 45 per cent. All the big cities in Britain and all those in the north-eastern industrial heartland of the United States (and many elsewhere) were acutely affected by this decline, experiencing devastating losses in very short periods.

By the late twentieth century, none of these cities could any longer be regarded as industrial. The former US steel capital, Pittsburgh, had just 8.5 per cent of its workforce in manufacturing in 1990 (USBC, 1994). Cleveland was the most industrial city on the US list with 23.1 per cent, while Detroit and Newark each had just over a fifth. Most of the rest – Chicago, Philadelphia, Baltimore and New York – had between a tenth and a fifth. Boston (and the south-eastern capital of Atlanta) were just under a tenth. The proportions in British cities were higher, but not by much (OPCS/RGS, 1994). Thus in 1991 Birmingham had almost a quarter of its workforce in manufacturing; Sheffield and Leeds almost a fifth. Manchester, Liverpool, Bristol and Glasgow all stood at just over 15 per cent. Newcastle had just 12.9 per cent and inner London 8.7 per cent.

The reasons for this spectacular de-industrialization of the cities were both structural and spatial. Quite simply cities contained more of the declining industrial sectors and more of the older plants of those industries. They also suffered from the general outward shift of manufacturing into suburban and small town locations (Knox *et al.*, 1988, p. 127). As early as 1963, there was more manufacturing in the American suburbs than in the core city areas (Jackson, 1985, p. 267). Partly because of planning policies which restricted suburban-ization, the shift was less dramatic in Britain but it was still present (Fothergill and Gudgin, 1982).

Faced with employment decline on this huge scale, with its serious implications for social well-being and city tax revenues, civic leaders soon realized they needed to fill the gap with new sources of economic activity. Given the long term trends of manufacturing locational prefer-ences, the chances of bringing in new factories were decidedly limited. Some cities certainly tried but, sooner or later, all realized that their futures lay in reinventing themselves as post-industrial service centres. To achieve this vision and attract the investors and visitors to give it reality they needed to market themselves.

In the United States the boosterist traditions of city leadership had, in most places, lain dormant and largely forgotten for many decades. But the memory was certainly recoverable; it was not an alien tradition. As economic decline brought greater fiscal strain, cities returned to the old ways. Moreover, if they decided to act entrepre-neurially and pull themselves up by their boot-straps, American legal precedents were that neither federal nor state administrations would seriously try to stop them. Cities could not literally do as they wished without reference to law (Wolman and Goldsmith, 1992, pp. 69–99). They were subject to some broad financial and other controls. But they operated in a rather more flexible legal framework than their British equivalents.

In Britain, a stronger tradition of central financial assistance ensured that fiscal necessity, which was the mother of urban re-invention in America's core cities, has never been quite so pressing. The general thrust of national political rhetoric and actual changes in 1980s' Britain certainly played a part in encouraging a more 'American' entrepreneurial approach by the cities. Yet, to a greater extent than under the American system, British local government rested on the legal proposition that cities could only take actions for which they had specific powers (Wolman and Goldsmith, 1992, pp. 72–74). Paradoxically, this tradition of tight central supervision was intensified even as the Thatcher government tried to cut local financial dependence on the centre. The overall effect was that British city governments were nothing like as free in choosing policy options as their American equivalents.

As unemployment grew alarmingly, Britain's local authorities therefore had few options. Many turned to section 137 of the 1972 Local Government Act (s83 of the equivalent Scottish legislation) (Widdicombe, 1986a, pp. 175–204). Tucked into major reforms of local government, these sections gave a general power to levy a small local tax (up to £0.02 in the £) for any purpose for the benefit of the local population. By 1979, when Mrs Thatcher came to power, these sections were being widely used to fund local economic policies, mainly promoting manufacturing investment.

There was already a strong undertow of central disapproval of using local revenues in this way. One opinion was that the powers were an open invitation to local rashness. The early 1980s' actions of some of Socialist authorities, creating

local enterprise boards that seemed intent on encouraging co-operatives rather than private capitalism, was certainly evidence enough for many Conservatives (Totterdill, 1989; Eisenschitz and Gough, 1993, pp. 77–79). Another view, however, was that such powers were a potential way of spreading the Thatcherite ethos of competition and enterprise, in effect the marketing approach, to local government. If this second is a correct reading, it certainly seems to have been borne out by subsequent events as left wing municipal socialism gave way to a more moderate local Labour entrepreneurialism.

In making this shift, cities were heavily influenced by Thatcherite initiatives. Thus the centrally designated Urban Development Corporations, created from 1981, became showpieces of a new, more market-oriented approach to planning and development (Imrie and Thomas, 1993). Other initiatives, such as Enterprise Zones, Urban Development and City Grants, encouraged city councils to adopt similar approaches. Meanwhile the generally less tendentious attitude of central government in Scotland allowed Labour councils to discover urban entrepreneurialism slightly earlier.

By the end of the 1980s central-local government tensions over urban economic policies had calmed somewhat. Both were now singing from what approximated to the same entrepreneurial hymn sheet. Under the 1989 Local Government and Housing Act, all local authorities were accordingly granted an unambiguous power to spend on promotion (Eisenschitz and Gough, 1993, pp. 19–20). In a highly centralized governmental system like Britain's, so dependent on the granting of explicit powers, this recognition made the Act into a landmark.

Meanwhile an even more fundamental change was occurring during the mid-late 1980s. In the main cities at least, these economic policies came increasingly to reflect de-industrialization as a permanent condition. All the capitals of the former industrial regions gradually, and with many regrets, accepted their uncertain destinies as post-industrial cities (Taylor, Evans and

Fraser, 1996). Marketing, both narrowly defined and as a broader ethos suffusing many of their activities, now became the principal means by which they sought to realize this re-invention of themselves.

The Nature of the Post-Industrial City

But what exactly is the post-industrial city, this new ideal that was being promoted? We readily grasp the general nature of the resort, the suburb or the industrial city because they are well established phenomena. It is more difficult to reach an equivalent perspective on the contemporary city. The problem is compounded because individual post-industrial cities prefer to emphasize their distinctiveness. Generic characteristics are kept in the background. Yet these rhetorical propositions of individuality barely conceal a phenomenon that is now becoming more easy to stereotype. As we will see in the next chapter, the post-industrial city has already begun, unknowingly, to caricature itself.

Our notion of the post-industrial city has evolved gradually as developments in particular cities began to suggest new ways of coping with the disappearance of manufacturing and the redundant spaces and lives it has left behind (Harvey, 1989, pp. 76–95; Taylor, Evans and Fraser, 1996). Most fundamental is an employment structure completely dominated by services. The most successful post-industrial cities have a solid employment base in offices, usually in marketed business services such as finance, software, advertising and other professional activities. Company headquarters also form a particularly attractive component because they signify the presence of important decision-makers, creating a demand for other high level service activities. The role of public sector services varies greatly. Some, such as universities and research institutes, are invariably key ingredients of the post-industrial mix.

Inevitably, even in the most successful cities, many service jobs will be lower paid. Most

declining industrial cities have, at some time, tried to mitigate the effects of decline by maintaining high manual employment in municipal and other non-marketed services. These approaches have not proved viable in the long term, however, without other changes to strengthen marketed activities. Successful post-industrial cities also tend to have a healthy retailing industry, providing many lower paid service jobs and contributing to a sense of vitality in central areas. As well as the traditional types of downtown shopping, there will usually be specialist districts, offering a more distinctive retailing experience. This is closely linked to one of the most critical elements in post-industrialism, the growth of tourism (Law, 1993). Most obviously manifest in a development of convention centres, exhibition spaces and hotels, tourism offers scope for many lower paid jobs. It also provides a way of mitigating some of the effects of generally declining city populations by bolstering retailing and public services.

A key element in the success of tourism is the development of attractions. Successful post-industrial cities usually show large investments in their cultural capital. Museums, art galleries, theatres and concert halls are particularly important (Bianchini and Parkinson, 1993). Less 'high brow', more popular leisure activities are also usually apparent, such as aquaria or sports stadia. Much will be made of the historic fabric of the city, with adaptive re-use of older structures. There will, however, be at least some more recent buildings, usually of striking design and showing high quality of finish (Neill, Fitzsimons and Murtagh, 1995, pp. 1–49). Public art, historic and ultra-modern, adorns public spaces, themselves carefully designed and maintained to create interest (Goodey, 1994). Nightlife is also particularly important (O'Connor and Wynne, 1996a). The successful post-industrial city has to offer a good range of restaurants, nightclubs and entertainments.

The majority of these most distinctive characteristics of post-industrialism are found in the downtown/central areas. A really successful post-industrial city will, however, have pushed these characteristics outward, typically into adjoining waterfront, dock or former industrial areas. In addition to the usual mix of activities characteristic of the post-industrial city, here will usually be found high income housing, either as new build or in adapted older structures. This will offset the long established trend to population decline, offering further support to local services in the heart of the city.

Those managing the post-industrial city will ensure that this urban landscape, especially its public spaces, exhibition and convention facilities and its water, presents a scene of continuing human animation. With apparent spontaneity, street entertainers will entertain and street traders will ply their carefully regulated trade. Pavement cafes will tempt the passerby with tokens of international sophistication. There will be a full calendar of well publicized events, sporting spectacles and cultural festivals designed to draw in both residents and tourists. And, because much of this animation depends on pedestrian movements, great efforts will have been made to encourage the large scale use of public transit, to limit the intrusive effects of motor cars. In many ways, indeed, public transit is one of the critical underpinnings of the post-industrial city as a whole. As an urban experience it rests on the value of centrality and concentration, an antidote to the bland functional prairies of car parking that surround suburban malls.

If we exclude special cases such as capital cities, the bulk of these characteristics were achieved first in Boston (O'Connor, 1993). Strictly speaking it had never been an overwhelmingly industrial city in the literal manner of Detroit, Cleveland, Sheffield or Birmingham. Its main blue collar employment had been more diverse, related to its port and its wholesaling and distribution trades as well as its factories. But it had clearly been a city of the industrial age. Its banking and insurance houses had long been important, servicing the whole New England industrial region. These had stagnated as the once mighty regional textile industry shrank, but they

provided an important base for the new post-industrial economy.

By the early 1970s the city already had a clear majority of its workforce in services, and was especially strong in the favoured sectors of finance and business services (Ganz and Konga, 1989). The university and research infrastructure was, with neighbouring Cambridge, superb. It had excellent public transit, being one of a handful of cities on the North American continent never to relinquish the street car. Its downtown and Back Bay areas presented an often excitingly juxtaposed mixture of historic and strikingly modern buildings. Downtown retailing was comparatively strong and was greatly enhanced with the opening, in 1976, of the Quincy Market to create a scheme which soon came to epitomize the very essence of the post-industrial city (Rouse, 1984; Frieden and Sagalyn, 1989, pp. 1–7; O'Connor, 1993, pp. 271–279). Developed in conjunction with the flamboyant Baltimore developer, James Rouse, the scheme was the first of a rash of festival marketplaces that quickly spread across American cities. It involved the adaptive re-use of historic market buildings to create a tourist-oriented, pedestrianized shopping quarter.

Tourism was already strong, building on the city's historical importance in the creation of America. A heritage trail, possibly the first in the world, was created as early as 1951 to provide a focus for this (O'Connor, 1993, pp. 48–49). Its galleries, museums and high culture, a rich legacy from its traditional financial elite and now reinforced by deliberate policies, further strengthened tourist appeal (Wynne, 1992b, pp. 88–89). Business tourism was encouraged by the provision of modern convention facilities in 1965, with major extensions in the mid-1980s (Law, 1993, pp. 44–45). And it was in Boston, in 1969, that the post-industrial age of aquaria dawned with the opening of the hugely popular New England Aquarium, an important focus for harbour front renewal (Kennedy, 1992, p. 181). The 1970s saw the impetus spreading further outwards from downtown as the Charlestown

Navy Yard was turned over to civilian use (BRA, 1979: 22; Perkins, 1986). By the early 1990s it had become a mixed activity district with offices, housing, medical research and, of course, tourism focused on a major historic area.

Other cities were more impressive in particular aspects of their post-industrial landscapes. Cities such as Baltimore, or Glasgow, attract interest because, in effect, the raw material of their transformations was so much more unpromising. Many of the individual things that have been consciously done to re-invent Boston have certainly been done better elsewhere. And other cities, as we will see, have definitely been more memorable for the *chutzpah* of their marketing messages. They have needed to be. But if it is valid to speak of a formula for the post-industrial city, Boston stumbled across it first.

MARKETING THE POST-INDUSTRIAL CITY

The Emergence of Post-Industrial City Marketing

During the late 1970s, as Boston's Quincy Market added the final dimension to an already impressive picture of a genuine urban renaissance, the city's Mayor, Kevin White, began staking its claim in the new post-industrial global order. Often, misleadingly, seen as the physical creator of the new Boston, White's role was more to use his instinctive feel for publicity and promotion to animate the physical structures and public spaces. As O'Connor (1993, p. 296) has observed, '. . . he demonstrated an imaginative flair for dramatizing the New Boston, advertising its commercial and cultural advantages, and drawing the attention of visitors and tourists to Boston's virtues as a world-class city'. Strictly speaking, it was a message spread more through public relations, through the creation of spectacle and the provision of newsworthy copy than through advertising proper.

By coincidence, the archetypal post-industrial city advertising campaign appeared at almost exactly the same time as White began his rhetorical re-positioning of Boston on the world stage. It was in 1977 that New York state launched its famous and much imitated 'I ❤ New York' campaign. Though not strictly a city marketing campaign, it was credited with pulling the city of New York back from the brink of bankruptcy (Holcomb, 1990, p. 31). Coinciding with Mayor Koch's attempts to restore probity to city finances, the message spoke both to residents of the 'Big Apple' (another promotional slogan, with obscure historic origins, revived by the Convention Bureau in 1971) and to the world. More than any previous marketing campaign it showed what advertising could do to create positive images of places that were perceived as tired, seedy and declining.

In Britain, meanwhile, growing fatalism about industrial decline and the growing sympathy for entrepreneurialism made cities more receptive to the ideas being pioneered across the Atlantic. It was Glasgow, traditionally perceived as hard, dirty and violent, a seemingly unstormable stronghold of the left, which took Britain into this new era of place marketing in 1983–84. And yet, improbable as it seemed at the time, there was a certain appropriateness about Glasgow's lead. The city had suffered decline more acutely than any other in Britain. Nowhere had experienced more severely the failures of established approaches, so that the larger framework of policy was already shifting more rapidly (and less confrontationally) than elsewhere in Britain (Boyle, 1990).

For all this, the conception of the deservedly famous 'Glasgow's Miles Better' campaign remained local and essentially idiosyncratic. The credit belonged to two men, Michael Kelly and John Struthers. Kelly was Lord Provost (Mayor) of the city in the early 1980s (Keating, M. 1988, p. 174; Boyle, 1990, pp. 121–123). Greatly impressed by the 'I ❤ New York' campaign, he took up the suggestion of John Struthers, senior partner in a local advertising agency, for a similar image-boosting campaign. The actual slogan was dreamed up by Struthers and his eleven year old son on the London Underground, after spending a train journey from Glasgow discussing different ways of projecting a positive and optimistic message (Struthers, 1986, pp. 8–10). The double meaning (smiles better/miles better) was a key part of this, to which the well known Mr Men cartoon figure, Mr Happy, replacing the O of Glasgow, added an immediate visual interest. The Mr Men, widely known through children's books, TV cartoons and growing use in product merchandizing, were created by Roger Hargreaves, a former advertising illustrator and colleague of Struthers. Hargreaves readily agreed to this unusual piece of merchandizing and the campaign was born.

Like 'I ❤ New York', it was targeted at both the local population and the wider world. After initial scepticism, the local launch in early 1983 proved successful and was taken beyond the city in the following year (Jack, 1984), backed by £50,000 city funding per year and growing private contributions. A minority local opposition continued to attack the approach. One critic, for example, spoke of 'a bland self-congratulatory hype, which found its true apotheosis in the insultingly patronising "Mr Happy" of "Glasgow's Miles Better"' (cited in Barnett, 1991, p. 168). Yet the dominant local view was very supportive (Wishart, 1991, p. 44). The original campaign ran until 1989 (though has recently been revived) (Gold and Gold, 1995, pp. 185; 191).

In 1984 London became the major national target, with advertisements on the sides of double decker buses, on taxis, on the Underground and in the main railway stations (Struthers, 1986). Meanwhile prominent advertisements were placed in the national press (e.g. *Sunday Times Magazine*, 5.9.84, pp. 10–11; 4.11.84, pp. 30–31; *Observer Magazine*, 18.11.84, pp. 68–69) and in international business journals. And there was much more besides. Struthers and the special city-led Miles Better Committee deployed videos, bumper stickers, tee shirts, endorsements by celebrities and much else, including the naval vessel, HMS Glasgow, to market the city.

Claimed as Scotland's most successful ever advertising campaign, 'Miles Better' caught the public imagination in Britain as no place selling campaign had done since 'Skegness is So Bracing'. Later it was extended beyond Britain, to other parts of Europe and North America. By 1986 there were French, Spanish, Italian and German versions of the slogan (partly intended, one suspects, to impress other parts of Britain with Glasgow's international profile). The only place where it failed immediately to strike a sympathetic echo was Glasgow's historic rival, Edinburgh, whose municipal authorities refused to carry the advertising on the city's buses. Kelly, though, secured a delicious revenge for this when, in 1987, Edinburgh decided to launch its own publicity campaign and turned to him as director (Keating, M., 1988, p. 194).

Alongside Struthers' New York-style advertising campaign, Kelly also adopted something of the public relations approach of Boston. Like Kevin White, Michael Kelly talked up his city as much as possible. He became its ambassador, impressing business men and opinion formers with Glasgow's unrealized potential. He had much less to boast about than White but this pioneering campaign, together with real changes that had already begun, pointed new directions for Britain's civic leaders. Succeeding Lord Provosts in Glasgow followed his lead and the approach became increasingly professionalized (Jack, 1984, p. 38). Press releases (the earliest composed, ironically, by a former Glasgow crime reporter whose sensational coverage of gangland terror had done much to blacken the city's reputation) were irrepressibly buoyant. Sceptics, if not quite silenced, at least began to recognize the potency of the new approach. By 1986 Glasgow was even winning media plaudits in the United States. The *New York Times*, for example, headlined one story 'Glasgow's Arising, on Its Own, It Says', while *Time Magazine* labelled it 'The City That Refused to Die' (Boyle, 1988, p. 83).

All this was in sharp contrast to contemporary British press coverage of other cities, embroiled in political confrontations or anxious to parade their problems. It was not long before these too began to change their tune. But Glasgow never lost the advantage that came from being first of the optimists.

Physical Form and Marketing

Yet marketing, narrowly defined, is not enough. Behind the fine words and images there has to be at least some physical reality of buildings, public spaces and activities that give some genuine promise of a re-invented city. Typically the physical re-invention is only partial. A few blocks beyond the gleaming office towers, harbour fronts or festival market places might typically be found all the familiar problems of a decaying industrial city. Large numbers of security and cleaning staff are typically needed to stop the inhabitants of this city of despair and desperation troubling the happy strollers in the post-industrial spaces.

Such physical change as was achieved would normally be seen as a flagship, a first step, giving a lead for what was to follow (Smyth, 1994). To achieve this, the first steps had necessarily to be impressive. They had to be conceived and executed with marketing priorities very much in mind. Such an approach is certainly not peculiar to the post-industrial city. The grandiose City Beautiful schemes in the American mid- and far-West of the early twentieth century betray something of the same sentiments. But never before had urban design and planning been used in quite such a systematically calculating way to re-image and sell places.

One of the most dramatic examples was Canary Wharf in the London Docklands (*Building*, 1991). Here a huge new financial district was planned and developed, not without problems, during the 1980s and 1990s. A deliberate challenge to the established financial centre in the

City of London, its design reflected the need to attract attention to a more distant and remote location. At the heart of the scheme was a vast tower, London's (and for a short time, Europe's) tallest building. Clad in stainless steel and glass, the combination of its great size and propensity to catch and reflect light ensure its visibility across wide areas of London, especially in the City, whose dominance it challenges.

None of this was accidental. Both G. Ware Travelstead, the American who had originated the development, and Olympia and York, the Toronto developers who carried it through, understood that the scheme had, by its form constantly to advertise itself (Brownill, 1994, pp. 143–146). Master architect-planners, Skidmore Owings and Merrill, brought an awareness of all the boosterist redolences of the early twentieth century American Beaux Arts styling which permeates the scheme. Finally the London Docklands Development Corporation saw it as a potential consummation of their regeneration efforts. To all these parties, the scale, form, layout and design of Canary Wharf were intended as a promotion statement. The hope, clearly, is that the central tower will become the icon of the re-invented, post-industrial Docklands, taking its place alongside the Houses of Parliament, the Tower and the other landmarks of London.

There was a formula in all this. Grand visual statements, a few 'signature' or 'trophy' buildings or structures designed by big name architects counted for a great deal (Crilley, 1993). One or two dramatic creations by the likes of I. M. Pei, Richard Rogers, Norman Foster, Cesar Pelli, Michael Graves, Philip Johnson, John Portman or Skidmore, Owings and Merrill were very bankable, especially in cities bidding for attention and investment on the world stage. Heritage, the marketing of the past, was another much used place marketing device that relied on the manipulation and presentation of urban form (Hewison, 1987). The refurbishment, repackaging and re-use of major historic structures, based on models such as Faneuil Hall and the Quincy Market in Boston, Covent Garden and St Katherine's Dock in

London or Albert Dock in Liverpool quickly became common. Even where most pre-existing buildings were removed, the retention of earlier structures, often moved to contrive the most artful placing in the new landscape, underscored a link with the past. In Manchester's Salford Quays, for example, original bridges, cranes and other dock paraphernalia are used to add interest in this way.

In turn this recycling of dereliction into heritage merged into another post-industrial city design favourite, public art (Goodey, 1994). The preferred form was intended to be popular and accessible. The intention was to highlight how much fun the post-industrial city could be and to reflect a more general interest in using culture as part of an urban regeneration strategy. Unusually, much more of the impetus here came from continental Europe than the United States. Of the British cities, Birmingham went farthest during the 1980s in using public art for promotional purposes (Beach and Noszlopy, 1996). A piece such as *Forward* in the new Centenary Square typified the approach. Flanked by a veritable inventory of flagship components of the post-industrial city – convention centre, theatre, festival market place and international hotel – it captures much of the spirit of the re-invented city.

However Birmingham's efforts already look likely to be eclipsed. 1996 brought an altogether more dramatic attempt to use public art with the opening of the Visual Arts UK festival across the whole, seriously de-industrialized, northern region. The largest single piece, *The Angel of the North*, an immense bronze angel on the outskirts of Gateshead, the metropolitan district adjoining Newcastle, promises to become a new Tyneside icon. Much more of this kind of thing also seems set to appear for the millennium celebrations in 2000, using funds provided by the National Lottery.

We could say much more about the physical promotion of post-industrial cities. But the essential point about all these devices – the flagship developments, the use of design, the references to the past and the use of public art – was that the

form and spaces of the post-industrial city had to be striking and imageable. Whether in the city marketeer's brochure or the lens of the tourist, the intention was to signal change in an arresting and eyecatching way.

Partnership and the Process of Re-invention

The physical creation of a critical mass of post-industrial growth on the substrate of a dying industrial city was itself only a further part of the process, however. It was part of, but it did not drive, the process of re-invention. Those city leaders who sought to distil the secret essence of success from American cities such as Boston and Baltimore were obliged to look beneath both the images and the physical realities of the new. What they found was an organizational model of how re-invention was to be achieved. It was a model that rested on entrepreneurialism and a spirit of deep co-operation between public and private sectors. This spirit permeated both the physical process of regeneration and propagation, through marketing, of the re-invented city. It can be summed up in a single word that has recurred repeatedly in discussions about regeneration and promotion. It soon became thought of, simplistically, as a talisman of successful urban re-invention. The magic word was 'partnership'.

In both the United States and Britain city leaders sought to build, or rebuild, a productive relationship between themselves and business leaders. These partnerships were doubly important. Ideally they would play an important direct role in bringing about new investments, priming the pump for future success. Indirectly partnership was also a litmus test for the reception a future investor might expect, a sign of the degree of local friendliness to external business investors. Either way partnerships were much trumpeted in promotional copy.

In Boston the groundwork which laid the basis for successful post-industrial partnership had come during the 1950s. Business estimation of Boston's city government was then at a low ebb. The traditional downtown business elite, the so-called Brahmins, Republican Anglo-Saxon Protestants, had been subjected to decades of tendentious bullying and punitive tax assessments on the part of an Irish Catholic, Democrat-dominated city hall (Kennedy, 1992, pp. 129–155; O'Connor, 1993, pp. 3–36). Successive Democrat mayors had since 1907 pursued essentially populist, anti-business policies.

The fiscal implications of this hit home as the descendants of the Brahmins and the Greater Boston Chamber of Commerce began to promote investment outside the city (Edel, Sclar and Luria, 1984, pp. 214–223). The 1950s saw a rapid growth of very advanced technology manufacturing on the 'Golden Industrial Semi-Circle' along the new orbital expressway, Route 128 (GBCC, 1959; Rosegrant and Lampe, 1992). Yet the decade also saw the first attempts to rebuild good relations. A more business-friendly city hall encouraged business to develop new ideas for modernizing the economic and physical structure of the city. Some specific initiatives, initially small-scale, but strongly suggestive of new directions, began to appear. It was, for example, public-private co-operation which created the pioneering 'Freedom Trail' referred to on page 190 (O'Connor, 1993, pp. 47–49).

By the end of the 1950s business was actively pressing city hall for tax abatements on new office developments (GBESC, 1959). Faced with a very weak tax base, roughly 25 per cent lower in 1960 than in 1935, the city and particularly the new Boston Redevelopment Authority (established in 1957), was eager to take this advice. New developments on which some potential local tax income was given as incentive were a better option than no development at all. One of the first tangible signs that the new partnership had been forged came in 1960 when the Massachusetts legislature passed an urban redevelopment act (Chapter 121A), with special provisions for the city of Boston, legalizing tax abatements on developments in blighted areas. Their immediate significance was to allow the

first big commercial development, the Prudential Center, to proceed (BRA, 1969; O'Connor, 1993, pp. 177–178).

Boston's public-private partnership moved decisively forward in the 1960s (e.g. GBCC/ACB, 1962). Public investments in a new government centre and many more Chapter 121A tax-abated private investments in office towers modernized the physical appearance of the city (Golden and Mehegan, 1983). Subsidies notwithstanding, they also greatly strengthened the city's tax base. This gave Boston the increasingly sound fiscal foundation on which to initiate crucially important developments such as the Quincy Market, again in partnership with a heavily subsidized private sector.

Yet the political road to this remarkably successful re-invention proved very rocky. Boston's blue collar neighbourhoods felt themselves neglected as investment boomed downtown. There were jobs for middle class commuters in the new office towers. There was also fun for tourists, but what was there to replace the harbour, warehousing and industrial jobs? In truth, there was, as all post-industrial cities eventually found, very little.

In 1969 Mayor White established a Development and Industrial Commission to stimulate jobs specifically for Boston residents (GBCC/EDIC/BRA, 1981, p. 13). Two years later it was reinforced by a development and marketing agency, EDIC/Boston (Economic Development and Industrial Corporation of Boston) (Ehrlich, 1987). Within a few years this archetypal post-industrial city was engaged in an active policy of developing and promoting industrial parks (Boston MOED, 1977). Yet the problems did not go away and have continued to pervade the political process throughout the 1980s and 1990s.

Other Routes to Partnership

In some respects, Boston's tradition of partnership, with city hall making almost all the main moves, was unusual amongst the other main US pioneers of the concept. It may account for the greater, if still imperfect, sensitivity to community interests compared to many other US cities. Certainly the civic role in early partnership initiatives in Baltimore, Pittsburgh and Atlanta was more limited. In all these the lead came much more from business, whose ideas were then taken up by city government. Such efforts formed part of a tradition of autonomous local business boosterism that has always been far more developed in US than in British cities. In Baltimore, for example, partnership can be traced back largely to the creation of the Greater Baltimore Committee on the initiative of business leaders in 1955 (Lyall, 1982; Hula, 1990). In Pittsburgh the equivalent moves occurred even earlier, in the late 1940s (Stewman and Tarr, 1982). And there was rarely a time when active private-public partnership did *not* exist in Atlanta. 1961, however, saw the Chamber of Commerce relaunching the 'Forward Atlanta' movement, a conscious revival (by the son of its originator) of its hugely successful, trend-setting 1926–29 promotional campaign (Henson and King, 1982).

Equivalent moves in Britain did not come until much later. The 1960s planning-led modernization of cities, though involving some degree of partnership, was far more of a public sector affair than in American cities. It was only as public spending was reduced from about 1976 that British eyes began to shift to the United States. The Thatcher Conservative government, especially the first Environment Secretary, Michael Heseltine, became very interested in American approaches as a way of regenerating Britain's cities using private sector funds.

Yet the hopes of the Thatcher administration were built on exaggerated assumptions about what had actually been happening in the United States. Public funding was actually very much higher on many of the admired US partnership developments than was usually supposed. Partly this reflected a widespread use of tax increment financing, committing future rather than current local tax revenues, and other kinds of overt or semi-concealed tax breaks, including private investor access to tax-exempt bond finance (Frieden and Sagalyn, 1989, pp. 248–252). But even direct public spending was often considerable. Actual ratios of public-private investment in US city regeneration were usually rather low, often much lower than the 1:4 minimum that the Thatcher governments tried to enforce in Britain.

There was, meanwhile, precious little enthusiasm for public-private partnership amongst the political leaders of many British cities (e.g. Lawless, 1990; Parkinson, 1990). Such were central-local government relations in the first half of the 1980s that everything Ministers proposed was viewed with suspicion. In some cities, such as Liverpool, London and Sheffield, the radical left was particularly strong. Even where it was not, its rhetoric often shaped local policy debate. It was hardly a conducive atmosphere for building closer links with business leaders.

But we should not solely blame the politicians. There was an even more fundamental problem in transferring the partnership ideal to Britain. The nature of business elites in British provincial cities was rather different to those in the United States. Britain's economy, especially its financial sector, was much more centralized on London (Robson, 1986). With the partial exception of Scotland, there was no longer a network of regional banks, as existed in the United States. This encouraged the migration of business headquarters or, at the very least, a shift in the locus of business decision-making to London. Either way the extent of local control over the local economy was seriously undermined.

From the point of view of promoting urban regeneration, the problem was simply that the ability of business leaders in Britain's regional cities to make things happen was much below their equivalents in US cities. Atlanta, for example, could call on the personal and corporate might of global players like Bob Woodruff of Coca Cola or Ted Turner of CNN TV to assist their promotional efforts (e.g. *Financial Times.*

1.11.94, Survey, p. 7). Glasgow or Birmingham, by contrast, no longer had such magnates in their midst. The problem was compounded by the exceptionally 'open' character of the British economy, with very large amounts of direct foreign investment, controlled often from the United States, Japan or other parts of Europe (Fine and Harris, 1985).

There was, therefore, no spontaneous emergence of local, American-style business-led regeneration partnerships in British cities. Much of what did happen involved centrally-legitimated initiatives such as the Urban Development Corporations and Enterprise Zones, referred to earlier. They played an important part in making the derelict tracts of inner cities attractive to private investors, usually with subsidies or tax incentives. They also became the focus of what were, for British cities, unprecedented amounts of place marketing. As we have seen, the city councils, led by Glasgow, once easily the hardest left of the big cities, increasingly took the hint. By the end of the 1980s their own regeneration efforts had begun to foster public-private partnership, especially in the specific area of property development (Harding 1992). Genuinely business-created partnerships had occasionally appeared, most notably The Newcastle Initiative (TNI) launched by the Confederation of British Industry in 1988 (Smyth, 1994, pp. 198–200). Yet even this was essentially the child of a national business lobby group, not a truly local initiative.

City Marketing and Partnership

As a central part of the new urban entrepreneurialism, city marketing in the narrow sense has mirrored the American and British approaches to partnership. In the United States it has been Chambers of Commerce or other more specialist business-led organizations which have usually taken the lead in marketing cities to potential investors and business contacts (Bailey, 1989, pp. 11–12). In general, municipal agencies have played their main entrepreneurial roles in matters such as promotional planning regimes,

site preparation, negotiation with developers and tax abatements. Marketing, narrowly defined, has been much more business-led. Typical marketing agencies in recent years have included the New Cleveland Campaign, the Civic Committee of the Commercial Club of Chicago, the Pittsburgh-based Penn's South West Association and yet another Forward Atlanta campaign.

As well as the leadership, much of the revenue for such marketing initiatives also came from private sources. Bailey's sample of 1980s campaigns showed the income mix at roughly 16 per cent public to 84 per cent private. The latter came mainly from a mixture of membership subscriptions, corporate sponsorship, income from advertising and sales and assistance in kind. Budgets, though very small by commercial standards, could still be extremely large compared to earlier episodes of place selling. The most recent Forward Atlanta campaign, for example, has been running at $1–2 million annual marketing spend, raised almost completely from member subscriptions (MACC, 1995; information from MACC). The New Cleveland Campaign was running at $1.1 million and the Chicago Civic Committee at $1 million per annum during the late 1980s.

Tourist marketing efforts are usually the preserve of each city's convention and visitors' bureau (Law, 1993, pp. 143–153). This form of public-private organization was very highly developed in the United States, with typical expenditures well in excess of those for more general economic promotion. The 1995 budget of the Atlanta Convention and Visitors Bureau (ACVB), for example, was $10.4 million (ACVB, 1995b). This compared to roughly $0.6 million for the economic development work of the Chamber of Commerce and about $1.5 million for Forward Atlanta, the main marketing campaign (MACC, 1995). Most of the funding for all the convention and tourist bureaux typically came from local hotel taxes. The remainder came from a mix of private and sometimes public contributions. Thus the ACVB derived 60 per cent of its income from the hotel tax with the remainder from private sources, including advertising and gifts in kind.

This typical US organizational dichotomy between economic development and tourism marketing is apparent to some extent in British cities. But there are some important differences in the organization of all aspects of city marketing. The promotion of city tourism is much more often a direct municipal role. Leeds, for example, operates City of Leeds Promotion and Tourism as an arm of the city council. In other cases, such as Liverpool, the Merseyside Tourism Board is a survival of the former metropolitan county tourism service. Many authorities deal with tourism promotion through their leisure services departments, alongside swimming pools, sports centres and parks. In other, usually smaller, towns and cities, municipal involvement has led to a close integration of tourist and economic development marketing in a single department.

In recent years, however, the US model of a more autonomous visitors and convention bureau has been adopted more widely, especially in the biggest cities. Glasgow, Birmingham and Manchester have all favoured this organizational form, serving an area larger than the core city alone. Yet the new US-style organizations have not been benefited from US-style funding. Their funding remains overwhelmingly reliant on general municipal revenues. The lack of a specific local tourist tax, essentially the same problem which dogged early moves for resort publicity, has made it difficult to fund such bureaux at anything approaching American levels. The Greater Glasgow Tourist Board and Convention Bureau has one of the largest budgets, at £2.2 million in 1991, followed by Birmingham with £1.4 million. Manchester's Bureau looked decidedly underfunded with £0.5 million (Law, 1993, p. 151). Moreover, voluntary contributions have not been at all dependable. Support comes from advertising in Bureau publications and gifts in kind but direct financial contributions from the tourist industry remain rare.

General economic development marketing in Britain has been even more reliant on public spending. The pace was set during the 1980s by the new Urban Development Corporations. Central government had made them the front line in the creation of entrepreneurial cities. By the early 1990s the UDCs were spending, on average, something like 2.5 per cent of their considerable budgets on advertising and marketing (Imrie and Thomas, 1993, p. 14). The highest spending UDC, the London Docklands Development Corporation (LDDC), spent £28 million on promotion and publicity between 1981 and 1992 (Brownill, 1994, p. 137). By 1993–94 its annual spend had risen to nearly £4 million (LDDC 1995, p. 44). Typical annual publicity spending varied between 1 and 4 per cent of total expenditure, more than on community programmes, for example.

Yet, although the absolute size of its promotional spending was high, LDDC was hardly exceptional in the relative scale of its activity. Smaller UDCs, such as Central Manchester (CMDC) which spent £1.1 million on promotion and publicity in 1992–93 (from a total budget of £17.2 million), tended proportionately to be much more active (CMDC, 1993). These figures exclude other UDC activities, such as assistance to private investments and site preparation, which were also promotional in intent. Such financial means allowed the UDCs to mount very impressive promotional campaigns that compared very well with the very slickest of US practice.

Elective local governments have also played a significant role. In fact though, the pattern of local authority marketing activity to promote business and investment remains elusive of precise definition. The most obviously relevant category of local government spending, economic development and promotion often excludes key dimensions of local marketing activity (CIPFA 1995*b*, table A). Typically, it is skewed more towards traditional industrial promotion than the figures we have been quoting from the US cities or the British UDCs. In many cities the critical spending may lurk under other heads, such as arts and recreation budgets. Moreover, as well as marketing, narrowly defined, economic development and promotion figures include site preparation and building provision. More seriously, the returns refer only to net expenditure falling on local taxation. They conceal the effects of sales, central grants and other income.

They thus give little away about the nature of public-private partnership involved in marketing. Since the figures cover only municipal expenditures, the full position of any promotional organizations to which cities may contribute is not apparent. What they do give, however, is a very general sense of the degree of municipal commitment to promoting and marketing their cities. In 1993–94, for example, inner London and the English metropolitan districts between them spent almost £40 million net on economic development and promotion. The six major core cities of the regional metropolitan areas – Birmingham, Leeds, Sheffield, Manchester, Liverpool and Newcastle – together spent nearly £16.5 million. Birmingham topped the list, spending £7.42 for each member of its one million plus population. Newcastle, spending £6.11 *per capita* and Sheffield with £5.19 *per capita* were also relatively high net spenders. Leeds (£2.84), Manchester (£2.78) and Liverpool (£2.69) were nearer the average for metropolitan districts (£2.85 *per capita*).

In Britain then, councils and, where they existed, UDCs were usually the main marketing organizations. Around them would cluster the efforts of public or quasi-public agencies (such as municipal airport companies or convention centre businesses). Outside the public sector Chambers of Commerce and *ad hoc* promotional organizations often also play some role, normally a rather minor one. It is rare for truly private organizations to have mounted major city marketing campaigns. The Newcastle Initiative, mentioned above, is one exception. Even here though, it has become only a subsidiary agency in marketing Newcastle (Wilkinson, 1992). The TNI experience does not drastically alter the general conclusion that the public sector has been expected to pick up the major part of the marketing bill.

Although some city councils were responsible for all marketing efforts, the typical large British regional city might well have several different promotional agencies. Even within city halls, there were normally splits between departments. There is clearly a real risk of fragmentation. Recently there have been moves to create umbrella marketing partnerships in some cities. Both Manchester and Birmingham made moves to develop such organizations in 1992–93. Marketing Manchester was created as a partnership of the city council, CMDC, Manchester Airport, the Greater Manchester Passenger Transport Executive, the Olympic Bid Committee, the City of Drama 1994 (both to be considered more fully later) and the Greater Manchester Visitor and Convention Bureau. The Birmingham Marketing Partnership (BMP) claims to be much more of a public-private coalition. In typical British fashion, though, the bigger businesses in the city have been reported as only lukewarm in their support (Aldersley-Williams, 1994).

Advertising

This growing emphasis on marketing during the 1980s brought an increasingly professional approach. Unlike the 'innocent crassness' (Zelinsky 1988, quoted in Holcomb, 1990, p. 39) of most earlier boosterist efforts, place selling campaigns were now more likely than ever to be the work of marketing experts. The use of advertising and public relations agencies became very common. In many cases local firms would be used, for example in Atlanta and, as noted above, Glasgow in its 'Miles Better' campaign. But the use of major agencies has become common (Bailey, 1989, pp. 20–21). American cities predictably moved earlier in this direction and the trend has recently spread to Britain. Newcastle City Council for example retained J. Walter Thompson in 1990 (Wilkinson, 1992, pp. 179–184) and Glasgow used Saatchi and Saatchi in the campaign to launch itself as European City of Culture in 1990 (Booth and Boyle, 1993, pp. 31–32). Cities are, of course, only minor clients compared to such agencies' commercial accounts. But handling a big city's publicity can bring great prestige, especially if their efforts can be portrayed as successful.

The main questions facing any city marketing body and its professional advisers relate to the nature of the promotional message and the mix of marketing methods to be used. The first of these we will address in the next chapter. On the second, the main methods available are print and other media advertising, direct mail and more selective publicity, public relations and special events. In practice most cities adopt their own blend of all or most of these methods. In any individual city the mix of marketing methods could also vary over time, reflecting shifting perceptions of what exactly needed to be done.

Thus Boston for many years placed little emphasis on advertising, relying more on public relations and, increasingly, simply on its impressive record of success. But it changed its policy quite dramatically in Autumn 1991. As was so often the case, this more assertive approach reflected insecurity rather than confidence. The city's economic development agency was quite open as to what had changed: 'Boston has an important story to tell . . . Yet for the past decade no one has told the story. We didn't need to. But, with the economy in recession, . . . it is time to get the message out' (EDIC/Boston, 1991, p. 1).

Atlanta, by contrast, was a city which traditionally has spent very heavily on advertising and publicity. In the mid-1980s, for example, the Chamber of Commerce was spending 60 per cent of a $1 million annual budget on economic development advertising and 20 per cent on collateral publicity (Bailey, 1989, p. 24). In 1995, however, Forward Atlanta decided to drop its routine advertising until after the 1996 Olympic Games. In part this was because the Games ensured continuing international media attention for the city (information from MACC, 1995). It also reflected fund raising difficulties. Local businesses preferred to sponsor the Atlanta Committee for the Olympic Games rather than Forward Atlanta.

In fact very few cities anywhere have ever had the funding to sustain expensive media advertising for long periods. The normal pattern is of particular campaigns being mounted and pursued, often quite intensively, and then dropped. Baltimore, for example, spent over $440,000 on economic development advertising in 1984, but less than $10,000 in 1986 (Bailey, 1989, p. 49). Even more dramatically, Cleveland spent nothing at all in 1985 and 1986 but over $170,000 in 1987. The same basic principles also apply to tourist advertising. Here too, themes are developed and disseminated in planned, finite campaigns. Bigger budgets, the need to reach big audiences and the regular seasonal nature of the business tend to mean, however, that the scale of activity is greater. In particular, TV advertising is more common in city tourism marketing than it is for general economic development.

All these basic principles apply to city advertising in Britain, though with generally lower funding. Glasgow, for example, ended up spending £1 million on the 'Miles Better' campaign but this was over six years. The initial campaign in 1983–84 enjoyed a budget, unprecedented in Britain, of £0.5 million, raised from public and private sources (Jack, 1984, p. 40; Struthers, 1986, p. 9). Only the UDCs have managed a very regular advertising presence in major national printed media. Yet the principle of the finite campaign still applied. One of the most prominent recent examples was the 'Knocker-Docker' advertisements, for example (which we will examine more fully in the next chapter) (Brownill, 1994). These were part of a very high profile campaign during 1992, involving full, sometimes double, page spreads in national broadsheet newspapers.

Brochures, Videos and Websites

A more continuous dimension of promotional action lay in general or, in US terminology, collateral publicity. This covered the range of brochures, fact packs, pamphlets, videos, websites and, often, novelty items that all serious city marketeers felt obliged to provide. Much of the printed matter was similar in basic conception to examples we considered in previous chapters. Yet the design, production and finish were invariably much higher than in earlier periods. This reflected the general rise in production standards of all advertising and publicity. Yet the bigger budgets of the big cities meant that their publicity standards were usually higher, too, than in contemporary resort or industrial promotion materials.

Some distinctively newer types of publicity have also appeared. Most obviously new, perhaps, are the videos. Many of these began as a kind of visual equivalent of the promotional handbook, managing usually to be even more cliché-ridden (cf Bailey, 1989, pp. 36–37). Thankfully, they are now used much more sparingly than ten years ago, reflecting the high costs of producing really professional and distinctive efforts in this form. Atlanta, predictably, retains a fairly convincing presence in this aspect of publicity, with three very professional videos on offer in 1995 (MACC, 1995). Some British cities have occasionally produced impressive materials in this field, amongst them Birmingham in the late 1980s. Yet high costs and low returns have generally reduced involvements by all cities.

By contrast, promotional magazines and newspapers, though not previously unknown, especially in the United States, have become much more prominent in recent city publicity. Although their purposes blur together, several different types can be identified. Most straightforward is that directed at the tourist. A very modest British example of this is *Leeds On*, produced by the city tourism department (CLPT, 1994). A much more highly developed version is *Atlanta Now*, produced by the ACVB in conjunction with a local publisher (ACVB, 1995d). Advertising income from local attractions is a critical element in the success of such publications which need good production standards and large print runs. Many cities, have however begun to use the magazine/newsletter/newspaper format for other target audiences, including

business investors and the local community. The more limited opportunities for advertising revenues, however, mean that these are either more modest or, if high standard, part of a more carefully planned strategy than is necessary for their tourist equivalents.

Another new promotional device has been novelty items, usually sent to opinion-formers in tourism and general business. In this aspect of promotion, originality is everything. To a target group well used to business free gifts, it is often difficult for cities to produce something which really stands out and has a clear link to the place. In this Cleveland has set new standards, with recordings of the Cleveland Symphony Orchestra as well as more predictable bumper stickers and 'I ❤ Cleveland' mugs (Bailey, 1989, p. 34; Holcomb, 1993, pp. 137–140). More usually, however, cities tend to associate such gifts with special events promotion, about which more is said below. Not only does this increase the impact, it means that costs can be shared with tourist souvenir sales.

Finally, we should note how place marketing sites on the worldwide web have proliferated since the mid-1990s. In general these have appeared earlier in the United States than in Britain. Everywhere, however, they are far more highly developed for city tourism marketing than for promoting business investment. The website offers a cheap and effective means of delivering marketing information to a large number of potential 'buyers' of a place. At present, though, it is inherently less effective for active promotion since it relies on the potential investor seeking information. Future improvements in electronic mail may well change this, however, allowing attractively presented website information to be sent directly to prospective investors.

Public relations

One of the most important changes of recent years has been the growth in public relations. As we have seen, several of the civic leaders who pioneered the selling of the post-industrial city, most notably Kevin White and Michael Kelly, were consummate masters of public relations. The term is something of a misnomer. Public relations staff did not deal as much with the public as with the major intermediaries who shaped public perceptions. What the term actually meant was ensuring the press and other media broadcast favourable impressions (Kotler, Haider and Rein, 1993, p. 169–171). To an extent that is not appreciated by the general public, much of the information about cities that appears in the mass media is at least partly dependent on press releases and other actions by public relations departments.

Promotional campaigns are invariably accompanied by press information packs and press launches, designed to highlight news values. As we will see in the next chapter, the invariably exaggerated notion of rebirth, of a city coming back from the dead has often proved irresistible. The biggest prizes, of course, have tended to go to those cities which were first in the game. In Boston and Glasgow inspired amateurism achieved great rewards for that very reason. Yet ruthlessly systematic campaigns which lobbied key journals and aggressively challenged negative stories also gained handsome rewards. This was especially so in the United States, where public relations was viewed with less suspicion than in Britain. Provided the public relations machine did not entirely lose contact with the truth, its efforts would be taken as a sign that the city really cared about its future. Conventional wisdom rates favourable editorial copy as worth three times as valuable as equivalent paid advertising (Bailey, 1989, p. 30).

Most notable during the 1980s were the public relations efforts of Cleveland and Indianapolis. With very big budgets (Indianapolis spent $720,000 annually by the end of the decade, split evenly between tourism and business), both were able to build impressive relations with the mass media. In order to foster media trust these successful campaigns had to admit negatives, but always accentuated positives. Both cities managed to make themselves the subjects of favourable articles in many major journals. For Cleveland, the culmination was a 1983 piece in *Readers Digest* (Methvin 1983). Indianapolis peaked a little later, with a 1987 article in *National Geographic* (Levathes, 1987).

The process does not stop with the publication of these positive pieces, however. To make absolutely sure their value is not lost, the articles become part of the supporting publicity. Few big cities now produce promotional packages that do not include facsimile offprints from *Business Week*, *Fortune*, *Financial Times* or other prestigious journals. For their part many business and trade journals, especially in the United States, regularly rank places for seemingly every aspect of living and working. For both parties this is valuable, generating advertising and syndication revenue for the journals themselves and much favourable copy for those places in the upper ranks. Always the credibility of such third party pieces is much higher than normal city advertising material. With luck they may legitimize existing promotional slogans, or even develop new ones.

Special Events and City Marketing

We have already noted how human animation and spectacle are essential components of success in the post-industrial city. The attraction of visitors and their willingness to part with money underpin a central part of the new urban economy, of course. But in a wider sense, such activity, by confirming the viability of existing investments, encourages further physical development. In a variety of other ways, too, including the generation of media interest, special events can also be made to change more general perceptions of place. Thus, it is hardly surprising that cities now devote a lot of marketing effort both to themselves promoting events and bidding for and staging major events that could go to any of many possible national or international locations. Particularly prominent events can allow cities to rise several notches in the national or global pecking order. In many cases, it is not always necessary actually to win a bid in order to derive some marketing mileage. Being taken seriously as a contender can bring benefits at national level. As such, bidding for special events has grown rapidly over a surprisingly short period. The competition for the most prestigious events has become at least as acute as that for more substantial investments.

One of the very first types of special events used to sell the post-industrial city in Britain was the garden festival. Originating in early post-war Germany to encourage the regeneration of war damaged areas, such festivals have also been used extensively in the Netherlands (Goodey, 1994, pp. 173–175). Their use in Britain has been specifically linked to post-industrial regeneration. Five bi-annual festivals were held between 1984 and 1992, mainly in city locations, such as Liverpool, Glasgow and Gateshead (adjoining Newcastle). In marketing terms, the intention was that the festival would boost local tourism, bring extensive media coverage and have a long term effect on the promotion of derelict sites for development. Unfortunately, poor planning limited the longer term impacts of most of them and the idea is now no longer favoured (PACEC, 1990).

Yet they played an important immediate role in encouraging former industrial areas to reorientate themselves to a post-industrial world based on tourism and the leisure industries. They also did something to change external perceptions of places traditionally viewed rather negatively. Beyond these simple objectives, much the most successful festival was that staged by Glasgow in 1988. Marketed as 'A Day out of this World', it benefited by being integrated into an already well developed strategy of promotion and regeneration (Gold and Gold, 1995, p. 185). It also maintained outside interest in the city in the run up to another great series of promotional events in 1990, based on culture.

The promotion of culture has become a centrally important theme in special events in all post-industrial cities (Wynne, 1992a; Bianchini and Parkinson, 1993). Virtually all big cities already have major cultural attractions, such as museums, galleries, theatres and orchestras, as a legacy of their years of prosperity. Most have recently sought to exploit the potential of these existing resources and many have extended their cultural industries as part of their regeneration (O'Connor, 1992; Wynne, 1992b). We have noted how Chicago was beginning to do this in the late 1980s, and how Boston, Cleveland and others used similar tactics. Manchester has recently begun to exploit its own potential in this direction and was named City of Drama in 1994 (Taylor, Evans and Fraser, 1996, p. 79).

But high culture is not the only form that can be marketed. Aware perhaps of how Liverpool had so dismally failed to capitalize on the 'Mersey Sound' during the 1960s, Manchester has begun to market its popular culture during the 1990s. In 1992, for example, the Greater Manchester Visitor and Convention Bureau, was launched not, as one might expect, at a major hotel, exhibition or conference centre but at the Hacienda, the city's premier music club and discotheque (O'Connor and Wynne, 1996, p. 84). Other northern cities, especially Leeds and Newcastle, have begun to try the same tactic, energized, like Manchester, with European ideas of the '24 hour city'. Yet neither of these can match Manchester's impressive concentration of smaller music venues, nightclubs, cafes and restaurants. The city's 'Gay Village' also gives it a very clear marketing distinctiveness, though one that, as we will see, has been exploited only cautiously.

No British city has so far taken cultural marketing further than Glasgow, however (Booth and Boyle, 1993, pp. 21–47). The 'Miles Better' campaign coincided with the opening of an impressive new museum to house the Burrell Collection, a remarkable 8,000 piece accumulation of art works built up by a major Glasgow shipowner and later bequeathed to the city. Other important developments in the 1980s strengthened Glasgow's cultural credentials in music, drama and other fields. By 1986, the combination of existing cultural resources and an active promotion strategy resulted in the city winning the nomination for European City of Culture 1990 (Gold and Gold, 1995, pp. 186–188). The title originated during the early 1980s when, following a suggestion from the Greek Minister of Culture, Melina Mercouri, the EC decided to invite nominations for this new title from different European countries in turn. Athens, predictably, was the first in 1985, followed by Florence, Amsterdam, Berlin and Paris.

When Britain's turn came, the Minister for the Arts invited local bids. With Glasgow, the resultant shortlist comprised Edinburgh, Cardiff, Swansea, Bristol, Bath, Cambridge, Leeds and Liverpool. Given the usual choice of capitals or major historic cities, Glasgow's selection was a surprise. Though it reflected the fruits of several years' work to build Glasgow's cultural industries, there is no doubt the title alone, passed on from Paris, boosted the city's image. The fact that it challenged so many preconceptions made it a compelling media story, especially as 1990 itself came nearer. In fact, as no city of culture before or since, Glasgow decided to make the most of its year in the cultural spotlight. By 1990 a new concert hall was opened and extensive stone cleaning and lighting undertaken to reveal its fine older buildings. The city also prepared a very full programme of events and activities, both high brow and popular. The total spend on the year was £53.1 million, virtually all from public sources (Booth and Boyle, 1993, p. 36). The city alone spent £35 million, compared to a roughly £18 million annual average over the preceding few years.

All signs are that this investment was handsomely repaid. Already tourist traffic had been growing markedly during the 1980s, reflecting both image promotion and real improvements. By the end of the decade visitor numbers were greater than other British provincial and even some major European cities, such as Amsterdam (Law, 1993, p. 159). During 1990, hotel and guest house room occupancy increased by 35 per cent and attendance at many major attractions increased even more dramatically – by nearly 80

per cent for the Burrell Collection, for example. There was an inevitable fall-back after 1990, but there were also lasting benefits. Thus the city took major conference bookings for several years in advance. The pace of business investment in services increased, creating several thousand permanent new jobs. (There were no equivalent manufacturing investments, however.) And the inexorable rise in Glasgow's external image has continued. In 1996 the city opened yet another gallery (of modern art) and celebrated the work of its great architect, Charles Rennie Mackintosh, as part of a year-long city Festival of Visual Arts.

Sports and City Marketing

Closely related to cultural promotion has been the growing interest in staging sporting spectacles. Much more than traditional high culture, however, sports events have a popular dimension that makes them relatively easy to justify locally. This is important in two main ways. Firstly, as many cities found, expensive programmes geared to tourists, external business investors and image boosting can often seem competitive with spending on more local matters. If they can be presented as offering enjoyment for locals as well, it can help give urban entrepreneurialism a broader political base. More simply, it can also strengthen citizens' commitment to 'their' city, especially important given that falling populations are one of the key symptoms of the broader syndrome of urban decline.

Both these points have particular potency in the United States where the attraction and retention of major sports teams are hard fought aspects of city competition. As the Mayor of Indianapolis exulted: 'If you ask people what the great cities in America are, I'll bet 99 out of a 100 cite an NFL [National Football League] city' (Frieden and Sagalyn, 1989, p. 279). Compared to Britain, the United States has relatively few teams playing in major leagues, often separated by greater distances than can be managed easily in a single day round-trip. This means that there is significant tourist potential amongst sports fans in cities that have such teams and therefore host games (Law, 1993, pp. 93–97). TV coverage and the extensive merchandizing of team kit and souvenirs also ensures that a city's name receives wide exposure. A premier team, provided it does well, can also serve as a powerful popular metaphor of a city intent on winning. Yet many cities have had to pay extraordinarily high prices for such image building.

For many years, individual teams and the leagues which grant franchises have forced cities to bid against each other in offering subsidies (Baade and Dye, 1988; Frieden and Sagalyn, 1989, pp. 277–280). Usefully, team names were constructed in such a way that the place name, though coming first, was only a secondary part of team identification and could be substituted without losing team identity. In fact, team relocation has become very common since the 1950s, especially from the north east to the west and south, a trend which paralleled broader economic and demographic shifts (e.g. Brandon and Marooney, 1987, pp. 41–42). The Atlanta Braves baseball team, for example, were originally the Boston Braves before moving to Milwaukee in 1953 and to Atlanta in 1966. To attract or keep teams, cities had to compete with new stadia (practically all of which have been publicly provided since 1960), favourable leases, guaranteed ticket sales and other subsidies.

In recent years, as de-industrialization has undermined so much of the vitality of older cities, the tendency has been growing for cities to pay to keep their teams. Baltimore, for example, lost the Colts football team to Indianapolis in 1984. Four years later, however, it managed to keep the Orioles baseball team when local business guaranteed $1 million in ticket sales for ten years (Kotler, Haider and Rein, 1993, p. 130). In the same year Pittsburgh managed to keep the Pirates baseball team when a public-private partnership bought the team. So far, at least, British cities have not experienced this particular variety of place wars and seem unlikely to do so in the future. Premier soccer teams such as

Manchester United and Liverpool have, however, been incorporated into city tourist and more general image promotion.

Despite these important differences in the sporting culture of cities, the pattern of attracting special sporting events is otherwise very similar in both countries. One type of sporting spectacle associated with the classic post-industrial harbour-front/dockside setting of cities such as Boston, Baltimore, Belfast, Liverpool and Newcastle is that with a leisure/maritime theme. Many such events may be fairly small and local in their impact. Most ambitious are yacht or tall ships regattas and races, such as Sail Boston 1992. These offer much to tempt the tourist gaze and enliven regenerated harbour areas, with great potential for promotional imagery. The tourist potential of such events in cities able to host them is clearly huge (BRA, 1992), if not always fulfilled. Moreover, like all such events they provide scope for the corporate entertainment as part of wider marketing concerns. Baltimore, for example, has its own tall ship, *The Pride of Baltimore*, which has been used to entertain key business decision makers during special maritime events (Bailey, 1989, p. 35).

Indianapolis has much the most highly developed strategy of using sports as a means of regeneration (Law, 1993, pp. 96–97). Its connection with motor racing (especially the famous Indianapolis 500 race) was long established. In the 1970s and, even more the 1980s, however, the city set out to build its reputation as a mainstream physical sports venue. A major new stadium, (the main bait used to attract the Colts from Baltimore) and other facilities were added and soon brought impressive rewards. During the 1980s over 200 national and international sports meetings were held in the city. Its biggest success was the Pan-American Games hosted in 1987. Overall, the approach generated a lot of media attention and was fully exploited by the city's formidable public relations machine.

Although Indianapolis was less well known in Britain than the east coast ports, some awareness of its strategy has filtered through. Sheffield, perhaps, has perhaps come closest to emulating its approach, especially its hosting of the World Student Games in 1991 (Taylor, Evans and Fraser, 1996, pp. 66–68. Unfortunately the Games attracted much less TV coverage and income than had been estimated, so that the immediate promotional and other benefits were rather limited. Other cities had already been badly burned when the financial projections for major sporting events had not been realized, most notably at Montreal, host city to the 1976 summer Olympics. The 1986 Commonwealth Games in Edinburgh had also turned out to be a financial disaster, because of a widespread boycott. Yet Sheffield was the first former industrial city to discover that winning bids and having to stage major sports events was not risk-free.

Marketing and Olympic Bids

The biggest world sporting event is, of course, the Olympic Games (Hill, 1992). Competition to stage the main summer Games has varied in intensity. It was certainly less keen by the late 1970s and early 1980s, reflecting the marring of three successive games by terrorism, huge financial loss and boycotts. The success, despite boycotts, of the 1984 Los Angeles Games (which the city had been awarded without contest) brought a dramatic change. It became clear that, properly staged, the Games could bring handsome profits and enhance the image of the host city throughout the world. Coinciding with a period when many western cities were already experiencing serious problems of economic decline and competing for increasingly mobile investment and tourism, the lesson encouraged many cities to try their luck. The location for 1988 (Seoul) had already been chosen, with only one other contender. But the competition was fiercer than ever before by the time the locations for the Games of 1992, 1996 and 2000 came to be chosen.

Competition began even at national level, because no country was allowed more than one

city bid. When Atlanta first put its name forward for 1996, it was one of fourteen cities competing to make the US bid (ACOG, 1990). In Britain, London, Birmingham and Manchester were in contention for 1992 and 1996, with London and Manchester again for 2000 (Hill, 1992, pp. 90–119). Wider city marketing motives were very strong, especially in Birmingham and Manchester. London's interest was at least partly motivated by a desire not to give the provincial cities a free run, reflecting a fear that any success might compromise its own position as Britain's only world city. In fact, the provincial cities actually produced much the most credible bids, partly because their leaders realized they had to compensate for their cities' lack of a global profile. It was largely the technical superiority of their bids that won national support. Birmingham became Britain's favoured host city for 1992 and Manchester for 1996 and 2000 (Bamford, 1995, pp. 55–58).

In the event all three British bids were ignominiously defeated. The last defeat was particularly painful (Taylor, Evans and Fraser, 1996, pp. 77–79). The Manchester bid, by now backed very enthusiastically by national government, promised urban regeneration by creating world class facilities in run down areas, mainly in the centre and east of the city. Yet the truth was that the city won practically no new support over its first attempt. The successful bidders, Barcelona, Atlanta and Sydney won because their bids were altogether more credible on wider, non-technical grounds. As places they conjured up far more attractive and progressive images than two rather drab British regional cities, whose greatest days seemed to have been in the nineteenth century. Both certainly were changing for the better, but even the kindest assessment would have to say that aspirations to international city status in the post-industrial world were premature.

None of the successful cities were without their own problems, however. Though it differed in many important respects from Manchester and Birmingham, Atlanta, the 1996 host city, is closer to their position than the other two. Certainly it has experienced many of the symptoms of core de-industrialization and outward shift (Duffy, 1995, pp. 33–70). But its troubled core is located within an extremely fast growing region, with one of the world's biggest hub airports. As we have seen, the city had lost few opportunities to promote itself since the late nineteenth century, initially for manufacturing, latterly more to service employers. Its boosterist efforts have been motivated by the historic fear of losing regional dominance to the cities of Florida and other sunbelt states. The Olympic bid (AOC, 1990) is thus part of a continuing tradition, trying to secure unchallenged regional dominance through world city status (e.g. *Fortune*, 14.11.94).

Olympic success clearly brings huge potential rewards. The Atlanta Games were expected to add approximately $5.1 billion to the Georgia economy between 1991 and 1997 (ACOG, 1992). No final figures are yet available, but these forecasts are reported to have been fulfilled. There are also important marketing benefits. We have already noted how the huge publicity spin off from the Atlanta Olympics has led to the suspension of more general city advertising for business. Remarkably though, even humiliated Manchester has gained considerably. Within the UK there was extensive media coverage of its bid. Some of it, certainly, was negative but far less than could reasonably have been expected. Bidding also brought marked increases in international business awareness of the city, something which sponsors readily recognized (e.g. CMDC, 1996,

p. 10). In contrast to the generally lukewarm approach of British businessmen to funding general city promotional campaigns on the US pattern, well-led, high profile campaigns with specific objectives did win ready business sponsorship. The Manchester 2000 organization, which organized the bid under the leadership of a local theatrical impresario, Bob Scott, was truly a private-public partnership, far more than the many other British place marketing initiatives that claimed the title.

Great publicity advantages came from the very prolonged choice process. Between the point at which Manchester was chosen as Britain's candidate and its international rejection, the city could truthfully be claimed as Britain's Olympic city. The CMDC particularly capitalized on this and ran an advertising campaign, targeted at business, on just this theme (e.g. *Evening Standard*, 11.5.92, p. 51). It is doubtful though whether a city marketing approach based on failed bids for the Olympic Games can be extended indefinitely. Business sponsors might be able to take a realistic, even cynical, view. But it is more difficult to motivate the actual campaigners (e.g. *Guardian*, 25.9.93, p. 19). There has been talk of further Olympic bids, but this now looks unlikely. Some of the investment in the city pledged by central government has gone ahead, allowing new facilities to be developed so that Manchester has been able to bid successfully for smaller events. Most notable has been the winning (against no serious opposition) of the Commonwealth Games in 2002 (Manchester 2000, 1994).

CONCLUSIONS

We can be certain then that, while the enthusiasms of individual cities may rise and fall according to their bidding successes, sports will retain or enhance their importance in the selling of the post-industrial city. Yet what these last examples really underline is how bewilderingly diverse the scope of city marketing has now

become. It has been marked by all the traditional approaches and techniques that we have discussed in previous chapters. Yet these have been pursued with ever greater professionalism, and they have been joined by many new approaches. The fact is that any activity which contains within it the possibility of competitive place advantage can become incorporated into the selling of a city. The decline of traditional sources of prosperity and employment has made cities willing to try new approaches. Fashion though has counted for a great deal. The most popular approaches in city marketing simply reflect what appear to have worked somewhere else.

The main innovations, as we have seen, have happened in the United States, with Boston and Baltimore having the biggest collection of 'firsts'. Increasingly though British experience has itself begun to provide more models, particularly Glasgow, an example which is now becoming well known in the United States and Europe. Within Britain, the examples of continental Europe are also becoming much better known. Cultural strategies in particular have probably borrowed more from European examples than from the United States. As regards the content of marketing policies, we may confidently expect a more conscious exploitation of the different dimensions, the sub-markets, of city culture. And there may well also be marketing possibilities in other aspects of city life which so far have been rather neglected as promotional ploys. In the next chapter we will extend these thoughts about the possible future of city marketing. Its main purpose, however, will be to probe the promoted imagery of the post-industrial city.

10

COME CELEBRATE OUR DREAM

It is inherently more difficult to decode the imagery and promotional language of the contemporary city. The dominant images of the resort, the suburb and the industrial town were formed at a time removed from present-day experience. Because of this they acquire a particularity that allows us more easily to probe their nature. We are less likely to miss their most obvious messages because we do not treat them any longer as obvious. It is not so easy when we consider a promotional episode which is being shaped before our eyes. There is a greater likelihood that we may share the assumptions of the creators of the promotional imagery and therefore not regard them as worthy of comment or examination.

Moreover, the sheer cleverness of the promotional imagery can be so beguiling as to befuddle even the most ardent cultural critics (cf. Williamson, 1978, p. 7). The risk of an excessively warm glow of nostalgia that pervades attempts to decode the place selling imagery of the past gives way to a sort of complicity with its present concerns. With this rather severe note of caution we try to make sense of the imagery and promotional messages of the contemporary scene. In some respects, these differ only by degree from those we have seen in the earlier parts of this book. Yet the greater panache with which even fundamentally tired place images are now presented is important. Slickness of execution has become an essential precondition for changing perceptions, securing the acceptance of an image

of city re-invention while the reality was still very incomplete.

Beyond this, however, the concern is to highlight those parts of promotional imagery which are more distinctively post-industrial. Here, incidentally, lies the greatest danger that the dimensions of the mundane will be overlooked. Perhaps, in time, we will understand the very concept of the post-industrial city as a purely promotional construct, devoid of real meanings. For the moment, however, its distinctiveness seems sufficient to warrant separate attention. Its promotional message is dominated by a jaunty optimism that goes beyond what we have found in the industrial town. It incorporates also a relentless emphasis on vibrancy, as if the city were host to a continual series of festivals and other celebrations of culture.

In turn, this has links to another powerful theme, the projection of uniqueness of place. While other types of place, and especially industrial towns, have seemingly projected their sameness, post-industrial city marketeers emphasize their city's distinctiveness. A critical theme is the social representation of the post-industrial city, where there are often tensions between the promoted ideal and the reality. Finally there is the associated issue of building local commitment to the changing city, an ideal which appears frequently, masking more complex realities. We begin, however, by considering some of the more routine elements of the marketing message.

A PEOPLE MADE OF STRONGER STUFF

Almost every literary and visual device (and cliche) we have met in earlier chapters has been recycled in the marketing of the post-industrial city. There are, in most cases, snappy slogans that use an array of literary techniques to achieve their effects. These include alliteration, ('Atlanta Advantage'); double meaning ('Glasgow's Miles Better' [Glasgow smiles better]); repetition ('Manchester the P*ositive City* for Business' [author emphasis]); rhyme ('Turning the Tide on Merseyside'); punning ('Pittsburgh To Go'); metaphor ('Birmingham: The Big Heart of England') and many other figures of speech (often, as the examples show, in conjunction). Direct or indirect imitation was very common.

Most obviously emulated was the 'I ❤ X' formula pioneered for New York. Several US cities also referred to New York's 'Big Apple' slogan, which seemingly had an authenticity that preceded its promotional use. Cleveland, for example, for a time in the 1970s used the slogan 'Cleveland's a Plum' (Holcomb, 1993, p. 139). More obviously, Minneapolis took to referring to itself as the 'Mini-Apple' (Frieden and Sagalyn, 1989, p. 275). For a (thankfully) short period the Indianapolis Convention and Visitors Bureau used the slogan 'Move over New York, Apple is our middle name' (Bailey, 1989, p. 22). In Britain a few smaller towns have imitated the slogans of the big cities. 'Glenrothes Better by far', for example, clearly shows the influence of 'Glasgow's Miles Better' (GDC, nd *c*1994).

The tendency to imitation was, however, offset by an increasing need to stress distinctiveness. Far more than we found in industrial promotion, where most places told very much the same story, all post-industrial city marketeers took great pains in weaving their own unique mythic vision of place. We saw how only the bigger industrial cities had bothered to do this in earlier years. Much industrial promotion had consisted merely of asserting the generic locational attributes needed for a mass industrial economy. As the framework of business action or tourism decision became ever more global and rootless, place distinctiveness came to be seen as a potential anchor point that might help give one city the edge over another (Harvey, 1989*b*, pp. 294–296).

As always, history provided a convenient way of doing this. Key heritage projects were one popular way of sending the 'right' message about the past. They also allowed tourist promotion to be linked to wider themes. The Merseyside Development Corporation's impressive renovation of the disused Albert Dock in Liverpool, for example, allowed the city to be punningly promoted as 'Vintage Port' (*Sunday Times Magazine*, 16.3.86, pp. 48). Like the drink, the often politically and industrially troubled city of Liverpool had now 'lost the violent purple of its youth and taken on the rich tones of age'. It had become a 'vintage port which is already making investors more than satisfied . . . which will only improve with age'.

Another approach to asserting distinctiveness was selective history, used to define special place qualities. Newcastle's 1990 image campaign was very much on these lines. It was, in copy framed by the J. Walter Thompson agency, 'A city made from coal and steel. A people made of stronger stuff' (Wilkinson, 1992, p. 181). Starting with the proud industrial past that encompassed ships, turbines, light bulbs and beer, the text promised that the 'success story doesn't end in the past'. The key point is the qualities of the people, who have 'never been backward in looking forward' and are not blindly committed to past economic structures. To prove this, there follow mentions and illustrations of successful and famous Newcastle people of today, covering the fields of fashion, pop music, athletics and comedy. The closing words punch home the point: 'New Era. New Attitude. Newcastle'.

Such approaches were familiar enough in the United States. Boston's mythic vision of itself relied heavily on a highly selective mingling of past and future: 'The city that sparked the

American Revolution is the hub of a new revolution for the 1990s: a resurgence of innovation and entrepreneurial vision' (*Business Week*, 25.10.91). Another favourite theme was the 'combination of Old World charm and a go-for-it attitude that is distinctly American' (EDIC, nd *c*1991). Chicago's preferred historical tradition was one of superlative achievement in everything: 'From the largest cow town in the world to the largest number of Nobel prize-winners in the world' (Lawson, 1989, pp. 68). (As always in claims of this kind, some of the links were tenuous in the extreme. T. S. Eliot, for example, was one of Chicago's Nobel prize winners, a connection which had eluded many of his readers.)

By contrast, Atlanta showed that it had lost nothing of its traditional mastery of the promotional game. Increasingly from the 1960s was fashioned the notion of a heroic place of destiny, 'a brave and beautiful city' in the title of the city's successful Olympic bid (ACOG, 1990). There was certainly something of the 'Atlanta Spirit' of earlier days, but reinforced now by 'the moral vision of Atlanta's civil rights heritage' (Forward Atlanta, 1991). The work of the city's Nobel laureate, Martin Luther King, and the foundations he laid for black political ascendancy and inter-racial co-operation were consistently stressed. Few cities could create such a vision of themselves and get away with it. Atlanta could and did, using it as a stepping stone to international recognition and greatness.

THE NEXT GREAT INTERNATIONAL CITY

Another very familiar aspect of promotional copy was the positioning statement. As we have seen, industrial towns and resorts typically adopted regional geographical slogans which positioned them within their region. Post-industrial cities were, however, generally larger and more self-important. Their sellers tended to favour positioning slogans that gave them dominance or placed them within a larger unit. A word which captured this sentiment exactly was 'capital'. It was rare indeed to find a city that did not fancy itself to be capital of something, usually its region. The trick was to exaggerate but not so much as to make the proposition unacceptable.

As always (in Britain at least), Glasgow did this miles better than anywhere else. Thus, it extracted maximum value from the European City of Culture title by rendering it, with unvarying consistency, as 'Cultural Capital of Europe' (Booth and Boyle, 1993, pp. 31). This helped give Glasgow a strong European identity shifting it, if only rhetorically, from being just another British regional city. Other cities have preferred, more modestly, to produce positioning statements that upgrade or consolidate their regional positions. Leeds Development Corporation, for example, claimed the city as 'Capital of the North of England' (*Evening Standard*, 11.5.92, pp. 52). In similar vein, if more ambitiously, Manchester 2000 (1993, pp. 8–9) claimed the would-be Olympic host as 'capital city of Britain's largest region' and 'a great international city'.

Such rhetorical bids for greatness are particularly well developed in the United States. Thus Boston emphasized its position as the 'economic, cultural and government capital of New England' (*Business Week*, 25.10.91). Similarly, Atlanta continues to project itself as 'business capital of the southeast' (MACC, 1995). Yet ambitious US cities such as these have also devised positioning statements that have presented them as global players. An early example was Kevin White's late 1970s' attempt to move Boston up a notch with his 'world-class city' slogan (Kennedy, 1992, p. 195). The theme regularly recurs in current publicity (BRA, 1993). More recently, the main US pretender to the somewhat imperfectly defined status of 'world city' has been Atlanta. Its currently favoured positioning phrase is the 'next great international city' (*Financial Times*,

Olympic bidding provided many opportunities to project cities for investment and tourism. During Manchester's second period as Britain's Olympic bid city, the Central Manchester Development Corporation made the most of the resultant window of marketing opportunity, as in this 1992 example.

1.11.94, Survey, p. 1). This provoked many sniggers when it first appeared but subsequent events have lent it more credibility. Other cities, for example Cleveland, have occasionally played this same game but cautiously (Bailey, 1989, p. 23). To work well the propositions have to be almost believable.

British provincial cities have faced similar problems. For many years, Birmingham themed its publicity as 'The Big Heart of England' (e.g. *Sunday Times Magazine*, 25.11.84, p. 26; *Sunday Times Business World*, 1.10.90). By 1986, as its abortive Olympic bid was reaching its climax, this somewhat parochial message was confusingly mingled with a rather overblown international tagline: 'Birmingham: One Of The World's Great Cities'. One advertisement in the series (*Sunday Times Magazine*, 21.9.86, pp. 28–29) promised that 'Even J. R. would feel at home in Birmingham' (a reference to J. R. Ewing of the TV soap opera *Dallas*). As the accompanying copy gushed:

Today a stranger on the streets of Birmingham might easily imagine himself in the heart of Manhattan. Or rubbing shoulders with the oil barons of Dallas.

Birmingham today is no stranger to the elegantly soaring pinnacles of business and finance that dominate the skylines of some of the world's great cities.

... Today a single glance at the city's bright new business district mirrors its status as one of the world's great cities.

Happily, the city soon abandoned such ridiculous posturing. Like Glasgow, Birmingham now emphasizes its European credentials, using its National Exhibition and International Convention Centres to become 'Europe's Meeting Place' (Aldersey-Williams, 1994; Hubbard, 1996). For British provincial centres, lacking any of the obvious attributes of world cities, Europe provides a rhetorical lifeline, allowing them, if only fancifully, to bypass London's dominance. Yet such propositions are not without deeper significance. As O'Connor and Wynne (1996b, p. 69) have written of Manchester's moves in the same direction:

[i]t was a negotiation of identity through a reworking of its location in the matrix of cultural space. 'Provincial' culture could now become semi-autonomous as it opened out into the 'Europe of the regions' and looked (enviously) to the great city-states of Europe.

A ROSE-RED CITY

As this rather implies, the best slogans are now very carefully considered and constructed. SWOT (strengths, weaknesses, opportunities, threats) analysis is usual. Public consultation, sometimes extensive, is not unknown, as happened with Atlanta's pre-Olympic sloganizing (*Guardian*, 7.10.93). And, much more than in previous periods, slogans are used in a rigorous and consistent way to theme advertising and publicity campaigns. Graphic and visual design have reinforced this trend, aiding recognition. Thus the heart and apple symbols were integral to New York's campaigns; Mr Happy was essential for Glasgow. There have also been dramatic improvements in presentation and general design standards. There is now more use of colour, finer photography, better quality paper with more subtle finishes, giving a slickness to marketing efforts that often runs well ahead of the actual content.

An important part of this slickness is the visual representation of place. The 'trophy buildings' and flagship developments are potential icons, or at least tokens, of the renewed city. The main way in which these are disseminated is through the photographic images which appear in promotional publicity. Typically these use all the conventional tricks of architectural photography to improve the presentation of place. Lighting conditions are usually dramatic, designed to highlight the qualities of the buildings depicted. In the promotional publicity of its now defunct Development Corporation, Manchester, for example, is typically bathed in the mellow light of the low evening or morning sun. This shows off the renovated older brick and stone buildings to particularly good effect. In many pictures filters strengthen the impression of a rose-red city and prevent bluish, cold shadows. Polarizing filters enhance reflections of waterside developments. There is a sharp contrast with 'before' shots, invariably taken under less flattering conditions.

Night or twilight pictures are also common ways of representing post-industrial cities, particularly in the United States. Nowhere has used

BOSTON

revolutionizing business opportunity

*"Boston's continued economic growth is the catalyst for the revitalization of the
New England economy. We have the ideal environment for business expansion
across a wide variety of industries. Our city demonstrates that when business
and government work together we can keep our people working and our economy growing."*

RAYMOND L. FLYNN
Mayor of Boston

Boston was a city which underwent the translation from industrial to post-industrial so effortlessly that for many years it needed little advertising. That began to change in the 1990s as the 'Massachusetts Miracle', on which Boston's prosperity partly rested, began to falter. This was an early effort, showing a characteristic mix of world city credentials, heritage, environment, high technology, sports and lifestyle.

this technique more in recent years than Atlanta. In both tourism and business advertising, general views of the city are usually photographed under these conditions. Daytime pictures are very rare indeed (as they are, incidentally, in postcards of the city). The projected image is one of a cluster of futuristic, towers, lit internally (and, increasingly, externally). They are set against the backdrop of a darkening, dramatically coloured sky. Graduated filters are used in many of these photographs to enhance sky colour. In the dark foreground the lights of city traffic are extruded as dramatic coloured lines by the photographer's time exposure.

The general effect is to make the city, particularly its downtown area, seem more exciting, modern and busy than could ever be suggested in a daytime picture. Marketing agencies were well aware of this rather magical visual effect. Thus the ACVB (1994) compared the city

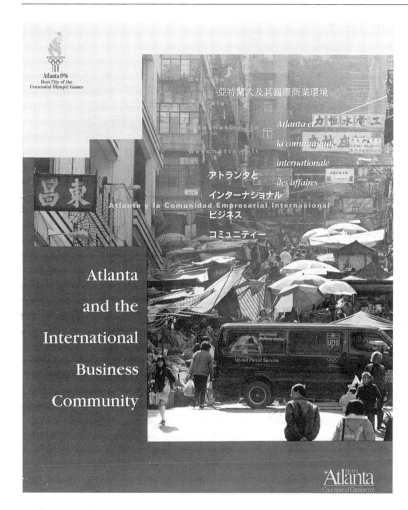

亞特蘭大及其國際商業環境

Atlanta et
la communauté
internationale
des affaires

アトランタと
インターナショナル
ビジネス
コミュニティー

Atlanta y la Comunidad Empresarial Internacional

Atlanta
and the
International
Business
Community

Asserting world credentials is common. Atlanta has laid down its marker to be the next great international city, though is often subtle in pressing this claim in publicity. This example, the cover of a brochure aimed at international business interests, simply shows one of Atlanta's global companies (United Parcels Service) at work in Hong Kong. The 1996 Olympic logo reinforces the point that the city is now a global player.

skyline to the land of Oz. Undistinguished buildings took on a new, more dramatic, aspect. Such representations also conveniently concealed the tawdriness of vacant lots and transformed visual clutter such as illuminated advertisements into something attractive. Most other cities have used something of the same approach. The growing fashion for external architectural illumination has encouraged many British cities to follow Atlanta. Manchester, for example, is sometimes represented in this way, though the focus, as we might expect, is more on its older buildings.

Overall then post-industrial city marketing has quickly developed its own promotional imagery, if drawing heavily on earlier place selling repertoires. In the sections which follow we explore a little more deeply the key propositions and associated images that are particularly characteristic of this evolving practice.

Dramatic photographic representations of the cityscape are characteristic aspects of contemporary city marketing. Atlanta does this extremely well, strongly favouring night or twilight shots of its city skyline. This approach, combined with architectural illumination, gives a sense of futuristic excitement to the city.

FORGET EVERYTHING YOU THOUGHT YOU KNEW ABOUT . . .

The very essence of re-invention was about changing existing perceptions. In many cases these perceptions were so completely negative that they had to be directly challenged. As we have seen, the public relations machines of US cities spent much of their time doing exactly this (Bailey, 1989; Holcomb, 1993, 1994). The perceived association of Chicago with crime was a crucial element in the late 1980s advertising drive to stress its cultural and other attractions (Lawson, 1989). In some ways, though, US cities have moved beyond this proposition, which tended to figure at an early stage in post-industrial advertising. Most of the clearest recent examples are drawn from British cities.

Glasgow's national 'Miles Better' campaign in 1984 was based centrally on this premise. One of the advertisements in the series began:

Forget everything you thought you knew about Glasgow. Here are a few facts about our little known but much maligned city . . . (*Sunday Times Magazine*, 4.11.84, p. 68)

One of the most commonly held perceptions was that Glasgow was a city of aggressive or

Other cities also made use of low light photography in promotional publications. Here the setting sun highlights the dramatic contrasts of Boston's skyline, between the older brick buildings of Beacon Hill and the modern glass and concrete office towers.

hopeless drunks, a view not without some historical basis (e.g. Oakley, 1975, pp. 187–188) and still widely held to be true. The city leaders were, however, understandably anxious to replace this view with a more continental 'European' image of civilized drinking. (Scotland broke dramatically with tradition by legalizing liberal licensing hours some years before the rest of Britain.) As another advertisement in the series promised:

The music-hall Glaswegian is a thing of the past. Frankly it's not an easy myth to dispel, but we know our sober citizens so well that altered traditional opening hours mean you can sink a pint almost any time of day (or night!). Thirsty Englishmen take note. Glasgow's miles better. (*Sunday Times Magazine*, 5.9.84, p. 10)

The same rewriting was applied to Glasgow cuisine:

Nouvelle tatties [potatoes] and mince? No. Not neeps [turnips] nicoises either. Glasgow's gourmet restaurants base their menus around fresh salmon from local waters or Scottish beef and succulent lamb. Even Monsieur Michelin has crossed cutlery with us. (*Ibid*)

and, if rather surreally, to the weather:

Contrary to popular belief, it does not rain 365 days a year in Glasgow. We get less rain than Miami (a lot less!) . . . (*Ibid*, pp. 10–11)

Glasgow was, of course, the British city that had to try hardest in this combating of negatives. But most cities adopted the tactic to some extent. Bradford, for instance, began theming its promotional publications with a 'Mythbreakers' slogan during the 1980s. One brochure included

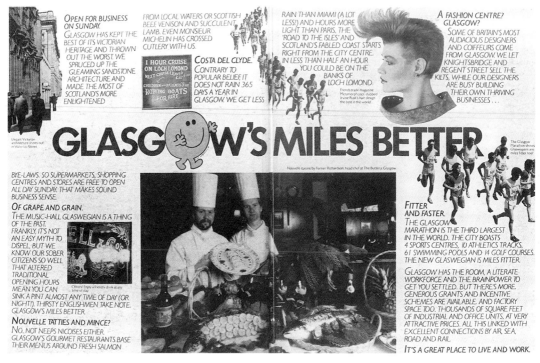

One of several colour supplement advertisements used in the national Glasgow's Miles Better campaign in 1984. Although something of a traditional tendency to recite facts about the city is apparent, it is done with wit and panache and striking images punctuate the text. The main slogan, punctuated by Mr Happy, ensures the principal message is not lost.

a section called 'We've heard all the jokes about Bradford', followed by detailed refutations (BEDU, nd *c*1985). Liverpool's 1990 promotional video was constructed entirely around the same basic theme. About the same time the Merseyside Development Corporation began to use a distorting mirror to emphasize the contrast between perceptions and the real Liverpool (Madsen, 1992, p. 636). Thus the MDC leaflet 'See yourself in Merseyside' incorporated a distorting mirror. With it came an invitation: 'In place of distorted images something new. Reality ... The new reality. A true reflection of Merseyside'.

Belfast is another, even more negatively perceived, city which has tried a direct confrontation with unfavourable perceptions in at least some of its publicity. There was, certainly, an ambivalence in the promotional imagery of the city's Laganside Development Corporation (LDC). The very name, the logo and much of its publicity serve to deny the Belfast connection (e.g. Neill, Fitzsimmons and Murtagh, 1995, pp. 88–90). It was not so much 'forget everything you thought you knew about Belfast' as 'let's forget about Belfast and hypothesize a new place, in the hope that we might get you interested in it before you realize where it is'. Without entirely departing from this approach, some LDC publicity did acknowledge Northern Ireland's problems. The advertisement 'And you think *we've* got troubles' tried to argue that these should be set against the area's positive features (Gold, 1994, pp. 23–27). Other cities had their

In Britain, a good deal of post-industrial promotion by provincial cities has been focused on London, where negative perceptions of older regional cities have often been most deeply entrenched. London's buses and Underground system were a favourite location for place advertising, as here by Liverpool's Merseyside Development Corporation in 1990.

own 'troubles', such as congestion, pollution, high rents and skilled labour shortages, of which Laganside (coyly identified as Belfast) was relatively free.

In the many cities which did not suffer (or were not prepared to admit to suffering) such negative preconceptions the message has been more implicit. This is especially so in advertising directly addressed at tourists. The possibility of a negative image is acknowledged rather more indirectly, by presenting the notion of a place holding surprises or secrets, a very familiar tourism promotional proposition. A 1984 advertisement for Birmingham, for example, promised 'One thing you can be sure of, if your passing knowledge of Birmingham is the view from Spaghetti Junction, the city has some very pleas-ant surprises in store for you' (*Sunday Times Magazine*, 25.11.84, p. 26).

Another nationally circulated advertisement from about the same time, for 'Capital Cardiff: The heart of Wales', carried the promise 'We'll let you into our secret!' (*Sunday Times Magazine*, 25.3.84, p. 40). The same broad tactic was very common in the (rather less well-funded) tourist publicity put out by, or on behalf of, the many former industrial towns. 'Unexpectedly, Wigan . . .' was a particularly entertaining example of the genre (ETB, 1988). More explicit was Torfaen: 'Anyone expecting to see a landscape ravaged by industrial exploitation, with coal miners emerging from pit heads will be surprised' (TBC, 1992). There were very many more in this general vein.

ALWAYS LOOK ON THE BRIGHT SIDE OF LIFE

For a few moments after the announcement, in September 1993, of Sydney's success in its bid to host the 2000 Olympics, the many thousands of people who had gathered in Castlefields, Manchester, stood before the nation's TV viewers in silent disappointment. The victory party they had hoped for was not going to happen. Fortunately, the public relations people realized that, win or lose, the prime time media exposure was precious. Soon two figures, dressed as the cuddly toy lion who would have been the mascot of a Manchester Olympics and TV's Mr Blobby, were on stage, leading the crowd in an enthusiastic communal rendition of 'Always look on the bright side of life'. As they did so, the image that was being transmitted suddenly changed. Here was a city which was not, in any fundamental sense, defeated. Its people had not given up. They did not feel sorry for themselves. Their spirit was unbowed. In its own way, it was a minor triumph.

It also captured, in a microcosm, one of the key themes in the promoted image of the post-industrial city. This was a place bouncing back, snatching at least some kind of victory from the jaws of defeat, not giving up or whining for sympathy.

In their own ways, practically all post-industrial cities projected this same story about themselves. It came across in advertising, for example, Detroit as the Renaissance City (Neill, Fitzsimmons and Murtagh, 1995, p. 128) or Pittsburgh Renaissance (Frieden and Sagalyn, 1989, p. 275). Even more it became the staple fare served up by city public relations bureaux and press releases. For their part the media were usually happy to reproduce and extend this narrative. In many ways it suited their purposes to exaggerate both the depths of former decay and the extent of present recovery to add drama to the comeback cities.

This was the message, for example, of one of the first of the *genre*, the well known *Readers Digest* article 'Cleveland Comes Back' (Methvin, 1983). Another was the *National Geographic Magazine* article 'Indianapolis: City on the Rebound' (Levathes, 1987). The latter piece lays bare, almost to the point of caricature, the essentials of this post-industrial saga of cities picking themselves up, dusting themselves off and starting all over again:

Once a rustbelt city on the skids, Indianapolis was laid low by cutbacks in federal aid and by an overdependence on the automobile industry. But those dark days are over, say residents, thanks to an aggressive partnership of government, business and philanthropy that has practically re-invented America's 14th largest city – complete with an upbeat new sports image and a taste for shopping malls, conventions, tourists, and entrepreneurs.

. . . Mayor William Hudnut III never tires of promoting his 'can-do city'. (*Ibid*, p.230)

The same air of jaunty optimism permeated the 'Glasgow's Miles Better' campaign and made it stand out from its British contemporaries in 1983–84. By coincidence the London Borough of Hackney began its own public relations campaign at about the same time in 1983 (Hackney LBC, 1983). The projected image was, however, radically different. Hackney publicized itself, mainly

Hackney's miles worse. About the same time Glasgow launched its miles better campaign, the London Borough of Hackney began a press and political campaign proclaiming itself as Britain's poorest borough. This pessimistic approach was much less successful, however.

to the media and to decision makers, as 'Britain's Poorest Borough'. This was actually a claim that Glasgow might have easily disputed – significantly, Hackney's supporting evidence ignored Scotland.

Yet this was not quite the point. The two approaches reflected entirely different social and political discourses. Fundamentally Hackney was asserting its case for special assistance from central government. Glasgow's campaign, by contrast, made no such calls on central funds. (But, compared to Hackney, it did not need to. Scottish central government agencies, never quite as uncompromisingly Thatcherite as their English equivalents, had already accepted Glasgow's case for special treatment.) The 'Miles Better' campaign was directed essentially at investors, possible residents and visitors. It was a particularly appealing contribution to the new political discourse of urban entrepreneurialism and won widespread admiration for the city.

Hackney's campaign, in sharp contrast, fell on stony ground. It won little sympathy with Ministers. Mrs Thatcher was strident in her general distaste for 'moaning minnies' who complained about problems such as unemployment and poverty. A city or borough which did so using local tax monies was hardly likely to appeal. And of course, telling the world how awful a place is does nothing to encourage investment or tourism, quite the reverse. At another time, in the 1960s, perhaps, Hackney's campaign might have been more effective in what it set out to do. But, set against the political realities of the 1980s, it was a major misjudgement. Other cities, more by default, sent out similarly negative signals, before realizing that optimism was essential (Madsen, 1992). By the 1990s positive messages had become universal. 'Sheffield Shines', adopted by the Sheffield Development Corporation in 1994, and Marketing Manchester's much ridiculed 'We're Up and Going' slogan of 1997 are recent examples (Taylor, Evans and Fraser, 1996, p.305; *Guardian*, 16.5.97).

Another typical dimension of the optimism syndrome was to stress 'success' or words that sent a similar upbeat message ('dynamic' or 'thriving', for example) in promotional copy. No cities were entirely immune from this. Merseyside Development Corporation, for example, in 1992 was boasting that 'Success after success is happening on Merseyside'. Bristol was 'a great European city competing successfully for trade and international investment' (*Evening Standard*, 11.5.92, pp. 57; 61). Also in 1992, the smart person (labelled, interestingly, 'The Docker', to which we will return below) '[k]nows beyond doubt that London Docklands will be a success' (*Guardian*, 8.9.92, p. 7). US cities were even more prone to the claiming of success, often on the flimsiest of pretexts.

Critics, not without reason, often attacked the mindlessness of such optimism. A particularly interesting recent study of US cities has found that perceptions and realities of 'urban success stories' between 1980 and 1990 were very different (Wolman, Ford and Hill, 1994). Pittsburgh, for instance, was the city most widely perceived as being successful. Certainly it received glowing coverage in the late 1980s in major newspapers across the country, such as the *New York Times* and the *Los Angeles Times* ('Blooming in the Rust') (Holcomb and Parisi, 1990, p. 8*a*; Holcomb, 1993, pp. 135–137). However, it was in fact towards the bottom of the rankings of improvements in economic well being amongst those cities classified as distressed in 1980. Many cities not perceived as successful had done much better. Only Boston (where the extent of success relative to other cities was actually underestimated), Atlanta and Baltimore showed anything like the real improvements that began to justify their perception as successful.

Where you can catch a few rays.

Spend a picture-perfect afternoon.

And get to know some crusty characters.

BALTIMORE IS A CITY OF HISTORY, CULTURE AND CHARM. A VIBRANT METROPOLIS WITH SMALL-TOWN CHARACTER. BUT MORE IMPORTANTLY, BALTIMORE IS A CITY OF ACTIVITY, WHERE EXCITING THINGS HAPPEN EVERY DAY.

HERE, YOU WILL FIND ATTRACTIONS LIKE THE NATIONAL AQUARIUM, HARBORPLACE AND THE MARYLAND SCIENCE CENTER. THE B&O RAILROAD MUSEUM AND RENOWNED INSTITUTIONS OF FINE ART. FORT MCHENRY AND ORIOLE PARK AT CAMDEN YARDS. SPECTACULAR SHOPPING AND SUPERB CHESAPEAKE BAY CUISINE. ALL CLOSE TO DOWNTOWN.

BALTIMORE IS ALSO EASILY ACCESSIBLE FROM VIRTUALLY ANYWHERE BY AIR, TRAIN OR HIGHWAY. PLUS, WE OFFER A FULL RANGE OF MODERATE-TO-DELUXE HOTEL ACCOMMODATIONS. SO WHETHER YOU ARE TRAVELING ALONE OR WITH THE ENTIRE FAMILY, YOU CAN BE SURE WE'LL PROVIDE THE EXACT LEVEL OF COMFORT AND VALUE YOU NEED.

THERE'S SO MUCH TO SEE AND DO HERE – AND SO MANY NEW THINGS UNDERWAY. WE INVITE YOU TO EXPERIENCE THE ENERGY, THE ENTHUSIASM, THE UNIQUE SPIRIT OF BALTIMORE. YOU'LL SEE WHY WE SAY THE EXCITEMENT IS STILL BUILDING.

Baltimore
Area Convention and Visitors Association
100 Light Street • 12th Floor • Baltimore, Maryland 21202

FOR MORE INFORMATION, CALL TOLL-FREE 1-800-282-6632 OR LOCALLY 410-837-4636.

Example of tourism advertising by a city that has played a critical role in refining western ideas about the nature of the post-industrial city. Note the punning references to specific attractions, namely the aquarium, art galleries and seafood.

IT'S CAPPUCCINO TIME

As we noted in the previous chapter, these extravagant claims often rested on impressive developments in culture and sport. These were designed, as we have seen, to bring an air of continuous animation to the urban scene. In the same fashion that British seaside resorts were, in an earlier era, supposed to be 'bracing', post-industrial cities everywhere now absolutely *had* to be 'vibrant'. Few cities, indeed, are presently able to resist using the word itself somewhere in their promotional publicity.

Baltimore, for example, 'is a city of history,

COME CELEBRATE OUR DREAM 223

culture and charm. A vibrant metropolis with small-town character' (*Mid-Atlantic Country*, 1996, p. 5). Glasgow 'is host to some of the most vibrant arts and cultural activities in the world' (Glasgow '96, 1996). Manchester has vibrancy coming out all over: 'Mix vibrant city centre shopping and nightlife with action-packed activities' (GMVCB, 1996, pp. 2–3); 'A thriving cafe bar culture adds to Manchester's vibrancy . . .' (MVSMCC, 1996*a*, p. 4); '. . . not only an excellent location for business, it is a vibrant cultural city' (MVSMCC, 1996*b*). Yet the advertising of cultural vibrancy is not itself remarkable. What is more important are the secondary discourses of such publicity, in other words, what they say about the supposed norms of post-industrial urban life – culture in its widest meaning.

While there were some broad parameters for the promoted culture of the post-industrial city, everywhere was not quite the same. There were significant variations in the exact construction of cultural vibrancy in different cities. The most prominent example of the 'high' cultural city was Glasgow. After the old Glasgow had been successfully refuted, the new promoted culture of celebration, leisure and the arts came in to replace it. Of 1990, Glasgow's year as European city of culture, the city's Saatchi and Saatchi-produced advertisements promised: 'If they're singing, dancing and painting the town in Glasgow, it must be Hogmanay (or March 4th, or June 17th, or August 9th, or September 22nd, or . . . ' (*Sunday Times Magazine*, 31.12.89, p. 46). This theme of year long cultural celebration was regularly reinforced throughout 1990 (e.g. *Sunday Times Magazine*, 28.1.90, pp. 56; 25.2.90, pp. 78; 8.7.90, p. 44). Even the graphic design of the distinctive typeface, derived from the style of Glasgow's famous architect/designer, Charles Rennie Mackintosh, sent the same message of culture (and underlined urban uniqueness). It was captured too in the punning theme slogan, 'There's A Lot Glasgowing on in 1990'.

This characteristic promotional mix of humour and 'high' culture continued after 1990:

'For those who know their art from their elbow, may we suggest a short break in Glasgow' (*Sunday Times Magazine*, 30.6.91, p. 53). The word play of this line (referring to the common saying that those lacking in worldly wisdom could not 'tell their arse from their elbow') effectively showed that the new 'cultural' Glasgow had not become so self-regarding that it had lost touch with the earthiness of the old city. All this changed with the 1992 'Glasgow's Alive' campaign, however. This involved the most ambitious propositions yet about the nature of Glasgow's new post-industrial European culture:

Early light, and a great European city gets to work. Down wide, bustling streets look up at Victorian and Georgian splendours built on an Imperial scale. Reflect on glass fronted edifices – inside the wheels of modern Glasgow carry the city ever forward. Laugh with the kids running to and fro in Princes Square, as grown ups take in the shops at their leisure. In the Italian Centre it's Cappuccino Time. Check out Gianni and Giorgio. The sun sets across the city as crowds rise to footballing heroes. The year of culture lives on at the Royal Concert Hall. People relax in the cafes, winebars, pubs and clubs and dishes from around the world are served up to expectant gourmets. All over Glasgow life speeds along its way, gathering energy, gathering warmth, gathering pace. *Another day and, more than ever, GLASGOW'S ALIVE.* (Gold and Gold, 1995, p. 190).

Here, clearly set out, was the promised post-industrial land. It was peopled by a new breed of international *boulevardiers*, who, on hearing the word culture, reached for their cappuccinos. To judge from the accompanying picture, they seemed to have stepped straight from the advertisements for smart clothes or cars on the adjoining pages of the glossy magazines. They certainly had no connection to the dirty, grimy world that had been industrial Glasgow. There had been mounting local criticisms of the cultural re-imaging of Glasgow. 1990 was, in one view, 'a year when an intellectually bankrupt and brutally undemocratic administration projected its mediocre image onto the city and ordered us to adore it' (cited Booth and Boyle, 1993, p. 21).

To those who already thought this way, the new campaign brought confirmation. Even to

The Saatchi and Saatchi agency were retained to promote Glasgow as European City of Culture in 1990. In the city's advertising, however, it was always rendered as 'Cultural Capital of Europe', an important rhetorical repositioning for the city. While naturally emphasizing culture, (even in the main typeface, derived from designs by Charles Rennie Mackintosh), the approach also keeps the humorous approach of the miles better campaign.

those who did not, the loss of the jokeiness that had pervaded the previous campaigns made a difference. The new Glasgow could be accepted, or at least tolerated, when it was asserted with jaunty humour. To the extent that sceptical receivers of the message smiled, even momentarily, they became complicit in the vision. Lacking this inclusive note of humour, the overblown language of 'Glasgow's Alive' was mere pretension. It was unintentionally funny because it so pompously presented a lifestyle far removed from ordinary experiences of the city. At any rate, the campaign was dropped in 1994. Mr Happy, Glasgow's equivalent of the jolly fisherman, returned for the Glasgow '96 Festival of Visual Arts. Like Skegness' famous marketing icon, he provided continuity, equipped with artist's brush, palette and beret.

These cultural tensions reflected in Glasgow's promotional imagery were more acute than elsewhere because city leaders had placed so much faith in 'high' culture as a basis for regeneration.

In a city which had experienced unparalleled industrial decline, bringing horrendous poverty and deprivation, it could hardly have been an inclusive vision.

JUST AS LIKELY TO WATCH A RUGBY LEAGUE MATCH . . .

The London Docklands experienced something of the same tensions, if for slightly different reasons. Here an established working class culture built around dock life was displaced by physical and cultural change. The conquering cultural force was not here the favoured Glasgow model of high European cafe culture. Instead it was the American-style 'yuppie' culture of hard working, high earning, hard playing and high spending. Docklands was, in a 1986 advertising campaign, 'your place in the city to work and play' (*Financial Times Survey*, 1.10.86). 'You' in this context were more than likely to have red braces and a Porsche. Another advertisement in the series called 'Working Lunch' showed a windsurfer talking on a mobile phone, an object very much associated at that time with 'yuppie' culture (Brownill, 1994, p. 142).

1992 saw a definite attempt to soften this image in the 'knocker-docker' publicity campaign (e.g. *Guardian*, 8.8.92, pp. 6–7; Brownill, 1994, pp. 146–148). In this the 'knocker' displays a wide variety of ultra-conventional attitudes. For example he (and the knocker is definitely a 'he') 'presses his jeans'; 'finds, in the spring, his fancy turns to thoughts of a new lawnmower'; 'doesn't move out of the middle lane of the motorway for anyone'; 'orders steak and chips in an Indian restaurant'; 'fears Vivian Westwood will catch a nasty cold'; and 'believes, on reflection, there's only one way to skin a cat'. Nor surprisingly, therefore, he has 'never visited London Docklands, even as a tourist' and 'would rather "lose" a few people than cut overheads by moving'.

The 'docker', rather predictably, was not burdened with such old-fashioned, suburban attitudes. Accordingly a 'docker' could be either new man (probably) or professional woman (possibly): 'is just as able to change a nappy as a tyre'; 'sees a secretary as a colleague not a slave'; 'went to gyms when Jane Fonda was still making movies'. He/she embraced the popular end of high culture: 'happily got wet to hear Pavarotti' (a reference to a then recent Hyde Park opera concert attended by the smart set, despite very heavy rain). But there was also a classless appreciation of popular culture: 'is just as likely to watch a Rugby League match as a Union Game'; 'is a fan of David Gower, Trevor Brooking and Andre Agassi'. Along with this, the 'docker' also approves of the Channel Tunnel 'even if it only means you get a decent croissant'; 'reveres Akio Morita, who went ahead with the Sony Walkman even though research said it would fail' and 'doesn't mind paying more for recycled paper'.

It therefore comes as no surprise that the 'docker' also realizes that 'an office isn't just space, it's a wavelength'; 'knows that cities, like businesses, must develop or they'll decay' and inevitably, as we have already noted, that London Docklands will be a success. Overall, the character sketch is of a reconstructed 'yuppie'. There is less of the amoral individualism of the 1980s. Respect for bold enterprise and its material rewards is still there but is now leavened by a self-congratulatory tone of social progressiveness and classlessness. The supreme cultural irony lies, however, in the 'docker' label, itself. Traditionally, the term conjured up a tough, male manual worker, a militant trades unionist, the main breadwinner in the close working class communities which grew up in the East End. Now, like the area itself, this traditional meaning of the label was being appropriated. It was part of the act of displacement, colonizing former working class cultural space.

IT'S QUEER UP NORTH

Manchester has been the British leader during the 1990s in using its nightlife to promote the city. A particularly distinctive aspect of the city is its music club scene, from which many prominent bands emerged in the 1980s. The city also has a well-developed gay sub-culture, discreetly referred to in this tourism brochure.

Manchester shows yet another way of using cultural imagery in place marketing, one that purports to be more genuinely socially inclusive than the other two examples. From the mid 1990s, the Greater Manchester Visitor and Convention Bureau began promoting city tourism under the slogan 'This is the life' (GMVCB, 1996). In truth, much of its content was fairly conventional tourist fare, with minor stately homes, heritage sites, shopping and 'high' culture. But there were clear references to the 'authentic' life of Manchester and surrounding towns, embracing a variety of popular and local sub-cultures. Thus the celebrations of the local, former textile, towns

around Manchester (such as the Rochdale Rushbearing Festival, 'always a lively event') are promoted as 'special days which have bound communities together and enriched the language and culture' (*Ibid*, p. 10).

The popular, commercialized mass culture of football and television forms important aspects of tourist promotion in Manchester. More unusual though, at least in a British context, is the promotion for tourism of the city's ethnic cultures. Chinatown, graced by a huge Chinese Imperial Archway provided by the city council in 1987 to promote the district and encourage Chinese investment, receives particular attention

Manchester's gay scene was much more overtly promoted in the gay press and through particular events such as this gay arts festival which had grown very dramatically since 1992.

(Bamford, 1995, pp. 28–29). Promotional photographs also acknowledge the presence of Manchester's other ethnic communities, if in a more token way. (Other provincial cities, for example Leeds, with its large West Indian Carnival, have gone further in this respect (CLPT, 1994).) Another more innovative aspect of promotional imagery, much more heavily pushed, is youth culture, especially the city's music clubs:

Any night can be a night to remember. Move with the music. You can feel the buzz. If it happens, it happens first in Manchester. (*Ibid*, p. 14)

Some of the accompanying illustrations convey the sweaty, crowded atmosphere of clubs such as the Hacienda or the Band on the Wall. But there is a distinct undertow of cultural conservatism about the dominant images. The young people most prominently featured in posed pictures are attractive, conventionally stylish male/female couples. In time-honoured place promotional fashion, the woman has greatest prominence, as if to signify the promise of the place itself. In many respects, these promotional figures are merely variants of archetypal post-industrial *boulevardiers*. Within a few years, or even at another time of day, their designer beers, drunk from the bottle, may well be replaced by cappuccinos and croissants.

Yet these general tendencies still represent a broadening, however cautious, of promoted images of urban culture. A further stage is the discreet incorporation of gay culture into promotional imagery (e.g. GMVCB, 1996, p. 14). This reflects the emergence of a distinct sub-culture in the city centred on the Whitworth 'village' area. Despite being widely known for its gay 'scene', this fact took some time to enter mainstream city marketing literature. Thus the CMDC, in whose area the Gay Village lay, did not finally 'come out' on this until its work had virtually ended (e.g. CMDC, 1996, p. 26; cf 1995, pp. 8–9). (This was despite partnership on particular developments between the Corporation and gay entrepreneurs.) By this time a lively gay sub-culture had been created, hosting a regular Gay Village Carnival and arts events such as 'It's Queer Up North'.

As others have commented, this represents a real and remarkable change in Manchester's urban culture (Taylor, Evans and Fraser, 1996, pp. 180–197). The traditional culture of northern industrial cities barely acknowledged the existence of homosexuality. Waterhouse's recent comments on Leeds would probably stand for all: 'certain men were known to be good to their mothers, and that was as far as it went' (Waterhouse, 1995, p. 61). Yet it is still only partially visible in promotional imagery. In effect, the cautious and partial incorporation into post-industrial Manchester's promotional imagery represents the continuing negotiation between two conflicting trends. On the one hand is a recognition of the power of the 'pink pound', manifest not only in consumption but also in a willingness to invest in more marginal urban spaces. On the other is a fear that being too overt might frighten off mainstream tourists, investors or residents.

COME CELEBRATE OUR DREAM

While such developments are still extremely unusual in British post-industrial cities, they have been known for some years in a few US cities, particularly San Francisco. There are, however, some important differences between the marketing imagery of American and British cities. Some, such as Boston (and, as we have seen, Chicago), have tended to promote themselves principally in a 'European' cultural language:

Blessed with big city vigor and small town charm, Boston – as America's most European city – is a paradise of cobblestones and gas lights on Beacon Hill, art galleries and haute couture in the Back Bay, Italian expresso cafes and pastry shops in the North End. (BRA, 1993)

Such words were certainly supplemented by much more completely American cultural references to the city's repertoire of spectator sports. But there were definite links here to the same high cultural mainstream that we have encountered in Glasgow. Other cities, such as Cleveland and Baltimore have also built similar 'high' cultural reference points into their publicity (e.g. Bailey, 1989, p. 34).

Yet many other US cities, particularly those where there is black political control, have begun to incorporate images of non-white communities more fully into place selling. We have seen that this is still treated very cautiously in British place publicity, confined to providing ethnic colour in food, dress and public celebration within a predominantly white mainstream. Ethnic minority businesses began to be taken seriously in most cities during the 1980s but overall this has remained a very minor theme. Tourism-oriented publicity, even where it acknowledges the existence of ethnic minorities in the host community, has almost completely ignored ethnic minority populations as tourists.

The imagery and targeting is significantly different in the predominantly black US city of Atlanta. We have already seen how business promotional publicity has referred to the city's civil rights tradition. This might be seen as little more than a token appropriation of history. Certainly business promotional publicity shows some black faces, but only in small numbers, usually as workers. Yet the imagery is amplified in the city's other promotional efforts. A case in point is the 1990 Olympic bid (AOC, 1990). Like Manchester's (later) bid (Manchester 2000, 1993), it reflects reality by showing black athletic prowess. Unlike Manchester, however, Atlanta's bid also portrays representatives of a powerful black professional middle class, such as Andrew Young (a former US ambassador to the United Nations), providing leadership alongside white business leaders. This portrays real differences between Atlanta and many other US cities (and all British cities).

Imagery deriving directly from African-American culture has also found an important, if still rather cautiously expressed, place in Atlanta's tourism promotion. In 1995 the ACVB launched a new theme slogan, 'Atlanta: Come Celebrate Our Dream', intended to span the Olympic period. It was designed specifically to encapsulate five major themes distilled from 5000 suggestions received from the public – hospitality, future, international, pride and dreams (*Guardian*, 7.10.93; *Financial Times*, 1.11.94, Survey, p. 1). As the ACVB explained in a press release (which incidentally casts some light on how place marketing slogans were formulated):

The breakdown is **Come** (representing an invitation – *hospitality*); **Celebrate** (focusing on up and coming events in Atlanta – *future/international*); **Our** (shared amongst the citizens of Atlanta – *pride*); **Dream** (highlighting the dreams of many Atlantans – *dreams*). (ACVB, 1995*a*)

Yet this somewhat mechanistic explanation was true only as far as it went. It omits a key part of the deeper meaning of the slogan, one readily acknowledged by ACVB marketing staff (*ex info* ACVB, 1995). The key notion of an inclusive dream directly and consciously echoes the famous visionary civil rights speech 'I have a dream' by the Reverend Martin Luther King, Atlanta's most famous son. It was a vision of all races standing together that, as world attention focused on the city in the run up to the 1996 Olympic Games, gave the slogan much deeper and more emotive resonances.

Within these overarching concerns, the ACVB has also promoted African-American tourism in the city, with specific publications targeted at black tourists. Again the Martin Luther King legacy has been central, with sites such as his birthplace, the church where he preached and the Martin Luther King Center heavily marketed. The same theme pervades many special events, such as the Black History Month featuring gospel singing, the African-American Philharmonic Orchestra and black history trivia contests – 'The more erudite may opt for the lectures, book-signings and exhibits' (ACVB, 1995*c*, p. 9). The Martin Luther King Week is another example:

. . . if you're not a youth who would benefit from attending a symposium aimed at curbing violence; chances are, you're a music lover for whom the prospect of the Atlanta Symphony's two-evening tribute to Dr King appeals. (*ibid*, p. 10)

The culmination is Coretta Scott King's 'State of the Dream' address, offering '. . . many opportunities for throat-catching emotion'.

The development of this imagery goes further than anything we have yet seen in Britain and much in other US cities. Holcomb (1993, p. 142), for example, notes the coyness of the publicity produced by Pittsburgh and Cleveland on race and ethnicity. Some cities target black tourists (for example Boston's Black Heritage Trail). Detroit, which has a bigger black population, absolutely and proportionately, than Atlanta, has also tried very hard to develop the promotional image of a 'black city' (Neill, Fitzsimmons and Murtagh, 1995, pp. 113–161). But it has proved a rather troubled vision, unable to transcend the negative image of Detroit as the United States' 'crime capital'. Neither white investors nor the black and white middle classes have been at ease with the marketing image. By contrast Atlanta has been able to sustain wider support for its black-inspired but more racially-inclusive image.

At one level this wider cultural reference in promotional imagery is entirely admirable. We should beware of confusing it with reality, however. The real Atlanta remains a city of immense inequalities (Duffy, 1995, pp. 45–59; Rutheiser, 1996). It regularly comes near the top of US murder and crime rate tables, often having a worse record than Detroit (e.g. Schaffer, 1991, p. 248). Desegregation and civil rights have produced some important changes. Yet a cynical view would say that they have simply allowed an already well established, rather conservative, black middle class to enjoy a position in society increasingly similar to their white equivalents. By contrast the position of the majority black working class population has changed much less. In some ways it is actually worse. Black neighbourhoods have decayed as the black middle classes have moved out to the suburbs. Moreover, the patronage of many traditional black neighbourhood small businesses has declined as black customers have no longer been confined by segregation to using them.

It is possible therefore to argue that Atlanta's use of a promotional imagery that draws on traditional African-American culture is just as false as any other, more mainstream marketing images. It appeals, in part, to a black ethnic and

This impressionistic collage of images promoting Atlanta to convention planners, key intermediaries in tourism marketing, says much about the city's current approach. Sports are naturally given priority in Atlanta's year as Olympic city, but culture, environment, nightlife and shopping also receive attention. Especially important is the emphasis on Atlanta's most famous citizen, Martin Luther King, whose words and sentiments are echoed in the promotional slogan. To reinforce the point a black couple are shown being served by a white waiter, reversing traditional stereotypes.

racial unity that is diminishing. It appropriates the emotive power of the King legacy to legitimate an alliance of black political and white business leaderships that has left many inequalities unaddressed. On balance, such a judgement is probably a little too harsh. As we have seen, social indicators have shown sufficient improvements to warrant limited claims of relative 'success'. The combination of promoted image and perceived reality are sufficient to draw many thousands of black migrants each year from both the rural south and northern cities such as Chicago or Detroit. One third of the city's black population has lived there less than five years (Duffy, 1995, p. 53). Less tangibly, there is a pervasive sense of optimism about the city, much more than in most other large older American cities.

SEALING LOCAL PRIDE

An example of Atlanta tourism publicity targeted on African-Americans. Heritage here has a specific meaning, beyond the very generalized notion that is familiar in Britain. Although Atlanta is something of a leader in this direction, more American cities are beginning to address the specific interests of black tourists.

These last points touch an extremely important aspect of city marketing, namely the securing of local approval or enthusiasm for a reinvented city. In marketing speak this concern is hidden within bland euphemisms such as 'sealing local pride' (e.g. CMDC, 1993, p. 18). It is, however, an issue which is taken very seriously by city marketing agencies. As we saw in the last chapter, there are inherent dangers that the re-invention of cities will generate local resentments.

It was not necessarily organized opposition that was feared. A more individualistic lack of positive local commitment to the re-invented city could seriously dent the overall image that was being promoted. New leisure spaces might be used inappropriately. Litter, graffiti and vandalism involving only a tiny minority of disenchanted local residents could tarnish the promoted image, especially if they were symptoms of more general indifference. Tourists might not be welcomed. Even with high unemployment, there might still be reluctance to fill the lower paid jobs. All other things being equal, places which displayed a positive spirit would be more attractive for investment or tourism or residence.

In other words, city marketing agencies have many reasons to sell the idea of the reinvented city to existing residents. To some extent, we have already seen some of the ways this was done. The jaunty optimism was usually intended as much to boost internal morale as to change external perception. Sports, whether in relation to the prowess of local teams or in bidding for major sporting events, were often of critical importance in sustaining or engendering local commitment. Manchester's bids for the Olympic and Commonwealth Games provided the pretext for locally targeted events, with much use made of themed balloons, teeshirts and other sports merchandizing. The sporting metaphor was doubly useful because it also embodied the notion of competition, underlining the importance of the need for the city itself to be competitive. It was rare, in

Marketing associated with bidding for sporting events is often deemed particularly effective. There has been huge popular support for Manchester's Olympics and Commonwealth Games bids, serving also to spread the idea that the city itself must be competitive

fact, to find a piece of sports related promotion that did not, more or less explicitly, make this point.

Yet there was also a distinctive branch of marketing efforts that sought to generate local complicity in post-industrial re-invention. Behind the scenes, tourist promotion bodies have fostered the ideal of the 'welcome host' in the hospitality industries (e.g. NWTB *et al.*, 1994). There have also been attempts to encourage this self-image amongst the wider population. This was particularly important where the common patterns of social interaction still tended to reflect a manufacturing rather than a service-oriented city. It was partly such reasoning which led Chicago to promote itself (largely to itself) as 'the friendliest city in the world' (Lawson, 1989, p. 73).

Many marketing agencies, particularly the British UDCs, also had a community liaison dimension to their operations that played an important role in engendering an imagery of local consent. This imagery is usually portrayed on the relevant pages of annual reports or in the more community-oriented publications. What is particularly striking is that the *boulevardier* or the yuppie who permeate the other dimensions of their advertising are here largely absent. Instead there is a different set of social types. Superficially, at least, there is a much closer correspondence with real life. There are many more people from ethnic minorities shown. There are children playing happily and young adults engaged in worthy acts. There are old people. There are people in wheelchairs or with other evident disabilities.

Yet the ways in which this more varied social cross section are portrayed indicate their essential purpose. Young people, for example, 'spruce up the city during a citizenship building training course' (CMDC, 1993, p. 16). Elderly people 'rediscover Manchester's rejuvenated waterways' (*Ibid*, p. 17). The disabled, and indeed all local people, are shown benefiting from enlightened policies. In fact, the essential role of these 'community' stereotypes is to bear witness to the intrinsic goodness of the re-invented city. Yet the benevolence of urban re-invention would be much more convincing if these figures, rather than the *boulevardier*, the yuppie or variants thereof, were accorded a more active role in post-industrial promotional imagery. In the usual state of things, these 'community' stereotypes are more marginalized. Their role is merely to be submissive and grateful.

The appropriation of genuine community imagery is sometimes done in a crude manner. The merest hint of local celebratory events in parts of cities that are being re-invented has been enough to set marketing antennae twitching. As we have seen, 'vibrancy' is a highly prized attribute in post-industrial city marketing. But marketing money and advice has meant that scenes from an essentially local cultural life have been re-imaged as spectacles to draw in visitors, as Thomas *et al.* (1996) have recently documented in Cardiff. We should not exaggerate this, however. There have, of course, been many other cases where local communities have themselves sought external interest and financial support. Yet it is inevitable that such commercialization, even where it has been welcomed and successful

in place marketing terms, has removed some of the original local meanings.

Sometimes the marketeers simply went too far in their attempts to appropriate local symbols. One of the most notable examples was J. Walter Thompson's original proposal for the Newcastle image campaign in 1990 (Wilkinson, 1992). The idea had been to base the campaign on the nationally famous and much-loved local cartoon character, Andy Capp. Never without his flat cap and cigarette, Andy's life revolved around the pub and betting shop. Work played no part in his scheme of things. At home he was often asleep in bed or on the sofa, waited on hand and foot by his long suffering wife, Flo. J. Walter Thompson had wanted to alter Andy's image to show how Newcastle, the main city of the north east, had itself changed. The new Andy would throw away his cap and smarten himself up with suit and tie.

It was actually a very clever idea, a Glasgow-type message of change smoothed by humour. Not unreasonably, the London-based advertising agency believed the area would be glad to shed this anachronistic stereotype. Yet, unlike Mr Happy, Andy Capp was, literally, rooted in his region. Even as they embraced change, north easterners did not entirely reject the working class culture of their industrial past. The incorrigible Andy Capp character, though never intended as typical, came directly out of this culture and can be readily identified in regional novels (especially Jack Common's *Kiddar's Luck*) and, more recently, television series (*The Likely Lads*). North easterners, and others, admired his roguish (and selfish) ability to live within but still break the conventions of working class society, living his own life in his own way.

When news leaked out, in May 1990, that Andy Capp was to become a yuppie there was an outcry. The notion that he was now going to be made to conform to a new set of post-industrial social disciplines was simply too much. The campaign was quickly dropped. It served as a graphic reminder of just how uneasily city re-invention and marketing sit with the complex local meanings and associations of place.

CONCLUSIONS AND PROSPECTS

As these last examples amply show, there is still much scope for refining the images post-industrial cities try to project. A 'golden age', comparable to that which resort and suburban promotion enjoyed in the early decades of the twentieth century, has not yet appeared. It may never come, of course. Already though, we would have to admit that 'I ❤ New York' and 'Glasgow's Miles Better' deserve a place alongside 'Skegness is So Bracing', 'Metro-Land', the many efforts of Samuel Eberly Gross and the first Forward Atlanta campaign as classic pieces of place selling. Yet, alongside these two outstanding campaigns are examples that deserve to live on only for their absurdity. (Not that the post-industrial city is alone in this respect, of course.)

What we do not know is whether the best is yet to be. Unlike the other major place selling episodes we have examined in this book, we have no clear sense of longer term development. Yet there is no reason to expect major changes in the broader frameworks for city marketing. In both North America and Britain, place competition seems to be becoming more, not less, intensive. In neither setting do political or other changes seem likely that will be sufficient to alter in any fundamental way the dominant notion of urban entrepreurialism.

In Britain, we may surmise that, with so much borrowing of promotional imagery, there is also likely to be a shift more in the direction of continental European approaches to place marketing. Here local promotional strategies are more likely to be negotiated and in large measure agreed between local, regional and national agencies. The promotion of the French post-industrial city of Lille for example, takes place within a far more co-ordinated framework than has been found anywhere in Britain in recent years. We could find essentially similar approaches in cities like Rotterdam or Liege. More obviously, too, the details of place marketing are likely also to follow more along European lines, as we have seen clearly over the last few years. The more

seriously British cities wish to position themselves as major players within Europe, the more they will need to borrow at least some ideas from that source.

Yet the US model of the post-industrial city as an independent self promoter, unaided and un-impeded by higher governments, remains very beguiling to the British. As we have seen, post-industrial city marketing has been essentially an American invention. The American pattern shows very little sign of changing in the future to become more 'European'. The American political agenda continues to eschew big government, so cities will be likely to remain on their own. No overall federal programmes seem likely to appear within which the promotional aspirations of individual cities will be able to nestle. There are also many signs of Britain continuing to go down this same road. Local government changes in 1996 and 1997 have created in more cities the sense of being 'on their own', as many remaining two-tier local government arrangements have been scrapped.

At the same time, the growing interest in the 'tiger' economies of Asia has begun to introduce other arguments for more city-based approaches to economic development than have been usual in the west. The spectacular recent growth of Hong Kong and Singapore has fuelled ideas of city states perhaps being the most efficient way of achieving economic growth. Shanghai, Kuala Lumpur and some other rapidly growing Asian cities show some signs of trying to reproduce such conditions. The idea is essentially that an individual big city, unencumbered by wider territorial concerns, is able more single-mindedly to pursue strategies that reflect its own growth imperatives. Quite how relevant such notions really are to post-industrial cities with very different problems is questionable. But the experiences of the Asian 'tiger' cities, the new 'world cities' of the twenty-first century, will certainly command a place in future British and American debates about city promotion.

Yet if the general economic and institutional frameworks encouraging urban entrepreneurialism seem unlikely to change dramatically, the more detailed substance of city marketing is very much more difficult to predict. Over the last few years there have, as we have seen, been many approaches used by cities, with a particular emphasis on culture, sports and special events. Each city has, in effect, tried to find unoccupied promotional niches within these general areas. Yet, even though the overall market for sports and culture is clearly growing, the field is becoming very crowded. All the presently recognized marketing niches within high and popular culture, sports and conventions and other events are now well colonized. The likelihood is that new ones will appear, or there will be greater differentiation of existing niches.

In the future we may expect to see more city marketing to specific social groups, along the lines of the promotion of Manchester's gay scene. Marketing to ethnic groups is also likely to increase. One area not yet strongly developed but seemingly with possibilities is the promotion of cities to retired people. It is not difficult to think of others. One beneficial consequence of such targeting will, of course, be that the social bases of promotional imagery will also have to broaden, embracing a wider population as active agents in city life. (In truth, post-industrial city marketing has already gone much further in this regard than any other episode of place selling we have examined. But, as we have noted, it still has far to go.)

The other possibility is that substantially new themes will be deployed to sell cities. Although much hyperbole remains, cities are now far more cautious than in the past about marketing pitches that lack at least some real substance. New marketing themes have, then, to be more than mere rhetorical fancy. Several possibilities immediately present themselves, however, particularly where cities gain a really distinctive edge over their rivals. The environment is one very obvious unclaimed niche. A city which is able to achieve a wide range of very visible and substantial changes in its approach to the environment will certainly be able to claim marketing and economic benefits. (How it will then manage them is another matter, of course.) New developments in electronic communications also suggest scope for a 'virtual' or 'net city'. Religion may also have some promotional possibilities, especially amongst minority populations. The reader can doubtless contribute other speculations, both of the 'wish' and 'fear' variety. Whatever the outcomes there will doubtless be much scope for further refinement of the observations and arguments in this book. We must now draw these together.

11

CONCLUSIONS

This book has focused on five main episodes of place selling activity. All have involved North America, particularly the United States, which may be considered the spiritual home of place marketing. All, except the first, have also involved Britain, though place selling activity here has usually occurred later and been less full blooded than across the Atlantic. Beneath this, we have also identified other important differences in place selling traditions, between continents and nations and between individual towns and cities. Yet, for all the differences, there are also some important similarities and convergences in particular aspects of place selling. This impression is not contradicted by our rather briefer glimpses at certain other European countries. In this concluding chapter we summarize the main features of the process of place marketing and promotion and make some generalizations about the nature of promotional language and imagery.

THE PROCESS

We begin by stating the obvious: place selling thrives in situations of economic change and instability. Episodes of place selling activity are mainly associated with periods of economic change and with urban systems or parts of urban systems which are experiencing that change. Not all place selling is the same, however. While the above few sentences may serve as a very broad brush summary, they do little to explain the actual forces which unlock and determine the propensity of places to sell themselves.

One crucial consideration involves the degree to which the place itself is synonymous with a recognized marketable commodity. The very act of place marketing is itself, of course, a commodification of place. But in many cases this commodification is more metaphorical than actual, since it may well be unclear exactly what the 'purchase' of the place involves. By contrast, landed property or real estate is a very tangible commodity that is integral to the concept of place in capitalist societies. In many aspects of place selling there has been a clear real estate sales imperative. On the frontier and in the suburbs, land and houses were literally being sold as an end result of the place marketing process. Similarly the rise of property-led urban regeneration in recent years has brought with it a commensurate rise in place marketing effort.

Yet, although it may be the most tangible aspect of place as commodity, landed property is certainly not the only such instance. Tourism, for example, involves the purchase of holiday services such as travel, accommodation and entertainment. Buying the suburb and the frontier also involves other purchases, for example of travel and other services. Accordingly, therefore, it becomes easy to see why so much effort has been (and still is) expended in tourism promotion by interests which benefit from purchases of travel, accommodation and entertainment. The active role of transport undertakings in the selling of the suburbs also makes more sense when it is equated with traffic receipts.

The different histories of settlement in the two continents were also important. Britain, and much of Europe, were long settled lands. Their settlement patterns had been substantially formed well before capitalism and a market system appeared. England's villages essentially owed their origins to bonds of tribe, kin and feudal obligation. While 'travellers' tales' no doubt played some part in the settlement process, there was certainly no market-based competition between different places, no 'bidding' for settlers.

In complete contrast, most of the habitable terrain of North America was colonized and its urban system laid down when capitalism was ascendant. As an integral part of the settlement process, the land itself became a marketable commodity. Formerly enjoyed collectively by indigenous American peoples, land could henceforth be bought and sold by individuals. The tracts of land opened up by different railroads, the public lands offered directly for settlement, those already appropriated by speculators and other intermediaries were competitively offered. Nowhere, before or since, did so much land become available for settlement in such a short time. A vast flow of colonists was necessary to fulfil this settlement imperative. Moreover, the most intense phases of agricultural colonization and urban growth coincided, fuelling further the phenomenon of place competition for settlers and investors. By contrast, the British, and in large measure the European, pattern, had been of towns and cities growing more organically out of their rural hinterlands.

These contrasting experiences were a fundamental underpinning for all that has followed. From the very beginning, the leaders of 'upstart' places in the United States realized that there was no pre-ordained, time-honoured pattern of change, such as there seemed to be in Europe. To survive and prosper, places had to assert them-

selves. Done with enough power and conviction, such promotional action could overturn the existing advantages or disadvantages of places. It could, literally, become a powerful force in the making of great cities.

Even the growth of industry in Britain brought surprisingly few changes. There were few entirely new towns and certainly none which became major cities. The regional industrial cities grew from what were already the main provincial urban centres before industrialization. And London's dominant position was never threatened. Overall, the essential features of the British urban hierarchy and the nature of functional interrelationships between places remained very stable for an extremely long period. Place competition, so far as most towns and cities were concerned, was rather muted.

The exceptions were, however, very important. Britain's true 'upstart' cities were its resorts and its residential suburbs. These were the only significant groups of new settlements to grow from almost literally nothing in the early-mid nineteenth century into important places a century later. Only within these groups of specialist urban places was there anything approaching the competitive instability and continual jockeying for position that pervaded most of North America's emergent urban system.

The general attitude to place marketing and promotion in Britain changed only as its industrial centres began to experience disinvestment. As traditional industries declined, it became increasingly clear that there were no longer enough local or regional capitalists willing or able to build new businesses. Progressively, British cities have become ever more dependent on external and highly mobile capital. To attract such investment, they have been obliged to adopt exactly the same tactics as those traditionally employed by North American cities.

Yet economics provides only the broader context. More specific to the local response were the institutional frameworks within which place selling occurred. That local marketing exists at all is in many ways a comment on the policies of higher governments. With a few exceptions, it has normally blossomed in settings where a higher government has tolerated local autonomy and encouraged fiscal self-reliance. By contrast, it has usually been both less common and more restricted under centralized government systems. Centrally-created development agencies such as Britain's Urban Development Corporations have been the only real exception to this generalization.

As we have seen, however, place selling has not been solely or even mainly the prerogative of government. A variety of other agencies, including privately-led business organizations, real estate developers and railway companies, have also played important roles. The varying nature of such agencies within different countries is another factor which has determined the character of place selling. In Britain, for example, we can note the generally weaker nature of business-led organizations compared to North America (and, indeed, other European countries,

such as France). The dual role of North American railroads, functioning also as major land and development agencies, automatically gave them greater importance as place sellers than their European equivalents.

Finally, specifically local factors have always been hugely important in shaping the character of place selling in particular places. This is especially so in those campaigns which have been particularly memorable or successful. Key local individuals have usually been very important. More important still has been the particular local relationship of business and political leaders. This is, unfortunately, something which has been more concealed than revealed by the use of the now universal label of 'partnership'. Crucial, too, has been the extent to which the promotional visions of the place sellers could be embraced, or at least tolerated, by the wider population. Usually this consent was won by promises of the benefits of growth and fears of stagnation or decline.

LANGUAGE AND IMAGERY

Equally important in all this was the nature of the promotional vision itself. In an almost timeless and placeless fashion certain messages and images have recurred in the selling of different kinds of places. Ever since place marketing began, frontier towns, resorts, industrial towns and post-industrial cities, have been heralded as 'gateways' and 'hearts', 'capitals' and 'centres'.

Without giving chapter and verse, we could go on to cite many other devices. These include positioning maps, perspective views, predictable assertions about accessibility and other place qualities, alliteration and assonance of place slogans and a litany of puns. Each type of place selling has its own particular repertoire of the mundane.

However we have also uncovered a less superficial stock of promotional images that are more expressions of time, place, society and culture. One example of wide importance is the recurrent

use of female figures to represent place. Although this traditional imagery is less apparent in post-industrial city marketing, we have noted its presence in all other areas of place selling. Thus the virgin, untouched and pure but promising abundant fertility, was used to sell the frontier. The sexual allure of the bathing belle, albeit often in the guise of the sporting woman, was used to sell the seaside. The domestic woman, tending home in the sylvan suburb while the man performed his masculine labours in the city, was another promotional staple. The promoters of the industrial town also used female imagery, though in a less consistent way, as if uncertain about the relationship with 'virile' industry.

In all these aspects, we can often find differences over time and between the patterns favoured in different countries. The sexual coyness of early British resort publicity compared to French is one important contrast. The more puritan British preferred to stress innocent fun, expressed through playing children or, most famously, the Skegness jolly fisherman. Another window on national character comes through the particular British preference for the promotional concept 'bracing'. The contrasts in suburban imagery between the rural ideal in Britain and North America provides a further example. And we could easily extend this list to cover matters of social class, race and, as we have noted in post industrial promotion, sexual orientation. In other words we can read the imagery and texts of place marketing as a mirror, albeit perhaps a distorting mirror, of a varied and changing wider world.

By virtue of visual or literary qualities, there has been a great deal of place marketing material that both provides innocent enjoyment and warrants serious artistic appreciation. Amongst commonplace efforts there is also much, more than we might expect, that is of real quality. The aesthetic qualities of poster art, much of it concerned with place promotion, are now widely recognized. The artists of the many resort and suburban posters produced by railway companies – Hassall, Cassandre, Purvis, Newbould and many others – are beginning to receive well deserved appreciation. (We can note in passing, though, that this brings with it another layer of commodification, this time of the posters themselves.) There is, however, much other material, usually produced by unnamed or unknown artists or agencies, that warrants similar attention.

Yet some promotional images and texts also deserve to be appreciated as more than art in the narrow sense. Campaigns such as 'Skegness is So Bracing', or 'Metro-land' or 'Glasgow's Miles Better' are, in their own ways, shining examples of this. We could add others, including several US campaigns, though these will serve to represent what is worthwhile in promotional image-making. Although they do all the 'wrong' things, they still have an emotional power to move all but the sternest cultural critic. To be sure, these campaigns have commodified places and denied or trivialized their subtle meanings.

But they do this with such skill, originality and integrity, that they actually add a layer of particularly vivid meaning to place.

There is a danger to all this, of course. Advertising has been criticized because it fosters a notion of unachievable perfection, far removed from real life. The images of place marketing can also do this. The idea is very well expressed in Philip Larkin's typically laconic poem 'Sunny Prestatyn' (1962), telling the bleak story of a promotional poster featuring a glamorous bathing belle. Within a couple of weeks of posting, the image was obscenely defaced. As Larkin says regretfully, '[s]he was too good for this life'.

At their best, other types of place marketing may also create images that are too good for this life. The better the quality of the campaign, the more beguiling its imagery, the greater the danger. The best place marketing campaigns articulate an ideal, an aspiration, which, rather like other forms of mass culture, can engage and involve the disinterested observer, sometimes with a surprising and insidious emotional power. Ultimately such ideals represent no more than a very fragmentary optimism about place. They sum up, let us never forget, what the originators wanted to say to encourage some target group to part with money.

Once created, however, promotional messages are partly liberated from their primary discourse of selling. To the extent that they strike a sympathetic chord within society, they become also part of more widely accepted ideals about places. In this sense Hassall's Skegness poster signifies what we would like the British seaside holiday to be. It has come to define our idea of a particular type of experience. Metro-land similarly epitomizes the suburban ideal as a bucolic fairy-tale. And we warm to Mr Happy because we want to think that former industrial cities really can be 'miles better'.

Moreover, place selling, though it may shift direction a little, is certainly not going to go away in the future. It is now much too deeply entrenched for that. And, if it is going to exist, we ought to do as much as possible to make sure it is done well. In superficial matters, this is already being done. But too often the more important themes are still being badly handled. Thus the linking of the deeper meanings of place with promotional imperatives is rarely done in a convincing way. Typical images still exclude much that makes up the reality of place. Or they appropriate aspects of place in ways that narrow meaning.

This, surely, can be improved. It must be worth trying to make more use of artists, particularly those with a genuine connection to the place they are helping publicize. The growing penchant for public art shows some willingness in this direction, exploring place representation and meaning. But other changes have also to precede or be part of such moves. Most fundamental is the political need to harness promotional imagery to the building of a genuinely inclusive vision of place. If it can do this, place selling will then truly deserve the central position it already enjoys in today's entrepreneurial cities.

BIBLIOGRAPHY

This bibliography consists only of the works actually cited in the text. The location of rarer materials, typically promotional brochures and pamphlets, is normally given in brackets.

ACC (Atlanta Chamber of Commerce) (1903) *Atlanta: A Twentieth Century City*. Atlanta: ACC (Library of Congress Local Collection).

ACC (1909) *Souvenir Album, Atlanta, Georgia*. Atlanta: ACC (Atlanta Historical Society).

Acme (Engraving) (1910) *London's Latest Suburbs: An Illustrated Guide to the Residential Districts Reached by the Hampstead Tube*. London: Acme (Bodleian Library).

ACOG (Atlanta Committee for the Olympic Games) (1990) *Chronology of Atlanta's Bid for the 1996 Olympic Games*. Atlanta: ACOG.

ACOG (Atlanta Committee for the Olympic Games) (1992) *The Economic Impact on the State of Georgia of Hosting the 1996 Olympic Games*. Atlanta: ACOG.

ACPB (Atlantic City Publicity Bureau) (1909) *Atlantic City New Jersey: America's Greatest Resort*. Atlantic City: ACPB (Library of Congress Local Collection).

ACVB (1994) *Atlanta: Look At Us Now*. Atlanta: ACVB.

ACVB (Atlanta Convention and Visitors Bureau) (1995*a*) *ACVB Announces New Theme Line for Atlanta*. Atlanta: ACVB Press Release.

ACVB (1995*b*) 1995 *Business Plan Summary*. Atlanta: ACVB.

ACVB (1995*c*) *Atlanta Heritage*. Atlanta: ACVB.

ACVB (1995*d*) *Atlanta Now: The Official Visitors Guide of the Atlanta Convention and Visitors Bureau*. September–October. Atlanta: ACVB/Attcomm.

Adams, G. L. and Pollard, C. A. (1936–37) The constitutionality of Mississippi's industrial program. *Mississippi Law Journal*, **9**, pp. 356–365.

Aitken, H. G. J. (1967) Defensive expansion: The state and economic growth in Canada in Easterbrook, W. T. and Watkins, M. H. (eds.) *Approaches to Canadian Economic History*. Toronto: McLelland and Stewart.

Aldersley-Williams, H. (1994) Cities bid to make their marque. *Management Today*, August, pp. 30–33.

Alderson, F. (1973) *The Inland Resorts and Spas of Britain*. Newton Abbot: David and Charles.

Aldridge, M. (1996) Only demi-paradise? Women in garden cities and new towns. *Planning Perspectives*, **11**(1), pp. 23–39.

Amulree Committee (1938) *Report of the Departmental Committee on Holidays with Pay* (Cmd 5724). London: HMSO.

AOC (Atlanta Organizing Committee) (1990) *Welcome to a Brave and Beautiful City*. Atlanta: AOC.

Artibise, A. F. J. (1970) Advertising Winnipeg: The campaign for immigrants and industry. *Historical and Scientific Society of Manitoba Transactions*, 3rd Series. **27**, pp. 75–106.

Ashworth, G. J. and Voogd, H. (1994) Marketing and place promotion, in Gold and Ward (eds.) *op. cit.*, pp. 39–52.

Ashworth, G. J. and Voogd, H. (1990) *Selling the City: Marketing Approaches in Public Sector Urban Planning*. London: Belhaven.

ASLR (Atlantic Shore Line Railway) (1909) *The Coast of Maine as Seen From the Atlantic Shore Line Railway*. Portland ME: Spear (Society for the Preservation of the New England Antiquities).

Atlanta (City Council and Chamber of Commerce) (1898) *Hand Book of the City of Atlanta: A*

Comprehensive Review of the City's Commercial, Industrial and Residential Conditions. Atlanta: ACC/ACCom (Library of Congress Local Collection).

ATSFRR (Atchison, Topeka and Sante Fe Railroad) (1876) *Ho! For the New Kansas! The Upper Arkansas Valley, 'The Best Thing in the West'.* Topeka: ATSFRR. (Library of Congress Broadside Collection).

Baade, R. A. and Dye, R. E. (1988) An analysis of the economic rationale for the public subsidization of sports stadiums. *Annals of Regional Science*, **23**, pp. 37–42.

Baglee, C. (ed Linsley, S.) (1979) *The North East Coast Exhibition of Industry, Science and Art.* Newcastle: Frank Graham.

Bailey, J. T. (1989) *Marketing Cities in the 1980s and Beyond.* Chicago: American Economic Development Council.

Baldwin, W. W. (1920) *Railroad Land Grants: A Statement of Their History, Their Value and Their Cost by W. W. Baldwin.* Chicago: CBQRR (Newberry Library).

Bamford, P (ed.) (1995) *Manchester: 50 Years of Change.* London: HMSO.

Barke, M and Harrop, K. (1994) Selling the industrial town: Identity, image and illusion, in Gold and Ward (eds.) *op. cit.*, pp. 93–114.

Barker, T. C. and Robbins, M. (1963) *A History of London Transport: Passenger Travel and the Development of the Metropolis: Vol I: The Nineteenth Century.* London: Allen and Unwin.

Barker, T. C. and Robbins, M. (1974) *A History of London Transport: Passenger Travel and the Development of the Metropolis, Vol II: The Twentieth Century to 1970.* London: Allen and Unwin.

Barlow Commission (Royal Commission on the Distribution of the Industrial Population) 1940: *Report.* Cmd 6153. London: HMSO.

Barman, C. (1979) *The Man Who Built London Transport: A biography of Frank Pick.* Newton Abbot: David and Charles.

Barnett, S. (1991) Selling us short? Cities culture and economic development, in Fisher, M. and Owen, U. (eds.) *Whose Cities?*, Harmondsworth: Penguin, pp. 161–171.

Barrett, H. and Phillips, J. (1988) *Suburban Style: The British Home, 1840–1960.* London: Macdonald Orbis.

Barrow (-in-Furness Corporation) (1931) *Barrow-in-Furness Commercially Considered.* Barrow: Corporation.

Bartels, C. P. A. and Timmer, M. (1987) City marketing: instruments and effects. Paper presented at the European Regional Planning Association Conference, Athens.

BCDC (Burnley Corporation Development Committee) (1935) *Burnley Means Business: Burnley and Its Industrial Facilities.* Burnley: Development Committee (Burnley Central Library, Local Collection).

BCDP (Benwell Community Development Project) (1978) *Private Housing and the Working Class.* Final Report Series no. 3. Newcastle: BCDP.

BCPC (Blackpool Corporation Publicity Committee) (1938) *Open the Door to Holiday Happiness.* Blackpool: Blackpool Corporation.

BCPC (1939) *Blackpool Official Guide.* Blackpool: Publicity Committee (Bodleian Library).

Beach, J and Noszlopy, G. T. (1996) Public art and planning in Birmingham. *Planning History*, **18**(1), pp. 22–28.

Bedfordshire Advertiser, as cited in text (Luton Museum, Chamber of Commerce Press Cuttings).

BEDU (Bradford Economic Development Unit) (nd c1985) *Living in Bradford.* Bradford: BEDU.

Beeby, D. (1984) Industrial strategy and manufacturing growth in Toronto, 1880–1910. *Ontario History*, **LXXVI**(3), pp. 199–232.

Begg, I. Moore, B. and Rhodes, J. (1986) Economic and social change in urban Britain and the inner cities, in Hausner, V. (ed.) *op. cit.*

Begg, I. and Eversley, D. (1986) Deprivation in the inner city: Social indicators from the 1981 census, in Hausner, V. (ed.), *op. cit.*

Berg, E. and L. (nd c1935a) *The Homes of Tomorrow with Sunshine Laid On.* New Malden: Berg (John Johnson Collection, Bodleian Library).

Berg, E and L. (nd c1935b) *The Tudor House*, London?: Berg (John Johnson Collection, Bodleian Library).

Berger, M. L. (1992) *They Built Chicago: Entrepreneurs Who Shaped A Great City's Architecture.* Chicago: Bonus.

Berwick [-upon-Tweed Corporation] (1940) *Berwick-upon-Tweed: 'A Jewel in the Bosom of the Border-land'.* London: G. W. May for the Corporation.

BHBC (Brookfield History Book Committee) (1994) *Brookfield Illinois: A History.* Brookfield: BHBC.

Bianchini F. and Parkinson, M. (eds.) (1993) *Cultural Policy and Urban Regeneration: The West European Experience*. Manchester: Manchester University Press.

BIB (Birmingham Information Bureau) (nd *c*1932) *Birmingham: The Hub of Industrial England* (German version). Birmingham: BIB (Birmingham Reference Library).

BIB (Birmingham Information Bureau) (nd *c*1939) *Birmingham: The City of a Thousand Trades*. Birmingham: BIB.

Biddle, G. (1990) *The Railway Surveyors: The Story of Railway Property Management 1800–1990*. London: Ian Allan; British Railways Property Board.

Binford, H. C. (1985) *The First Suburbs: Residential Communities on the Boston Periphery, 1815–1860*. Chicago: University of Chicago Press.

Bishir, C. W. and Earley, L. S. (eds.) (1985) *Early Twentieth-Century Suburbs in North Carolina: Essays on History, Architecture and Planning*. Raleigh: North Carolina State Museum.

BIP (Bureau of Information and Publicity) (1906) *Atlantic City New Jersey: America's Greatest Resort*. Atlantic City: Bureau of Information and Publicity (Library of Congress Local Collection).

Blackpool Corporation (nd 1896) *Premier Sea-side Resort for Health and Pleasure – Blackpool Lancashire Its Advantages and Attractions*. Blackpool: Blackpool Corporation (John Johnson Collection, Bodleian Library).

Bliss, M. (1982) *The Evolution of Industrial Policies in Canada: An Historical Survey*. Discussion Paper no 218, Ottawa: Economic Council of Canada.

Bloomfield, E. (1981) Municipal bonusing of industry: The legislative framework in Ontario to 1930. *Urban History Review*, **9**(3), pp. 59–76.

Bloomfield E. (1983*a*) Building the city on a foundation of industry: The industrial policy in Berlin, Ontario, 1870–1914. *Ontario History*, **75**(3), pp. 207–243.

Bloomfield, E. (1983*b*) Community, ethos and local initiative in urban economic growth: Review of a theme in Canadian economic history, *Urban History Yearbook 1983*. Leicester: Leicester University Press.

Bloomfield, E. (1983*c*) Boards of Trade and Canadian urban development. *Urban History Review*, **12**, pp. 77–99.

Bloomfield, E. (1985) Bonusing and Boosterism, *Planning History Bulletin*, **7**(2), pp. 23–29.

Bloomfield, G. (1978) *The World Automotive Industry*. Newton Abbot: David and Charles.

Board of Trade (1911) *Report of an Inquiry by the Board of Trade into Working Class Rents, Housing and Retail Prices together with the Rates of Wages in Certain Occupations in the Principal Industrial Towns of the United States of America* (Cd. 5609) (Parliamentary Papers, Accounts and Papers LXXXVIII). London: HMSO.

Bogue, A. (1994) An agricultural empire, in Milner, C. A., O'Connor, C. A. and Sandweiss, M. A. (eds,), *op. cit.*, pp. 275–313.

Bonsall, M. (1988) Local government initiatives in urban regeneration 1906–1932: The story of Derby's Borough Development Committee. *Planning History*, **10**(3), pp. 7–11.

Boorstin, D. J. (1965) *The Americans: The National Experience*. New York: Vintage.

Booth, P. and Boyle, R. (1993) See Glasgow, See culture, in Bianchini and Parkinson, (eds.) *op. cit.*, pp. 21–47.

Boston MOED (Mayor's Office of Economic Development) (1977) *Annual Report 1975/1976*. Boston: MOED (Boston Public Library).

Bourke, J. (1996) The great male denunciation: Men's dress reform in interwar Britain. *Journal of Design History*, **9**(1), pp. 23–33.

Boyle, R. (1990) Regeneration in Glasgow: Stability, collaboration and inequity, in, Judd, D. and Parkinson, M. (eds.) *op. cit.*, pp. 109–132.

Boyle, R. (1988) Private sector regeneration: The Scottish experience, in Parkinson, M., Foley, B. and Judd, D. (eds.), *op. cit.*, pp. 74–92.

BRA [Boston Redevelopment Authority] (1960) *Looking Forward With Pride . . . To a Better Boston . . . Through Urban Renewal*, Boston Revelopment Authority (Boston Public Library).

BRA (Boston Redevelopment Authority) (1969) The Prudential Center, Part One: Its Direct Impact on Boston. Boston Redevelopment Authority Research Paper no. 24.

BRA (Boston Redevelopment Authority) (1979) *Boston Harbor: Challenges and Opportunities for the 1980s*. Boston: BRA.

BRA (Boston Redevelopment Authority) (1992) *Sail Boston 1992: Economic Impact on Boston and Massachusetts*. BRA Research Paper no. 464, Boston: BRA.

BRA (1993) *Boston: A Tradition of Innovation*. Boston: BRA.

Brandon, D. and Marooney, J. (1987) *The Book of Baseball*. London: Sidgwick and Jackson.

Brendon, P. (1991) *Thomas Cook: 150 Years of Popular Tourism*. London: Secker and Warburg.

Briggs, A. (1967) *Victorian Cities*. London: Penguin (first published 1963, Odhams).

Brighton [Corporation] (*c*1929) *Brighton – Delightful at all Seasons*. Brighton: Brighton Corporation (John Johnson Collection, Bodleian Library).

Brown, C. V. (1985) Three Raleigh suburbs: Glenwood, Boylan Heights, Cameron Park, in Bishir, C. W. and Earley, L. S. (eds.) *op. cit.*, pp. 30–37.

Brown, D. (1995) *Inventing New England: Regional Tourism in the Nineteeth Century*. Washington: Smithsonian Institution Press.

Brown, R. H. (1948) *Historical Geography of the United States*. New York: Harcourt Brace and World.

Brownell, B.A. (1972) Birmingham, Alabama: 'New South' city in the 1920s. *Journal of Southern History*. **38**, pp. 21–48.

Brownill, S. (1990) *Developing London's Docklands: Another Great Planning Disaster?* London: Paul Chapman.

Brownill, S. (1994) Selling the inner city: Regeneration and place marketing in London's Docklands, in Gold and Ward (eds.) *op. cit.*, pp. 133–152.

Brunner, E. (1945) *Holiday Making and the Holiday Trades*. Oxford: Nuffield College.

BSSR (Bay State Street Railway Company) (1914) *Trolley Trips*. Boston: BSSR (Society for the Preservation of the New England Antiquities).

Building (special issue) (1991) *Canary Wharf: A Landmark in Construction*. (October). London: Builder Group.

Built Environment (1991) Special Number: Post-Suburban America. *Built Environment*. **17**(3/4).

Bunce, M. (1994) *The Countryside Ideal: Anglo-American Images of Landscape*. London: Routledge.

Burgess, J. A. (1982) Selling places: Environmental images for the executive. *Regional Studies*, **16**(1), pp. 1–17.

Burnley Express and News, as cited in text.

Burns (Report) (1980) *Review of Local Authority Assistance to Industry and Commerce – Report of the Joint Group of Officials of Local Authority Associations and Government Departments*. London: Department of the Environment.

Businessweek Special Advertising Section (1991)

Boston Revolutionizing Business Opportunity, 25 October.

Byatt, I. C. R. (1979) *The British Electrical Industry 1875–1914: The Economic Returns of a New Technology*. Oxford: Clarendon Press.

Cadbury, G. Jnr (1915) *Town Planning with Special Reference to the Birmingham Schemes*. London, Longmans Green.

Camard, F. and Zagrodski, C. (1989) *Le train a l'affiche: Les plus belles affiches ferroviaires francaises*. Paris: La Vie du Rail.

Camina, M. M. (1974) Local Authorities and the Attraction of Industry. *Progress in Planning*, **3** (2), whole issue.

Carpenter, C. C. (1879) *Grand Rush for the Indian Territory*. Independence: W. C. Branham (Library of Congress Broadside Collection).

Carr, M. C. (1982) The development and character of a metropolitian suburb: Bexley, Kent, in Thompson, F. M. L.(ed.) *op. cit.*, pp. 211–267.

Carter, H. and Lewis, C. R. (1990) *An Urban Geography of England and Wales in the Nineteenth Century*. London, Arnold.

Carter, H. (1978) Towns and urban systems 1730–1900, in Dodgshon, R. A. and Butlin, R A. (eds.). *An Historical Geography of England and Wales*. London: Academic Press: pp. 367–400.

Castells, M. (1977) *The Urban Question*. London: Arnold.

CBQRR (Chicago, Burlington and Quincy Railroad) (1881) *Burlington and Missouri River Railroad Land Grant 600,000 Acres Remaining*. Chicago: CBQRR (Newberry Collection).

CBQRR (nd *c*1883) *Suburbs of Chicago on the Chicago, Burlington and Quincy R. R.Illustrated*. Chicago: CBQRR (Chicago Historical Society).

CBQRR (nd *c*1900) *Suburban Homes Along the Chicago, Burlington and Quincy RR*. Chicago: CBQRR (Chicago Historical Society).

Chalklin, C. W. (1974) *The Provincial Towns of Georgian England: A Study of the Building Process 1740–1820*. London: Arnold.

Chase, S. M. (1995) Working Class Suburbs and Restrictive Covenants, 1900–1941. Paper presented at 6th National Conference on American Planning History, Knoxville.

Cherry, G. E. (1994) *Birmingham: A Study in Geography, History and Planning*. Chichester: Wiley.

Chicago Tribune, as cited in the text.

CIPFA (Chartered Institute of Public Finance and Accountancy) (1995*a*) *Financial and General Statistics 1995–6*. London: CIPFA.

CIPFA (1995*b*) *Local Government Comparative Statistics 1995*. London: CIPFA.

Clark, E. (1995) Samuel E. [G]ross: Dreiser's real estate magnate, in West, J. L. W. (ed.) *'Jennie Gerhardt' by Theodore Dreiser: New Essays on the Restored Text*. Philadelphia: University of Pennsylvania Press, pp. 183–193.

Clark, E. and Ashley, P. (1992) The merchant prince of Cornville. *Chicago History*, **XXI**(3), pp. 4–19.

Clawson, M. (1983) *The Federal Lands Revisited*. Washington: Resources for the Future.

CLPT (City of Leeds Promotion and Tourism) (1994) *Leeds On, Spring–Summer*. Leeds: CLPT.

CMDC (Central Manchester Development Corporation) (1992) *Annual Report 1991/92*. Manchester: CMDC.

CMDC (*c*1992*a*) *The Positive City for Development +061 Central Manchester*. Manchester: CMDC.

CMDC (*c*1992*b*) *The Positive City for Business +061 Central Manchester*. Manchester: CMDC.

CMDC (1993) *Annual Report 1992/93*. Manchester: CMDC.

CMDC (1995) *Annual Report 1994/95*, Manchester: CMDC.

CMDC (1996) *1988–1996 Eight Years of Achievement*. Manchester: CMDC.

CNWR (Chicago and North Western Railway) (1900) *The Beautiful Country Near Chicago*. Chicago: CNWR (Library of Congress Local Collection).

CNWR, (nd *c*1909) *Beautiful Suburban Towns*. Chicago: CNWR (Library of Congress Local Collection).

Coad, J. (1979) *Laing: The Biography of Sir John W. Laing, CBE (1879–1978)*. London: Hodder and Stoughton.

Cobb, J. C. (1984) *Industrialization and Southern Society 1877–1984*. Lexington, KY: University Press of Kentucky.

Cobb, J. C. (1988) Beyond planters and industrialists: A new perspective on the New South. *Journal of Southern History*, **44**, pp. 45–68.

Cobb, J. C. (1993) *The Selling of the South: The Southern Crusade for Industrial Development 1936–1990*, 2nd ed. Urbana/Chicago: University of Illinois Press.

Cobban, A. (1965) *A History of Modern France 1871–1962*. Harmondsworth: Penguin.

Cochran, T. C. (1953) *Railroad Leaders 1845–1890: The Business Mind in Action*. Cambridge: Harvard University Press.

Cole, B. and Durack, R. (1990) *Happy as a Sandboy*. London: HMSO.

Cole, B. and Durack, R. (1992) *Railway Posters 1923–1947 from the collection of the National Railway Museum*, York. London: Lawrence King.

Collinge, C. (1992) The dynamics of local intervention: Economic development and the theory of local government. *Urban Studies*, **29**, pp. 57–75.

Conservatoire de l'Affiche en Bretagne (nd *c*1994) *La Bretagne et la Mer: Affiches 1890–1950*. Rennes: Editions-Ouest.

Constandt, M. (1986) *Een Eeuw Vakantie: 100 Jaar Toerisme in West-Vlaanderen*. Tielt: Lannoo.

Cook, G. (1992) *The Discourse of Advertising*. London: Routledge.

Cook, T. (1922) *UK Brochure*. London: Cook (Thomas Cook Archives).

Cook, T. (1936) *UK Brochure*. London: Cook (Thomas Cook Archives).

Cook, T. (1951) *UK Brochure*. London: Cook (Thomas Cook Archives).

Cook, T. (1993) *The Thomas Cook Travel Archive Poster Collection*. London: Thomas Cook Travel Archive.

Cook's American Traveler's Gazette, as cited in text (Thomas Cook Archives).

Cook's Australasian Traveller's Gazette, as cited in text (Thomas Cook Archives).

Cook's Excursionist, as cited in text (Thomas Cook Archives).

Cook's Oriental Traveller's Guide, as cited in text (Thomas Cook Archives).

Cooke, P. N. (1983) *Theories of Planning and Spatial Development*. London: Hutchinson.

Coppock, J. T (1964) Dormitory settlements around London, in Coppock, J. T. and Prince, H.C. (eds.) *Greater London*. London: Faber, pp. 265–291.

Costin, F . and C. (nd *c*1935) *Costin Houses: Such Stuff As Dreams Are Made On*. Kenton: Costin (John Johnson Collection, Bodleian Library).

CPE (Croham Park Estate) (1908) *Croham Park Estate: South Croydon, Surrey*. Croydon: CPE.

Craig, P. (1986) The House That Jerry Built? Building societies, the state and the politics of owner occupation. *Housing Studies*, **1**(2), pp. 87–108.

Crilley, D. (1993) Architecture as advertising:

Constructing the image of redevelopment, in Kearns, G. and Philo, C. (eds.) *op. cit.*, pp. 231–252.

Cross, G. (ed.) (1990) *Worktowners at Blackpool: Mass Observation and Popular Leisure in the 1930s.* London: Routledge.

CSO (Central Statistical Office) (1984) *Annual Abstract of Statistics.* London: HMSO.

CSO (Central Statistical Office) (1988) *Annual Abstract of Statistics.* London: HMSO.

CSO (Central Statistical Office) (1995) *Annual Abstract of Statistics.* London: HMSO.

Daniels, S. and Rycroft, S. (1993) Mapping the modern city: Alan Sillitoe's Nottingham novels. *Transactions of the Institute of British Geographers*, New Series, **18**, pp. 460–880.

Darby, H. C. (ed.) (1973) *A New Historical Geography of England.* Cambridge: University Press.

Dare, H. (nd *c*1933) *Dare's Distinctive Houses.* Birmingham: Dare (Birmingham Reference Library).

Daunton, M. J. (1990) American cities, in Daunton, M. J. (ed.) *Housing the Workers: A Comparative History, 1850–1914.* Leicester: Leicester University Press.

Daunton, M. J. (1987) *A Property-Owning Democracy? Housing in Britain.* London: Faber.

Davis Estates Ltd (nd *c*1936) *This is Worth Looking Into: The Davis Mystic Oracle Solves the Homeseeker's Problem of Today.* London: Davis (John Johnson Collection, Bodleian Library).

DBDC (Derby Borough Development Committee) (nd *c*1928) *Derby as an Industrial Centre.* Derby: DBDC (Bodleian Library).

DCDC (Dundee City Development Committee) (1931) *Do It At Dundee.* Dundee: DCDC.

DCPC (Derby Corporation Publicity Committee) (nd *c*1933) *Derby: The City of Vital Industries.* Derby: Publicity Committee (Bodleian Library).

Denbigh, K. (1981) *A Hundred British Spas.* London: Spa Publications.

Dennis, R. (1995) Landlords and housing in depression. *Housing Studies*, **10**(3), pp. 305–324.

DOE (Department of the Environment) (1986) *Local Government Financial Statistics 1984/85.* London: HMSO.

DOE (Department of the Environment) (1992) *The Relationship Between House Prices and Land Supply.* London: HMSO.

DOE (Department of the Environment) (1995) *Local Government Financial Statistics England No 5 1994.* London HMSO.

Dreiser, T. 1981 (orig. 1947): *The Stoic*, New York: Signet

Drummond, I. *et al.* (1987) *Progress Without Planning: The Economic History of Ontario from Confederation to the Second World War.* Toronto: University Press.

Drummond, I., Cain, L. P. and Cohen, M. (1988) Canadian historical review dialogue: Ontario's industrial revolution. *Canadian Historical Review*, **LXIX**(3), pp. 283–314.

Duffy, H. (1995) *Competitive Cities: Succeeding in the Global Economy.* London: Spon.

Dumke, G. S. (1944) *The Boom of the 'Eighties in Southern California.* San Marino, CA: Huntington Library.

Dyer, J. and Dony, J. (1975) *The Story of Luton*, 3rd ed. Luton: White Crescent Press.

East, W. G. (1965) *The Geography Behind History.* London: Nelson.

Ebner, M. H. (1988) *Creating Chicago's North Shore: A Suburban History.* Chicago: University of Chicago Press.

Ebner, M. H. (1993) Prospects for the dual metropolis in the US. *Planning History*, **15**(3), pp. 13–21.

EDC (Edinburgh Development Committee) (1932) *Place Your Factory in Edinburgh.* Edinburgh: EDC.

Edel, M., Sclar, E. D. and Luria, D. (1984) *Shaky Palaces: Home Ownership and Social Mobility in Boston's Suburbanization.* New York: Columbia University Press.

EDIC (Economic Development and Industrial Corporation/Boston) (1991) *Setting the Record Straight: Doing Business in Boston.* Boston: EDIC/Boston.

EDIC (Economic Development and Industrial Corporation/Boston) (nd *c*1991) *Target Boston.* Boston: EDIC/Boston.

Edwards, A. M. (1981) *The Design of Suburbia: A Critical Study in Environmental History.* London: Pembridge.

Ehrlich, B. D. (1987) The Politics of Economic Development Planning: Boston in the 1980s. Unpublished Master of City Planning Dissertation, Massachusetts Institute of Technology.

Eisenschitz, A. and Gough, J. and (1993) *The Politics of Local Economic Policy: The Problems and Possibilities of Local Initiative.* Basingstoke: Macmillan.

Elias, J. W. (1983) *Los Angeles: Dream to Reality 1885–1915*. Northridge, CA: Santa Susana Press/ California State University, Northridge Libraries.

EMG (Eastbourne Marketing Group) (1994) *History of Eastbourne Marketing Group*. Press Release. Eastbourne: EMG.

Engelhardt, G. W. (1902) *Richmond Virginia: The City on the James: The Book of the Chamber of Commerce and Principal Business Interests*. Richmond: Engelhardt (Virginia State Library).

English, J. and McLaughlin, K. (1983) *Kitchener: An Illustrated History*. Waterloo: Wilfred Laurier University Press.

ETB (English Tourist Board) (1988) *Wigan Mini-Guide* (ETB/408/88PCE/1132/30M/11/88). London: ETB.

ETB (English Tourist Board) (1991) *The Future for England's Smaller Seaside Resorts: Summary Report*. London: ETB.

ETB (English Tourist Board) (1992) *Shorelines: Seaside Development and Marketing Initiatives*. London: ETB.

ETB (English Tourist Board) (1993) *Turning the Tide*. London: ETB.

Evening Standard, as cited in text.

Expansion Management (1994) *Expansion Management 1994 Atlas and Guide*. Boulder: New Hope Communications.

FAC (Forward Atlanta Commission) (nd *c*1930) *Report of the Forward Atlanta Commission 1926–1929 Being A Detailed Statement of the Administration of the Forward Atlanta Fund for the Years 1926 – 1927 – 1928 – 1929*. Atlanta: FAC (Atlanta Public Library, Local Collection)

Farewell, J. E. (1973) (reprint of 1907 original) *Ontario County*. Belleville: Mika.

FDIDC (Forest of Dean Industrial Development Committee) (1940) *Forest of Dean Industrial Estates*. Gloucester: FDIDC.

Felsdale (nd *c*1920) *Felsdale in Winchester: A Rural Community for Modern Homes of Artistic Harmony on the Eastern Hillslopes of Winchester Massachusetts*. Winchester: Felsdale Land Company (Society for the Preservation of the New England Antiquities).

FGC (First Garden City Ltd) (1908*a*) *Letchworth as a Manufacturing Centre*. Letchworth: FGC (John Johnson Collection, Bodleian Library).

FGC (First Garden City Ltd) (nd *c*1908) *The Best Location in England for Manufacturers is The New Industrial Town of Letchworth (Garden City)*. Letchworth: FGC (John Johnson Collection, Bodleian Library).

FGC (First Garden City Ltd) (nd *c*1909) *Why Manufacturers Move to Letchworth (Garden City)*. Letchworth: FGC (John Johnson Collection, Bodleian Library).

Financial Times, as cited in text.

Fine, B. and Harris, L. (1985) *The Peculiarities of the British Economy*. London: Lawrence and Wishart.

Finer, H. (1941) *Municipal Trading*. London: Allen and Unwin.

Finer, H. (1950) *English Local Government*, 4th ed. London: Methuen.

Fishman, R. (1987) *Bourgeois Utopias: The Rise and Fall of Suburbia*. New York: Basic Books.

Fishman, R. (1992) The American garden city: Still relevant? in Ward, S.V. (ed.) *The Garden City: Past, Present and Future*. London: Spon, pp. 146–164.

Fitte, G. C. (1966) *The Farmer's Frontier 1865–1900*. New York: Holt, Rinehart and Winston.

Fogarty, M. P. (1945) *Prospects of the Industrial Areas of Great Britain*. London: Methuen.

Fogarty, M. P. (1947) *Plan Your Own Industries: A Study of Local and Regional Development Organizations*. Oxford: Blackwell.

Fortune, as cited in text.

Forward Atlanta (1991) *Business At Its Best: A Study in Momentum – Headquarters Atlanta*. Atlanta: Chamber of Commerce.

Forward Atlanta (1994) *Downtown Atlanta: A Strategic Business Location*. Atlanta: Chamber of Commerce.

Forward Atlanta (1995) *Atlanta and the International Business Community*. Atlanta: MACC.

Fosler, F. S. and Berger, R. A. (eds.) 1982: *Public-Private Partnership in American Cities: Seven Case Studies*. Lexington: Heath.

Fothergill, S. and Gudgin, G. (1982) *Unequal Growth: Urban and Regional Employment Change in the UK*. London: Heinemann.

Frames (Tours) (1927) *Brochure*. London: Frames (John Johnson Collection, Bodleian Library).

Frazer, W. M. (1950) *A History of English Public Health*. London: Balliere, Tindall and Cox.

Frieden, B. J. and Sagalyn, L. B. (1989) *Downtown, Inc.: How America Rebuilds Cities*. Cambridge: MIT Press.

Funnell, C. E. (1975) *By the Beautiful Sea: The Rise and High Times of that Great American Resort, Atlantic City*. New York: Knopf.

Ganz, A. and Konga, L. F. (1989) Boston in the World Economy, in Knight, R. V. and Gappert, G. (eds.) *Cities in a Global Society*. Newbury Park: Sage, pp. 132–140.

Garofalo, C. P. (1976) The sons of Henry Grady: Atlanta boosters in the 1920s. *Journal of Southern History*, **XLII**(2), pp. 187–204.

Garreau, J. (1991) *Edge City: Life on the Frontier*. New York: Doubleday.

Gaston, P. (1970) *The New South Creed: A Study in Southern Mythmaking*. New York: Knopf.

Gates, P. W. (1934) *The Illinois Central Railroad and Its Colonization Work*. Cambridge, MA: Harvard University Press.

Gates, P. W. (1973) *Landlords and Tenants on the Prairie Frontier: Studies in American Land Policy*. Ithaca: Cornell University Press.

GBCC (Greater Boston Chamber of Commerce) (1959) *Boston's Golden Industrial Semicircle*. Boston: GBCC (Boston Public Library).

GBCC/ACB (Greater Boston Chamber of Commerce and the Advertising Club of Boston) (1962) *The New Boston: Its People – Its Places – Its Potentials*. Boston: GBCC/ACB (Boston Public Library).

GBCC/EDIC/BRA (Greater Boston Chamber of Commerce/Economic Development and Industrial Corporation of Boston/Boston Redevelopment Authority) (1981) *Boston Guide to Development*. Boston: GBCC (Boston Public Library).

GBESC (Greater Boston Economic Study Committee) (1959) *A Report on Downtown Boston*. Boston: GBESC (Boston Public Library).

GDC (Glenrothes Development Corporation) (1994) *Glenrothes Better By Far*. Glenrothes: GDC.

Gee, H. L. (ed.) (1949) *1899–1949 Bridlington: 50 Years a Borough*. Bridlington: Borough Council.

Georgia Laws, as cited in text.

Georgia (1773) *[By His Excellency Sir James Wright, Baronet, Captain General, Governor and Commander in Chief of his Majesty's said Province, Chancellor, Vice-Admiral and Ordinary of the same] A PROCLAMATION, Land Secured by treaty from Indians for Settlement*. Washington: Library of Congress, Broadside Collection.

GER (Great Eastern Railway [Row, P. and Anderson, A. H. (eds)]) (1911) *By Forest and Countryside: A Guide to the Residential Localities on the Great Eastern Railway*, 2nd ed. London: Homeland Association for Great Eastern Railway.

Girard, L. (1965) Transport, in Habukkuk, H.J. and Postan, M. (eds.) *The Cambridge Economic History of Europe*, Vol VI: *The Industrial Revolution and After: Incomes, Population and Technological Change (1)*. Cambridge: Cambridge University Press, pp. 212–273.

Glasgow '96 (1996) *Festival of Visual Arts*. Glasgow: Greater Glasgow & Clyde Valley Tourist Board.

GLRO (Greater London Record Office) MET 1/27: Metropolitan Railway Board Minute Book No 27.

GLRO MET 1/30: Metropolitan Railway Board Minute Book 1927–31.

GLRO MET 1/34: Metropolitan Railway: Appendix to Board Minutes Book No 3.

GLRO MET 1/38: Metropolitan Railway Appendix to Board Minutes Book No 7.

GLRO MET 1/115: Metropolitan Railway General Manager's Reports to Board 1925–9.

GLRO MET 1/116: Metropolitan Railway General Manager's Reports to Board 1929–33.

GLRO MET 4/13: Collection of handbills, notices, letters, booklets, maps, photographs etc.

GLRO MET 10/89: Metropolitan Railway: Development of Northwick Park Estate and Construction of Northwick Park and Kenton Station.

GLRO MET 10/152: Moor Park Estate: Metropolitan railway Country Estates Propectus Etc 1919–1927.

GLRO MET 10/322: Metropolitan Railways Country Estates Ltd – Purchase of Land from Metropolitan Railway at Neasden and Chalk Hill Estate, Wembley 1912–1922 – Formation of Company: Agreement of 1919.

GLRO MET 10/327: Metropolitan Country Estates Ltd: Land and Property at Kingsbury Garden Village, Neasden and at Chalk Hill Estate Wembley also Land at Hillingdon 1921–1928.

GLRO MET 10/339: Metropolitan Railway: Halden Estates Co Ltd re Hillingdon Halt 1922–26.

GLRO MET 10/442: Metropolitan Railway – Hillingdon Station: Various Photographs/ Timetables/ Halden Estate Brochures/Plans Etc 1923.

GLRO MET 10/559: Come to Britain Movement (Correspondence and Literature regarding support for the movement by the four main line companies, 1926–28).

GLRO MET 10/617: The Travel and Industrial Development Association of Great Britain and Ireland 1928–1933 Various Papers etc.

GLRO MET 10/712: Metropolitan Railway: Growth of Population in Metro-Land 1928.

GLRO MET 10/756: Metropolitan Railway Company and the Metropolitan Country Estates Ltd – Copy Agreement setting forth the details of the Business relationship between the two companies, statements, reports, correspondence etc 1919–1930.

GMVCB (Greater Manchester Visitors and Convention Bureau) (1996) *This is the Life: Short Breaks Guide 96–97 Greater Manchester: the life and soul of Britain*. Manchester: GMVCB.

GNR (Great Northern Railway) (1906) *Where to Live: Illustrated Guide to Some of London's Choicest Suburbs*. London: GNR (Bodleian Library).

Gold, J.R. (1974) Communicating Images of the Environment. Occasional Paper no. 29, Centre for Urban and Regional Studies, University of Birmingham.

Gold, J. R. (1994) Locating the message: Place promotion as image communication, in Gold and Ward (eds.) *op. cit.*, pp.19–37.

Gold, J. R. and Gold, M. M. (1990) 'A Place of delightful prospects': Promotional imagery and the selling of suburbia, in Zonn, L. (ed.) *Place Images in Media: Portrayal, Experience and Meaning*. Savage, Maryland: Rowman and Littlefield, pp.159–182.

Gold, J. R. and Gold, M. M. (1994) 'Home at last!': Building societies, home ownership and the imagery of English suburban promotion in the interwar years, in Gold and Ward (eds.) *op. cit.*, pp. 75–92.

Gold J. R. and Gold, M. M. (1995) *Imagining Scotland: Tradition, Representation and Promotion in Scottish Tourism since 1750*. Aldershot: Scolar.

Gold, J. R. and Ward, S. V. (eds.) (1994) *Place Promotion: The Use of Publicity and Marketing to Sell Towns and Regions*. Chichester: Wiley.

Golden, D. and Mehegan, D. (1983) Changing the heart of the city. *Boston Globe Magazine*, 18.9.83, whole issue.

Goldsack, B. (1993) *A Century of Fun: A Pictorial History of New England Amusement Parks*. Nashua: Midway Museum.

Goodey, B. (1994) Art-full places: Public art to sell public spaces, in Gold, J. R. and Ward, S. V. (eds.) *op. cit.*, pp. 153–179.

Goodrum, C. and Dalrymple, H. (1990) *Advertising in America: The First 200 Years*. New York: Abrams.

Goodwin, M. B. (nd *c*1932) *Goodwin's Homesteads of Distinction*. Hounslow: Goodwin (London Transport Museum).

Green, O. (1990) *Underground Art: London Transport Posters 1908 to the Present*, London: Studio Vista.

Gross, S. E. (1883) *Homes in Lakeview*. Broadside, Chicago: Gross (Chicago Historical Society).

Gross, S. E. (1886) *The House That Lucy Built or A Model Landlord*. Chicago: Gross (Chicago Historical Society).

Gross, S. E. (1888*a*) *The Home Primer*. Chicago: Gross (Chicago Historical Society).

Gross, S. E. (1888*b*) *Illustrirter Katalog von S. E. Gross' Bauplatzen, Hausern, Cottages*. Chicago: Gross (Chicago Historical Society).

Gross, S. E. (1891) *Tenth Annual Illustrated Catalogue of S. E. Gross' Famous City Subdivisions and Suburban Towns*. Chicago: Gross (Chicago Historical Society).

Guardian, as cited in text.

GWR (Great Western Railway) (1935) *Cornwall*. London: GWR (John Johnson Collection, Bodleian Library).

GWR/Looe (1931) *Looe, South Cornwall: Where Sea, River and Countryside Make an Ideal Holiday Land*. London/Looe: GWR/Looe (John Johnson Collection, Bodleian Library).

Hackney LBC (London Borough Council) (1983) *The Case for Hackney: Britain's Poorest Borough*. Hackney: London Borough of Hackney Council.

Hall, P., Gracey, H., Drewett, R. and Thomas, R. (1973) *The Containment of Urban England*, 2 Vols. London: Political and Economic Planning/Allen and Unwin.

Hansard, H[ouse of] C[ommons] Deb[ates] 5th s[series].

Hansard, H[ouse of] L[ords] Deb[ates] 5th s[eries].

Harding, A. (1992) Property Interests and urban growth coalitions in the UK: A brief encounter, in Healey, P., Davoudi, S., Tavsanoglu, A., O'Toole, M. and Usher, D. (eds.) *op. cit.*, pp. 224–32.

Harris, R. (1990) Working class home ownership in the American metropolis. *Journal of Urban History*, **17**, pp. 46–69.

Harris, R. (1994) Chicago's other suburbs. *Geographical Review*, **84**(4), pp. 394–410.

Harris, R. and Hamnett, C. (1987) The myth of the promised land: The social diffusion of home ownership in Britain and North America. *Annals of the Association of American Geographers*, **77**(2), pp. 173–190.

Harvey, D. (1989*a*): *The Urban Experience*. Oxford: Blackwell.

Harvey, D. (1989*b*) *The Condition of Postmodernity: An Enquiry into the Origins of Cultural Change*. Oxford: Blackwell.

Harvey, D. (1989*c*) From managerialism to entrepreneurialism: The transformation in urban governance in late capitalism. *Geografiska Annaler*, **71B**.

Haug, C. J. (1982) *Leisure and Urbanism in Nineteenth Century Nice*. Lawrence: Regent's Press of Kansas.

Hausner, V. (ed.) (1986) *Critical Issues in Urban Economic Development*, Vol. I.Oxford: Clarendon Press.

Hawson, H. K. (1968) *Sheffield: The Growth of A City*. Sheffield: Northend.

Healey, P., Davoudi, S., O'Toole, M. Tavsanoglu and Usher, D. (eds.) (1992) *Rebuilding the City: Property-led Urban Regeneration*. London: Spon.

Heaton's (Annual: The Commercial Handbook of Canada and Boards of Trade Register), Toronto: Heaton's Agency, years as cited in text.

Hembry, P. (1990) *The English Spa 1560–1815: A Social History*. London: Athlone.

Hen Wlad Fy Nhadu (Land of My Fathers) Official Journal of Industrial Development Council of South Wales and Monmouthshire.

Henson, M. D. and King, J. (1982) The Atlanta public-private romance: An abrupt transformation, in Fosler, F. S. and Berger, R. A. *op. cit.*, pp. 293–338.

Hewison, R. (1987) *The Heritage Industry: Britain in a Climate of Decline*. London: Methuen.

Hewitt, J. (1995) East coast joys: Tom Purvis and the LNER. *Journal of Design History*, **8**(4), pp. 291–311.

Hill, C. R. (1992) *Olympic Politics*. Manchester: Manchester University Press.

Hobson, O. R. (1953) *A Hundred Years of the Halifax: A History of the Halifax Building Society 1853–1953*. London: Batsford.

Hoig, D. S. (1933) *Reminiscences and Recollections*. Oshawa: Mundy Goodfellow.

Holcomb, B. (1990) *Purveying Places: Past and Present*, Centre for Urban Policy Research, Working Paper no 17. Piscataway: Rutgers University.

Holcomb, B. (1993) Revisioning place: De- and re-constructing the image of the industrial city, in Kearns, G. and Philo, C. (eds.), *op. cit.*, pp. 133–143.

Holcomb, B. (1994) City make-overs: Marketing the post-industrial city, in Gold and Ward (eds.), *op. cit.*, pp, 115–131.

Holcomb, B. and Parisi, P. (1990) Press and Place: Equivocal Relations in the Redeveloping City. Center for Urban Policy Research, Rutgers University, Research Paper no. 20, Piscataway, New Jersey.

Hood, M. M. (1967) *Oshawa: The Crossing Between the Waters*. Oshawa: Public Library.

Houseland Gazette (1931–) (John Johnson Collection, Bodleian Library)

Howkins, F. (1938) *Development of Private Building Estates*, 2nd ed. London: Estates Gazette.

Hubbard, P. (1996) Re-imaging the city: The transformation of Birmingham's urban landscape, *Geography*, **81**(1), pp. 26–36.

Hudson, E. G. (nd *c*1933) *Particulars of Properties for Sale on the Sunnyside Estate, Cowley (Oxford's Greatest Housing Scheme)*. Oxford: Hudson (Centre for Oxfordshire Studies).

Hula, R. C. (1990) The two Baltimores, in Judd, D and Parkinson, M. (eds.) *op. cit.*, pp. 191–215.

Huntington, E. (1915) *Civilization and Climate*. New Haven: Yale University Press.

Hussey and Robinson (1865) *Nantucket as a Watering Place and Summer Residence*. Nantucket: Hussey and Robinson (Library of Congress, Broadside Collection).

Hutchings, C. (1995) Wishing you were here . . . *Geographical Magazine*, September, pp. 12–15.

Hutchison, H. F. (1968) *The Poster: An Illustrated History from 1860*. London: Studio Vista.

ICRR (Illinois Central Railroad) (1853) *Maps of the Cairo City Property Comprised in the 1st Plat of the City of Cairo, Illinois*. Chicago: ICRR (Newberry Library).

ICRR (1854) *2 Million 5 Hundred Thousand Acres of Land in Illinois Belonging to the Illinois Central Railroad Company*. Salem: Observer (Chicago Historical Society).

ICRR [Dupuy, C. M.] (1855) *The Illinois Central Railroad Company Offer for Sale over 2,400,000 acres Selected Prairie, Farm and Woodlands in Tracts of Any Size to Suit Purchasers on Long Credit At Low Rates of Interest*. New York: Oliver (Newberry Library).

ICRR (1859) *A Guide to the Illinois Central Railroad Lands: The Illinois Central Railroad Company Offer for Sale over 2,400,000 acres Selected Prairie, Farm and Woodlands in Tracts of Any Size to Suit Purchasers on Long Credit At Low Rates of Interest.* Chicago: ICRR (Newberry Library).

ICRR (1878) *Why Go To The West When You Can Get Fine Farming Lands in the State of Illinois?* Chicago: ICRR (Newberry Library).

ICRR (1896a) *Railroad Lands for Sale Owned By the Yazoo and Mississippi Valley Railroad Company in the Famous Yazoo Valley of Mississippi.* Chicago: Illinois (Newberry Library).

ICRR (1896b) *Railroad Lands for Sale By the Illinois Central Railroad in Southern Illinois.* Chicago: ICRR (Newberry Library).

ICRR (nd c1900) *Flossmoor: A model high class south side suburban home-site located only 24 miles south of the Court House on the Illinois Central Railroad.* Chicago: ICRR (Chicago Historical Society).

ICRR (1912) *Illinois Central Magazine.* (Newberry Library).

ICRR (nd c1912) *Country Clubs on the Suburban Line of the Illinois Central Railroad.* Chicago: ICRR (Chicago Historical Society).

ICRR (nd) *The Illinois Central Railroad: Facts concerning its incorporation, land grant, construction and resulting development, Charter Taxes and Charter Law Suit.* Chicago: ICRR (Newberry Library).

IMPB (Isle of Man Publicity Board) (nd c1925) *Official Guide to the Isle of Man.* Douglas: IMPB.

Imrie, R. and Thomas, H. (eds.) (1993) *British Urban Policy and the Urban Development Corporations.* London: Paul Chapman.

ITCS (Indian Territory Colonization Society) (1879) *A Large Area of the Beautiful Indian Territory Open to Homesteaders.* ITCS (Library of Congress Broadside Collection).

Jack, I. (1984) The repackaging of Glasgow. *Sunday Times Magazine,* 2 December, pp. 37–45.

Jackson, A. A. (1986) *London's Metropolitan Railway.* Newton Abbot: David and Charles.

Jackson, A. A. (1991) *Semi-Detached London: Suburban Development, Life and Transport 1900–39,* 2nd ed. Didcot: Wild Swan.

Jackson, K. T. (1985) *Crabgrass Frontier: The Suburbanization of the United States.* New York: Oxford University Press.

Johnson, B. M. (Real Estate Investment and Development Company) (1926) *Loopway Park, Florida.* Bradenton: Johnson (Library of Congress Broadside Collection).

Johnston, R. J. (1984) *Residential Segregation, the State and Constitutional Conflict in American Urban Areas.* Institute of British Geographers Special Publication 17, London: Academic Press.

Jones, G. (1988) Foreign multi-nationals and British industry before 1945. *Economic History Review,* 2nd series, **XLI**(3), pp. 429–453.

Judd, D. and Parkinson, M. (eds.) (1990) *Leadership and Urban Regeneration: Cities in North America and Europe,* Volume 37: *Urban Affairs Annual Reviews.* Newbury Park: Sage.

Kain, R. (1980) Deauville/Trouville, *Connoisseur,* **204** (820), pp. 140–147.

Kaiser, T. E. (1921) *Historic Sketches of Oshawa.* Oshawa: Oshawa Reformer.

Karn, V (1977) *Retiring to the Seaside.* London: Routledge and Kegan Paul.

Karr, R. D. (1984) Brookline and the making of an elite suburb. *Chicago History,* **XIII**(2), pp. 36–47.

Kearns, G. and Philo, C. (eds.) (1993) *Selling Places: The City as Cultural Capital, Past and Present.* Oxford: Pergamon.

Keating, A. D. (1988) *Building Chicago: Suburban Developers and the Creation of a Divided Metropolis.* Columbus: Ohio State University Press.

Keating, M. (1988) *The City that Refused to Die – Glasgow: The Politics of Urban Regeneration,* Aberdeen University Press.

Kellett, J. R. (1969) *The Impact of Railways on Victorian Cities,* London: Routledge and Kegan Paul.

Kelly, B. M. (1993) *Expanding the American Dream: Building and Rebuilding Levittown.* Albany: State University of New York Press.

Kennedy, L. W. (1992) *Planning the City upon a Hill: Boston since 1630.* Amherst: University of Massachusetts Press.

Kirwan, R. (1986) Local fiscal policy and inner city economic development, in Hausner, V, (ed.) *op. cit.*

Knox, P. L., Bartels, E. H., Bohland, J. R., Holcomb, B. and Johnston, R. J. (1988) *The United States: A Contemporary Human Geography.* Harlow: Longman.

Kotler, P., Haider, D. H. and Rein, I. (1993) *Marketing Places: Attracting Investment, Industry, and Tourism to Cities, States, and Nations.* New York: Free Press.

Laing, J. (nd *c*1930*a*) *The Little Palaces of Colindale.* Mill Hill: Laing (John Laing Archives).

Laing, J. (nd *c*1930*b*) *The Palaces of Golders Green.* Mill Hill: London (John Laing Archives).

Laing, J. (nd *c*1933) *Laings Queensbury Estate.* Mill Hill: Laing (John Laing Archives).

Laing, J. (1935*a*) Open letter, 1.1.35. (John Laing Archives)

Laing, J. (1935*b*) Olympia 1935. Typescript address to Olympia salesmen by John Laing, 18.3.35. (John Laing Archives).

Laing, J. (nd *c*1936) *The Laing Estates at Belmont and Canons Park, Edgware.* Mill Hill: Laing (John Laing Archives).

Laing, J. (nd *c*1937*a*) *From a Woman's Point of View.* Mill Hill: Laing (John Johnson Collection: Bodleian Library).

Laing, J. (nd *c*1937*b*) *Laings 10 Estates.* Mill Hill: Laing (John Laing Archives).

Laing Press Cuttings, dates as cited in text (John Laing Archives).

Lash, S. and Urry, J. (1994) *Economies of Signs and Space.* London: Sage.

Law, C. M. (1981) *British Regional Development Since World War I.* London: Methuen.

Law, C. M. (1993) *Urban Tourism: Attracting Visitors To Large Cities.* London: Mansell.

Lawless, P. (1986) *The Evolution of Spatial Policy.* London: Pion.

Lawless, P. (1990) Regeneration in Sheffield: From radical intervention to partnership, in Judd, D. and Parkinson, M. (eds.) *op. cit.,* pp. 133–151.

Lawrence, C. G. (1873) *Health, Comfort and Pleasure. A Delightful Summer Resort Among the Green Mountains: The Brooks House.* Brattleboro VT: Lawrence (Society for the Preservation of the New England Antiquities).

Lawson, M. (1989) Whose kind of town? *Independent Magazine,* 11 November, pp. 68–74

LCC (London County Council) (1937) *London Housing.* London: LCC.

LDDC (London Docklands Development Corporation) (1995) *Annual Report and Financial Statements for year ended 31 March 1995.* London: LDDC.

Leach, E. H. and Morrison, R. L. C. (1928) *Tenby.* London: Health Resorts Association for the Corporation.

Lemmon, S. M. (1966) Raleigh – An example of the 'New South'? *North Carolina Historical Review,* **43**(3), pp. 261–285.

Levathes, L. E. (1987) Indianapolis: City of the rebound. *National Geographic Magazine,* **172**, pp. 230–259.

Levet, J.-M. and de Montry, A. (1992) *A vendre: Affiches immobilieres.* Paris: Elina/Sofedis.

Lewis, R. (1980) Seaside resorts in the United States and Britain: A review. *Urban History Yearbook,* pp. 44–52.

Lewis, S. (1922) *Babbit.* London: Vintage (reprinted 1994).

LHSPC (*Lawnsdale Hustler and Shedd's Park Cyclone*), as cited in text (Newberry Library).

Lidster, J. R. (1983) *Yorkshire Coast Lines: A Historical Record of Railway Tourism on the Yorkshire Coast.* Nelson: Hendon.

Liverpool (Housing Department) (1937) *Liverpool Housing.* Liverpool: Corporation.

LIDC (Lancashire Industrial Development Council) (1932) *Lancashire: An Introduction to the Commercial and Industrial Resources of the World's Greatest Manufacturing Area with Some Account of Its Past History and Present Activities.* Manchester: LIDC (Manchester Central Library, Local Collection).

LLEC (Liberal Land Enquiry Committee) (1914) *The Land,* Vol 2, *Urban.* London: Hodder and Stoughton.

LNIC (Luton New Industries Committee) (1900) *Luton as an Industrial Centre.* Luton: LNIC.

LNIC (1905) *Luton as an Industrial Centre,* 2nd edition. Luton: LNIC.

LNWR (London and North Western Railway) (1911) *The Spas of Central Wales.* London: LNWR (John Johnson Collection, Bodleian Library).

Loebl, H. (1988) *Government Factories and the Origins of British Regional Policy, 1934–1948.* Aldershot: Avebury.

Loftman, P. and Nevin, B. (1996) Pro-growth Local Economic Development Strategies: Civic Promotion and Local Needs in Britain's Second City 1981–1995. Paper delivered at the Urban Geography Study Group, Annual Conference of the Institute of British Geographers, University of Strathclyde, Glasgow.

Logan, J.R. and Molotch, H.L. (1987) *Urban Fortunes: The Political Economy of Place.* Berkeley, CA: University of California.

Lombaerde, P. (1983) Belgian urban development, Spa, Ostend and Antwerp in the 19th century. *Planning History Bulletin*, **5**(1), pp. 33–37.

Lowe, R. and Roberts, R. (1987) Sir Horace Wilson, 1900–1935: The making of a mandarin. *The Historical Journal*, **30**(3), pp. 641–662.

LTM (London Transport Museum), items as cited in text.

LUER (London Underground Electric Railways) (1907) *Healthy Homes: Illustrated Guide to London's Choicest Suburbs Made Easy of Access by the New Tube Railways*. London: Underground Electric Railways of London (Bodleian Library).

Luther, M. L. (1923–24) *The Boosters*. Indianapolis: Bobbs-Merrill.

Luton News, as cited in text (Luton Museum, Chamber of Commerce Press Cuttings).

Lyall, K. (1982) A bicycle built-for-two. Public-private partnership in Baltimore, in Fosler, F. S. and Berger, R. A. (eds.) *op. cit.*, pp. 17–58.

M'Gonigle, G. C. M. and Kirby, J. D. (1936) *Poverty and Public Health*. London: Gollancz.

MACC (Metro Atlanta Chamber of Commerce) (1995) *1994 Annual Report*. Atlanta: MACC.

Madsen, H. (1992) Place-marketing in Liverpool. *International Journal of Urban and Regional Research*, **16**(4), pp. 633–640.

Mair, D. (1986) Industrial derating: Panacea or palliative? *Scottish Journal of Political Economy*, **33**(22), pp. 159–170.

Mais, S. P. B. (nd *c*1930) *Wild Woods and Vast Vistas*. London: Ottershaw Park Investment Co. (John Johnson Collection, Bodleian Library).

Mais, S. P. B. (nd *c*1933) *Live in Brighton or Hove*. Brighton/London: Brighton and Hove Chamber of Commerce/Southern Railway/Brighton and Hove Corporations (John Johnson Collection, Bodleian Library).

Manchester 2000 (1993) *The British Olympic Bid: Manchester 2000 – Bid Document Summary*. Manchester: Manchester 2000.

Manchester 2000 (1994) *The English Commonwealth Bid*. Manchester: Manchester 2000.

Manzoni, H. J. B. (1939) *The Building of 50,000 Municipal Houses*. Birmingham: Corporation.

MAP Magazine (nc *c*1930) (John Johnson Collection, Bodleian Library)

Marr, W. C. and Paterson, D. G. 1980: *Canada: An Economic History*, Toronto: Macmillan.

Martin, J. E. (1966) *Greater London: An Industrial Geography*. London: Bell.

Massey, D. (1984) *Spatial Divisions of Labour: Social Structures and the Geography of Production*. Basingstoke: Macmillan.

Masters, P. (1994) European Support for Seaside Towns. Paper presented to TCPA Conference on the Future of Seaside Towns, Eastbourne.

May, G. W. (nd *c*1904) *Health Resorts Association*. London: Health Resorts Association (John Johnson Collection, Bodleian Library).

MCC (Manchester Chamber of Commerce) 1931: *Manchester Chamber of Commerce Handbook 1931–2*, Manchester: Chamber of Commerce (Bodleian Library).

MCC (Manchester Chamber of Commerce) (1937) *Manchester: Heart of the Industrial North*. Manchester: Chamber of Commerce (Bodleian Library).

McCulloch, A. (1990) A millstone round your neck: Building societies in the 1930s and mortgage default. *Housing Studies*, **5**(1), pp. 43–58.

McKelvey, B. (1963) *The Urbanization of America*. New Brunswick, NJ: Rutgers University Press.

McLaughlin, R. S. (1954) My eighty years on wheels: R. S. McLaughlin as told to Eric Hutton, Toronto: reprinted from *Maclean's*, 15.9.54; 1.10.54 and 15.10.54. (Oshawa and District Historical Society).

McMichael, S. L. (1949) *Real Estate Subdivisions*. New York: Prentice Hall.

Mercer, L. J. (1982) *Railroads and Land Grant Policy: A Study in Government Intervention*. New York: Academic Press.

Methvin, E. H. (1983) Cleveland Comes Back, in Porter, P. R. and Sweet, D. C. (eds.) (1984) *op. cit.*, pp. 65–70.

MH (Ministry of Health) (1926) *7th Annual Report of the Ministry of Health, 1925–6*, Cmd 2724. London: HMSO.

Mid-Atlantic Country (1996) **XVII**(2), *Destination Maryland*.

Middleton, D. J. and Walker, D. F. (1980) Manufacturers and industrial development policy in Hamilton, 1890–1910. *Urban History Review*, **VIII**(3), pp. 20–46.

Miller, M. (1989) *Letchworth: The First Garden City*. Chichester: Phillimore.

Miller, M. (1992) *Raymond Unwin: Garden Cities and Town Planning*. Leicester: University Press.

Mills, S. (1994) Seaside Towns – A National

Resource. Paper presented to the TCPA Conference on The Future of Seaside Towns, Eastbourne.

Milner, C. A. (1994) National Initiatives, in Milner, C. A., O'Connor, C. A. and Sandweiss, M. A. (eds.), *op. cit.*, pp. 155–193.

Milner, C. A., O'Connor, C. A. and Sandweiss, M. A. (eds) (1994) *The Oxford History of the American West*, New York: Oxford University Press.

Ministry of Health (1926) *Seventh Annual Report of the Ministry of Health 1925–6* (Cmd. 2724). London: HMSO.

Morris, R. J. (1989) The reproduction of capital and labour: British and Canadian cities during industrialization. *Urban History Review*, **18**, pp. 48–63.

MR (Metropolitan Railway) (1909) *Country Homes: The Official Guide of the Metropolitan Railway Company Residential Districts of Buckingham, Hertford and Middlesex*. London: Acme, for Metropolitan Railway (Bodleian Library).

MR (1920) *Metro-land*. London: MR (London Transport Museum).

MR (1921) *A Tour Through Metro-land: Visit of Press Representatives July 26th 1921*. London: MR (London Transport Museum)

MR (1923) *Metro-land*. London: MR (London Transport Museum).

MR (1924) *Metro-land*. London: MR (London Transport Museum).

MR (1926) *Metro-land*. London: MR (London Transport Museum).

MR (1927) *Metro-land*. London: MR (London Transport Museum).

MR (1932) *Metro-land*. London: MR (reproduced in facsimile with an introduction by Oliver Green, 1987: Oldcastle/London Transport Museum).

MVSMCC (Marketing and Visitor Services, Manchester City Council (1996*a*) *Manchester: The City Guide 1996*. Manchester: MVSMCC.

MVSMCC (1996*b*) *Manchester*. Promotional envelope folder. Manchester: MVSMCC.

Myres, S. L. (1982) *Westering Women and the Frontier Experience 1800–1915*. Albuquerque: University of New Mexico Press.

NASDA (National Association of State Development Agencies) (1993) *Directory of Incentives for Business Investment and Development in the USA: A State by State Guide*. Washington: National Council for Urban Economic Development/ The Urban Institute.

Nash, R. (1973) *Wilderness and the American Mind*, revised ed. New Haven: Yale University Press.

Naylor, R. T. (1975) *The History of Canadian Business 1867–1914 II: Industrial Development*. Toronto: James Lorimer.

NBSC (Nantasket Beach Steamboat Company) (nd *c*1907) *Daytrips between Boston and the far famed Nantasket Beach and Historic Plymouth*. Nantasket Beach, MA: NBSC (Society for the Preservation of the New England Antiquities).

NCPC (National City Publicity Company) (1922) *Atlantic City: The World's Playground*. Atlantic City: NCPC (Library of Congress Local Collection).

Neill, W. J. V., Fitzsimmons, D. S. and Murtagh, B. (1995) *Reimaging the Pariah City: Urban Development in Belfast and Detroit*. Aldershot: Avebury.

Newcastle Evening Chronicle, as cited in text.

Nix, J. (1995) The Fashioning of Landscapes and Identities: Nottingham's Lace Market 1850s–1920s. Paper delivered to the London Group of Historical Geographers, London.

Nordhoff, C. (1874) (orig. 1873): *California for Health, Pleasure and Residence: A Book for Travellers and Settlers*. New York: Harper.

NWTB (North West Tourist Board), Manchester Training and Enterprise Council and Marketing Manchester (1994) *Welcome Host Manchester*. Manchester: NWTB.

NYNHHRR (New York, New Haven and Hartford Railroad) (1910) *Narragansett Pier*. New Haven CT: NYNHHRR (Society for the Preservation of the New England Antiquities).

NZGDTHR (New Zealand Government Department of Tourist and Health Resorts) (nd *c*1906) *New Zealand*. Wellington: NZGDTHR.

Oakley, C.A. (1975) *The Second City*, 3rd ed. Glasgow: Blackie.

O'Barr, W. M. (1994) *Culture and the Ad: Exploring Otherness in the World of Advertising*. Boulder: Westview.

O'Connor, J. and Wynne, D. (eds) (1996*a*) *From the Margins to the Centre: Cultural Production and Consumption in the Post-Industrial City*. Aldershot: Arena.

O'Connor, J. and Wynne, D. (1996*b*) Left loafing: City cultures and postmodern lifestyles, in O'Connor J. and Wynne, D. (eds.) *op. cit.*, pp. 49–89.

O'Connor, J. (1992) Local government and cultural policy, in Wynne, D. (ed.) *op. cit.*, pp. 56–69.

O'Connor, T. H. (1993) *Building a New Boston: Politics and Urban Renewal 1950–1970*. Boston: Northeastern University Press.

Oak Hill (Company) (1926) *Oak Hill Village – Just Imagine*. Boston: Oak Hill Company (Society for the Preservation of the New England Antiquities).

Observer Magazine, as cited in text.

OCC (Oshawa Chamber of Commerce) (1928) *Manufacturing Data of the City of Oshawa, Ontario, Canada*. Oshawa: OCC (Oshawa and District Historical Society).

OCRR (Old Colony Railroad) (1889) *Suburban Homes on the Old Colony: A Directory for those who seek a Suburban Residence*. Boston: OCRR Passenger Department (Society for the Preservation of the New England Antiquities).

Official Catalogue of the Great Exhibition of Industry of All Nations (1851) *Official Catalogue Advertiser*. Oxford: John Johnson Collection, Bodleian Library.

Oliver, P., Davis, I. and Bentley, I. (1981) *Dunroamin: The Suburban Semi and Its Enemies*. London: Barrie and Jenkins.

Ontario (Government of) (1896) Return Shewing the Municipal Indebtedness of the Various Municipalities of the Province on the 31st December 1894 . . . etc. Published Sessional Paper no 68. (Ontario Legislative Library).

Ontario (1897) 60 Vict Ch 45 *Municipal Amendment Act*.

Ontario (Government of) (1900) Return to an Order Passed by the Provincial Assembly on the 30th March 1899 Regarding Municipal Aid to Manufacturing Industries. Unpublished Sessional Paper no 69 (Provincial Archives of Ontario).

Ontario (1910) 10 Edw VII Ch 85, *Municipal Amendment Act*.

Ontario Reformer (1911) Special Souvenir Number (Oshawa and District Historical Society).

Ontario Reformer, issues as cited in text (Provincial Archives of Ontario)

OPCS/RGS (Office of Population Census and Surveys/Registrar General for Scotland) (1994) *1991 Census Key Statistics for Local Authorities Great Britain*. London: HMSO.

Oshawa Bylaws, as cited in text (Provincial Archives of Ontario).

Oshawa (1898) *Oshawa: The Manchester of Canada*. Toronto: Canadian Souvenir Publishing Co. (Oshawa and District Historical Society).

Oxford Times, as cited in text.

PACEC (PA Cambridge Economic Consultants) (1990) *An Evaluation of Garden Festivals*. London: HMSO.

Pacione, M. (1995) *Glasgow: The Socio-Spatial Development of the City*. Chichester: Wiley.

Paddison, R. (1993) City marketing, image reconstruction and urban regeneration. *Urban Studies*, **30**, pp. 339–349.

Pakenham, S. (1967) *Sixty Miles from England: The English in Dieppe 1814–1914*. London: Macmillan.

Palin, M. (1987) *Happy Holidays The Golden Age of Railway Posters*. London: Pavilion in Association with Michael Joseph.

Parfitt, J. A. (1979) Laing Pre-War Private Housing. Typescript by former employee of J Laing. (John Laing Archives).

Park, R. E., Burgess, E. W. and McKenzie, R. D. (1925) *The City*, Chicago: University of Chicago Press.

Parkinson, M. (1990) Leadership and regeneration in Liverpool: Confusion, confrontation, or coalition, in Judd, D. and Parkinson, M. (eds) *op. cit.*, pp. 241–257.

Parkinson, M. and Bianchini, F. (1993) Liverpool: A tale of missed opportunities, in Bianchini and Parkinson (eds.), *op. cit.*: 155–77.

Parkinson, M., Foley, B. and Judd, D. (eds.) (1988) *Regenerating the Cities: The UK Crisis and the US Experience*. Fulbright Papers no. 4. Manchester: University Press/Fulbright Commission.

Parr, J. (1990) *The Gender of Breadwinners*. Toronto: University Press.

Parsons. D. W. (1986) *The Political Economy of British Regional Policy*. London: Croom Helm.

Paterson, R. (1989) Creating the packaged suburb: The evolution of planning and business practices in the early Canadian land development industry, 1900–1914, in Kelly, B. M. (ed.) *Suburbia Re-examined*. Studies in Sociology no 78. New York: Greenwood Press, pp. 119–132.

Payne, P. L. (1988) *British Entrepreneurship in the Nineteenth Century*, 2nd ed. Basingstoke: Macmillan.

Perkin, H. (1975) The 'social tone' of Victorian seaside sesorts in the North West. *Northern History*, **XI**, pp.180–194.

Perkins, G. W. (1983) Twenty-two Years of Boston's Fiscal Record: A Review of Expenditure and Revenue Trends for Boston City Government,

1960–1982. Boston Revelopment Authority, Research Paper no. 151.

Perkins, G. W. (1986) Boston's Waterfront: A Storied Past and a Brightening Future. Boston Redevelopment Authority Paper no. 268. Boston: BRA.

PIIC (Pecos Irrigation and Improvement Company (c1891) The Pecos Valley: The Fruit Belt of New Mexico. Eddy, NM: PIIC (Library of Congress Map Collection).

Pimlott, J.A.R. (1976; orig. 1947) The Englishman's Holiday: A Social History. Hassocks: Harvester.

PLC (Park Land Company) (nd c1926) Highland Park: 'A Community of Beautiful Homes'. Boston: PLC (Society for the Preservation of the New England Antiquities).

Pollard, S. (1962) The Development of the British Economy 1914–1950. London: Arnold.

Powell, W. R. (ed.) (1973) Victoria County History of Essex, Vol IV. Oxford: University Press.

Pred, A. (1965) Industrialization, initial advantage and American metropolitan growth. Geographical Review, 55, pp. 158–85.

PRO BT 56/38/CIA 1800/1 & 2 (together): Industrial Development: New Industries in Depressed Areas.

PRO BT 56/38 CIA 1800/11: Proposed Establishment of Birmingham Information Bureau.

PRO BT 56/39 CIA 1800/27: New Industries: Industrial Development Proposals by Teesside Chamber of Commerce.

PRO BT 56/39 CIA 1800/29: New Industries: West of Scotland Development Board.

PRO BT 56/40 CIA 1800/64: New Industries – general: Possible co-operation of railways etc to encourage establishment of industries in depressed areas.

PRO BT 56/41 CIA 1800/121: Industrial Development Publicity: Local Development Associations.

PRO BT 56/41/CIA/1800/123: Industrial Development Publicity

PRO BT 104/1: North East Development Board.

PRO BT 104/11: Jarrow Town Council Proposed Bill for the Financing by the Corporation of Industries in the Town.

PRO BT 177/1823: Birkenhead Corporation Bill 1954.

PRO HLG 29/179: Local Authorities (Publicity) Bill 1930.

PRO HLG 29/233: Health Resorts and Watering Places Bill 1936.

PRO HLG 30/64: Lancashire Industrial Development Council: Special (Derelict) Areas – Industrial Areas (Lancashire).

PRO HLG 52/114: Local Authority Publicity (Health Resorts and Watering Places Act 1921).

PRO HLG 52/115: Local Authorities Publicity – Proposed Amendments to the 1921 Act.

PRO HLG 52/116: Local Authority Publicity – Legislation – suggesting amended legislation 'Come to Britain' Movement.

PRO HLG 52/117: Health Resorts and Watering Places Act 1921 – Amendment to Secure Additional Advertising Powers for Holiday Towns.

PRO HLG 52/1069: Local Authority Procedure – Powers of Local Authorities to Make Advances to Industrialists (1942).

PRO HLG 52/1392: Local Authorities Publicity: Development Associations: Subscriptions by Local Authorities.

PRO HLG 52/1393: Local Authorities Publicity: Publicity Organizations Approval under Local Authorities (Publicity) Act 1931.

PRO HLG 52/1395: Local Authority Publicity British Travel and Holidays Association Formation Local Authorities Publicity Act 1931.

PRO HLG 54/265: Liverpool Corporation Bill 1936.

PRO HLG 54/574: Land: Powers of Local Authorities 1) To purchase 2) To develop surplus and specific (including for industrial purposes).

PRO HLG 57/357: Felling UDC – Legality of Expenditure: Tyneside Advertising Campaign.

PRO RAIL 226/236 Great Central Railway 1908: Guide to Holiday Resorts and London's Rural Retreats.

PRO RAIL 268/206: Great Western Railway, Homes for All: London's Western Borderlands, 1914.

PRO RAIL 410/1998: London and North Western Railway c1912: Manchester and Where to Live on the London and North Western Railway.

PRO RAIL 425/7: London Midland and Scottish Railway: Advertising and Publicity: Copy Minutes, Reports Relating to Various Advertising Media 1923–1929.

PRO RAIL 429/17 London, Midland and Scottish Railway 1929: Residential Districts in the London Area.

PRO RAIL 645/26: Southern Railway, Law Medical and Traffic and Continental Committees, January 1932–July 1939.

PRO RAIL 645/89: South Eastern and Chatham/ Southern Railway Meetings of Publicity Representatives 1922–23.

PRO RAIL 652/29 Southern Railway c1929: *Country Homes at London's Door.*

PRO RAIL 652/32: Southern Railway, nd c1932: *Southern Homes.*

PRO RAIL 652/33: Southern Railway, 1939: *Southern Schools*

PRO RAIL 1080/581: Railway Clearing House Minutes of Meetings of Advertising Representatives, 12.2.19–4.9.23.

PRO RAIL 1080/583: Railway Clearing House Minutes of Meetings of Advertising Representatives, 5.1.26–25.1.28.

PRO RAIL 1080/584: Railway Clearing House Minutes of Meetings of Advertising Representatives, 8.3.28–21.11.28.

PRO RAIL 1080/586: Railway Clearing House Advertising and Public Relations Committee Minutes, 11.6.30–31.12.34.

PRO RAIL 1080/589: Railway Clearing House Advertising and Public Relations Committee Minutes, 1.1.39–18.1.40.

PRO RAIL 1080/590: Railway Clearing House Advertising and Public Relations Committee Minutes, 15.4.40–24.10.47.

PRO ZPER 12/4, *Southern Railway Magazine*, Vol 4, 1926.

PRO ZPER 12/5 *Southern Railway Magazine*, Vol 5, 1927.

PRO ZPER 12/7: *Southern Railway Magazine*, Vol 7, 1929.

PRO ZPER 12/10: *Southern Railway Magazine*, Vol 10, 1932.

PRO ZPER 12/16A: *Southern Railway Magazine*, Vol 16, 1938.

PRO ZPER 38/17: *Great Western Railway (London) Lecture and Debating Society*, No 179, 1925.

PRO ZPER 39/36 *Railway Magazine*, Vol. XXXVI, January–July 1915.

Punch, as cited in text.

QBCC (Queens Borough Chamber of Commerce) (1920) *Queens Borough, New York City: The Borough of Homes and Industry.* New York: QBCC (Library of Congress Local Collection).

Quiett, G. C. (1934) *They Built the West: An Epic of Rails and Cities.* New York: Appleton-Century.

RCB (Residential Centres Bureau) (nd c1910) *Cardiff and District as a Place of Residence.* Cheltenham: Burrows (John Johnson Collection, Bodleian Library).

RCC (Richmond Chamber of Commerce) (1907) *Richmond Virginia: The Most Important Commercial and Manufacturing City in the South Atlantic States.* Richmond: RCC (Virginia State Library).

RCC (nd c1923) *Industrial, Commercial and Financial Advantages of Richmond, Virginia.* Richmond: RCC (Virginia State Library).

RCC (1927) *Richmond, Virginia: Down Where The South Begins.* Richmond: RCC (Virginia State Library).

RCC (1933) *Studying Richmond's Hand in the 'New Deal'.* Richmond: RCC (Virginia State Library)

Rea, K. J. (1985) *The Prosperous Years: The Economic History of Ontario 1939–1975.* Toronto: Univerity Press.

Rees, J. (1983) Regional economic decentralization processes in the United States, in Hicks, D. A. and Glickman, N. J. (eds.) *Transition to the 21st Century: Prospects and Policies for Economic and Urban-Regional Transformation.* Greenwich, CT: JAI Press, pp. 241–78.

Reid, S. J. (ed.) (1902) *Memoirs of Sir Edward Blount 1815–1902*, 2nd ed. London: Longmans.

Reinders, P. and Oosterwijk, W. (1989) *Neem de Trein! Spoorwegaffiches in Nederland.* Utrecht/ Antwerp: Veen Reflex.

Reps, J. (1965) *The Making of Urban America.* Princeton: Princeton University Press.

Richardson, H. W. and Aldcroft, D. H. (1968) *Building in the British Economy Between the Wars.* London: Allen and Unwin.

Roberts, R. (1983) The corporation as impresario: The municipal provision of entertainment in Victorian and Edwardian Bournemouth, in Walton, J. K. and Walvin, J. (eds.), *op. cit.*, pp. 138–157.

Robson, B. T. (1973) *Urban Growth: An Approach.* London: Methuen.

Robson, B. (1986) Coming full circle: London versus the rest 1890–1980, in Gordon, G. (ed.) *Regional Cities in the UK 1890–1980*, pp. 217–231.

Rosegrant, S. and Lampe, D. (1992) *Route 128: Lessons from Boston's High-Tech Community* New York: Basic.

Rouse, J. W. (1984) The case for vision, in Porter, P. R. and Sweet, D. C. (eds.) *op. cit.*, pp. 22–32.

Rudin, R. (1982) Boosting the French Canadian town: Municipal government and urban growth in

Quebec, 1850–1900. *Urban History Review*, **XI**(1), pp. 1–10.

Runte, A. 1991: Promoting the Golden West: Advertising and the railroad. *California History*, **70**, pp. 62–75.

Runte, A. (1992) Promoting wonderland: Western railroads and the evolution of national park advertising. *Journal of the West*, **31**, pp. 43–48.

Runte, A. (1994) *Trains of Discovery: Western Railroads and the National Parks* (collector's edition). Niwot, CO: Roberts Rinehart.

Russell, J. M. (1988) *Atlanta 1847–1890*. Baton Rouge: Louisiana State University Press.

Rutheiser, C. (1996) *Imagineering Atlanta*. London: Verso.

Ryans, J.K. jr. and Shanklin, W. (1986) *Guide to Marketing for Economic Development: Competing in America's Second Civil War*. Columbus, Ohio: Publishing Horizons.

Saunders, P. (1981) *Social Theory and the Urban Question*. London: Hutchinson.

Schaffer, D. (1991) After the suburbs. *Built Environment*, **17** (3/4), pp.242–256.

SE (Sanderstead Estate) (nd *c*1912) *Sanderstead Estate Illustrated*. Sanderstead: Webster and Hawkes (John Johnson Collection: Bodleian Library)

Senior, E. K. (1983) *From Royal Township to Industrial City: Cornwall 1784–1984*. Belleville: Mika.

Shackleton, J.T. (1976) *The Golden Age of the Railway Poster*. London: New English Library.

Short, J. R., Fleming, S. Witt, S. J. G. (1986) *Housebuilding, Planning and Community Action: The Production and Negotiation of the Built Environment*. London: Routledge and Kegan Paul.

Smithies, E. D. (1974) The Contrast between the North and South in England 1918–1939: A Study of Economic, Social and Political Problems With Particular Reference to the Experience of Burnley, Halifax, Ipswich and Luton. Unpublished Ph.D thesis, University of Leeds.

Smyth, H. (1994) *Marketing the City: Flagship Developments in Urban Regeneration*. London, Spon.

Soane J. V. N. (1993) *Fashionable Resort Regions*. Wallingford: CAB International.

Southall, H. (1988) The origins of the depressed areas: Unemployment, growth and regional economic structure in Britain before 1914. *Economic History Review*, 2nd series, **XLI**(2), pp. 236–258.

Southport [Corporation] (1931) *Sunny Southport: England's Seaside Garden City*. Southport: Southport Corporation.

SR (Southern Railway) (1931) *Come to Weymouth for Happy Days*. London: SR (John Johnson Collection, Bodleian Library).

Stafford, F. and Yates, N. (1985) *The Later Kentish Seaside (1840–1974) – Selected Documents*. Gloucester: Sutton/Kent Archives Office.

Stephenson T. (ed.) (1921) *Industrial Edinburgh*. Edinburgh: Society for the Promotion of Trade in conjunction with the Edinburgh Chamber of Commerce and Manufacturers.

Stewman, S. and Tarr, J. A. (1982) Four decades of public-private partnerships in Pittsburgh, in Fosler, F. S. and Berger, R. A. (eds.) *op. cit.*, pp. 59–128.

Stilgoe, J. R. (1983) *Metropolitan Corridor: Railroads and the American Scene*. New Haven: Yale University Press.

Struthers, J. (1986) *Glasgow's Miles Better: 'They said it' About Glasgow*, Glasgow: Struthers.

Sunday Times Magazine, as cited in text.

Sunderland (Corporation) (nd *c*1921) *Sunderland and Its Industries with Notes Upon the Town as a Residential Centre*. Cheltenham: Burrow.

Sunderland (Corporation) (1931) *Sunderland: The Official Industrial Handbook*. Cheltenham: Burrow.

Sutcliffe, A. (1981) *Towards the Planned City: Germany, Britain, the United States and France, 1780–1914*. Oxford: Blackwell.

Swenarton, M. and Taylor, S. (1985) The scale and nature of the growth of owner-occupation in Britain between the wars. *Economic History Review*, 2nd series, **XXXVIII**(3), pp. 373–392.

Taylor, F. S. 1952: *The Century of Science*, 3rd ed. London: Heinemann.

Taylor, I., Evans, K. and Fraser, P. (1996) *A Tale of Two Cities: Global Change, Local Feeling and Everyday Life in the North of England. A Study of Manchester and Sheffield*. London: Routledge.

TBC (Torfaen Borough Council) (1992) *Contrasts in Torfaen*. Pontypool: TBC Economic Development Unit.

The Househunter's ABC (nd *c*1910) (John Johnson Collection, Bodleian Library).

The Housefinder (1905–) (John Johnson Collection, Bodleian Library).

The Standard House-hunter's Guide to London

(1908–) (John Johnson Collection, Bodleian Library).

Thomas, G. E. and Doebly, C. (1976) *Cape May: Queen of Seaside Resorts*. Philadelphia: Art Alliance Press.

Thomas, H., Stirling, T., Brownill, S. and Razzaque, K. (1996) Locality, urban governance and contested meanings of place. *Area*, **28**(2), pp. 186–198.

Thompson, F. M. L. (ed.) (1982) *The Rise of Suburbia*. Leicester: University Press.

Tindall, G. B. (1963) Business progressivism: Southern Politics in the twenties. *The Southern Atlantic Quarterly*, **LXII**(1), pp. 92–106.

TIDC (Tyneside Industrial Development Conference) (1926) *Interim Report of the Investigating Committee: New Industries on Tyneside*. Newcastle: TIDC.

Toronto Globe, as cited in text (Provincial Archives of Ontario).

Torquay Corporation (nd *c*1925) *Torquay: The English Riviera*. Torquay: Corporation/Chamber of Commerce/Hotels, Caterers and Apartments Association.

Totterdill, P. (1989) Local economic strategies as industrial policy: A critical review of British development in the 1980s. *Economy and Society*, **18**, pp. 478–526.

TPE (Trafford Park Estates) (1923) *Trafford Park: Britain's Workhouse and Storehouse*. Trafford Park: TPE.

Traveller's Gazette, as cited in text (Thomas Cook Archives).

Traves, T. (1987) The development of the Ontario automobile industry to 1939, in Drummond *et al.*, (eds.) *op. cit.*, pp. 208–223.

Tronrud, T. J. (1990) Buying prosperity: The bonusing of factories at the Lakehead, 1885–1914. *Urban History Review*, **XIX**(1), pp. 1–13.

Urry, J. (1987) Holidaymaking, Cultural Change and the Seaside, Lancaster Regionalism Group Working Paper 22. Lancaster: University of Lancaster.

USBC (United States Bureau of Census) (1994) *County and City Data Book*. Washington DC: US Government Printing Office.

Wakefield (City of) (1932) *Wakefield Commercially Considered*. Wakefield: City Corporation (Wakefield Central Library, Local Collection).

Walton, J. K. (1978) *The Blackpool Landlady*. Manchester: Manchester University Press.

Walton, J. K. (1983*a*) *The English Seaside Resort: A Social History 1750–1914*. Leicester: Leicester University Press.

Walton, J. K. (1983*b*) Municipal government and the holiday industry in Blackpool, 1876–1914, in Walton, J. K. and Walvin, J. (eds.), *op. cit.*, pp. 160–185.

Walton, J. K. and Walvin, J. (eds.) (1983) *Leisure in Britain 1780–1939*. Manchester: University Press.

Walvin, J. (1978) *Beside the Seaside*. London: Allen Lane.

Ward, S. V. (1984) List Q: A missing link in interwar public investment. *Public Administration*, **62**, pp. 348–358.

Ward, S. V. (1986) Implementation versus planmaking: The example of list Q and the depressed areas 1922–1939. *Planning Perspectives*, **1**(1), pp. 3–26.

Ward, S. V. (1988*a*) *The Geography of Interwar Britain: The State and Uneven Development*. London: Routledge.

Ward, S. V. (1988*b*) Promoting holiday resorts: A review of early history to 1921. *Planning History*, **10**(2), pp. 7–11.

Ward, S. V. (1990) Local industrial promotion and development policies 1899–1940. *Local Economy*, **5**(2), pp. 100–118.

Ward, S. V. (1991) Municipal Policies and the Industrialization of Ontario 1870–1939: The Example of Oshawa. *Canadian Studies Research Award End of Grant Report*, CSRA 90/36.

Ward, S. V. (1994*a*) *Planning and Urban Change*. London: Paul Chapman.

Ward, S.V. (1994*b*) Time and place: Key themes in place promotion in the USA, Canada and Britain since 1870, in Gold, J.R. and Ward, S.V. (eds.) *op. cit.*, pp. 53–74.

Ward, S.V. (1995) Place Marketing: A Comparison of British and North American Experiences. Paper presented at the Society for North American City and Regional Planning History, Knoxville, Tennessee.

Warner, S. B. (1978) *Street Car Suburbs: The Process of Growth in Boston, 1870–1900*, 2nd ed. Cambridge, MA: Harvard University Press.

Waterhouse, K. (1995, orig. 1994) *City Lights: A Street Life*. London: Sceptre.

WBC (Worthing Borough Council) (1959) *Residential Worthing*. Worthing: WBC Publicity Committee.

WBT (Wichita Board of Trade) (1887) *Wichita, Kansas, 1887*. Wichita: Board of Trade (Library of Congress, Map Collection).

Weaver, J. C. (1982) *Hamilton: An Illustrated History*. Toronto: James Lorimer/National Museums of Canada.

Wechsberg, J. (1979) *The Lost World of the Great Spas*. London: Weidenfeld and Nicolson.

Weightman, G. and Humphries, S. (1984) *The Making of Modern London 1914–1939*. London: Sidgwick and Jackson.

Weightman, J. (1970) The solar revolution: Reflections on a theme in French literature. *Encounter*, December, pp. 9–18.

Weill, A. (1994) *L'invitation au voyage: L'affiche de tourisme dans le monde*. Paris: Somology.

Western Mail, as cited in text (Luton Museum, Chamber of Commerce Press Cuttings)

Whitelock, D. (1972) *The Beginnings of English Society*, revised edition. Harmondsworth, Penguin.

Wichita Eagle (1888) *Wichita: Metropolis of the South West The Largest City in Kansas. A city of fine educational institutions, Magnificient Business Blocks, Elegant Residences and Extensive Manufactures, with more railroads, more Wholesale Trade, more manufacturing, more enterprise than any city in the South West*. Wichita: Wichita Eagle (Library of Congress Rare Book Collection).

Widdicombe (Committee) (1986) *Report on the Conduct of Local Authority Business*, Cmnd 9797. London: HMSO.

Wilkinson, E. (1939) *The Town That Was Murdered*. London: Gollancz.

Wilkinson, S. (1992) Towards a new city? A case study of image-improvement initiatives in Newcastle upon Tyne, in Healey, P., Davoudi, S., Tavsanoglu, A., O'Toole, M. and Usher, D. (eds.) *op. cit.*, pp. 174–211.

Williams, R. (1980) Advertising: The magic system, in *Problems in Materialism and Culture*. London: Verso.

Williamson, J. (1978) *Decoding Advertisements: Ideology and Meaning in Advertising*. London: Marion Boyars.

Wilson, R. B. (1987) *Go Great Western: A History of GWR Publicity*, 2nd ed. Newton Abbot: David and Charles.

Wilson, W. H. (1989) *The City Beautiful Movement*. Baltimore: Johns Hopkins University Press.

Wishart, D. (1987) Settling the Great Plains 1850–1930: Prospects and problems, in Mitchell, R. D. and Groves, P. A. (eds.) *North America: The Historical Geography of a Changing Continent*. London: Hutchinson, pp. 225–278.

Wishart, R. (1991) Fashioning the Future: Glasgow, in Fisher, M. and Owen, U. (eds) *Whose Cities?* Harmondsworth: Penguin, pp. 43–52.

Wolman, H. L., Ford, C. C. and Hill, E. (1994) Evaluating the Success of Urban Success Stories. *Urban Studies*, **13**(6), pp. 835–850.

Wolman, H. and Goldsmith, M. (1992) *Urban Politics and Policy: A Comparative Approach*. Oxford: Blackwell.

Worcester (City Council) (nd c1909) *The Industrial Advantages of Worcester*, Worcester: City Council.

World Jewry, as cited in text (John Laing Archives).

Wynne, D. (ed) (1992*a*) *The Culture Industry: The Arts in Urban Regeneration*. Aldershot: Avebury.

Wynne, D. (1992*b*) Urban regeneration and the arts, in Wynne, D. (ed.) *op. cit.*, pp. 84–95.

Yankton Press (1871) *Uncle Sam is Rich Enough To Give Us All A Farm HOMES IN THE WEST THE FREE LANDS OF DAKOTA!* Yankton: Yankton Press (Library of Congress Broadside Collection).

Yates, N. (1988) Selling the seaside. *History Today*, **38**, August, pp.20–27.

Zube, E. H. and Galante, J. (1994) Marketing landscapes of the Four Corners States, in Gold and Ward (eds.) *op. cit.*, pp. 213–232.

Zube, E. H. and Kennedy, C. (1990) Changing images of the Arizona Territory, in Zonn, L. (ed.) *Place Images in Media: Portrayal, Experience and Meaning*. Savage: Rowman and Littlefield, pp. 183–203.

INDEX